GW00363302

DREAMING OF DAMASCUS

DREAMING OF DAMASCUS

Arab Voices from a Region in Turmoil

Stephen Glain

JOHN MURRAY
Albemarle Street, London

© Stephen Glain 2003

First published in 2003
by John Murray (Publishers) Ltd,
50 Albemarle Street, London W1S 4BD

The moral right of the author has been asserted

All rights reserved. No part of this publication may be reproduced in
any material form (including photocopying or storing it in any medium
by electronic means and whether or not transiently or incidentally to
some other use of this publication) without the written permission of
the copyright owner, except in accordance with the provision of the
Copyright, Designs and Patents Act 1988 or under the terms of a
licence issued by the Copyright Licensing Agency, 90 Tottenham Court
Road, London W1T 4LP. Applications for the copyright owner's
written permission to reproduce any part of this publication should be
addressed to the publisher.

A catalogue record for this book is available from the British Library

ISBN 0-7195-5543 4

Typeset in Monotype Bembo 12/13.5
by Servis Filmsetting Ltd, Manchester

Printed and bound in Great Britain by
Clays Ltd, St Ives plc

For my parents.
And for Danny.
'How dull it is to pause, to make an end,
To rust unburnish'd, not to shine in use.'
Tennyson, *Ulysses*

Contents

Illustrations   ix
Maps   x

Introduction   1
1. Lebanon: The Sluice Gate   22
2. Syria: The Circle   58
3. Jordan: The Royal Expediency   105
4. Palestine: The Last Colony   136
5. Iraq: The Show   177
6. Egypt: The Towering Dwarf   212
   Conclusion: Whither *Asabiyya*?   257

Chronology   274
Sources   280
Bibliography   285
Glossary   290
Acknowledgements   292
Index   297

Illustrations

1. François and Charbell Bassil, Le Chef, Beirut
2. Nazem Ghandour and Tarik Arafiri, mushroom magnates, Tripoli
3. Mohammad Hijazi, medical technician and ex-Hezbollah fighter, Beirut
4. The Umayyad mosque, Damascus
5. Palestinian refugees, Hai Qaissieh district Amman
6. Jordanian journalist Qassem al Katib, Ma'an
7. Palestinian refugee Subhi Abu Suleyman, Jenin
8. Dr Mustafa Barghouthi, Ramallah, West Bank
9. Israeli-controlled checkpoint, Nablus, West Bank
10. The remains of a Nablus soap factory after Operation Defensive Shield
11. Iraqis celebrate Saddam Hussein's sixty-fifth birthday, Tikrit
12. Foreign dignitaries at the birthday celebrations in Tikrit
13. Abbasid palace, Baghdad
14. The sheik of the Al Jabur tribe, Baghdad
15. Baghdad's oldest barber, Hikmat Mahmoud Al Hilli
16. The Brazilian Coffee Shop, Alexandria
17. Saber Mohammad Abu Leila, octogenarian street historian, Alexandria
18. Al Azhar mosque, Cairo
19. The Cairo and Alexandria Stock Exchange
20. Abdel-Raouf Essa, imitation-furniture baron
21. Ben Ezra synagogue, Cairo
22. Dr Mohammad Morsi, Zaqaziq University
23. Clinic sponsored by the Muslim Brotherhood, Zaqaziq
24. Greek Club regulars, Cairo
25. Egyptian dissident Saad Eddin Ibrahim

All the photographs were taken by the author

Mediterranean
Sea

- Aleppo
Latakia
- Hama
- Homs
Tripoli
Beirut
LEBANON
SYRIA
Damascus
ISRAEL Haifa
Tel Aviv Nablus
Amman
Jerusalem
JORDAN
Gaza
Damietta
Alexandria
Port
Said
Zaqaziq
Cairo
Suez
Ma'an

River Nile

EGYPT

Red Sea

Medina

SUDAN

Mecca
Ta

Aydhab

Caspian
Sea

Mosul

Kirkuk

Tikrit

Baghdad

IRAQ

IRAN

SAUDI
ARABIA

Basra

KUWAIT

Persian Gulf

N
W E
S

THE
MIDDLE EAST

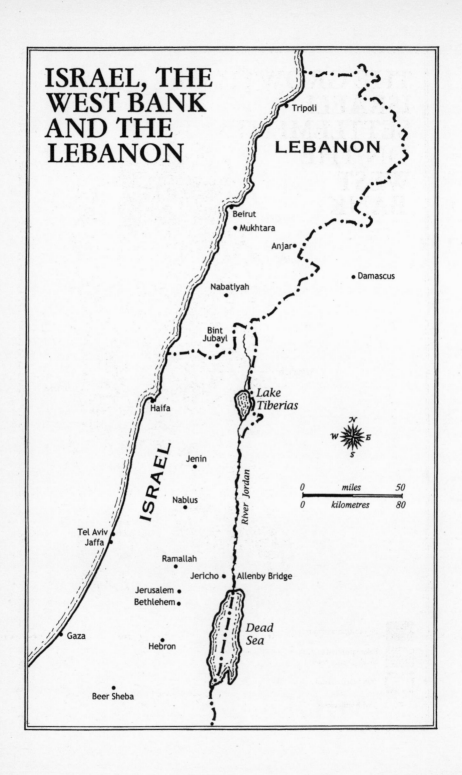

ISRAEL, THE
WEST BANK
AND THE
LEBANON

LEBANON

Tripoli

Beirut
Mukhtara

Anjar

Damascus

Nabatiyah

Bint
Jubayl

Lake
Tiberias

N
W E
S

Haifa

ISRAEL

Jenin

0   miles   50
0   kilometres   80

Nablus

River Jordan

Tel Aviv
Jaffa

Ramallah

Jericho   Allenby Bridge

Jerusalem
Bethlehem

Dead
Sea

Gaza

Hebron

Beer Sheba

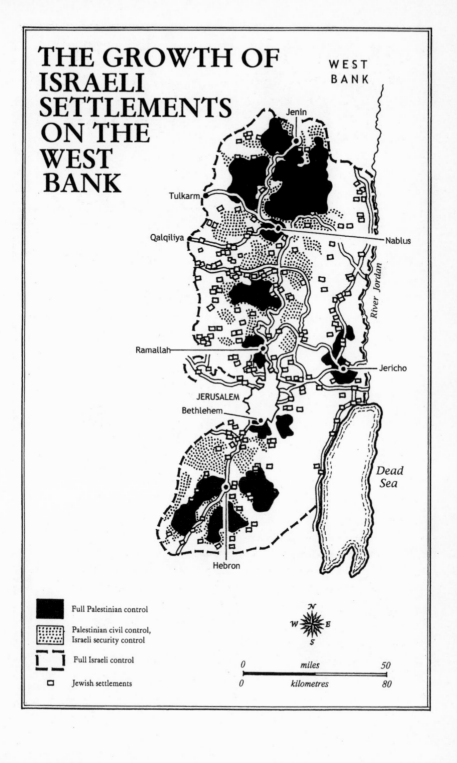

THE GROWTH OF ISRAELI SETTLEMENTS ON THE WEST BANK

WEST BANK

Jenin

Tulkarm

Qalqiliya

Nablus

River Jordan

Ramallah

Jericho

JERUSALEM

Bethlehem

Dead Sea

Hebron

■ Full Palestinian control

▦ Palestinian civil control, Israeli security control

⌐_⌐ Full Israeli control

◻ Jewish settlements

N
W   E
S

0   miles   50
0   kilometres   80

THE CHANGING SHAPE OF ISRAEL

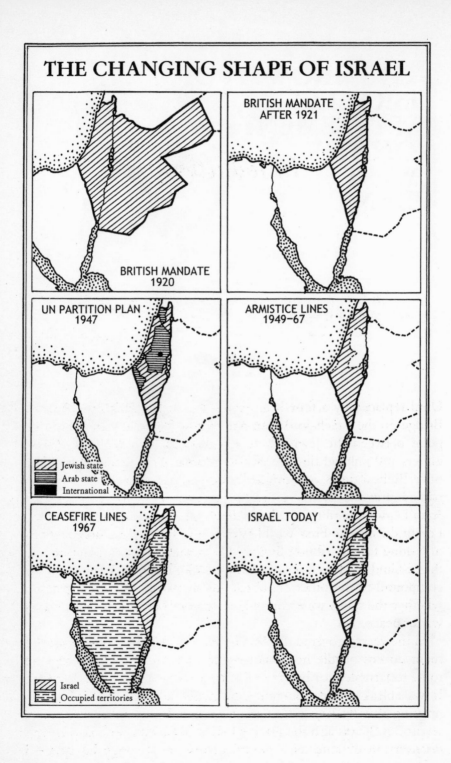

BRITISH MANDATE
1920

BRITISH MANDATE
AFTER 1921

UN PARTITION PLAN
1947

ARMISTICE LINES
1949–67

Jewish state
Arab state
International

CEASEFIRE LINES
1967

ISRAEL TODAY

Israel
Occupied territories

Introduction

Be kind to the people of the covenant . . . for they are our brothers and allied to us by marriage.

The Prophet

Until replaced by a four-lane expressway in late 2000, the Allenby Bridge on the Israeli-Jordanian border was the main surface crossing point between the Jewish state and the Arab world. Built of steel girders and railroad ties it straddled a Jordan River sadly diminished since Biblical times, and originally formed part of a border complex named after the British general who, with T.E. Lawrence and the Arab Legion guarding his flank, drove the Ottoman Turks from the Levant during the First World War. It stood in the middle of a two-mile-long tarmac ribbon linking the Jordanian immigration post to the east and the Israeli post to the west. Getting from one side of the compound to the other could take up to two hours, depending on whether the buses were running on schedule and the region was at war or peace.

In the years I covered the Middle East for *The Wall Street Journal*, I spent dozens of idle hours waiting to cross the Allenby Bridge en route to Jerusalem or back to my bureau in Amman, Jordan's capital. It was a bleak but peaceful refuge from the violence of the Palestinian uprising that by late 2000 had consumed Israel and the occupied territories. It was also the place where – like a desperate lawyer who discovers an obscure legal precedent that may salvage his case – I found reason to be hopeful about the Middle East.

I was returning to Amman after a week's reporting in Palestine. Israeli immigration had disgorged me along with a handful of NGO workers and Australian tourists, and together we crossed the border in one of the buses owned and operated by Jordan Express Tours. It was dusk and the shimmer from the Dead Sea was extinguishing itself as we made our way through the grey, lunar wasteland that is the lowest place on Earth. A full moon revealed itself on the horizon; it was amber-coloured and seemed perilously close.

By the dim reading light on the console above my seat, I squinted through the final pages of *The Life and Times of Muhammad* by Sir John Bagot Glubb, a British Orientalist. The author, better known as Glubb Pasha, is not fondly remembered in the Arab world. Britain imposed him on Jordan's King Hussein as a military adviser and to the Arabs he embodied everything pernicious and arrogant about Western imperialism. In 1956, pressured by the rise of Arab nationalism, the young King Hussein dismissed him and his detail of British officers. It was a timely move; two years later, King Faisel II of Iraq, Hussein's cousin and a fellow British proxy, was brutally murdered in a military coup.

Arrogant or not, Glubb could write. His book, an inspired and sympathetic account of the origins of Islam, concludes with a vivid survey of the great Arab-Muslim civilization that flourished less than a generation after Mohammad's death in AD 632. 'The Arab expansion from a tangle of mutually hostile nomadic tribes in a remote desert to the world's greatest empire,' Glubb wrote, 'is one of the most astonishing and dramatic incidents in world history.'

For nearly 400 years beginning in the late seventh century, the Mediterranean was a Muslim-controlled economic bloc administered by an enlightened and tolerant Arab empire. Jews, Christians, and Muslims co-existed peacefully. Arab caliphs commissioned great mosques, schools and hospitals, and Persian architects and Byzantine artisans built them. Jewish astronomers and Christian poets cultivated a scientific and cultural flowering that pre-dated the European renaissance by hundreds of years. Before Dante, there were the Arab philosophers Al Kindi and Averroës and the great Persian physician Avicenna, and preceding Leonardo da Vinci the remarkable fourteenth century traveller Ibn Battuta.

Less than a century after the birth of Islam, Damascus – not Rome or Paris – was the cultural capital of the world. A corpus of scientific knowledge was translated into Arabic from Greek, Coptic, Indian, and Persian texts. A seventh century Jewish physician of Persian origin named Masarjawayh translated a Syriac medical treatise, originally composed in Greek by a Christian priest in Alexandria. It was the first scientific textbook written in the Arab language. Inspired by a maxim ascribed to the Prophet – 'Science is two-fold: that which relates to religion and that which relates to the body' – Arab physicians synthesized and enhanced medical theory from the empires that preceded them. Muslim surgeons lectured their Christian counterparts in Sicily and Constantinople; and even Guillaume de Harsigny, the court physician to Charles V, Holy Roman Emperor and King of Spain in the sixteenth century, studied under Arab instructors in Cairo.

The Muslim enlightenment expanded as far as southern Spain, where *Al Andalus*, the Muslim enclave known today as Andalusia, marked the westernmost reaches of the Muslim empire and became a fount of intellectual and artistic expression. The eighth century Great Mosque of Cordoba stands today as a triumphant mix of pious aesthetics and engineering skill. Among the most sophisticated cities of its time, Cordoba was Europe's vestibule to modernity and light; its streets were illuminated at night and its air was redolent with the scent of lush gardens when London and Rome were backward and dark.

Until that evening, jostled about No-Man's Land in the tour bus, I had thought of the Arabs as a people – proud but miserable. I had yet to think of them as a *civilization* responsible for great contributions to art and science. In Spain a year earlier, I had marvelled at the Alhambra, the spectacular Moorish palace in Granada built in 1354; the do-it-yourself, cassette-tape tour told me it was the jewel of an Islamic empire that dominated the Mediterranean for centuries. I had seen the Umayyad Mosque in Damascus and toured Cairo's Old City, the extravagant seat of the Fatimid dynasty. Yet so vast was the contrast between the spectacular Alhambra and the dilapidated slums of Gaza and southern Lebanon that I failed to associate Islam's dreary present with its glorious past.

I decided to write a book comparing the Arab economy of today – parochial, intolerant, corrupt – with the ancient, but enlightened Islamic caliphates. It would be a tragic, but illustrative and hopeful story; what was once an established cosmopolitan society could be so again. The Arabs, like people everywhere, are prisoners of their environment; if solid institutions, legitimate government and a prosperous middle class create a stable society, lawlessness, despotism and prolonged economic decay undermine it. Any policy that failed to deal aggressively with the Arab world's jaundiced economies would never remove the real sources of instability. Rather than selling Arab governments tanks and fighter jets, it should be compelling them to lower trade barriers and restructure their capital markets. Just as the bankrupt Weimar Republic – and the vindictive terms of Versailles – provided the seedbed for Fascism in pre-war Germany, so poverty and despair have nourished Islamic extremism. In the West, it is naturally assumed that a shrinking economy leads to rising crime. Why not apply the same logic to help unearth the root causes of Middle East instability and radical Islam?

About a year later, I walked out of my Capitol Hill apartment in Washington, DC and nearly collided with panicked legislative aides – a flying wedge of Brooks Brothers suits, laminated tags, and faux-pearl earrings – streaming out of Congress. The capitol was being evacuated. A sonic boom announced a flight of F-16s storming over-head, too high to see. By the end of the day, more than 5,000 people would be feared dead.

It was the morning of September 11, 2001. An old war had been carried, grotesquely, to a new front.

This was not, however, the time for a sober examination of the root causes of Middle East instability and radical Islam; any chance for a restructuring of US policy in the region was buried in the rubble of the Pentagon and the World Trade Center. American ignorance about the Arab-Muslim world metamorphosed from benign to bel-ligerent. There was no appetite for nuance, only absolutes.

'Why do those people hate us?' I was brusquely asked in a TV interview a week after the attacks. The question was strange to me. Working in the Middle East, I had countless interviews, encounters and casual conversations with Arabs from Baghdad to Cairo who were overwhelmingly friendly. Almost everywhere I travelled in the Arab world, I was treated as an honoured guest consistent with the ancient traditions and protocols of Arab hospitality.

Once, while reporting in Mosul in northern Iraq, I found myself in the home of Bader Suhel Salih Al Zeidi, a sheik of the Al Zeidi tribe. The Al Zeidis migrated to Iraq from Yemen 400 years ago and were now thoroughly urbanized. Sheik Al Zeidi's residence was a suburban, ranch-home dwelling. He sat me down at the far end of a large rectangular reception room known as a *diwan* alongside a framed photograph of a beaming Saddam Hussein enlarged several times life-size. The sheik's brothers, then his cousins and second cousins joined us. Finally, his frail grandfather shuffled in on crutches and was seated on a special cushion.

The growing assembly greeted each newly arriving guest with a handshake and a bow, right hand over heart, in a gesture of respect.

'*Salam Aleikum*,' each man murmured to the other.

Within 20 minutes or so, I was encircled by two-dozen tribal elders, some in traditional robes and headdress, others in ill-fitting, western suits. Almost all of them were threading worry beads through their fingers.

I was offered tea. 'This is a great honour,' Sheik Al Zeidi told me. 'Many of us have never met an American before.'

Then the bombs started falling.

The explosions were very distant. I probably wouldn't have noticed them if it hadn't been for the concussion that sent tiny ripples through my tea.

The sheik detected my concern. 'Those are your fighter jets,' he said in English. (Most of the others spoke only Arabic but sat upright and attentive throughout the interview.) 'Almost every day they come. Sometimes, they kill children and old people. Why does your government do this to us? We like Americans. We were once good friends with America. We bought your grain and cars. Now your government drops bombs on us. Why is this?'

His manner was passive, almost gentle. I stumbled over an explanation about the complexity of US foreign policy and managed to get through the interview. As we parted, the sheik repeated what would become the leitmotif of my years spent covering the Middle East:

'We are not against Americans. *We are against American policy*.'

I am quite certain that Sheik Al Zeidi was horrified by footage of innocent civilians leaping from the burning World Trade Center Towers shortly before they collapsed. While the sheik may have agreed with some of Osama bin Laden's objectives, he would certainly oppose his methods as antithetical to the spirit of Islam.

But with over 3,000 Americans killed in an obscene act, few Americans were interested in the distinction. A gallery of politicians and pundits declared the attacks on the Pentagon and World Trade Center to be nothing less than the first assault in an epic clash between the forces of light – the Judeo-Christian West – and the forces of darkness, the Muslim East. Islam was a primitive faith, the Arab world an antediluvian backwater. There was little discussion of how and why America's Middle East policy – in reality a domestic

policy masquerading as foreign policy – had succeeded in antagonizing an Arab world made up of moderate Muslims, Christians – and
yes, a smattering of Jews.

Many Americans had no idea that Washington used the Middle
East as a market for US weaponry in exchange for cheap oil, with
little regard for the consequences of its failing economies. They were
unaware that US troops had for years been deployed in Saudi Arabia,
the land of the Islamic holy cities of Mecca and Medina, which pious
Muslims considered a profanity and secular Arabs regarded as a violation of Arab sovereignty. Only a handful of Americans had any idea
that US and British fighter jets were engaged almost daily in a largely
ineffectual bombing campaign over Iraq, or that a US-led sanctions
regime on Baghdad had asphyxiated what had been the region's most
important economy. While Americans routinely watched news
footage of Palestinian teenagers throwing rocks at Israeli soldiers, few
understood what provoked them – an illegal occupation that has
strangled their economy.

There was little, if any, analysis of the Arab world's failed economies and how systemic poverty, oppression and hopelessness breed
extremism, or how the colonial powers at the end of the First World
War had segregated what had been a prosperous trading bloc into
cantons of tiny markets. Few commentators pointed out that while
Osama bin Laden is rich and educated, his populist appeal is strongest
in the lowest strata of an impoverished society educated in *madrassas* –
schools financed by fundamentalists, and popular where the state has
failed to provide a minimum level of secular education. Overlooked
too was the fact that Somalia, Sudan, and Afghanistan – the countries
where bin Laden found refuge – have an average annual per-capita
income of $240.

Viewed from the ruins of the Arab economy and the rising tide of
Arab hopelessness, Osama bin Laden could be seen for what he was –
a particularly vile mutation of a much larger disease.

That was eighteen months ago. The West has yet to prevail in its war
on radical Islam because it has yet to come to terms with what causes
it. The popular impression of the Middle East continues to be
informed by evocative images on 24-hour newscasts: Israeli buses
demolished by fanatics, women dehumanized under the veil, imams
bellowing anti-Western slogans from the minarets or *minbars* (pulpits)
of crowded mosques. These are consequences, not the cause, of a

deeper problem that is hard to capture on video or in a photo essay. They mislead viewers and readers into thinking that the Middle East has been, and always will be, locked in conflict.

Any useful analysis of what ails the Middle East must begin with a thorough understanding of its economics and politics. To ignore either is to perpetuate a foreign policy that, in collusion with corrupt Arab regimes and vested US interests, has plundered the Middle East and, by widening the gap between the ruled and their rulers, now endangers the West.

One by one they arrived in Beirut: a cavalcade of sheiks, emirs, monarchs, and presidents-for-life, an illegitimate ruling elite, the bastard sons of Old World imperialism, estranged as much from their people as from each other. They stepped down from their official jets to a tarmac festooned in green, black and red – the colours of the ancient Islamic caliphates – and the ritual blather of Arab diplomacy.

Security was ultra-tight. To accommodate the arrivals of the leaders and their retinues, commercial flights in and out of the airport were cancelled or postponed and highways leading into Beirut were cordoned off. Each delegation was escorted in steel-plated limousines to the Phoenicia Intercontinental Hotel, a polished-marble smoke-screen for Lebanon's economic and political disarray.

It was 27 March 2002. Another Arab summit was inflicting itself on the Arab people.

It was billed as the most important summit in years. On the table was a Saudi Arabian proposal to bring peace to the Middle East. The plan was ultimately endorsed by league members but not before they nearly drowned each other out in comic-opera discord. The prime minister and parliamentary speaker of Lebanon boycotted the welcoming ceremony, reportedly miffed at being upstaged by the president; the Palestinian delegation walked out temporarily after the Lebanese cancelled plans for Yasser Arafat – incarcerated in his West Bank headquarters by Israeli tanks – to address the assembly by satellite link. The Lebanese said they feared Israeli prime minister Ariel Sharon, who controlled the airwaves around Arafat as well as the roads, would cut into the feed and begin haranguing Arab leaders at their own summit – a virtual invasion of Lebanon that would have been as terrifying in its way as the real one Sharon carried out in

1982. The Palestinian delegation implied the Lebanese move was payback for Arafat, whose unruly exile in Lebanon decades earlier provoked the Israeli invasion in the first place.

It was all there – the full panoply of tribal double-dealing, animosity and oafishness. An exception was Saudi Arabia's de-facto leader, Crown Prince Abdullah ibn Abdulaziz, and his stately appeal to Israelis, if not to Sharon, to accept his offer of normal relations between the Jewish state and the Arabs in exchange for an Israeli withdrawal from occupied Palestinian land. This was followed by Syrian President Bashar al Assad and his 45-minute, meandering tirade against Israel and in support of the Palestinians' 18-month long Intifada, the resistance to a 35-year Israeli occupation, that erupted in September 2000. The United Arab Emirates downgraded its delegation in protest of what it said was inept management of the proceedings; as if in empathy with the Arab League's own debility, a Saudi delegate suffered a stroke.

Most of the officials who spoke did so in mangled Arabic, a reflection on the level of education possessed by Arab rulers. At least the older generation of leaders – Egypt's Gamal Abdel Nasser and King Hussein of Jordan among them – could inspire in the tradition of the great Arab orators.

'This is a farce,' Chibli Mallat, a human-rights lawyer told me. 'It's symptomatic of a leadership with little legitimacy. They quarrel over silly rituals. They can't even speak correctly. It's embarrassing.'

Half the 22 heads of state invited to the summit failed to appear, including the custodians of the only two peace treaties between Israel and the Arab states – Egyptian President Hosni Mubarak and Jordanian King Abdullah II – apparently in protest of Sharon's restrictions on Arafat. The meeting was even deprived of an appearance by Libyan leader Moammar Gadhafi, the Arab League's honorary court jester and carnival barker, with his female bodyguards, coffee-house antics and flamboyant Afro-Bedouin wardrobe. Gadhafi stayed home, officially because he was angry with the League for rejecting his own peace plan, though Lebanese officials said privately he was afraid of the country's large Shiite-Muslim population, who suspected he plotted the demise of a prominent Lebanese imam in 1978.

Arabs had long ago dismissed their leaders as a fraternity of nabobs and despots capable of little more than feudal bickering, and the Beirut summit further alienated the rulers from those they ruled. If the Saudi proposal was applauded by Western leaders as a desirable first step towards peace – though within hours it would be swept away by a scorching escalation of Palestinian-Israeli violence – it was a far cry from what ordinary Arabs wanted. On college campuses, city streets, and in living rooms, Arabs urged their leaders to use what leverage they had – oil, peace treaties, the Suez Canal, anything – to pressure the United States into imposing peace terms on the Israelis and ending sanctions on Iraq. It was a genuine expression of pan-Arab outrage and an appeal for the kind of stability that could lead to economic rehabilitation and ultimately, democracy.

The men who meet, spend and squabble at Arab summits have no interest in economic reform, let alone democracy. Since the Second World War, few if any Arab leaders have been elected in a vote that wasn't bought, rigged, or gerrymandered. After all, reform that favours the popular welfare would come at the expense of their own. The best thing that can be said about Arab leaders is that the Arab people are not responsible for them. That distinction goes to the French and British, at least until the end of the Second World War, and to the Americans after that. Surprisingly, the best place to begin an examination of Middle Eastern decay is in a small city in northern England.

Hull is a long way from the Middle East. Yet in the Hull University archives, the yellowed papers, maps, and documents of Sir Mark Sykes, a little-known civil servant, show why a once-prosperous part of the world has for the last century known little but sectarian conflict and hardship.

Sir Mark, together with a French diplomat named François Picot, secretly carved up what used to be called the Levant into an assortment of dissonant monarchies, mandates and emirates. The Sykes-Picot agreement, hatched in smoke-filled salons in Paris, London and Cairo, enshrined Anglo-French imperialist ambitions at the end of the First World War. Syria and Lebanon were tucked into the French orbit, while Britain claimed Iraq, the Gulf States and the Palestinian Mandate – what is now Israel, Jordan and the Palestinian Authority. It also sealed British support for a Jewish state, a triumph for the increasingly influential World Zionist Organization.

If the many ghosts of the Middle East conflict could somehow be summoned to reflect on what they had wrought, the one with the most to say might be Sir Mark. In a way, the first victim of the West's tumultuous intervention in the Middle East was Sir Mark's peaceful vision for it.

He was born in 1876, the sixth baronet to the Sykes clan, and raised in a snakepit; his father was a drunkard who used to beat his son regularly, and his mother was a spendthrift. Yet his difficult upbringing fortified him for what would be a distinguished, if tragically short, career. He went to Cambridge, wrote several best-selling travelogues about his frequent visits to the Middle East, served in the Boer War where he met Winston Churchill and compensated for the abuse he suffered as a child by becoming a model husband and father.

In 1911, Sir Mark was elected to a seat in parliament from which he was plucked three years later when war broke out, being assigned to the War Office as an Arab expert. From the hundreds of memos and reports about what to do with the Arab world should the Bedouin armies succeed in driving out the Ottoman Turks comes a tale of the limits and dangers of Great Power intrigue and influence. With the burden of hindsight, trolling through Sir Mark's papers was like listening to the black-box recording of a doomed airliner.

Picot, a veteran diplomat, believed subject peoples like those in the Middle East should remain under the imperial thumb. But Sir Mark defended both Arab nationalism and Zionism. He wrote enthusiastically of how their agreement would pave the way for a peaceful and productive 'Arab-Jewish combine'. In a memo dated July 18, 1917, he decried the 'eight centuries of slavery' the Arabs endured under the Ottoman Turks and proclaimed Britain's post-war policies to be 'the liberation of oppressed peoples', both Arab and Jew.

Memos written in the early phase of the war reveal a cheery vision of Arab-Jewish harmony free of foreign meddling, creating a Middle East entente 'with no spheres of influence . . . that must differ strategically and politically from anything that has existed in the past'. His optimism is parried by Gilbert Clayton, Britain's chief representative in Cairo. In a letter to Sykes dated 15 December 1917, he responds prophetically to Sir Mark's support for a Jewish homeland and the prospects for its peaceful co-existence with Muslim and Christian Arabs.

'We will try it,' Clayton writes, 'but it must be done very cautiously and, honestly, I see no great chance of any real success. It is an attempt to change in a few weeks the traditional sentiment of centuries.'

Clayton also warns of an Arab backlash in response to Britain's perceived pro-Zionist bias. 'We have to consider whether the situation demands out-and-out support of Zionism at the risk of alienating the Arabs,' he writes. 'By pushing them as hard as we appear to be doing, we are risking the possibility of Arab unity becoming something like an accomplished fact and being ranged against us.' (In the margins of the letter, an unidentified hand notes, 'This happened.') In a handwritten postscript Clayton reiterates, 'I wish to point out clearly the dangers and difficulties which exist here.'

But Sykes-Picot prevailed and the Arab states were parcelled up and divided out.* When news of the agreement leaked out in late 1917 – the Soviets released it after taking power in Moscow – the Arabs condemned it as violating Anglo-French pledges for post-war independence. 'The promises to the Arabs was a dead paper,' wrote T.E. Lawrence in his memoirs. Pockets of resistance were easily overcome. Having driven the Turks from Damascus in 1918, a Syrian militia two years later found itself at the gates of the city to confront French troops. It was strafed by French warplanes and fled.

The colonial powers installed as their proxies a collection of pliant emirs that presided over small countries with tiny populations. What had been by the end of Ottoman rule a borderless economy of 40 million consumers was subdivided into small markets around which trade barriers and tariffs inevitably calcified. As late as 1914, the value of Egypt's total trade was worth nearly half its gross domestic product (GDP), a ratio close to that of Great Britain's. Today, trade among any of the Arab states is negligible. The economies of Syria and Lebanon, which in many ways represent the greatest potential of the Arab economy, did not recover their pre-First World War vitality until the late 1920s.

The Cold War turned the Middle East into a battleground molten with big-power rivalry and wars of national liberation. The Eisenhower Doctrine – you're either with us or against us in the War on Communism – chased Egypt, Syria and other Arab states into the Soviet orbit, which reciprocated with arms, technology, and subsidies. (This was predictable; like everyone else, the Arabs don't mind being bribed but hate being blackmailed.) A generation of Anglo-French colonial meddling and Bolshevik-style, planned economics doomed what had once been a large, borderless and prosperous market into a Balkanized, authoritarian heap. Arab living standards

---

* In 1919, a US panel known as the King-Crane Commission recommended temporary mandates be set up for Syria, Palestine, and Iraq with the US presiding over the former two and the British over the latter. France was to be deprived of any post-war role in the Near East, the commission concluded, because of the low regard Arabs had for her. The panel also found against the Zionists' plan for a 'Jewish Commonwealth' in Palestine and in favour of a highly restricted and gradual Jewish migration.

have been declining ever since. In *Jihad, the Trial of Political Islam*, an authoritative account of the evolution of radical Islam, Gilles Kepel writes of the *hittistes* – the unemployed youths of Algeria who became foot soldiers for the radical Muslim orders that challenged Algeria's secular regime in the late 1980s. A decade later, the *hittistes'* shadow covers the entire Arab world.

Sir Mark Sykes never saw the long-term results of his diplomatic endeavours; he died in 1919 in the great 'flu epidemic that killed more people than the First World War. After visiting Hull, I asked Christopher Sykes, Sir Mark's great-grandson, how Sir Mark would find the Middle East today.

'He would have been horrified,' Christopher replied. 'He was a man of peace. The idea he was a cause of war and strife would have devastated him.'

I agreed to cover the Middle East largely because I needed a change. For the previous seven years I had worked as a *Wall Street Journal* correspondent in East Asia, where I covered booming economies and hungry conglomerates. I wrote about shipyards and auto works, corporate mergers and rights issues, infrastructure projects and regional trade. It was much more an economic than a political story; US diplomatic missions were staffed by dozens of commercial attachés who lobbied on behalf of American business interests eager to participate in Asia's burgeoning economies. The ancient animosities and suspicions that prevailed among Asian states – between Burma and Thailand, Vietnam and China, North and South Korea, and Japan and everybody else – were subdued beneath a carapace of rising living standards and a growing middle class.

In the Middle East, I found a region fractured by sustained economic decay into rival camps – between haves and have-nots, rulers and ruled, modernists and medievalists and, ultimately, between its own bloc of corroded economies and the rest of the world. The authority of many Arab regimes was unravelling; from Lebanon to Iraq to Egypt, entire populations of disenfranchised citizens were retreating to the mosque or the tribe for basic civil services. While American embassies in the region – often huge, vault-like compounds – were top-heavy with political and military officers who coordinated weapons sales and collected electronic intelligence, commercial attachés were conspicuous by their absence. With the exception of the Israeli high-tech sector, revenue from which underwrites an as-yet-unreformed command economy, there was little in the Middle East to interest *Wall Street Journal* readers.

The US is well into its war on terrorism. It has been more than a decade since the Middle East peace process began in Madrid and two and a half years since the fateful visit by Ariel Sharon on 28 September 2000 to the Harem al Sharif, the holiest Muslim site in the Old City of Jerusalem that is also venerated by Jews as the site of Solomon's temple.* The image of Sharon and a thousand security guards trampling about the Al Aqsa Mosque and the Dome of the Rock was considered an insult to Islam. Riots broke out and catalyzed into the second Intifada the next day.†

Hopes for a peace dividend from the Oslo peace accords were exhausted years ago.‡ Washington has failed to appreciate anaemic levels of foreign investment as a leading indicator for instability. Israel is still allowed to protect the West Bank and Gaza, among its largest export markets, from Arab products. Although Washington enthusiastically endorses its Arab allies' feeble and often fraudulent gestures towards economic reform, those few governments who once embraced privatization have indefinitely postponed it. Egypt has yet to sell its state-owned airline, telephone company, or a bank. In Jordan, government monopolies have engineered a series of backroom deals between existing monopolies and foreign – usually corrupt – public utilities that do little to enhance competition or reduce user prices. Few, if any 'privatized' companies in Jordan have been listed on the Amman Stock Exchange.

Investment in Arab countries is inhibited by inadequate credit systems. The proliferation of bounced cheques in the few countries that extend credit to retail customers has been climbing steadily for

* The uprising that followed Sharon's visit is known as the second or Al Aqsa Intifada and still rages at the time of writing; the first Intifada began in 1987 and ended with the Oslo peace accords in 1993.
† A fact-finding commission launched by the Clinton administration and led by former US Senator George Mitchell debunked the notion that Palestinian leaders used Sharon's visit as a pretext for the uprising. 'We have no basis on which to conclude that there was a deliberate plan by the [Palestinian Authority] to initiate a campaign of violence at the first opportunity,' the Mitchell report concluded.
‡ In October 1993, after months of secret talks in Oslo, Norway, Israel and the PLO signed a declaration of principles for peaceful coexistence between Israel and an independent Palestine, which was to be declared five years later. This included a proposal for the dismantling of most Israeli settlements on the West Bank and in Gaza.

years. Arab capital markets, a primary source of funding for new businesses and investment elsewhere in the world, are derelict; most global money managers and venture capitalists now ignore them. Local financial institutions are ill equipped to harness the vast pool of unrecorded income that keeps Arab economies afloat; some 80% of Egyptians have no bank account, yet hold personal savings worth fifty-five times the value of Egypt's total foreign direct investment. Young entrepreneurs seeking capital for enterprises that could create wealth and jobs are forced to pool their families' wealth – a limited source of funding that only adds to the region's chronic illiquidity. The Middle East is the only region in the non-developed world where the broadest measure of the liquid-money supply – known as M3 – is dropping. From 1990 to 2000, M3 in the Arab world declined from 62% of GDP to 60%. In East Asia during the same period, the ratio nearly doubled, from 64% to 120%; the average ratio among low- and middle-income nations, rose from 43% to 62%.

A direct line leads from low volume on the Palestine Securities Exchange to a young boy throwing rocks at Israeli soldiers in Ramallah. But most policymakers in the West fail to see it.

The extent of Arab economic degeneration is as ominous as it is vast. Interest rates throughout the Arab world are prohibitively high, owing to a fear of inflation and runaway debt that siphons consumption and investment. Overvalued currencies make Arab exports uncompetitive relative to their Asian, East European and Latin American counterparts. Foreign direct investment in the world's 22 Arab economies, both in value and as a percentage of GDP is less than half the global average. The Vancouver-based Fraser Institute each year ranks more than 100 countries based on the openness of their trade and investment policies. Not a single Arab country made the top half of the 2001 list. The highest-ranking Arab state was Oman, at 59. Iraq, Libya, Saudi Arabia, Sudan and Yemen were excluded from the study because they lacked the necessary data. In Egypt, exports equal around 8% of GDP compared with 15% for Mexico and Thailand and 44% for South Korea. Overall, the value of trade between Arab countries as a percentage of aggregate GDP – excluding oil products – is about 4%, the lowest level of any bloc of countries, including Africa.

Today's Arab states – some knowingly, some not – have opted out of the global economy and the impact can be measured in a single, chilling statistic: between 1990 and 1999, real per-capita income in the world's 22 Arab countries averaged less than 1% growth, *about a quarter the rate of its population growth during the same period.* Increasingly, living standards in the Arab world are more closely associated with those in Africa than in the West. The Arab middle class – a vital bulwark between the haves and the have-nots – is eroding, exposing an entire generation of disenfranchised, unemployed young men to the lure of extremist groups. They included Saeed Hotary, a 22-year-old electrician from Zarqa who left home in 1999 to look for work in the West Bank. Having found none, he settled for divinity; on 1 June 2001, according to the Associated Press, he blew himself up in front of a Tel Aviv disco, killing 19 Israeli teenagers and injuring 90 others. Until then, Hotary had no record of political activity.

Oil is no longer the economic elixir it was in the 1970s and 1980s. Gulf economies are so weak they have no choice but to sell crude oil at reasonable prices, or else their regimes would collapse. Saudi Arabia, with much of the world's petroleum reserves, suffered an economic contraction of 1.1% in the ten years between 1989 and 1999. Kuwait, with one of the Arab world's highest per-capita incomes at $13,500, is burdened with a huge government payroll – 93% of all employed Kuwaitis are civil servants – and a drop in global oil demand would strain what amounts to a welfare emirate. The Organization of Petroleum Exporting Countries (OPEC), once the spoiler of the global economy, now has as much interest in stable fuel prices as net oil-importers. Analysts project a glut, not a shortage, that will keep prices in the $20 to $30 range for much of the next generation at a time when the world's largest gas guzzler, the United States, is lessening its dependence on imported fuel. This could have a devastating impact on the oil economies of the Arab world, resulting in reduced employment opportunities in the Gulf for workers from non oil-producing Arab states like Lebanon, Egypt, and Palestine. That, in turn, means fewer wages remitted home, an important source of capital for the oil-poor Levantine economies.

For ten years after the end of the Cold War the West got away with ignoring the Arab world. Under the Clinton administration, America's Middle East policy was confined largely to a monster F-16 sale to the United Arab Emirates and a snap peace summit imposed on the Palestinians with tragic consequences. Efforts to produce a peace dividend prior to the second Intifada by encouraging trade and investment were perfunctory and largely ignored, particularly by Israel.

Until September 11, George W. Bush wanted nothing to do with the Middle East so long as oil prices traded below $30 a barrel and the Intifada was confined to a local turf fight. Continued economic decline in North Africa and the Levant threatened to fuel the migration to Europe of restless, job-seeking youths. But beyond that, the consequences of the Arab world's malaise seemed comfortably remote.

What happened on September 11 changed everything – and nothing. Washington continues to focus on Muslim extremism in isolation from the rage and frustration that fuels it. Militant Islam, in one incarnation or another, has been stalking the Middle East since the death of the Prophet. Osama bin Laden, it was suggested in the pop psychology that proliferated after the attacks, was trying to turn back the clock and re-impose a fundamentalist Muslim empire on the Middle East. But there never *was* a fundamentalist Muslim empire. True, the early caliphs proclaimed fidelity to the Koran. But they administered a realm that was largely secular in spirit, tolerant and congenial to foreign ideas, cultures and religions – everything Al Qaeda opposes.

It is that long history of Muslim tolerance that radical Islam is trying to repeal. Osama bin Laden – either dead or alive – and his associates have found a growing constituency among an Arab people punch-drunk from a century of Western imperialism, Zionism, Pan-Arab nationalism, Ba'ath (Resurrection) Party Socialism and two Intifadas. In a world pushing itself inexorably if chaotically toward democracy, Middle Eastern Arab leaders steadfastly deprive their people of basic freedoms and civil liberties, with succession increasingly ordained by bloodline, not the ballot box. The Saudi Arabian and Jordan monarchies show no sign of introducing genuine suffrage, and corrupt dynasties are congealing around the 'republics' of Syria and Iraq. In Egypt, officially a democratic republic, parlour gossip centres over whom President Hosni Mubarak will anoint as his successor. The short list of candidates usually includes the president's son or another military man, all of this despite the Arab craving for genuine representational government even as they are consigned to another generation of despotic rule and economic decay.

The strength of radical Islam lies in the weakness of the Arab leaders it confronts. If Osama bin Laden could turn the clock back, he'd be exactly where he was on September 11 – a terrorist lurking in the shadows of Islamic society and resisted by the established elite. In short, he'd be a *Kharijite*, a member of a militant, puritanical Islamic group. The *Kharijites* – or Outsiders – were strongest when caliphal authority was weakest. So it is with Al Qaeda.

For 1,300 years, the history of the Muslim world was, more or less, a history of peaceful commerce with the odd civil war, power struggle, and foreign invasion tossed in. Today's Middle East was once the heart of a vast Muslim empire stretching from the Central Asian steppes to the Straits of Gibraltar. Until then, no civilization had ruled such an immense and resource-rich domain, nor established its authority in such a short period of time. Islam took less than a generation to evolve into the world's dominant monotheistic religion; Christianity, which eventually replaced it, took centuries.

Mohammad, a merchant who married into wealth, was as much a statesman and diplomat as a holy apostle. Persecuted by the pagan burghers of Mecca, known as the Quraysh, Mohammad and his small group of followers escaped to Medina in 622. There, he was honoured for his humble manner and skilful arbitration of local disputes. The people of Medina became the Prophet's 'Helpers' – early converts to Islam and the vanguard in the Islamic revolt against the Quraysh. Mohammad and the early Muslims prevailed in late 629. In January 630, they returned to Mecca.

Outnumbered by members of the prevailing religions, Mohammad understood that his young faith would appeal only through conciliation. His largely peaceful capture of Mecca, was followed by only a few executions and no forced conversions. Mohammad drew a distinction between the *umma* – the Muslim community – and the surrounding pagans, so Jews and Christians were largely left alone. However power struggles were inevitable. In 624, the Prophet moved against the Banu Qaynuqa, a clan of Jewish silversmiths who controlled the economy in Medina and were allied to one of the few challengers to Mohammad's authority. The Muslims routed the Qaynuqa, who were executed on the Prophet's command. Not long after that, he ordered the evacuation of the Banu'l-Nadir, the wealthiest among the surviving Jewish clans of Medina. But once Islamic authority was in place, the three monotheistic religions co-existed peacefully.

It was subtle diplomacy rather than the sword that established the Muslim empire, as demonstrated by the conversion of the Bedouin Beni Tameem, a huge tribe from the central Nejed desert in what is today's Saudi Arabia. In 631, a delegation of the Beni Tameem

arrived in Medina after a three-day ride in search of Mohammad.
Finding no one to greet them, the tribesmen entered the village
square and declaimed a crude summons to the commander of this
now-formidable faith.

Mohammad emerged from his mosque to receive their challenge.

'O Mohammad,' the chief of the delegation called down from his
mount, 'we have heard you Muslims are men of inspired poetry and
song. Let us see if they can best the elders of the Beni Tameem.'

Contests of poetry and oratory were a common way of settling disputes among the early Arabs and Mohammad was honour-bound to
accept. It was also a charade; the tribesmen had not come to challenge Islam but to surrender to it.

A member of the visiting team, coaxing his camel to kneel, slid to
the ground and opened with a declaration of the power and wealth of
the Tameem. Mohammad called upon one of his oldest allies to
respond. The man praised God and the Koran, as revealed to
Mohammad, the messenger of God.

The preliminary round complete, the poetry contest began. After
an exchange of compositions, the Muslims were declared the
winners.

'By the life of my father,' hailed the chief of the Tameem, 'this man
has some ready helpers. His orator and his poets are better then ours
and their voices are more melodious.'

The delegation immediately converted to Islam and returned
home with gifts from the Apostle. This face-saving pantomime was a
diplomatic coup that allowed the proud tribal leaders to submit to the
growing authority of a mere shopkeeper, Apostle of God notwith-
standing.

Mohammad died a year later. The appeal of Islam spread throughout the Middle East, gradually supplanting Byzantine and Persian
suzerainty in the region. From the Arabian Peninsula the Muslims
elbowed the Byzantines from what is Egypt, Palestine and Syria in
the west and the Persians from the interior of today's Iraq in the east.
Both powers were atrophying due to what we call 'imperial over-
stretch', creating a vacuum that Islam filled like quicksilver. Like most
successful religions, Islam triumphed more as a social rather than a
spiritual revolution; it promoted tolerance among the monotheistic
faiths and appeared to its growing flock to be an inspiring and egalitarian theology – absent the stifling hierarchy of Byzantine
Christianity and the Persians' musty Zoroastrianism.

By 638, the Muslims had reached Jerusalem, the third most holy site in Islam. Jews and Christians welcomed the Muslims as a pious alternative to the corrupt Byzantines and were declared *dhimmis* – protected minorities under Muslim administration.

From Mecca the seat of the Muslim world would migrate to Damascus, where the empire was expanded and refined under the Umayyad dynasty. The shift foreshadowed the division of Islam between what would become the mainstream, Sunni Islam, and their Shiite rivals.*

In 750, the increasingly decadent and corrupt Umayyads would be crushed in a revolt led by the Abbasid clan and the empire's centre of gravity shifted to Baghdad. In the late tenth century, the Fatimids, a Shiite tribe from Tunisia, seized the mantle of Muslim leadership after conquering Egypt. For over two centuries, the Fatimids presided over the most resilient and prosperous of the Islamic caliphates until corruption and the trauma of foreign invasion – first by Seljuk Turks, then Crusaders and Mongols – finally manoeuvred the Arabs into the smothering embrace of the Ottoman Empire.

Though distinguished by different clans and sects, the Islamic empires continued the tradition of religious tolerance. Until the end of Ottoman rule in 1918, the three monotheistic religions had mingled far more peacefully under the Muslims then they ever did in Europe. After King Ferdinand expelled the Jews from Spain in 1492, the sultan in Constantinople welcomed them. This ensured the Muslim economy enjoyed a favourable balance of trade with Europe for years after. Religious tolerance was perhaps the Islamic world's greatest achievement then, just as intolerance is its biggest liability now.

This book is about the progeny of the great Arab empires – Jews and Christians as well as Muslims. They constitute both the Arab world's declining middle class and the vital middle ground in the West's war on terror, which is a war over demographics. The prevailing one – an Arab population of 250 million people growing four times faster than its economy can absorb – is working in the *Jihadists'* favour. So long as the Middle Eastern economy is poorly managed

---

* Ali, the Prophet's nephew and beloved for his piety, served briefly as the fourth caliph in 656. In 661 he was murdered by a fundamentalist *Kharijite* for negotiating a power-sharing agreement with the profanely secular Mu'awiya, who became a legendary Umayyad caliph. In 680, following Mu'awiya's death, Ali's supporters in the Iraqi city of Kufa demonstrated in favour of Ali's second son, Husain. Mu'awiya's son and successor Yazid ordered Husain's assassination. When Husain and his clan were slaughtered at Kerbala, in Iraq, Husain was the last to die, his infant son in his arms. The atrocity fuelled the gradual break between Shiites, the followers of Ali, and the Sunni mainstream.

and its people unjustly led, radical theology will be a viable alternative to the status quo. What is left of the region's middle class will
disappear and the corrupt regimes they leave behind could face
an uncertain future.

It may be too late. Economic malaise in the Arab world is so
advanced and Arab regimes so inept and corrupt that some kind of
revolution could be inevitable – perhaps even desirable. In 20 years,
perhaps less, Iran will be a powerful democracy and a solid US ally.
Having ejected its own western stooge and endured an indigenous,
orthodox replacement, the Iranians realize there is no alternative to
liberal democracy. If the Arab world is entering a pre-revolutionary
phase, Iran is in a post-revolutionary one. The Iranian polity is
already more dynamic than many of its Arab counterparts. Its demographics – a growing population of young, secular reformers and a
dwindling pool of ageing clerics – are working in favour of stability.
    Unfortunately, Iran took more than 20 years to get this far. How
stable is a perimeter of democracies – Iran, Turkey, and Israel –
perched alongside a cauldron of impoverished and angry Levantine
Arabs?
    There could still be time. Most of the people profiled in this book –
educated, proud of their heritage and profoundly secular – could be
the embryo of a revived, progressive and solidly pro-Western Middle
East. But since September 11, the United States has reduced the
Middle East to a chessboard, its cultures and values defined by neat
squares of black and white, thereby creating a new orthodoxy in the
region. This orthodoxy, rooted in a deep contempt for the US
government and its foreign policies, particularly its support of Israel,
transcends spirituality, ethnicity and nationality. It is embraced by
Christians as well as Muslims, Arabs as well as ethnic Armenians,
Greeks, Druze, Chaldeans, Circassians, Turcomans and Kurds, and
will proliferate unless US policies are transformed to suit the complex
and increasingly grim realities of the Arab world.
    Without this transformation, the West cannot win its war on terror.
It must adjust its policies to challenge those vested interests that hold
its current ones hostage – particularly its near-unconditional support
of Israel and Israel's proliferating and corrupting occupation of
Palestinian land. It must insist friendly regimes in the region – Egypt
and Jordan first and foremost – aggressively restructure their economies even as existing aid programmes are modified to reward progress

and penalize lethargy. This will require political and diplomatic back-bone to match the courage that moderate Arabs demonstrate every day by resisting the lure of an exit visa or the path of extremism.

This book is based on the years I covered the Middle East beginning in mid-1998 and ending in a two-month reporting trip to the region during the spring of 2002. It retraces the migration of power during the first 400 years of Islam, from what was once called Greater Syria, then Iraq and finally Egypt. While these countries have long since evaporated as the world's great centres of culture, trade and enlight-enment, they are critical to the Arab identity and the prospects for an Arab revival.

This is a book about a region in decay, but also about human resilience and hope for the future.

1

Lebanon

The Sluice Gate

If someone does not know how to manage his own household, how can
he take care of God's church?

First Letter of Paul to Timothy 3:5

One order of couscous, *with a sniper on the side . . .*
Like most former French colonies, Lebanon is known for its food.
Imperial France may have strip-mined entire economies, denuded
local culture and inspired wars of national liberation, but it could
cook. If the legacy of British imperialism is an efficient postal service,
the French made the world safe for soufflés.

So it is no exaggeration to say Beirut, set like a gemstone along the
bountiful Mediterranean, has the Middle East's finest restaurants.
One could then argue, by combining Cartesian logic with a pinch of
Oriental hyperbole, that the best restaurant in the Arab world is Le
Chef, a tiny café in the Gemayze district of West Beirut.

Le Chef is run by Charbell Bassil and his 60-year-old father,
François. The Bassils are Maronite Christians who live in the predominantly Christian village of Daroun just north of Beirut.* Every
morning at 5.30 a.m. – except Monday, when Le Chef is closed –
Charbell and François make the half-hour drive along a new

---

* The Maronites are among the largest Eastern-rite communities of the Roman Catholic Church.
They trace their origins to St. Maron, a Syrian hermit of the late fourth century and its early adherents
settled in the Lebanese mountains to escape persecution. In 684, under the leadership of St. John
Maron, patriarch of Antioch from 685 to 707, the Maronites established their independence by routing
the invading Byzantine armies of Justinian II.

highway, named after the current prime minister and real estate mogul, Rafik Hariri, to the city to buy and prepare the day's produce. Le Chef opens at 7 a.m. and closes at 6.30 p.m. But if a party arrives before closing, the Bassils will keep the kitchen open until the last patron leaves.

Le Chef has dark wood panelling but is brightly lit from windows that look out on to rue Gouraud. The main wall is painted with a Monet-inspired street scene, and faded newspaper columns praising François' gastronomy – including a mention in the *Lonely Planet Guide to Lebanon* – are displayed in the corner. Bottles of liquor, wine, beer and pickled radishes line the wall that separates the kitchen from the dining area. The tables – no more than seven or eight – are covered with white cloth protected by a plastic veneer and the chairs with red vinyl. Renderings of Christ and Virgin Mary are tacked onto the wall over the cash register.

Charbell, who was educated at a Jesuit school and dropped out of college to work with his father, sees to the customers. He knows most of his patrons by name and greets them warmly.

'My favourite part of this job is to meet our French and English customers,' says Charbell. 'I like people from foreign countries coming here. We serve them from our hearts.'

The patrons are usually well dressed and Christian. They come for the convivial ambience, the cosmopolitan buzz that was once so vital to Beirut when it was a haven for international bankers, businessmen, socialites, and arms dealers. But most of all, they come for le chef, François. His specialty is *Kharouf Mihshi* – lamb stuffed with rice, meat and nuts – but he also makes a mean *Soujuk*, an Armenian sausage.

It takes some coaxing to get François out of the kitchen but the breakfast crush has peaked and he can talk. Today he is unshaven. He has speckled grey hair and a missing front tooth, but his Gallic nose, patrician forehead and white chef's tunic with the double row of buttons on the front, give him a quietly potent authority.

François first came to Beirut at the end of the Second World War, when his village was very poor. His uncle owned a restaurant near the old president's palace and he worked there for room and board. A year later, he got a job at Sa'ad, one of Beirut's top clubs. He was paid LLP50 (50 Lebanese pounds) a month and shared a room with three other boys. The monthly rent was LLP4 each.

By 1955, François was 17 years old and the assistant chef at the Regent Hotel, then one of Beirut's best hotels. The Regent's owner also had a café in the Lebanese mountains, so François would be based in Beirut through the winter and in the mountains during the summer. He also worked at the Bristol, the Select, and the Normandy – all famous hotels, all, like the Regent, later destroyed.

A year later, a top hotelier in Riyadh, Saudi Arabia, hired François and provided him with a staff of two-dozen junior chefs, assistants, and underlings. At 22 he was poached by one of Baghdad's most powerful nightclub owners to be the head chef at a famous nightclub called the Oberge. It was 1958 and Iraq and Jordan had formed a political union to offset a similar alliance between Egypt and Syria. François arrived just in time to arrange a huge banquet for Iraq's young King Faisel II and his cousin, King Hussein of Jordan.

'Neither king paid his respects,' François remembers, 'but their vice-regents did. It was a wonderful meal of fish, *Kharouf Mihshi*, toasted pine nuts, and salads. The vice-regents later called me from the kitchen to offer their compliments.'

One morning, not long after the banquet, François awoke to find tanks in the streets. The king and his retinue had been murdered in a military coup led by a general named Kassem.

'I found myself in the middle of a revolution,' François says. 'I was told I was a foreigner and was kept indoors for two months. When I finally had the chance to go, I was ordered to leave my money behind – all the money I'd been saving.'

François sewed his cash into his clothes, walked across the Syrian border and returned safely to his village in Lebanon – and to a civil war then brewing between ruling Christians on one side and disenfranchised Druze and Sunnis on the other.* The Middle East was changing. The US, fearing the possibility of a wider war, landed 14,000 marines on the beaches of south Beirut.

The civil war was snuffed out, the marines remained and business was good. François was making $300 a month running the officers' club at the famous St Georges Hotel and at least that much working nights at the Riviera. The Lebanese pound was trading at LLP2.25 to the dollar (100 piastres = LLP1.00) and 60 piastres (27 cents) to the Deutschmark.

'Back then,' François recalls, 'there were lots of tourists and money. I worked more at night than at day. The big boss of the US Sixth

---

* The Druze are members of a secretive sect of Islam inspired by the eccentric eleventh century Fatimid Caliph, Al-Hakim (996–1021) who finally went insane and proclaimed himself divine in 1020. He inexplicably vanished in February 1021, although some accounts say he was murdered by his sister over a succession-related quarrel. The Druze believe that he was transported to heaven, one day to return to earth in triumph. Druze teachings draw on the Koran, the Bible and Sufism.

Fleet would come to the Riviera. He was the most powerful man in Lebanon.'

Eventually, the marines withdrew, sectarian violence resurfaced and in 1975 a more ferocious civil war broke out. The Bassils retreated to Gemayze and Le Chef, which François was already operating with his brothers. Although rue Gouraud was a favourite target area for snipers in a high-rise office more than a mile away, the patrons still braved high-velocity bullets for François' celebrated *Kharouf.*

François lights a cigarette. The restaurant is nearly empty now. Charbell joins us to talk about the war.

'Occasionally,' Charbell says, 'we had to close the restaurant but most of the time we kept it open. Every morning my father would listen to the radio to see how bad the shooting would be. Sometimes it would be very bad and he would stay home. Other times he would leave and things would get bad and he would have to stay in Beirut. We might not see him for four or five days.'

I asked if Lebanon would ever recapture its former glory.

'We can't go back as before,' François says. 'Especially after September 11. There will be no peace. Next America will attack Hezbollah, Syria and Iran.* That will leave us Christians in the middle. After twenty years, most Christians have already left. We are already down to less than a third of the population.'

'We dream to go to America,' says Charbell. 'But things are different now, after those nineteen students did this thing in New York. Where is your CIA? In movies America is always the winner. Now look. We need peace. We were born to war, twenty years of war and nothing to show for it. And now George Bush talks of a second crusade. Why? I am a Christian. Why does he say things like that?'

What will happen to Le Chef?

'Business depends on politics,' Charbell says. 'I have a brother who has worked here and we would like to continue the restaurant after my father retires. Our father has created the name but we will never close Le Chef.'

François returns to the kitchen. The lunch crowd is filtering in and Charbell gets up to greet them.

The fastest way to make a million dollars in Lebanon, so goes a popular Lebanese joke, is to come in as a billionaire.

* The militant Shiite group, Hezbollah – Party of God – emerged in southern Lebanon during the civil war. Backed by Iran and Syria, its political wing holds seats in Lebanon's parliament.

It doesn't seem that way to the first-time visitor. At Beirut's striking new airport, arriving passengers are enveloped by spacious arrival lounges, whisked to the immigration counters on conveyor belts and spoiled by duty-free shops offering the widest range of luxury goods between Istanbul and Dubai. The visa counter, where visitors obtain their $15 tourist stamp, can even give change for a fifty-dollar bill.

It all makes for a heartening first encounter. It is also a fraud. Beirut International Airport deceives visitors into thinking Lebanon is sleek and progressive instead of a country where national trauma has been replaced by administrative paralysis. Once a robust financial capital and tourist draw, Lebanon is saddled with a public debt that exceeds 170 per cent of its gross domestic product, flat growth and a population expanding by nearly 3 per cent a year. Syria's imperial grip provokes the occasional rocket strike from Israel and the second Intifada soured investors on the country's badly needed privatization programme. Like so many Arab states, Lebanon's economic potential is exceeded only by the political forces arrayed against it.

The country was regarded as a rock of ecumenical stability, having rehabilitated itself from the vicious civil wars of the mid-nineteenth century when Muslims killed thousands of Maronite Christians. In 1943, a national charter allocated Maronites the presidency, Sunni Muslims the premiership and Shiites the head of parliament. This reflected the numerical superiority of Christians over Muslims and it preserved the peace until the 1970s, when the Christian advantage gave way to a burgeoning Muslim population.

The Maronite elite refused to accept Lebanon's changing demographics. War clouds gathered and by 1975 sectarian clashes had mushroomed into full-scale civil war. For two decades, Maronites, Druze, Shia, Sunni, and the Palestinian Liberation Organization alternatively allied with and betrayed each other, often serving more powerful patrons – America, the Soviet Union and in the case of the Maronites' Phalange militia, Israel. Damascus intervened on the invitation of the Maronites, with tacit American encouragement. In November 1989, the warring factions signed a peace treaty, the Taif accord, named after the Saudi Arabian city where it was negotiated. This obligated Syria to withdraw from Lebanon; yet more than a decade later, tens of thousands of Syrian troops are still there. Since May 2000, when Israel withdrew from southern Lebanon after its defeat by Hezbollah guerrillas, Lebanon has been peaceful.

Unfortunately, it is not the kind of solid peace that encourages foreign investment and Beirut's revival seems to have been freeze-dried. True, property developer Solidere has expertly renovated the downtown business district straddling the Green Line that during the war divided the Muslim west and Christian east. Fashionably dressed women patronize the boutiques of rue Hamra and students mill about in coffee shops outside the American University of Beirut. Yet much of the city remains blighted and the atmosphere, particularly since the advent of the second Intifada and the September 11 terrorist attacks on America, is tense. Villas restored to their French-colonial splendour alternate with buildings gutted by everything from small-arms fire to mortar rounds. Squatters occupy them and hang their laundry to dry from shattered windows. Bills advertising shampoo and women's underwear are plastered alongside posters of long-dead Shiite mullahs and Muslim *shaheeds* – martyrs. Syria's holy trinity: Hafez al Assad, the late president of Syria, his eldest son Basil – who perished in a car crash – and surviving son Bashar, the current Syrian president, survey their proxy state from countless portraits.

There has been no process of national reconciliation, no cathartic post-mortem of how and why the violence erupted. The Taif accord provided for a peace so fragile it dares not redress the past. As late as spring 2002 people were talking about a devaluation of the Lebanese pound and an inevitable economic collapse. Few investors will underwrite so uncertain a future, and who can blame them? Only a dullard would invest in an electrical grid that could be turned overnight by Israeli warplanes into a linguine of twisted metal.

At least not any more. In the hopeful aftermath of the Oslo peace accord, Lebanon attracted billions of dollars in foreign investment, due in part to the charisma of the then-prime minister, Rafik Hariri, who pushed through an ambitious government plan to redevelop the country's devastated infrastructure. He also chaired Solidere, the company entrusted with rebuilding Beirut's war-torn financial district. The government pledged to sell off state assets, restructure an over-banked financial sector, and overhaul the country's anaemic capital markets.

Hariri reduced inflation and strengthened the pound. The banking sector, which had never defaulted on a transfer in 20 years of civil war, began rebuilding itself. But most of the $23 billion set aside for development was hijacked by parliament and funnelled into payrolls for civil servants, the army and intelligence agencies. In 1998, Hariri resigned after losing a power struggle to President Emile Lahoud. Re-elected in 2001, he has since been groping with an inert economy, a stalled restructuring plan and a high-risk currency. Three decades after François Bassil was running the officers' club at the St Georges Hotel, Lebanon embodies nearly everything that ails the Arab economy: slow-to-flat growth, galloping population rates, a payroll-engorged public sector, an unrealized commitment to privatization and a small, inefficient capital market.

Furthermore, Lebanon's educated elite is bleeding away: up to 3,000 Lebanese aged between 25 and 50 emigrate each month against a monthly birth rate of 5,000. Thus a declining number of working-age citizens are increasingly responsible for a swelling number of the non-working young and elderly. Economic reform becomes less palatable politically as it becomes more urgent, economic decay spirals on, and emigration accelerates. The spectral clutch of fundamentalist Islam, expressed by growing numbers of veiled women and new mosques, tightens at modernity's elbow.

There are two ways to reverse this cycle: investment from without and reform from within – ideally, both together. The Lebanese government, like many Arab regimes, is on its own after doing the one thing no developing economy can afford to do: it pissed off the suits.

Bankers, heal thyselves . . .
In general, the men and women who inhabit the corridors and boardrooms of the great merchant banks in London didn't get there because of blood ties or piety. Success in corporate finance is measured in stark and unforgiving terms. The objective is to anticipate the meeting point along a latitude of greed and a longitude of fear where the price of a stock or a commodity becomes acceptable. Too many mistakes on either side and you're just another loser on Cheap Street. It is an elegantly simple world. The market rarely blinks, flatters, or lies. Capital pursues value and ignores everything else.*

The corporate world's three allied subcultures – stock-broking, research, and investment banking – generate the capital that underwrites the world's business and propels its economies. The first group is rewarded for the volume of shares it trades with fund managers and high net worth individuals. Investment bankers identify a company with an innovative product or service to sell, often in concert with a team of research department analysts, and persuade it to list all or

---

* In between, of course, the epochal bingeing periods symbolized by Drexel Burnham Lambert in the late 1980s and Enron in the early 2000s.

some of its equity on a capital market. This is often known as an initial public offering, or IPO. In return, the bankers' company receives a commission calculated as a percentage of the value of the initial offering, and often a small share of equity from the listing.

In the mid-1990s, the most lucrative corporate finance markets were in the developing world. From Latin America to Asia to the former Eastern Bloc, the number of little known, underfunded companies seemed endless. Merchant banks established emerging markets desks and dispatched their executives to obscure capitals to identify potential IPOs, including the apparently pacified Middle East. They fanned out, laptops slung over their shoulders, like missionaries spreading the gospel. In the wake of the Taif accord and the beginning of the Arab-Israeli peace process a year later in 1991 at a conference in Madrid, the Middle East seemed poised for a boom. Suddenly, the Arab world evolved in the popular consciousness as less a collection of authoritarian states hell-bent on destroying Israel than an untapped market of 250 million people with a common language and culture.

And so the bankers came – to Cairo, to Amman, to Beirut. Negotiators may have hammered out a Middle East peace, but the suits would decide what the peace was worth.

One of them was Aboudi Najia, a stockbroker at Nomura International plc, the London arm of the venerable Japanese trading house. The Nomura building, near St. Paul's Cathedral, is Edwardian on the outside and postmodern, corporate gothic inside. The lobby bustles with expatriate Japanese, exiles from a forgotten empire, and visitors are escorted to an intimate reception room and offered green tea by Japanese service girls.

Aboudi greeted me there three years ago in blue pin-striped suit, yellow tie and braces – the 'power look' that began in the 1980s and has survived numerous bear markets and the sartorial anarchy of casual Fridays.

He was ten years old when the Lebanese civil war started. His family fled to London, the vanguard of a vast Lebanese Diaspora. Unlike his father's generation, which followed more staid professions like medicine and engineering, Aboudi and his peers were lured by finance. After three years working the foreign exchange and commodities desks at American Express, Aboudi was tempted away by Nomura, which was starting up a Middle East trading division.

It was 1995, two years after Oslo, and it seemed peace in the Middle East would finally prevail. History had pronounced in favour of free market capitalism, and Arab governments from Morocco to Qatar were promising aggressive economic liberalization. State-owned cement makers, public utilities, airlines, and banks were to be sold and subjected to free market disciplines. Shimon Peres, the quixotic visionary and Israel's then-prime minister, referred dreamily to 'the New Middle East'. The potential for new business – what bankers call 'deal flow' – was lavish.

So it seemed. In fact both sides were talking past one another.

'They talked the talk about things like "shareholder value",' Aboudi said. 'It turned out they didn't know what shareholder value is.'

In 1994, Nomura launched the first Middle East investment fund. A trickle of bond issues and equity listings followed. By 1996, the deals were gushing in and Nomura, one of the first players in a near-virgin market, was commanding transaction fees of as much as 5 per cent. By the late 1990s, however, the deal flow starting drying up. Privatization plans sputtered and relations between foreign investors and Arab governments – particularly Egypt, the region's largest market – chilled. Not long after Cairo's Commercial International Bank issued a global depository receipt (GDR) – a kind of IPO – its directors moved to vote themselves the right to buy their own stock at L.E10 (10 Egyptian Pounds) a share when the shares were trading at L.E60. Board members voted down the proposal, but foreign investors, unnerved by the attempt, phoned Aboudi with orders to sell.

As Arab share prices stagnated, Arab executives were less inclined to submit themselves to interrogation by investors. When Aboudi asked some senior executives at an Egyptian Bank to accompany him on a roadshow they declined, fearful their chairman would accuse them of angling for extra vacation time. The chairman of a Tunisian bank, during a presentation to promote a share offering, abruptly walked out when asked about the bank's bad loans.

'He just left me there,' Aboudi recalled. 'The investors were shocked. How can you market a company under those circumstances?'

Then came the listing of Arab Re-insurance Group, which Nomura helped manage. The agency, co-owned by insurers in Libya, the United Arab Emirates and Kuwait, specialized in re-insuring transport companies, but was entering the life and medical sectors that cash-strapped Persian Gulf governments could no longer afford to subsidize. The group's shares were listed on stock markets in

Bahrain, Oman, Egypt and Kuwait. The issue raised $200 million and the company's shares rose 20 per cent on the first day's trading to $19. On a roadshow two months later, the insurers assured Aboudi and the investors their prospects were bright.

Within days after Aboudi returned to London, Reuters reported that ARG's sales were 50 per cent below expectation. The company had been deluged with last-minute claims from Saudi Arabia, where policyholders can wait until the end of the year to file claims. Aboudi quickly arranged a conference call with investors and the company promised to be more vigilant. Six months later, ARG released an earnings report that was 15 per cent below estimates and its share price plummeted.

So too, has interest in Arab capital markets. Like most merchant banks, Nomura disbanded its Middle East team and has no plans to form a new one. Aboudi has abandoned whatever ambitions he once had about returning to Lebanon and rebuilding its economy.

'Growing up, we thought peace with Israel would change things,' Aboudi said. 'But Israel's out and things have only gotten worse.'

Among the anticipated dividends of Taif was an overhaul of Lebanon's banking sector. As a financial centre, Lebanon could always punch above its weight; its 55 banks have total assets of only $47 billion, compared with the $500 billion or so held in Hong Kong, but their superb credit rating and financial expertise attracted funds from investors all over the Middle East that they hoped fearless Lebanese bankers would leverage into huge gains.

Today, most Lebanese bankers would just as soon not lend money. If Lebanese banks are profitable, it is because they hold the majority of the country's public debt, which the government finances at 10 per cent in dollars and 16 per cent in Lebanese pounds. Civil war and over-regulation has made Beirut's once-nimble and cosmopolitan bankers risk-averse. Nepotism is chronic; managers are usually pro-moted for their filial ties to the chairman rather than their compe-tence as bankers. Lending officers are trained to offer credit against a borrower's collateral, usually real estate, rather than cash flow. That favours big, established companies at the expense of smaller, more innovative ones.

Collateralized lending is common among most banks in the devel-oping world, where transactions are often done in cash instead of credit due to weak legal codes and a lack of transparency. Financial products the West takes for granted, such as small-business loans and home mortgages, are rare. The exodus of Lebanon's young, educated elite is driven by something as prosaic as the preponderance of collateralized lending; smart people go where the money is cheapest.

It is this that makes Michael Rowihab and his work so important. Michael is a Lebanese banker who has spent much of his 30-year career as the Mr Fixit of international finance. As BankAmerica's specialist in emerging markets, he has travelled the world turning troubled banks around – in Egypt, Kuwait, South Korea and Hong Kong. All his assignments posed the same challenges: reduce bad debt, introduce the latest management and computer technology, cut staff levels, bring in Western-educated managers – almost always from local sources – and develop a lending standard that values cash flow over collateral.

Michael has worked all over the world but never in Lebanon. There he was assigned perhaps his most daunting professional challenge: the revival of Banque Libanaise Pour Le Commerce, Beirut's oldest and at the time most distressed financial institution.

In August 2000, BLC announced its second attempt at a merger in as many years. Investors applauded the deal, valued at more than $200 million. A few weeks later, BLC's portfolio of bad loans were revealed to be far larger than was estimated. The shareholders in the new bank – still known as BLC – bickered with each other, credit committees rarely met and the payroll hadn't been updated in years. There were no computers; accountants still entered transactions involving its 80,000 accounts in ledger books. Overlap was chronic; bank branches operated within shouting distance from each other. At one point, BLC had four treasurers for one treasury. One 'employee' on a 20-year contract was revealed to be the spouse of a man killed in an auto accident several years ago by the wife of a previous BLC chairman.

Into this chaotic breach stepped Michael. BLC had just issued its first consolidated earnings report, announcing a net loss of $110 million for 2000. Its share price on the Beirut stock exchange had halved from its 1997 high.

Michael first assembled a team of accountants and managers to clear the minefield of BLC's hidden, non-performing loans. He bought computers and laid off hundreds of employees. He pleaded, cap in hand, for fresh funding from the handful of Persian Gulf billionaires who emerged with control of the bank. When BLC's books revealed a bad loan from a Sudanese borrower, Michael flew to Khartoum to reschedule it.

He also lobbied the bank's best and brightest to stay. Three months before his arrival, capital markets chief Samer Khalaf, shell-shocked by years of mismanagement, was eager to accept BLC's redundancy compensation. Michael changed his mind. 'Since Michael took over,' Samer told me, 'committees have been set up and decisions are made on the spot. Things are moving like clockwork.'

A team of some 20 accountants was charged with defusing BLC's bad-loan bomb. Non-performing assets – loans that can range in value from $5,000 to $6 million – account for a debilitating $180 million of the bank's total portfolio of $600 million.

It could take years for BLC officers to recover those loans, so many of them would be rescheduled or written off. Michael introduced me to Lama Khalif, one of his 'special asset' committee leaders. Lama classifies loans on a scale of one to five: Unclassified, Special Mention, Standard, Doubtful, and Lost. She calls the debtors, then works with them to recover as much of the loans as possible. Last year, she and her committee redeemed $1.2 million in bad loans.

Most debtors will strike a deal; no one wants to go to court and be seen as a deadbeat borrower, the commercial kiss of death in a small country like Lebanon. Those who default because of the moribund economy usually get a second chance. 'If they can survive a downturn like this, they become very good customers,' Lama told me. 'We just hope the economic climate improves.'

Lama was clearly a natural for the job. Correct, concise, she sat bolt upright in the chair before me. Her hands, clasped together, never strayed from her lap. No one should default on a loan from the Banque Libanaise Pour Le Commerce for fear of getting The Call from Lama Khalif.

'When you define the problem and set a strategy, you find a solution,' she said, resoundingly clear and straightforward in a country known for shadow-play and subterfuge.

Michael had discovered Lama as an auditor working on the BLC merger. She supervises a team of over 15 seasoned accountants, a degree of authority for a businesswoman as refreshing in the Middle East as it is rare.

'My job,' she told me with a slightly menacing half-grin, 'is my pleasure.'

Once the bad debt is mopped up, Michael said, BLC would introduce products overlooked by its rivals. He is eyeing retail business like mortgage lending, an underdeveloped market in Lebanon because of a cumbersome legal process that can delay property repossession for years after a foreclosure. He wants to move aggressively into small-business lending, another neglected market – assuming he can get the board of directors to stump up.

'I want to train people to know our primary source of revenue will come from a company's revenue stream, not its land bank,' Michael told me. 'If it works, others will follow.'

The quiet revolution at BLC comes far too late for people like Nazem Ghandour. But no matter: in Lebanon, when life gives you shit, you grow mushrooms.

In the mid-1950s, Nazem's father opened a sugar-mill in the Ghandour hometown of Tripoli. The refinery had been shuttered during the civil war and after the Taif accord Nazem returned to Lebanon after getting a computer science degree in London to help resurrect the family business. Within three years, the company controlled half of Lebanon's sugar market. Then the government announced that it would help producers of sugar from domestic beet with $30 million in subsidies. Nazem, who was refining high-grade imported beet, was suddenly priced out of the market by cheaper, inferior products. In 1996, the mill had to close when banks called in their loans.

'We took all the financial precautions,' said Nazem. 'We were hedged. We lost the business because of factors beyond our control. The financiers failed us. That is the reason most Middle East businesses fail.'

I visited Nazem and his partner, Tarik Arafiri, at the old refinery, abandoned and run down, to hear their story. The offices were empty and the windows smashed. But I hadn't come all the way to Tripoli to see a rusting sugar mill.

I had come for the mushrooms.

In less than five years, Nazem and Tarik had transformed themselves from failed sugar refiners into Lebanon's celebrated mushroom magnates. Having lost his father's business to greedy creditors, Nazem opened two restaurants in downtown Tripoli, hoping to exploit the peace boom. But the boom broke, so Nazem searched for a new enterprise. He settled – with no experience in agribusiness – on mushrooms.

'My experience told me that the biggest problem with running a restaurant was having to import specialty products like fresh vegetables and meat,' Nazem said. 'So I started thinking about growing mushrooms.'

Why mushrooms?

'We had a cold-storage area that went along with the sugar refinery,' Nazem said. 'It was used for potatoes but I thought it would do well for mushrooms.'

Nazem ordered a copy of *The Mushroom Cultivator* by Paul Stamets, the high priest of mushroom culture, through Amazon for $65. He began with 'spawn', or seed production. When that didn't work, he imported seeds and grew mushrooms in a container he picked up for free from a local oil refinery.

After an initial investment of $2,000 and a few months of experimentation, Nazem was harvesting his first batch of *agaricus bisporus* – white button mushrooms. He christened the company 'Le Champignon Parfait' – The Perfect Mushroom. Within six months its daily yield filled six cold-storage rooms. Now, the company is Lebanon's top mushroom producer, employs 21 people and generates average annual revenues of $400,000. It has averaged sales growth of 40 per cent each year, a rate Nazem expects to sustain for the next several years. And he is expanding into asparagus.

Nazem met Tarik several years ago while buying chemicals. They make an odd pair; Nazem is soft-spoken with a slight lisp. He is a businessman and is interested in mushrooms as a means of making money. Married with an eight-month-old baby boy, he is tall, squarely built and calm, almost serene. His eyes seem heavy-lidded.

Tarik is a 60-year-old chemist by training but – as he carefully points out – is a smelter by profession. He is short and wiry, with a scientist's passion for complex methods and processes and the only atheist I have met in the Middle East.

'Religion gets in the way of science,' Tarik says. 'I don't go out at night because I'm afraid of the fundamentalists.' He pointed at a Jeep Wagoneer parked outside. 'See my big car? I buy American for safety.'

Tarik has bright eyes, speaks with a kind of lilt and is easily excitable. He sits literally at the end of his seat as Nazem, sprawled out comfortably on an easy chair, guides me through the arcana of mushroom cultivation. Mushrooms grow in cycles of 40 days, he tells me. Harvest lasts three to four days and consists of four picks – 'flushes' in mushroom parlance – per day. Typically, the first two flushes yield a ton of mushrooms each, followed by successive flushes equal to about 40 and 20 per cent respectively of the first two.

But all of this is secondary to the real art of mushroom rearing.

'The trick,' Nazem says, sliding like Tarik to the end of his chair, 'is in the compost.'

'Compost is an art!' declares Tarik, *'A science!'*

'In the US,' Nazem continues, 'there are companies that make and deliver compost, but we had to develop our own. We had to find the right mix of temperature and the right amount of oxygen. We experimented with the development cycle, the fermentation process. It wasn't until this year we got everything computerized. We've removed the factor of human error from the compost process.'

We toured the factory, built inside the sugar mill. Some equipment from the old refinery had been cannibalized for mushroom production and much of the original staff had been reassigned for mushroom work. A chief mechanic is now chief compost-maker and an electrical engineer the farm manager.

We entered the compost room which reeked of fresh chicken and horse manure – the vital ingredients of compost that are mixed with straw, stacked in a heap and drenched with water under a sprinkler boom.

Once the compost is properly hydrated it is transferred to a huge container where it is fermented for four days, pasteurized and conditioned. A $7,000 computer network produced by Janssen Kessel, a Dutch composting systems company, runs the whole process. The mainframe and monitor installed on the container wall showed everything fermenting swimmingly at an optimum temperature of 58 degrees Fahrenheit.

We returned to the office. Nazem wanted to boost sales by exporting, but this meant increasing production to achieve the proper scale.

'Exporting is complicated!' Tarik exclaimed. 'It is time consuming, wasteful, humiliating . . .'

Humiliating?

'He means the procedures you have to go through to get the proper licensing,' Nazem said. 'But also, we don't really even have a marketing team. We have six people . . .'

'Drivers, really . . .'

Greater production demands greater capacity, which requires new investment, Nazem said. That means fresh capital, but the banks are not lending.

'The banks here look at your name,' he said, 'and if they find you've screwed up once they won't issue you credit. Something has to be done in this country. I have a friend who started a cell-phone system in 1995 after the war destroyed all the landlines. Lebanon is a $2 billion-a-year cell-phone market. We speak more on cell phones than anyone, because . . .'

'Because we love to talk!' Tarik said, nearly shouting. 'We're feeble-minded, we're . . .'

Nazem cut Tarik off calmly. 'It's because we got so used to cell phones when there were no landlines during the war. Anyway, my friend charged $3,000 per connection and got rich. But then the politicians came in with their own system and they squeezed him out.'

'If you want to be successful in this country,' Tarik told me, 'you have to be an insider. They pick on us, they over-regulate us, they smother us!'

Nazem accused Tarik of exaggeration and the two began to argue. Both were saying more or less the same thing but clearly enjoyed arguing for the sake of it. They agreed on one thing: reform – both political and economic – was desperately needed.

'We cannot express our opinions,' said Nazem. 'We see corruption but can do nothing about it. The poor are uneducated and passionate. They cannot say a word about their government, so they condemn the West. We want democracy.'

'Yes, democracy!' Tarik echoed.

'And transparency . . .'

'Transparency . . . and tolerance!'

'Tarik,' Nazem said, 'we have tolerance.'

'Not any more! Look at my car, see how big it is!'

They were at it again. It was getting late, so I signalled between rebuttals it was time for me to go. They graciously invited me back, and presented me with a crate filled with cartons of fresh mushrooms and trial asparagus, which had been marked and bowed by a hailstorm the night before.

The Deadly Embrace

In addition to a common language and culture, Arabs share a sense of violation, both from within and without. There is the corruption, brutality and ineptitude of their own regimes and the inequities they believe have been imposed on them from abroad. The Palestinians have Zionism, the Iraqis Saddam Hussein and the US-led embargo, the Jordanians their increasingly weak and corrupt British-installed monarchy.

The Lebanese have Syria.

'Look at them,' gestured 22-year-old Radwan, a driver who once picked me up from the airport. He motioned to some scruffy young men milling under a highway overpass who, even to my untrained eye, stood out among the fashion-obsessed Lebanese. 'They come here and take our jobs. Everyone hates them. It's time for the Syrians to go home.'

Radwan wore a silk shirt and his hair was thoroughly moussed. I couldn't imagine him lugging bags of cement on a construction site wearing a threadbare polyester T-shirt and plastic sandals. But his outrage over what the workers represented – Syrian violation of Lebanese sovereignty – was genuine.

In addition to being a cauldron of competing religious sects, Lebanon – once a prosperous Mediterranean enclave – had become a sluice gate for the slurry of its neighbour's excess. Syrian politicians used Beirut's banking-secrecy laws to deposit their private fortunes in Lebanese banks; Syrian generals launder drug-money through Lebanese accounts. Until recently, Syria's young elite – including the new president, Bashar al Assad – surfed the Internet via Lebanese servers before Syria developed its own.

Hezbollah, supported by both Syria and Iran and hailed as a liberator for driving out the Israelis, is now regarded as a potential liability. While happy to regain control of the south, most Lebanese would like to see Hezbollah consolidate its victory by leaving the Jews alone.

Plain-clothed Syrian intelligence agents man border checkpoints. An estimated 30,000 Syrian troops remain in Lebanon – in contravention of the Taif accord – since their deployment during the civil war, part of a 'protection force' that many Lebanese grumble is a praetorian guard for Syrian interests. Syrian militias, for example, run oil refineries in the Lebanese cities of Tripoli and Sidon. Once owned by a consortium of Iraqi investors and a joint venture between Mobil and Caltex, they were shut down in 1978, but still 'employ' 500 Syrian emigrants.

As many as half-a-million Syrians could be in Lebanon doing unskilled jobs, though the Lebanese labour ministry lists only 530 guest workers in the country. When they commit a crime they are brought before a Syrian security agent, not a Lebanese police officer. They are to the Syrian economy what the Lebanese Diaspora is to Lebanon; Syrians work for the equivalent of a few dollars a day, two-thirds of which is remitted to Syria. They demand no medical insurance or social services, which is good for employers; they pay no taxes, which is bad for Lebanon.

The depths of popular resentment against Damascus are difficult to plumb, as few people are prepared to speak out openly against occupation for fear of provoking Syria. In 2000, several judges who called for a Syrian withdrawal were assassinated and Damascus figured prominently as the chief suspect. However, nearly two years after the Israeli pullout and a perceived softening from Damascus since the 'election' of Bashar al Assad, the resentment is beginning to seep through.

'The Syrians will stay,' said Michael Young, a political analyst and columnist for Beirut's *Daily Star*, 'but pressure is mounting for them to go, and the Americans will have to take notice of this. A lot of young people are fed up. They have less to lose. They are the motor of this movement.'

A number of Lebanese leaders are fuelling it. One of them is Nasrallah Sfeir, the patriarch of the Maronite Church. While travelling abroad in March 2001, Sfeir vocally condemned Syria's occupation and was welcomed by some 100,000 Christians when he returned home. A few months later, he announced during a visit to North America he would not meet Pope John Paul II during his historic visit to Damascus. Within days, Sfeir received a courtesy call from Druze leader Walid Jumblatt, who during the war waged a bitter guerrilla fight against the Maronites for control of the Chouf Mountains in southern Lebanon. The two sides were well into a rapprochement inspired largely by their mutual desire to see the back end of the Syrians. In September, two dormitories housing Syrian workers were attacked in southern Lebanon with sticks of dynamite. Though no one was hurt, it was a particularly violent expression of discontent. Not long after, Syrian troops staged a redeployment disguised as a partial withdrawal that suggested at least mild unease in Damascus.

A week after the Christians celebrated Sfeir's return, 300,000 Shia Muslims congregated in Beirut's southern suburbs on a Muslim holy day to hear their spiritual leader and Hezbollah Secretary-General, Sayyed

Hassan Nasrallah, praise Syria for doing its 'national duty' by policing Lebanon against the profane designs of the Zionist oppressor, Israel.

The man who called upon Nasrallah Sfeir, Walid Jumblatt, is the son of a pacifist-turned-guerrilla leader and lives in a pink stone palace named Mukhtara, after the village where it nestles deep in the mountains of the Chouf. To get there you head south along the coast from Beirut on Route One, then east along the inland highway and snake for about 90 minutes through mountain passes and dramatic switchbacks. Maronite villages – clusters of medieval stone villas with red-tiled roofs and rusted-metal storm shutters – hug the road.

I first met Jumblatt in May 2001 through Khaled Yacoub Oweis, a friend and correspondent in the Reuters' Beirut bureau. The invitation came at short notice, but we immediately packed ourselves into Khaled's battered Porsche; an offer of coffee and pistachios with a Lebanese warlord should never be refused.

For much of the civil war Walid continued in his father's role as reluctant warrior. He battled the Maronites, who had lined up behind Israel to the horror of an Arab world struggling to keep a united front against the Jewish state. The Druze were first led by Walid's father, Kamal, who fought alongside Palestinian groups exiled to Lebanon after being driven from their de facto occupation of Jordan in September 1970. Kamal, a Gandhian who also led the Lebanese left, wanted to reverse 140 years of Christian rule. But the late Hafez al Assad, the Syrian dictator, feared such a conflict would give Israel an excuse to 'rescue' its Christian proxy by invading Lebanon and even marching on Damascus for good measure. An all-out war in the Middle East – only three years after the 1973 Arab-Israeli conflict nearly precipitated a great power nuclear exchange – seemed imminent.

In March 1976, the United States endorsed a Syrian intervention to subdue the crisis, an abrupt volte-face from Washington's previous warnings that Damascus should not get involved. On 1 June 1976, Syrian forces moved into Lebanon. Kamal Jumblatt condemned Assad as an adventurist fascist dictator. On 16 March 1977, gunmen intercepted Kamal as he was being driven to Mukhtara from the Druze stronghold of B'aqlin and blew out the back of his head.

Walid Jumblatt, among many others, held the Syrians responsible for his father's assassination. Nevertheless, when Walid finished the customary 40-day mourning period he found himself in Damascus before Assad, the godfather of Syria, for the ritual sanction.

Assad greeted his young visitor warmly. 'How closely you resemble your father,' he remarked. Such is the shadow under which Walid Jumblatt – and Lebanon – dwells.

Over the last two years, Walid has been testing the limits of Damascene tolerance. He condemns the Syrian presence and its support for Hezbollah's occupation of the south, both on moral grounds and for its corrosive effect on the Lebanese economy. Damascus, in response, proclaimed him *persona non grata* and an 'insignificant, isolated leader unworthy of any care'. He has rebuilt ties to the Maronite community, correctly identifying them as the lynchpin of the country's dwindling middle class.

Upon arriving at the gates of the castle, built in 1650 by Jumblatt's ancestors, the guards comprising the modest security detail cheerfully motioned us through. Having parked Khaled's Porsche on a clearing overlooking the vast Mukhtara valley, we made our way to the stone steps of the reception villa, which was set apart from the main palace.

It was Saturday and the warlord was hearing petitions from his people. We wandered into the complex of elaborate *diwans,* Hellenic statues and mosaics embellished the courtyard. The spacious reception rooms were filled with antique furniture from around the world: a walnut campaign desk from England, leather chairs from Italy, rugs from Central Asia. Flamboyant lamps of brightly coloured stained glass hung from the ceilings.

Objects of war were everywhere. German Mausers and British Enfields were mounted alongside a huge oil depicting Russia's calamitous 1905 naval engagement with Japan in the Tsushima Straits, between Japan and the Korean peninsula. On his desk was the French translation of a book on how the Allies broke Germany's secret codes in the Second World War. Elaborate uniforms displayed on dummies manned the corner of each room.

On Walid's office desk were two loaded Smith & Wesson automatic pistols with extra clips and a Kalashnikov automatic rifle by the door. These were not for show.

We positioned ourselves near the entry of the *diwan* where Jumblatt was sitting, patiently listening to a laundry-list of complaints and requests – land squabbles, family disputes, pleas for jobs on the government's already bloated payroll. Each party presented him with supporting documents, testimonials, and calling cards. He examined them respectfully before passing them to an aide for follow-up.

It was a poignant look at how civic affairs are administered in a world where local authorities are filling a vacuum created by a weakened central government. A Beirut that lacks the funds or willpower to provide civil and legal services relies on leaders like Jumblatt to meet the needs of his people. This ruthless and successful guerrilla leader was now little more than a tribal sheik, a paternal mediator of petty disputes in a fragile peace.

We waited for ten minutes or so. Finally, the tall, lanky patriarch walked over and gestured, without acknowledging us directly, to follow us into another, smaller *diwan*. He whispered a few, final instructions to an aide before bidding us sit down on a sofa that extended the length of the room and was covered in an antique kilim. Paintings and sketches of his father were spot lit reverently by tiny, halogen lamps.

He sat down, flanked by the two of us with Khaled on his right. He was wearing faded jeans, a blue blazer, and a hastily knotted blue tie. His eyes projected that strange haunted melancholy frozen in countless, grainy news photos.

Walid waved his hand wearily: 'Ask what you like.'

Khaled generously let me ask most of the questions: routine queries about his thoughts on Israel's withdrawal, his most recent, forceful comments on the occupation and overall prospects for peace against the terrible backdrop of the current Intifada. He anticipated prolonged violence, with Lebanon in the middle and no peace in sight. Only Washington could end the conflict, he said, but it has no incentive to get involved. Syria will continue its occupation, consigning a once-robust financial centre into a decaying Damascene satellite while chasing out its most important asset – a prosperous and multi-religious, white-collar class.

'I'm stuck here,' he told us. 'I have to look to the interests of my people, though anyone else able to find a job outside is leaving. The Lebanese elites, especially the Christians, are leaving the country. Unless the trend is reversed Lebanon will soon be like all Arab countries – predominantly Muslim and totalitarian.'*

Earlier that month, Hezbollah killed an Israeli soldier in a disputed area on the foothills of the Golan Heights, prompting an Israeli strike on a Syrian radar battery in Lebanon. Damascus responded, as always, with a fiery pledge to teach the Zionists a stiff lesson. As always, it did

---

* I tried to confirm a rumor that Sfeir, the Maronite patriarch, had asked the US embassy to help reverse the brain drain by rejecting Christian applications for visas to America. My calls to the embassy, a sprawling, walled community on the outskirts of Beirut, were unreturned.

nothing. Nonetheless, Walid noted, even the occasional air strike is enough to keep investors away from Lebanon. That means less money available to pay down the country's huge public debt or to invest in its ailing infrastructure.

'Hariri's whole plan for bringing investment to Lebanon is at stake,' Walid said. 'He's in bad shape. One scenario is the economy collapses and the government is replaced by the military. That would suit the Syrians. They don't like him.'

I asked about Bashar al Assad, who had just taken over Syria after his father's recent death.

'The best way for Bashar to consolidate his power is to declare the crusade of Palestine,' said Walid. 'He has nothing to lose. America doesn't care about Arab public opinion and democratization. So long as the Arabs produce cheap oil and buy US weapons, American interests in the Middle East are being served. Why should the US give a damn about the Christians of Lebanon?'

Walid's soft voice was barely audible through the torrent of water that cascaded from the top of the mountains and funnelled into the cisterns and aqueducts of Mukhtara. He ended by warning that war in Lebanon could resurrect itself, ghoul-like, unless Washington pressured Syria to quit Lebanon and control Hezbollah. Only that, he told us, could lead to real economic recovery.

The interview over, we thanked Walid and said goodbye. As we walked out, I took some photos of the palace. Walid reappeared and gave us a personal tour of the grounds. He seemed to have relished a visit from someone in pursuit of his opinions rather than his patronage.

Khaled leavened Walid's spirits with humour. Jumblatt partly owned a vineyard in the Bekka Valley named Khafraya. The Syrians had recently deployed two Soviet-built tanks just outside the winery, and Khaled suggested they be featured on the label of Khafraya's next limited-edition Burgundy-style wine.

Walid smiled. 'Comme "Estate du T-72",' he quipped.*

We parted again, this time for good. 'I speak a little French,' he said. 'Keep me in mind if your newspaper needs a translator.'

On the way back to Beirut Khaled and I took a detour to see the Umayyad ruins at Anjar. The Syrian-Lebanese relationship hasn't changed much since the first Arab-Muslim dynasty over thirteen

---

* 'Like "From the T-72 Estate",' he quipped.

centuries ago. Then, as now, Lebanon was a Damascene satellite. Sadly for contemporary Lebanese, vassalage was much easier under the caliph than under the Assads. In Umayyad times, between the seventh and eighth centuries, Lebanon prospered as an important gateway to Mediterranean markets. No borders restricted the flow of goods and people into what was even then a service economy built around trade.

The caliph ruled with a light hand; in the summers, he moved his court to the milder climes of Anjar, in the foothills of the Lebanon Mountains. Anjar today is populated largely by Armenians, the progeny of refugees who escaped the genocide committed against them by the Turks a century ago. Homes of plaster-covered cinder-block painted in faded pastels cling to a latticework of roads and side streets. At the centre of town stands an Armenian church with a large fountain. It is a prosperous rural community blessed with nitrate-rich soil and a mild climate. The head of the Syrian intelligence agency in Lebanon – known in Arabic as the *mukhabarat* – heads the Syrian garrison in the country from his headquarters in Anjar.

Few tourists come to Anjar; the Roman cities of Ba'albek and Tripoli have long overshadowed the appeal of a 1,300-year-old shopping mall and summer palace where the caliph relaxed when he wasn't embroiled in court intrigue in the capital. Those who bother to make the trip are greeted at the main gate by a hapless camel lashed to a rail and poised for the next thrill-seeking tourist eager for a ride. A covey of young guides loiter in the shade of a whispering pine, seemingly content sipping Armenian vodka and soda water bought from a nearby concession stand. They charge the equivalent of $3 for an hour-long tour. Our tour had to be cut short, however; Syrian soldiers had occupied the northeast corner of the ruins and Faris, our guide, didn't want to disturb them. We could see their laundry drying on a clothes line suspended between the ramparts.

'No Lebanese ruin would be complete without Syrian soldiers sleeping in them,' said Khaled.

Not far away, we stumbled over the broken glass plate that covered a spotlight used to illuminate the ruins after dark. Someone had made off with the halogen bulb. 'It must have happened recently,' Faris muttered. 'I didn't notice it this morning.'

The Anjar ruins are of worn pink stone and mud brick consumed by a firestorm of mustard-weed blossoms and dried, golden reeds. Lizards, well camouflaged against the dung-coloured brick, flattened themselves in the heat. Faris gave us a lazy account of the city's history. The centrepiece was a palace built in 700 AD by the Islamic caliph, 'Abd al Malik, who often summered here away from Damascus. At its heart was a large courtyard where the caliph would hear petitions. Like most Islamic palaces, there was a mosque on one side and special quarters for the royal harem on the other – symbols of the caliph's competing secular and spiritual appetites. The royal baths, as important to the early Muslims as the Romans, heated water drawn from a nearby reservoir. Potable water was pumped throughout the complex for drinking and ablutions before prayer, then recycled for irrigation and the watering of livestock.

Anjar straddled the trade routes linking the Mediterranean with the spice markets of India and the Arabian Peninsula and was an established entrepot long before the arrival of Al Malik. It was the caliph, however, who rebuilt the city on an ancient Roman plan. Bisecting arcades – known to the Byzantines as *cardo maximus* and *documanus maximus* and designed to match the Christian cross – overflowed with shops hawking textiles, leather goods, silver and gold jewellery, garments, and spices imported from Syria, Turkey, Palestine, and the Orient. A community of merchants and craftsman – mostly Jews and Christians – lived together outside the city.

The arcades, covered by a vaulted, cedar-wood roof, crossed at a square supported by sixteen pillars bundled at each corner into clusters of four. The pillars are joined by Arabesque arches and feature Roman-style shafts and Byzantine capitals hewn in Italy. The cosmopolitan Al Malik delighted in hybrid motifs that served both form and function; the stone walls are interrupted every five feet or so by three rows of tiling running parallel to the earth. This gave the structure flexibility in earthquakes, an innovation thought to be introduced by Roman engineers and enhanced by the Persians.

The palace was discovered in 1959, Faris told us, and remains one of the most complete early Islamic sites. Prior to the Second World War, most archaeologists considered the early Muslim era as unimportant and many of its ruins were cleared away to reach the more glamorous Byzantine and Roman strata underneath them. Only recently have Medievalists, even Arab ones, come to appreciate the depth of early Islamic culture.

I tipped Faris and thanked him for the tour. Returning to Khaled's car we passed the camel, now on all fours and masticating mechanically, as camels do.

Occupation Lost

The Lebanese haven't lost their talent for trading. In southern
Lebanon, a few hours drive south from Walid's castle in Mukhtara are
the remains of what was once one of the Arab world's most robust
economies. Unfortunately, that was when it was also a war zone.
When the war ended, so did the economy.

Until three years ago, the strip of land along Lebanon's southern
border was occupied by Israeli troops to protect northern Israel
from missile attacks by Hezbollah. This cost Israel two or three
young soldiers killed each month by Hezbollah guerrilla strikes.
On 15 May 2000, the then-Israeli prime minister, Ehud Barak, fulfilled a campaign pledge to withdraw from southern Lebanon,
frantically yanking troops out and leaving their proxy militia, the
Christian-dominated South Lebanese Army, to fend for itself.
Commentators in Washington warned Hezbollah would shower
northern Israel with Katushya rockets, provoking a hellish response
on targets in Lebanon and possibly Syria. Instead, Hezbollah
leaders displayed considerable restraint. It set up medical facilities
and repaired some damaged infrastructure. Some suspected SLA
leaders were tried for collaborating with the enemy but their sen-
tences were relatively light. Within a year, many of the 6,000 SLA
members and civilians that sought refuge in Israel had returned
home.

Militant Islam has always flourished in the south, in part because
Beirut always neglected it. While Hezbollah and a fundamentalist
group and rival to Hezbollah known as *Amal* – The Deprived –
tended to the south's Muslims, Israel helped enrich the SLA
members, paying them some $500 a month and allowing a member
of each militiamen's family to work in Israel. Many southern
Lebanese were employed in Israel as day labourers. Bilateral trade –
some legitimate, most not – between the occupied zone and Israel
was brisk. A hospital in Bint Jubayl run by Lebanese doctors, stocked
with the best pharmaceuticals and medical supplies from Israel,
offered free medical care to anyone with a $10 insurance card. By
some estimates, per capita income in the zone averaged twice the
national average.

Business once boomed at the Château de Pins, a resort complex
in Ayn Ibil, a largely Christian village with a population of 900
people. With a large dining room and an outdoor café overlooking
an Olympic-sized swimming pool, the 'château' is run by Imad La
Clauss, once a maintenance chief for a United Nations peace-

keeping unit deployed in 1978. On weekends, it would be filled with Beiruties fleeing the dust and grime of the capital. SLA militiamen would bring their families here for the afternoon. The dining room was booked solid with wedding receptions. Even Israeli soldiers would come to lounge by the pool and drink Lebanese wine.

'Even before 1975,' Imad said, 'there was no infrastructure, no companies, no factories. When the Palestinians brought their war here from Jordan we were shelled every day by the Israelis. Four people died in my village. So we decided to prohibit the Palestinians from attacking Israel.'

The Lebanese Army split into pro- and anti-Palestinian camps. The people of Ayn Ibil opposed the PLO and were rewarded with Israeli work permits. Traders brought items from Israel that were channelled into the smuggling trade between Lebanon and Syria. Some Ayn Ibil families, Imad said, made as much as $3,000 a month. They neglected agriculture, southern Lebanon's traditional, legitimate industry, in favour of smuggling.

'Now,' Imad said, gesturing to the empty swimming pool and vacant deck chairs, 'we are in a very drastic situation.'

When the Israelis and the SLA fled they took much of the economy and infrastructure with them. The Israelis controlled water, power, telephone and hospitals; when they left they shut everything down. There is little, if any, foreign investment. Coincidentally, a conference of expatriate Lebanese businessmen opened in Beirut only a week after the Israeli withdrawal. With Lebanon at last free of foreign occupation, could investment be far behind?

'I doubt it,' said Imad Jaber, an ex-parliamentarian in his villa near Nabatiyah, south Lebanon's commercial centre just north of the zone, after the Israeli withdrawal. 'I have a son in Africa, making potato chips. Why would he come back to this?'

Imad, a tobacco farmer, was lamenting the government's disregard of the south. There are no factories, he pointed out, just an inefficient, woefully subsidized tobacco industry. The World Bank and International Monetary Fund has pledged $5 billion to help rebuild the region, but no new projects have been announced. A programme to build an irrigation canal and improve the roads had yet to be implemented. Whatever money Beirut had for infrastructure was siphoned away to pay down the national debt.

'The central government has a budget that is barely enough to rebuild our houses destroyed in the war,' Imad said, overlooking his fallow tobacco fields. 'The money will have to come from outside.'

Shortly after Israel's withdrawal, Lebanese from all over the country gathered in the south in a crush motivated by profit as well as patriotism; many were seeking luxury items from the smuggling trade. Chivas Regal scotch – $15 a litre in the south, compared with $40 in Beirut – and Davidoff cigarettes were in particularly high demand.

When the crowds came, Mahmoud al Mawla, the governor of Nabatiyah, spent the whole day directing traffic. When I met him he was grappling with the reality of the Israeli exodus and a provincial district that for 22 years had been neglected by the central government. Roads and ports were in disrepair and electricity intermittent at best. An Israeli company had dug a well and pumped water to it from inside Israel but stopped after the withdrawal because it knew it wouldn't get paid. If Hezbollah reaped the glory from Israel's defeat, Mahmoud was harvesting the mess.

Mahmoud, like all provincial governors in Lebanon and much of the Middle East, was appointed by the central government but is popular with his constituents. Fadi Ali Ahmad, a consultant I knew, had introduced us. 'People like Mahmoud,' Fadi had told me. 'He's an honest one.'

Mahmoud was 45 years old when Israel pulled out. When we met he was wearing a pine-tree green, double-breasted suit. His office, a typical *diwan*, had chairs lining the walls and long tables for traditional rounds of bitter Turkish coffee. Fadi and I arrived at about 9 a.m. to a municipal office complex teaming with officials and tribal sheiks for the first weekly meeting to be held since the withdrawal.

'We never thought the Israelis would leave,' he told me. 'But we're doing our best with the resources we have.'

The empty boxes and Styrofoam packing of a new Panasonic telephone system cluttered the corridors and Mahmoud's calls kept getting misdirected. A delegation of northern governors and mayors arrived to celebrate the south's victory and be photographed for the afternoon papers. No one flinched when the electricity went out; Mahmoud's personal computer and fax machine still functioned, powered by a car battery under his desk.

The politicos departed, their egos suitably stroked. In walked a police officer with two silver stars on his epaulettes. He whispered into Mahmoud's ear the latest developments in a case involving a lawyer who two days earlier shot someone dead. The murder was an isolated event, Mahmoud told me, but he wanted to keep the investigation quiet to prevent a vendetta that could shatter the relative calm that followed Israel's exodus.

More deputies entered. A blocked sewage line was fouling a nearby intersection. A debate ensued on how to deliver a batch of documents to Beirut. Who should they send? Would the driver need gas money? A cluster of families in a remote village wanted to subdivide a parcel of land but there are no deeds because the Israelis kept no such records. Mahmoud referred the matter to the Lebanese equivalent of a circuit-court judge. The city of Bint Jubayl had gone without water since the Israelis switched off the pipes. Tanker trucks had arrived but there was insufficient electricity to pump the water they carried into local cisterns. Chain-smoking Marlboros, the governor ordered electricity diverted from the city of Tyre, some 20 miles away.

We sat down to watch the morning TV news. It led with footage of Mahmoud inspecting what he told me was a pump diverting water from Lebanon's Al Wazani river into Israel. Armed troops were filmed standing guard on the Israeli side, firing warning shots at anyone who got too close to the pump. At El Khiam, 25 miles to the east, Israeli trucks were shown carting off what was reported to be lush Lebanese topsoil.

Water and land, the Middle East's twin clarion calls. 'This has been going on for six, seven months,' Mahmoud said, slouched in a chair, his eyes fixed on the screen. 'We're trying to resolve it through diplomatic means.'*

Mahmoud showed his deputies how to draw up bills for the development company tasked with repairing the south's dilapidated roads. 'Write everything up and report it,' he told them. 'Don't bother me with any charges under $2,000.'

A few hours later, after lunch, we were relaxing over glasses of Chivas Regal at Mahmoud's villa. He had changed into shorts and a T-shirt emblazed with the Johnny Walker Scotch logo. He gestured toward the hills that until a few days ago were crested by Israeli artillery positions. The withdrawal was a step towards real peace, he said, but only a small one.

'The Israelis are gone, and we're in control,' he said. 'But it will be a long time before we can trust them. That's for the next generation.'

---

* A foreign ministry official later confirmed that one of the items Beirut is demanding from Israel as compensation is, in fact, Lebanese dirt.

How will you redevelop the economy?

'Just because we didn't expect the Israelis to withdraw, it doesn't mean we didn't have a plan. Wait a year, and then come back.'

So I did.

Actually, it was two years later. The Arab summit held in Beirut had just ended, the second Intifada was in its eighteenth month and Israel had just launched what would be a three-week siege of the West Bank. Ariel Sharon was whacking Yasser Arafat's 'terrorist infra-structure' following a suicide bomb attack on a restaurant in Netanya that killed nearly two-dozen Israelis celebrating Passover. The Palestinians said the attack was in response to an unprovoked Israeli assault on Palestinians celebrating an Islamic holy feast in Gaza a week earlier. Moral authority still mattered in the Middle East even as it entered its sixth decade of conflict.

Nabatiyah was cloaked in banners condemning Israel and glorify-ing the recently martyred. There were anti-American riots in Beirut, Cairo, Amman and throughout the Persian Gulf. The weather was unseasonably cold and wet and the municipal office complex draughty; employees wore gloves and leather jackets as they worked. The atmosphere was tense. A day earlier, Israel accused Hezbollah of firing a Katushya rocket into northern Israel and there were fears of retaliation.

A secretary led me into the governor's office. Mahmoud was smartly dressed in matching suede leather waistcoat, jacket and cravat. He appeared to have lost weight. The car battery was still there and he was still entertaining constituents. One of them pre-sented him a gift of scented *nesbaha*, or worry beads, which someone had purchased while on pilgrimage to Mecca.

The visitors prepared to leave, though Mahmoud insisted they take a handful of sweets from a silver tray on the coffee table in front of his desk. He closed the door behind them, sat down and immediately began fingering the beads.

'All that surrounds us is depressing,' Mahmoud told me. 'Look at what is happening in Palestine. There is no sign of peace. Lebanese people, and those in the south especially, were behind the peace process and they were surprised and disappointed to see Israel elect Ariel Sharon. If you're going the way of peace, you need a man of peace.'

Mahmoud, with some help from Beirut, had managed to rebuild schools, hospitals, roads, water works and a telephone grid. 'But things work very slowly in Lebanon and they still haven't delivered what they promised – the things we discussed two years ago. We were to be an important part of the economy. We were ready for many, many projects. But how can we provide our people with opportunity when we haven't progressed in peace?'

There was no foreign investment, Mahmoud said. The political risk was too high and the future too bleak. 'The Israelis say we fired a Katushya at them but we can't confirm this. It means they are preparing something. Why should anyone invest here? It is not stable. What if the Israelis invade again?'

I asked Mahmoud if his constituents approach him for government jobs, traditionally the employer of last resort in Lebanon and just about everywhere else in the Arab world.

'Every day,' he said. 'People come to my office and ask for help. I have to tell them there is a moratorium on civil service hires.'

Turned away by the government, I suggested, jobless Lebanese call on Hezbollah, with its *madrassas*, hospitals and day-care centres.

Mahmoud fidgeted. 'Hezbollah is under the law,' he said. 'We have 1,500 soldiers and police here to maintain order. But they don't tell us when they will launch an operation.'

How can there be peace if an influential group like Hezbollah refuses to recognize Israel?

'If there is a real peace, there will be real co-existence,' Mahmoud said. 'If Israel accepts the pre-1967 borders as legitimate, even Hezbollah will recognize Israel. But only if they get their land back. Suicide bombers are not terrorists. They have a right to resist the occupation. We need America to stop this. Most educated Arabs hold the US as an ideal for democracy, liberty, tolerance. Why don't we have better relations? Because of Sharon? This man of blood? The Jewish lobby in America? I don't hate the Jews. The people killed in those cafés by suicide bombs are not all Ariel Sharons. Do you think any Arab wants this? But when you see what the Israelis are doing . . .'

Mahmoud put his beads on the desk. It was getting late and he had allowed me more than the hour he said he could spare. As we shook hands, he offered me chocolates from the coffee-table tray.

There would be no lunching *alfresco* today. There wasn't the time and it was too cold out.

As a group, Hezbollah – 'Party of God' – evolved during the Lebanese civil war and was inspired by the Iranian revolution of

1979. It attained notoriety after Israel's 1982 invasion of Lebanon and the subsequent US deployment there to stabilize the region. Hezbollah is supported by Iran and Syria and its stated objective is to establish the Middle East as an Islamic Republic. The group has been associated with some of the bloodiest acts of violence in Lebanon's long history of sectarian strife, including the 1983 car bombing that killed 241 US marines as they slept in their barracks.

Hezbollah is still committed to the destruction of the Jewish state – which irks a Lebanese government concerned less with jihad than rebuilding its economy. There is ample evidence that Damascus and Tehran continue to fund the organization and it occasionally goads Israel by attacking or kidnapping Israeli soldiers wandering into what it claims is Arab land. Every so often Hezbollah Secretary-General, Sheik Hassan Nasrallah, speaks ominously about a looming confrontation with Israel that will open a new front in the current Intifada and enflame the region in conflict. This appeared imminent early in 2001; news reports – many from off-the-record briefings provided by Israeli intelligence officers – warned Hezbollah was hoarding weapons and girding for a prolonged assault.

A contrarian voice came from Israel's daily newspaper, *Ha'aretz*. 'The absurdity of attributing to the Hezbollah a strategic threat' wrote Reuven Pedatzur in the 7 February 2001 edition, 'is symptomatic of a certain routine on the part of [Israel's] senior command. It can't operate without identifying – and nurturing – new threats. The senior officers need the shadow of threats, whether real or rhetorical. That's how they justify ever-increasing budgets for new weapon purchases.'

Whether Hezbollah was genuinely planning an assault may never be known. At the time of writing – well after Israel quit Lebanon – Hezbollah has stopped short of the kind of provocation that would give Israel a green light to move back in.* It is unclear if such restraint can be attributed to Damascus, Tehran, or even Hezbollah itself. What is clear is that Hezbollah has spent as much time insinuating its way into the daily routine of the average Lebanese – what used to be called 'ward-heeling' in the US – as it has confronting Israel. Hezbollah administers schools, hospitals, a construction company and an agricultural cooperative called the Jihad Development

---

* As late as March 2002 in a story headlined 'Hezbollah "prepared" for all-out war in South', Beirut's *Daily Star* reported Lebanon's southern border was a 'tinderbox set to ignite [...] All the elements for a flare-up are there,' a UN observer as was quoted as saying. The tension eased in time for Israel's invasion of the West Bank.

Association. It has also developed a growing bureaucracy and even has seats in the Lebanese parliament.

In rhetoric at least, Hezbollah is as provocative as ever. Having dropped the pretence of representing Lebanon's parochial interests, it sounds more like the militant, pan-Arab, radical group that it is. Hezbollah's success against Israel almost certainly inspired the militarization of the Palestinian Intifada. Nasrallah has shown little interest in the banality of Lebanese politics – finding jobs for apparatchiks and ladling out patronage. In 2001, a Hezbollah security operative named Imad Mugniyah and two of his colleagues were placed on the US government's list of most-wanted terrorists.

Nonetheless, Hezbollah has yet to match its words with actions and it appears caught in a perpetual bind; pursuing its primary objective by attacking Israel with missile and guerrilla attacks would cost Hezbollah its greatest asset – the legitimacy bestowed upon it by average Lebanese for showing restraint in victory. Too long at peace and it becomes just another constituency in Lebanon's fragile democracy. Like other extremist groups, Hezbollah is like a log in a blazing hearth; take it out of the fire and it extinguishes itself.

'It's difficult to define Hezbollah's political ambition,' Michael Young told me. 'The end of the resistance was bad for it because there is nothing for it to rally around. Nasrallah's ambition is to fight Israel. He wants to be the regional vanguard and the violence in Palestine gives him that chance. He wants a fight but Syria and the Lebanese don't.'

Hezbollah headquarters is located in a squalid neighbourhood in Dahiya, a southern suburb of Beirut. The telephone grid is inadequate; phone cables stream out like festive ribbons from the windows of apartment buildings and tap directly into a trunk line suspended from metal poles. Across the street are the studios of Al Manar, Hezbollah's satellite-television channel. Images of dead Palestinian suicide bombers and three times life size portraits of Hassan Nasrallah are everywhere, as are the trio of Shiite Islam's modern heroes: Ayatollah Khamenei, Iran's current spiritual leader, Musa Al Sadr, the missing Imam allegedly eliminated by Moammar Gadhafi, and Ayatollah Khomeini.

I wanted to interview someone who could speak authoritatively about Hezbollah's platform. First, I had to submit to a routine interrogation from Haider, one of Hezbollah's media handlers and press spokesmen – who was I, which newspaper did I represent, where I had been in the region? He carefully wrote down my answers on a yellow legal pad.

Our meeting was interrupted by calls to one of Haider's *five* telephones – two on his desk and three cell phones. He patched each call to his headset by toggling a mini-switchboard as if shifting gears in a sports car. Give this kid a seat on the Beirut Stock Exchange, I thought, and he could move the index ten points in either direction.*

Haider was polite and professional. I was to call him in a few days to confirm the time and place of the interview.

A week later, I was in the office of Abdul Halim Fadallah, acting vice-president of the Consulting Centre for Studies and Documentation, not far from Hezbollah headquarters. The Centre was established ten years ago as a research centre for the party. It has a library and a database and occasionally provides data and research for NGOs and journalists, sometimes for a small commission. When I arrived, the reception hall was filled with students. All the women wore *hijabs*, the traditional Muslim head cover.

Fadallah, who I guessed to be in his mid-thirties, has a degree in economics. I asked him about Hezbollah's position on Lebanon's fiscal and monetary policy.

'We oppose government subsidies for industry unless there is a social reason to do so,' he said. 'For example, we endorse subsidies to tobacco farmers in the south where there is no opportunity. The government's policies, however, are not clear. Extreme market forces lead to monopolies and we oppose this. When government wants to intervene, it does not do so on a regular basis.'

Fadallah explained why Hezbollah favoured a 'social-market' system over socialism. 'We tried socialism and it didn't work. If the government keeps doling out subsidies it will run out of funds. Labour should be stronger – only 8 per cent of the Lebanese work force is unionized – but unions should work in concert with corporate players in society. In Denmark, for example, labour and companies cooperate. When they freeze or raise wages, it's a holistic thing.'

Michel Aflaq and Salah al-Din Bitar, the pioneers of Ba'ath Party socialism, must have been turning in their graves.

'The main reason for the economic crisis,' Fadallah went on, 'is because of the government spending that has pushed our total debt to 170 per cent of gross domestic product. This is one of the highest in

* Not a difficult thing to do actually, considering the market's chronically low trading volume.

the world. The only remedy is a currency devaluation or reduction of the public sector. The government has no desire to devalue the currency and privatization is too heavily politicized to go through. We are for privatization, so long as it doesn't penalize the end user or create more corruption.'

What about Israel, I asked. Was Hezbollah prepared to recognize the Jewish state?

Fadallah drew a breath. 'Politically and ideologically, we will never accept Israel. How can you accept as legitimate a state that was built on another state? Israel is not really a state. It is a product of Western hegemony, first British and now American. But Hezbollah is part of society and we would never do anything that would isolate us from society. If the Lebanese people say yes to peace with Israel, so be it.'

I was impressed. I had expected fundamentalist cant and found instead finely tuned, subtle equivocation. Later that day I consulted my notes. Fadallah had committed Hezbollah to everything and nothing – privatization, labour issues, currency rates, pushing the Jews into the sea. Everything was negotiable, reactive, status-quo oriented.

As a political party, Hezbollah had arrived.

Haider had also arranged a tour of Al Rassoul Al Azzam, Hezbollah's flagship hospital in Beirut. Every reporter who requests an interview with Hezbollah gets to see it. To be fair, it is impressive. Opened in 1988 for basic triage, it has expanded to 140 beds and 100 physicians (including one Christian) and offers every medical service except open-heart surgery. With a daily average of 30 to 40 outpatients, 125 regular patients and 100 emergency cases, it is a non-profit enterprise and most basic services are subsidized. Patients cover the cost of treatment through Lebanon's national healthcare system.

Mohammad Hijazi, head of the technical department, met me at the hospital. He graduated from American University of Beirut, he said, 'so I'm somewhat Americanized'. Mohammad was a thickset, balding man with a full beard and an easy manner. He escorted me into his office, produced two packets of Nescafé instant coffee with non-dairy creamer, and filled an electric kettle with water.

'This is not America,' he said. 'There's not always hot water on demand.'

Mohammad opened the packets with the kind of dog-legged surgical scissors that are used to cut away the clothes of emergency victims. I half-expected some out-of-breath intern in bloody surgical scrubs might burst in and gasp '*There* they are!'

Mohammad noticed my concern. 'Relax,' he said, 'someone gave these to me in Saudi Arabia. I worked for the medical arm of [oil giant] Aramco for eleven years.* We called it South Africa because the Americans got everything six times better, including pay, than the Arabs. Even the security guards were dressed like Los Angeles cops so the Americans would feel at home.'

Mohammad prepared the Nescafé. He was a member of Hezbollah, he said, but was now dedicated to building institutions like hospitals. As we talked, Mohammad revealed himself to be more a Lebanese nationalist, perhaps even a pan-Arabist, than an Islamist – a follower of militant Islam. His sincere candour contrasted with Fadallah's precise ambiguity.

'I was alive when Nasser lost the battle [against imperialism and Zionism],' Mohammad said. 'The Arabs are looking for anyone who can give us back our pride. Hezbollah is restrained; it can only shoot from the border. This is Hezbollah. It's not just hospitals and water systems, but pride and resistance. We can't rely on the Americans – lies, lies, lies. Slobodan Milosevic is on trial in The Hague and not only is Ariel Sharon not on trial, you Americans call him a man of peace. The hero of Sabra and Shatila a man of peace?'†

I asked Mohammad: Will Hezbollah ever accept a Jewish state in Palestine?

'Muslims are obligated to liberate any Muslim territory held by an infidel,' he replied. 'Yes we want to liberate all of Palestine. The question is ability. Israel is like a cancer. Without chemotherapy, it will spread. Look at this map' – he pointed to a wall map of the Levantine Middle East – 'all those cities have had Arab names for over a thousand years. Palestine is Arab. A small number of Jews came here from Europe and that changed everything. No one can give Israel legitimacy. It was implanted by the law of the jungle with the strong prevailing over the weak. If Arafat is killed he becomes a martyr, and whoever follows him cannot accept anything less than what Arafat would have accepted.'

---

* Aramco began in 1933 as an oil concession granted to US oil companies by the Saudi monarchy. It was dominated by US interests until 1980, when it was effectively nationalized by the Saudi government.
† During Israel's invasion of Lebanon in 1982, Christian militias allied with Israel broke into two Palestinian refugee camps and over the next two days massacred up to 2,000 unarmed men, women and children. An Israeli commission of inquiry condemned the then-defence minister, Ariel Sharon, for 'not ordering appropriate measures for preventing or reducing the chances of a massacre'. In response to the commission's findings, Sharon was stripped of his defence portfolio.

And this justifies the killing of innocent people in suicide attacks?

'What people in the West don't understand is that when you believe in something very strong, when you are driving a superior foe from your land, suicide bombers and martyrs are something great, an alternative to repression. If one side has very little and the other has so much, what else can you do? We've had United Nations resolutions for 22 years.* What good has it done?'

Mohammad drained his coffee mug and began my tour of the hospital. It was clean and seemingly well managed. There was an auditorium named after the Ayatollah Khomeini and some of the latest medical equipment, including a panoramic X-ray and ultrasound device.

In the medical imaging department, Mohammad proudly showed off the hospital's brand-new, Open Magnetic Resonance Imaging machine.

'This will save a lot of lives,' he told me.

* In November 1967, the UN Security Council passed resolution 242, which calls for Israel to withdraw its forces from occupied Palestinian territory. An earlier UN resolution establishes the right of Palestinian refugees to return to their homes in what is now Israel. Israel rejects the resolution as a threat to the Jewish character of the state.

2

Syria

The Circle

Keep your friends close but keep your enemies closer

Al Pacino as Michael Corleone in *The Godfather, Part II*

Inside looking out . . .

Long before the publication of Sir Richard Burton's accounts of his nineteenth-century exploits in Central Asia and the Arab world, the West had perceived the Eastern Hemisphere as forbidding and inscrutable. What used to be called the Orient – Victorian shorthand for the land mass that stretches from the Bosporus to Russian Sakhalin – is a netherworld obscured by cultural swamp-mist and vapours. One doesn't understand Asia; one *penetrates* it. It is a 'yes-means-no' world littered with the bleached bones of Westerners who tried, as Kipling wrote, to 'hustle' it. Searching for a straight answer in the Orient is like trying to get traction on an oil slick.

It is a simplistic and ethnocentric way of interpreting a foreign land. It is also, at least in the Middle East today, more or less accurate. Arab leaders enter alliances with the West while funding extremists who are damaging, if not deadly, to Western interests. They publicly condemn Israel while privately negotiating with it. Compacts are sealed with a wink and repealed with a nod. In the Middle East, convergence is driven by expediency, not by principle.

It is tempting to attribute this to a chemical imbalance, as if Arabs and their leaders possessed some kind of duplicity hormone. In fact, justice and authority are negotiable in any society, Oriental or

58

Occidental, where there is no rule of law. Throughout the developing world the institutions that interpret and enforce the law are weak and vulnerable to manipulation by the elite. In China, this is known as *guanxi*. The Arabs call it *wasta*.

The primacy of relationships over legality subverts every layer of Middle Eastern life. While Westerners bemoan their litigious societies, the Arabs crave one. A friend of mine, a cardiologist from a prominent Jordanian family, once explained to me the real source of American power that had nothing to do with its $380 billion-a-year military. His father had developed minor respiratory problems while the two were vacationing in California. They checked into a hospital and waited an hour for treatment.

'That is the beauty of America,' my friend said.

Waiting for an hour in a hospital?

'Waiting an hour because you know you can't manoeuvre your way to the head of the line,' he replied. 'If I was in Jordan, I would simply call a friend who knows the hospital director and get to see the doctor immediately. Or I'd just bribe the orderly, regardless of how sick the person ahead of me was. But in America riches and influence only go so far. You have institutions. We have *wasta*.'

In a society without credible institutions, where personalities loom larger than the law, flexibility is the key to survival. Where authority can be bought or stolen overnight and lost again just as quickly, no one wants to identify themselves too closely with what could be a fleeting regime or policy. Western models of governance are built around a moderate 'centre'; Arab autocracy rests on a circle of complicity held together by coercion, incentive, and charm.

Dennis Ross, Middle East special envoy under President Clinton, once wrote how Yasser Arafat 'prefers to co-opt, not confront [. . .] he never closes doors. He never forecloses options. He never knows when he might want to have a particular group, no matter what its ideology or purpose, on his side.' It was a fine profile of the Palestinian president, applicable to just about every leader and power broker in the Arab world.

The West prescribes freely elected democratic government for the Arabs. In fact, autocracy can be legitimate provided it delivers competent civil administration and sustained economic growth. In 1961, Park Chung Hee, a South Korean army general, seized power and ruled with an iron hand. He muzzled the press and emasculated the unions. He also built the foundation for a world-class, industrialized economy and formed institutions to manage it. Today, his people honour him as the father of modern Korea, now a thriving democracy, and as one of the enlightened autocrats who helped build the Asian economy.

Many of today's Arab leaders assumed control in the same way as Park Chung Hee, but they have failed to earn legitimacy by developing stable economies. On the contrary, the world's 250 million Arabs are huddled in a cluster of *de facto* if not *de jure* garrison states – supported in some cases by the US government – under regimes paralyzed by fear and ineptitude. Educated, middle-class Arabs with the means emigrate; those who remain try to protect themselves by bartering their way into the ruling circle. A shrinking economy starves the regime of funds for patronage. Lacking the carrot, it turns to the stick. The circle tightens.

Ibn Khaldun, the fourteenth-century medieval historian developed a theory of social cohesion called *asabiyya*. Translated roughly as 'solidarity' it refers to a complex of culture, language and customs that connect the nodes of traditional society – family, clan, tribe, kingdom and nation. With urbanization, *asabiyya* dilutes and society atomizes – Ibn Khaldun measured the process in cycles of four generations – unless the leadership adapts *asabiyya* to suit an urban milieu.*

While Far Eastern nations like Korea and Taiwan have managed this transition, most Middle Eastern ones have not.† Like a bone drained of its marrow, Arab societies have been leached of *asabiyya* and are susceptible to radical ideas and ideologies. In the absence of compelling alternatives, the state resorts to neutralizing, intimidating or destroying potential challengers. As a means of preserving power this is a tactic, not a strategy, and a tactic without a strategy is by definition not sustainable.

Behind the anti-Israel demonstrations that packed Arab streets in spring 2002 lay a wadding of discontent with the local ruling elite. The brutality and ineffectiveness of Arab leaders goes unchecked and unreformed, but not unnoticed.

The road from Beirut to Damascus passes through the Lebanese-Syrian border crossing in the Lebanon Mountains, just north of

---

* Interestingly, Ibn Khaldun's writings are hard to find on the syllabi of today's *madrassas* because conservative headmasters consider them too 'scientific'.

† The clash between urban and rural culture bedevilled even the Prophet; he often remarked in exasperation of his stubborn Bedouin converts: 'If they are told, "Obey the law God sends you!" they reply, "We obey the customs of our fathers!"'

Mount Hermon. On the Lebanese side a scrum of Syrian money-lenders rushes travellers as they approach the immigration office. The going exchange rate at the border is 50 Syrian Pounds (SL50) to 1 US dollar, though experienced visitors know they can get about SL55 or so to the dollar from exchange dealers in Beirut. Damascus – known as the 'Queen of Cities' and the 'Garden of the World' in Umayyad times – occupies the fertile seat of Syria's Duma valley, shadowed by Mount Qasyoon to the southwest and bisected by the Barada River. In the eighth century Damascus was the fulcrum of the Umayyad Dynasty, the largest empire the world had yet known and more prosperous than ancient Rome. The world's most accomplished scientists, physicians, artists and musicians came to Damascus under the patronage of the Caliph. Against the delicate splashing of a water fountain in the palace *salam*, or main courtyard, astrologists measured the quarter-movements of the stars, and poets and preachers celebrated the virtue of romantic love. Some Arab historians even hold Medieval Arabs pioneered the theory of blood circulation, an achievement which they also assert was ardently claimed a thousand years later by the royal physicians of Victorian Britain.

The empire's centrepiece was the Umayyad Mosque, completed in 715 under Caliph Al Walid I. It was built on the ruins of a Roman temple of Jupiter that the emperor Constantine demolished after his conversion to Christianity in the fourth century. He dedicated the church he built on the temple ruins to John the Baptist and it is here that the saint's itinerant head, having been toted about the Holy Land for years, was finally laid to rest. After the Islamic conquests Muslims and Christians shared the church as a place of worship until Walid ordered it rebuilt as a great mosque. Construction took a decade, although, poignantly, Walid died hours before the first prayers were to be sung.

The Umayyad Mosque gracefully allies Byzantine, Hellenistic and Arab motifs. Visitors entering the courtyard from the western entrance walk under an imposing, atypically square minaret that looks like a tower from a Christian church. When the mosque opened, so the story goes, the mu'uezzin lacked the lungpower to reach the street, so he lowered from his perch a huge white sheet to signal the time to pray. It has since been known as the 'bride' minaret. The mosque's other minaret, marking the spot where many expect Christ will return on judgment day, is known as 'Jesus'.*

---

* The Saviour has been double-booked; He is also scheduled to appear at the Golden Gate, east of Jerusalem's Old City.

The vast courtyard is pure Byzantium. The plan follows the lines of a normal Christian basilica; an arcade of columns and capitals enamelled with a glittering mosaic on the eastern wall contains scenes of Mediterranean villas and sweeping vistas. It is a stately monument to early-Islamic multiculturalism.

Today, a vast shantytown of cinder block and corrugated steel consumes Mount Qasyoon. Modern Damascus is all too similar to most capital cities that developed under the crush of mid-twentieth-century urbanization; a dormitory for the low-income families who can afford to live there, a back-breaking day trip for commuters from its ramshackle outskirts.

Yet the city's charm and integrity have survived generations of pell-mell development, war, coups and countercoups. Many of the neighbourhoods that appear in grainy black-and-white photographs in books about a painfully innocent Arab world are little changed. Damascene life still flourishes with Kurdish, Armenian and Greek traditions. The Christian quarter, a honeycomb of conjoined stucco warrens with exposed timber-rail roofs, is more or less as it was under Ottoman rule. Though Damascus' minority communities have been depleted over the years – non-Arabs account for only 10 per cent of the total, compared to nearly 30 per cent a century ago – only its once-thriving Jewish population has all but vanished.

For centuries, Syria straddled the great trade route from Europe and Anatolia to Mesopotamia, Iran, and India. Unlike many Arab urban centres, cities like Damascus, Homs and Aleppo prospered under the Ottoman Empire and suffered the most in the early 1920s when the French and English imposed a border with Turkey on Syria that was just 50 kilometres north of Aleppo, its industrial heartland. By the middle of the century, Syria's purely agricultural economy had evolved into a more sophisticated, manufacturing one. It developed a robust light industrial sector – textiles, canned goods and building materials – to complement its traditional merchant activities. It boasted a spirited middle class and a political culture unparalleled in the Arab world for its diversity.

All this came to a halt with the rise of the socialist Ba'ath Party, the brainchild of two Lebanese – a Christian named Michel Aflaq and a Muslim, Salah al-Din Bitar. Both were highly respected leaders of a pan-Arab nationalist movement then proliferating in response to Western imperialism. Although Egypt's Gamal Abdel Nasser never adopted the Ba'ath, he did agree in 1958 to a short-lived union with Syria known as the United Arab Republic. It was a vindication for socialism. It also stifled whatever hopes the Syrian economy may have had of overcoming the constrictions – the arbitrarily drawn borders, travel restrictions and tariffs – that followed Sykes and Picot. The UAR would soon disintegrate because of squabbling over who would lead the fight against British, French and increasingly American hegemony. But its legacy – an inefficient, state-run industrial sector, centrally planned growth, bloated government payrolls – would linger for generations.

Syria, like most Arab countries, is still a nation of traders – but mostly of non-Arab manufactured products. Syrian merchants import finished goods from Europe and Asia, paying with revenue generated by the country's petroleum sector. Oil, along with agriculture, the country's largest source of jobs, cranks the Syrian economy along. Syrian oil exports cover an estimated 70 per cent of its total import costs; thus the country is using a diminishing resource to pay for everything from toilet paper to machine tools. Although Syria expects to export refined petroleum products long after it becomes a net crude-oil importer by 2010 or so, diplomats and oilmen say the country's energy resources are not managed prudently and such projections are over-optimistic.

The Syrian government has welcomed foreign help in developing its oilfields, particularly those near its north-eastern border with Turkey and Iraq, but the response has been underwhelming. This is not surprising. Why put up with Syria's corruption, red tape and paranoid bureaucrats when richer fields beckon in Central Asia and the Gulf States? An executive from a British energy firm and consultant to the Syrian government once told me about a visit to the petroleum ministry to inspect some public documents. The photocopies he requested needed approval from a host of departmental heads. He returned with the requisite stamps a week later and had to submit the documents to a security guard posted at the photocopy machine, who rigorously inspected each one for state secrets.

Then there is the capriciousness and rapacity of Syria's civil service. In 2001 a British-based division of Japanese electronics giant JVC sold digital cameras and editing facilities worth £375,000 to Syria's state-owned television broadcaster. The Syrians stipulated that the invoice be stamped by the Syrian embassy in London. This cost JVC £6,000 – just over 1.5 per cent of the value of the transaction. Like many other companies, JVC now factors such fees into any offers it makes when dealing with the Syrian government.

As in most Arab countries, conclusive economic data in Syria is hard to find. The country has a gross domestic product valued at $17.9 billion and an average annual income of $970. It estimates the economy grew by 3% in 2001 and forecasts 4% growth in 2002. No one believes this. In the late 1990s, when the government was announcing growth rates of between 2% to 4%, the US embassy in Damascus issued a report estimating the economy was actually shrinking by as much as 4% a year. A Syrian businessman I know concluded that in 2001 the economy shrank by 1%. Unemployment, according to the government, is 5%; the true figure is probably one quarter of the working-age population.

Many Syrians blame their economic woes on Israel. To be sure, confrontation with the Jewish state has allowed the military to monopolize most of the country's resources and justifies the kind of Gestapo-like security measures that smother innovation and enterprise. Yet peace could prove traumatic to the Syrian economy, at least in the short term. The Syrian army employs some 500,000 soldiers. You see them everywhere – restless, uneducated young men dressed in patched, ill-fitting uniforms. They slouch arm-in-arm through the streets of major cities and huddle inside battered trucks and armoured vehicles – gifts from the long-expired Soviet proletariat – en route from one make-work assignment to the next.* Syrian troops rarely train due to a shortage of spare parts and fuel; they spend the rest of their time filling potholes and fixing ageing tanks – anything to keep them out of the mosques.

Should Damascus ever make peace with Israel, many of these uniformed urchins would be decommissioned, unleashing an army of idle hands on to the job market. Unless Syria liberalizes and diversifies its economy away from agriculture and petroleum, it could find the only thing more destabilizing than a cold war with Israel is peace with it.

The Lion Cub
'The Umayyads are a set of tyrants,' went a popular saying under the reign of Abd Al Malik, the fifth Umayyad caliph and the Arab world's first world-class despot. 'They arrest on surmise, judge according to their caprice and kill to gratify their anger.'

---

* Syria hasn't purchased a modern weapons system in two decades; the last time the Syrian air force engaged Israel, it was destroyed in a 12-minute dogfight over Lebanon's Bekka Valley.

The dynasty that rules Syria today comes not from Arabia but from a north-western village in the Alawi highlands. Long an impoverished, disenfranchised minority, the Alawite clans and sub-clans by the late 1960s were well represented in Damascus by the then-defence minister, Hafez al Assad. In November 1970, Assad – 'Lion' in Arabic – deposed Salah Jadid's vastly unpopular government in a bloodless coup and for the next 30 years ruled as a giant among Arab leaders with absolute but not unchallenged authority. In its 1982 war with the Muslim Brotherhood, the government massacred an entire population of innocent civilians at the Islamist stronghold of Hama; two years later, Assad survived a coup led by his brother, Rifat. Though Rifat was exiled to London, tensions between the two men simmered until months before the president's death in June 2000. In October 1999, government troops commanded by Assad's son, Bashar, battled with guards protecting his uncle's residence in the port town of Latakia, where Rifat still enjoyed considerable influence. The government said the troops were smashing a narcotics ring and that three people were killed – all part of a get-tough campaign on corruption.

A few months after the attack I met Latakia's governor, Nawaf El Faves. He said he had no details to give me about the shoot-out. There was no evidence of smuggling anywhere in his province – no drugs, no cigarettes, no liquor – no contraband of any kind. He attributed this to the benevolent influence of the president's ophthalmologist son and heir-apparent, Bashar al Assad, depicted in a dozen portraits, sculptures, and photographs throughout his office.

'We all love Dr Bashar,' he told me, as if the bronze bust of the good doctor on the coffee table wasn't proof enough. 'He is civilized, democratic in nature, sincere to the country, and polite. He is very polite.'

For diplomats, the Latakia incident was a classic Middle Eastern power play. The attack, according to their intelligence, ended with 30 people dead and was the ruling clan's signal to Rifat and other prospective challengers that Bashar had the proper instinct for Syria's Shakespearean brand of hardball politics.

Middle East analysts in Washington had warned Hafez al Assad's death could be disastrous for the region. Civil war would break out. The army would revolt. Hezbollah would march on Haifa. In fact the transfer of power after Assad's death by natural causes in June 2000 was, unsurprisingly, smooth; when it comes to political succession in closed, authoritarian states, Washington almost always gets it wrong. Diplomats speak to reporters darkly of the instability to come 'once the old man kicks'. The new blood is usually character-ized as neophyte, lightweight and unable to hold competing factions at bay.*

The reason for this is simple. No one in the Beltway Biosphere – a complex of wonks, pundits, ex-diplomats and retired generals – really wants a smooth transition when a looming power struggle makes for much better chat-show theatre.† China was supposed to split up into warring fiefdoms when Deng Xiaoping died. North Korea would implode or invade South Korea – perhaps both – with the elevation of Kim Jong Il after his father's death; after all, it was argued, the younger Kim drank too much, stuttered and – worst of all – had never met an American. Moroccans would rise up against their monarchy when King Hassan expired just as Jordan's ethnic Palestinians would revolt against the Hashemites with the passing of King Hussein.

None of these happened (Kim Jong Il, as it turns out, speaks perfectly well), largely because no one in the ruling circle had an interest in anything less than a peaceful succession. The less nuanced the analysis of authoritarian rule, the more it attributes absolute authority to one man while overlooking the sometimes obscure but influential constituencies that keep him in check. It is easier to fit caricatures into sound bites than a sober analysis of a particular regime and the motivations and prerogatives of its component parts.

Coming from a minority tribe, like the early Muslims, Hafez al Assad was a master at keeping rival clans as allies and prudently balanced the various ethnic and religious groups by wooing them more or less equit-ably. This included Syria's minorities – Catholics, Greek Orthodox, Maronites, Chaldeans, Ismaelis – because together they comprised a constituency relatively cheap to satisfy and easy to motivate. Those relationships have held well past his death. The more powerful con-stituencies, such as Syria's Sunni business elite, required a higher price. But all remained status quo players with a stake in a peaceful status quo.

Though Assad's death was a surprise, the government responded with impressive agility. A media centre was established for the hundreds of

---

* Diplomats and policy wonks still wring their hands over the prospect of a post-Castro Cuba. However the most important change will probably be the end of the 12-hour political monologue and what ordin-ary Cubans will do with all that free time.
† The Washington 'Beltway' refers to the political, bureaucratic and diplomatic nerve-centre that hums inside the city's main ring road.

journalists descending on Syria. Reporters' visas, which ordinarily took weeks to process, were issued immediately. Broadcast facilities were provided and transportation arranged. A normally reclusive nation was turning itself out for the world.

Damascus in mourning was fairly impressive in a part of the world where the venality of a recently deceased leader can be measured by the apparent sincerity and spontaneity of the bereaved. I arrived to a city festooned in black. Students flooded the streets in black T-shirts and held aloft portraits of the two Assads with black sashes clipped to the right-hand corners. They chanted 'God loves Hafez al Assad' and waved black flags. Black banners ran down the fronts of entire buildings and black ribbons were tied to the radio antennas of automobiles.

A shortage of five-star hotel rooms for the expected onslaught of foreign dignitaries was resolved by kicking lesser guests out, with foreign correspondents the first victims. Bounced out of the Meridien, I was assigned with a covey of other reporters to the dismal Fardos Tower Hotel on the other side of town. My new lodging was only slightly roomier and brighter than a confessional booth; when I threw open the curtains, I found myself staring at the back of an enormous black banner.

'I hate funerals,' I muttered.

The Ba'ath-dominated Syrian parliament quickly amended legislation to enable Bashar's succession. Clerics recited the Koran from minarets and television studios. His father interred, the young Assad was shown on state-run TV in a reception line, accepting condolences from world leaders. In a span of 16 months the Arabs had lost two of their most prominent ruling patriarchs – King Hussein of Jordan and now Hafez al Assad. The men who raised the modern Middle East were leaving it, contused and bleeding, to another generation.

The transition was complete. The 'beating heart of Arab nationalism', as Nasser once described Syria, was now firmly in the hands of a 35-year-old, internet-surfing, British-trained eye-doctor.

Months before his father's death, Bashar agreed to speak on the record to me and Howard Schneider of the *Washington Post*, the first Western reporters to interview him. We were covering a seminar in Damascus hosted by the Syrian Computer Society, which Bashar chaired, and the soon-to-be president-for-life apparently decided that on 26 April 2000 he should introduce himself to the non-Arab world.

Bashar was thought to be friendly to Western ways because of his studies abroad and his fascination with computers and the Internet. Most people wanted to believe it would be the junior Assad who would open Syria to the global economy.

Howard and I waited in a receiving room below the conference hall. Bashar arrived only a few minutes late, urbane and garrulous in a well-tailored grey suit. His English was good but he preferred to speak through an interpreter in Arabic. He was easy-mannered, even charming. He did not appear like someone looking over his shoulder for the glint of cold steel.

Howard, his Beltway readers' interests in mind, delved into high diplomacy. He peppered Bashar with questions about the peace process (the Second Intifada was still five months away), the paradox of promoting the Internet in a police state and Syria's support of Hezbollah. Bashar competently parried Howard's questions. Syria has never supported terrorism, he said; Hezbollah was 'a reality that imposes itself' on the region due to Israeli excess; Syrian troops are in Lebanon to 'achieve stability' and will withdraw when Beirut requests it; Syria is a victim of Israel's illegal occupation of Arab land, not an aggressor.

'We are a sympathetic people,' he told us. 'But do we have to show sensitivity by letting [Israel] occupy our territory? No one can accuse Syria of committing massacres or terrorism. Throughout history, Syria has been tolerant of others. The proof is in the mosaic of our society.'

Howard asked Bashar if he would extend his promotion of the Internet to other media – Western movies, for example.

'As a point of principle,' he said, 'I would like everyone to see everything, because more knowledge means more development. Just crossing the street, you learn something new. Guidelines should not be imposed by governments; society must choose.'

Bashar volunteered reading and photography as his twin passions. He told us he listens to Phil Collins, Faith Hill, and Whitney Houston. He is an enthusiast for those photo-shop websites that allow people to 'morph' pictures into different shapes. He was cool, self-assured.

'Should foreigners invest in Syria?' I asked. This softly lobbed question was an easy opportunity for Bashar to market Syria's natural and human attributes to the handful of Wall Street investors who could point to Damascus on a map.

Bashar hesitated.

'Legislation has not been issued to regulate in this manner,' he began. 'Some want strict measures [of control], some want just the opposite, and others want a reasonable balance. You can't separate the progress of development from society. If you take what you hear from your discussion, you get many different perspectives. I can't really give an answer whether there should be strict control or openness. It is complicated, dealing with traditions in this manner.

'Economics is a product of society and other domains which reflects back on society. Therefore, if you want to lead to progress, you have to establish common positions. Deciding our priorities of where to begin need discussion and dialogue.'

Clearly, Bashar felt much more comfortable in Howard's ballpark than in mine. Perhaps rumours of his reformist credentials were over-blown. Maybe he found economic matters as boring as his father did and hadn't given them much thought. Yet he may have understood only too well both the importance of reform and its consequences for the vested interests that have calcified around the presidency.

It was difficult to tell. Official blather is hard to decipher at the best of times, especially so against the reflected twilight of a bankrupt regime.

Under Hafez al Assad, a reporter in Syria could interview practically anybody about anything – except politics. A year into Bashar's rule there was a glimmer that things were changing. Within six months after Bashar assumed power, Syria had released dozens of political prisoners. Discussion groups, or salons, proliferated. *The Lamplighter*, the country's first privately owned newspaper, appeared in February 2001 and sold out its initial print run within hours. There were increasingly vocal debates in parliament, and Syria's business commu-nity was making tepid appeals to the Alawites for deregulation, a long-delayed banking code and other reforms.

'Something has changed, and it may even be irrevocable,' a Western diplomat told me.* 'The genie isn't out of the bottle, but it almost is.'

Bashar al Assad's apparently tentative efforts toward liberalization triggered cautious optimism among Syrians that the worst of 40 years

---

* 'Western diplomats' and 'Western sources' are shorthand for representatives of Syria's foreign commu-nity who, due to the impenetrability of Syrian politics, know only slightly more about what's really going on than a first-time visitor. They are, however, a valuable and generous resource.

of repression was finally over. One could sense a collective exhaling among a people who referred to Bashar's father only as 'Him', or simply with a mute, jerking glance upward. That alone was regarded as a major achievement.

'Bashar welcomes change,' Waddah Abd Rabbo, the editor of a current affairs magazine called *Al-Shahr* and a self-described 'Basharian', once told me. Waddah, the son of a wealthy Syrian trading family, spends much of his time in Beirut both for business and pleasure. He wanted me to understand how capable Bashar is and how sincere are his ambitions to liberalize Syria. He told me *Al-Shahr*, one of Syria's few privately owned magazines, has been openly critical of corruption in government.

'This is possible only because of Bashar. He wants an open country with the right reforms, but he knows it will take time. He has to move slowly, to prevent a collapse like in Eastern Europe. We need foreign investment, tourism, and private banking. We need to have a unified currency. But there are people benefiting from the situation who don't want change.'

Fair enough. But the Syrian elite, like their counterparts throughout the Arab world, fail to understand that the kind of volatility that battered Eastern Europe following the abrupt collapse of communism was an essential by-product of reform and progress. It is true that Poland, the Czech Republic, Hungary and the Baltic States suffered from the trauma and dislocation of change. Yet they quickly recovered and today are among the few developing markets that attract significant foreign investment.

By mid-2002, Syrian 'liberalization' was on life-support. Several intellectuals were threatened and beaten after amplifying calls for greater freedom. Nizar Nayyouf, a journalist and democracy activist was abducted by *mukhabarat* agents and held for two days before his scheduled appearance at a press conference about human rights violations. Riad Saif, a member of parliament, was charged with 'illegally' trying to amend the constitution. He was sentenced to five years in jail.

Like most other Arab leaders, President Bashar displays all the symptoms of a bi-polar disorder. He displays one 'Intifada' face to the West and another to his own people. He tells the world he opposes Zionism, not Judaism, while keeping in his cabinet Mustafa Tlas, a man known for his shrill, anti-Semitic remarks. He keeps the door open to a peace with Israel – and the prospect of aid and arms from the West – but along with Iran finances Hezbollah, which is officially committed to retaking Jerusalem.

Even his association with Hezbollah is hedged. The extremist group enjoys a legitimacy denied many Arab leaders for driving Israel out of Lebanon and providing the Lebanese with basic civic services. It also launches the occasional strike against Israeli troops in disputed territory in the Golan Heights that provokes a counter-strike against Syrian positions in Lebanon – like the raid in May 2001 that resulted in the Israeli destruction of the Syrian radar battery. Hezbollah leader Hassan Nasrallah urged Syria's 'young leader' to retaliate. Not only did Syria not respond, it kept its troops on a low state of alert. There was no cancelling of leave, counting of ammunition, or husbanding of petroleum and other supplies. The bodies of those killed in the missile strike were brought home quietly and buried without ceremony.

'The appropriate response to the attack would have been to disperse the troops,' said a diplomat in Damascus. 'But this is a reckless regime that doesn't care much about men in uniform. I wonder what junior officers think when they see their seniors with cars and big salaries, compared with what they have in the field. Everybody here is outside the law and everyone can be arrested for corruption.'

The episode highlighted the dilemma in Damascus, a microcosm of the paradox facing other Arab leaders. Bashar talks tough at Arab summits, likening the Israelis to the Nazis, but carefully avoids provoking the Jewish state. Syrian troops are highly exposed in Lebanon but removing them might signal to Israel it was redeploying for an attack, handing the Jewish state an excuse to hit Damascus as well as Lebanon. Most important, it would reduce Syria's influence over Lebanon, of far greater importance to Damascus economically and politically than the Golan Heights, occupied by Israel since the 1967 Arab-Israeli war.

Officially, Damascus maintains its troops in Lebanon to 'protect' its tiny neighbour from Israeli aggression; in reality Syria can't protect itself. Bashar's soldiers, both in Lebanon and at home, are hiding from Israel in plain sight – in the open for all to see, but careful not to do anything that might provoke the very country they are deployed to confront. The absurdity of Syria's condition is increasingly conspicuous to a people informed by Al Jazeera and frustrated by a contracting economy.*

* Al Jazeera, a Qatar-based Arab satellite news channel, has evolved into the BBC of the Arab world and has inspired a galaxy of independent, or at least independently minded, media programmes in a region where information was once tightly controlled by the state.

Re-drawing the Ba'ath

In 1988, during a meeting with a dozen or so parliamentarians, Hafez al Assad predicted the collapse of the Soviet Union. As Syria had built its economy on the Soviet model, this caused concern.

What, he asked the assembled rubber stamps, was Syria's fate? Had he erred in embracing command economics? Would Syria be overtaken by Israel?

These were of course rhetorical questions. Whether anyone present realized it at the time, they were not about to suggest that yes, like North Korea, Cuba and Vietnam, Syria had been standing in the wrong line all along.

Nearly 15 years later, the Ba'ath Party appears to be accepting that its Soviet roadmap is somewhat dated. Its new slogan, roughly translated as 'Prepare to share power in business, but not politics,' indicates it may be considering the Chinese model for economic reform.* It also suggests the Ba'ath understands that the concept on which it was built – exporting a pan-Arab identity – exhausted itself years ago.

Some changes have already taken place. In 2001, the government introduced tax cuts on imported automobiles, with the steepest reductions for the smallest cars. The plan offered the owners of vehicles over 40 years old incentives to buy new models if they took their existing cars to a recycling facility. Two years after the plan was launched, the same incentives would apply to those with 30-year-old cars, and so on.

This well-meaning bit of legislation aimed to rid Syria's streets of unsafe, fuel-inefficient automobiles. But it has had mixed results. Government vacillation on the value of the final tax cut and the high recycling facility fees meant that many consumers postponed trading in their clunkers. The majority of new cars are not economy models from Korea and Malaysia but brand-new luxury ones from Europe – BMWs, Mercedes, Volvos, Audis – which can cost Syrians as much as $300,000 even with the tax cut. Many of the vehicles' licence plates identify their owners as senior government officials.

The government also tried gamely to deregulate the country's real-estate market. Until recently, rents in Syria were pegged at 1960s levels. Therefore tenants have no incentive to move out and landlords any reason to do proper maintenance. The new law would allow for apartment owners to evict renters in return for compensation to be

---

* The fact that Chinese banks are estimated to have on their books an estimated $300 billion in bad loans suggests just how desperate the Syrians are for fresh ideas.

settled by an arbitrator. This, it was hoped, would enhance liquidity in the property sector and create a demand for new, better housing.

'It was fine in theory,' a diplomat told me. 'But landlords still can't charge more than what the market will bear. Remember, a police-man in Damascus makes the equivalent of $3 a day.'

The biggest challenge facing Syria is building a modern financial system. The country has no banks except for a handful of state-owned, Soviet-style lending windows. As in most Arab countries, businessmen hoping to invest in existing or new operations must do so from cash flow or other private sources. Small businessmen have to pool their family's resources.

Few Syrians have bank accounts; most keep their savings at home where they earn no interest. People carry bundles of cash in plastic bags. Merchants drive the day's earnings home in the trunks of their cars. Each year, the winner of the Damascus lottery carts his win-nings away in a vinyl suitcase. Syrians won't take cheques let alone credit cards, though some retailers will accept American Express for large purchases. I once used my Amex card to buy a trove of antique carpets from an Aleppine merchant. He called an associate in Beirut who checked my card number through a friend in Dubai before I was finally declared an acceptable risk. The whole process took three hours.

During the Islamic empire, Arab currency was held from Scandinavia to China and a draft order signed against a Damascus account would be honoured in Canton. (The draft orders were known in Arabic as *sek*, which inspired the English 'cheque'.) Trade and finance as a part of the Arab identity pre-dated the Prophet and informed the character of Islam. Part of Muhammad's appeal was his reputation as an honest merchant and arbiter in disputes between businessmen. His first wife, Khadija, was a successful merchant. The most revered caliph in Muslim history, the pious Omar I, is reputed to have wanted to die in the market place 'buying and selling for my family'. The *hajj*, or pilgrimage to Mecca, was an enormous business; 'May your *hajj* be accepted, your sins be forgiven and your merchan-dise not remain unsold,' went a contemporary salutation.

Today, Syria is parched of liquidity. In April 2002, it began accept-ing applications for foreign banks interested in opening Syrian branches. According to the World Bank, three banks – including one Lebanese – have formally expressed an interest in planting their flag in Damascus. Active Lebanese participation is crucial; if Lebanon's top banks waded into the Syrian banking market, so the betting went, other banks would follow. After all, Lebanese banks already have a strong Syrian client base – for both legitimate and non-legitimate transactions. The Lebanese and Syrians share a language and the most prominent Lebanese bankers are in fact, Syrian.

'Frankly, I'm not sure they'll be coming in force,' a European diplomat in Damascus told me when the government's draft banking law first came out. A week earlier, the diplomat had met a delegation of Lebanese bankers who were not impressed. 'They told me that after looking at the environment they decided it was too risky. To hear the Lebanese say they didn't think the conditions were right was eye-opening.'

The diplomat then told me why he was at once pessimistic and hopeful for Syria's future. He was the last scheduled speaker at a recent conference in Damascus attended by European Union and Arab leaders. The penultimate speaker, a prominent Syrian official, delivered a searing attack on what he described as the European Union's predatory designs on Syria. The diplomat felt compelled to defend the EU's motives. The following day he was condemned by a columnist in the state-controlled press as a presumptuous foreigner who thought himself an expert on the Syrian economy a mere six months into his assignment.

Later that morning, the diplomat phoned the columnist and suggested lunch. He wanted to explain in person his sincere wish to promote equitable EU-Syrian trade and to encourage Syrian economic reform.

'Sure,' the columnist replied. 'But there's really no need. I agreed with everything you said.'

The Ba'ath Party never was a great forum for domestic issues. The last time it dabbled in local affairs was in 1963 when it engaged in Soviet-style land distribution. Since then, the party has predicated itself on regional politics. It engaged Nasser when he held aloft the banner of Arab solidarity, then dumped him when his charisma threatened to shoulder Damascus aside. It allied against Iraq during the Second Gulf War and now appears to favour a rehabilitated Baghdad at the expense of its ties with Iran.

In the 1970s, the Ba'ath party became a preserve of the Assads and the Alawites, who used regional instability to justify absolute rule. However brutal his method, Assad's control of the party ended decades of coups and countercoups, which is why his funeral, while not as emotional as the event of King Hussein's death, was sombre and respectful nonetheless. Syrians may have hated Assad and the corrupt Alawites, but they appreciated his strength and the continuity of his rule.

Though King Hussein and Hafez al Assad were of opposite styles and temperaments they left their sons the same legacy – a state based not on the rule of law but on a circle of power. In Jordan, a key component of this is the army – poor but loyal. In Syria it is the all-powerful Ba'ath. Like two vehicles involved in a high-speed collision, the Ba'ath and the Syrian economy are fused. To reform one is to disrupt and distort the other. The only incentive for the Ba'athists to break free is the prospect of a severe economic crisis, and this may be what motivates the few, isolated moves toward change at the expense of meaningful, comprehensive reform.

Until the crisis is imminent, the Ba'ath will confine itself to minor tinkering. Its responsibilities are minimal. There is no real concern about monetary policy because there is no monetary system. Fiscal policy consists of buying local farm products with petrodollars and selling them to consumers at a discount. The state employs 1.6 million people but only needs about 300,000 to run things.*

The Syrian economy survives off a vast reservoir of unofficial activity. A brisk smuggling trade, mostly with Iraq, has sidelined the traditional bourgeois layer of the economy – the middle-class merchants in Damascus, Hama and Aleppo. The value of this underground commerce is unquantifiable; possibly a quarter of gross domestic product or possibly half. Not all of it is illegal, but it is unrecorded and therefore untaxed. Like other Arab states, Syria's tax revenue – the lifeblood for any civil society – is a fraction of what it should be.

A shadow economy is by nature corrupt; businessmen say the compounded costs of bribery and extortion in Syria can inflate the price of a finished good by 18 to 20 per cent. An ex-vice president of parliament once complained to me how he had to pay the minister of health a bribe of SL5 million just for a license to open a pharmaceutical factory. Traffic police pay their superiors hundreds of thousands of pounds each year for the right to patrol areas around Damascus' five-star hotels, the choicest spots for small-time extortion.

Without a crisis, Syria will continue to tap the proceeds of its grey-market economy no matter which hazily defined 'model' it may

---

* A ministry of planning study once concluded the average Syrian puts in a workday of 37 minutes.

adopt for whatever reforms it may consider under whichever circumstances that may arise to demand it. Not only is there no pressure from within the Syrian regime to change, there are no rival power centres that might promote a credible alternative. If they exist, they are not organized. If they attempt to organize, they are eliminated – sometimes through force, more often by assimilation. An Aleppine merchant once told me how his hometown, disenfranchised by rival Damascus, sided with the Muslim Brotherhood in its war with the state in the late 1970s. Rather than move on Aleppo, Hafez al Assad assigned a handful of intelligence agents to the city with a mandate to traffic in the black market. So active were they that they effectively bribed Aleppo's burghers into submission.

Assad adopted similar tactics with Syria's Druze community. When Druze militias became too powerful after subduing restive tribes in the south, he simply gave them a share of the synthetic-opium traffic coming from Turkey to Israel and the Gulf States. Within months the tribesmen were too busy fighting each other over the spoils of the trade to challenge the regime.

'When you corrupt something,' the merchant told me, 'you make it ineffective.'

The Islamists are another case in point. One of the most important Islamic institutions is the *wakf*, or charitable trust. The concept goes back to Islam's earliest age. Essentially a fund that includes income-generating assets, such as real estate or a taxable utility, the dividends support some civic or religious service – a *sabeel*, or public water fountain, a bathhouse, hostel, or a mosque. The assets are donated by public officials as well as private individuals. Rich men and women can thereby dispose of their assets to pre-empt inheritance disputes between siblings in a world without probate law.

The *wakf* and a strong tradition of private charity are among the many admirable and endearing features of Islamic and Arab society.* In my years reporting throughout the Middle East I have always been touched by people – regardless of their financial condition – going out of their to way to give money, or alms, to someone in the street. Such compassion radiates through the *wakf* on a much larger scale.

The *wakf* is also big money. The right to manage its assets has

---

* Almsgiving is among the five Pillars of Islam, along with profession of the faith, prayer, the fast of Ramadan, and pilgrimage to the holy places.

inspired as many power plays and double-deals as anything in the history of Islam.* Imagine a bidding war for the mandate to control a fund relative in size to the California Public Employees Retirement System and you get the idea.†

The senior religious leader in most Islamic societies is the Grand Mufti, and his power and influence derive principally from his control over the *wakf*. Traditionally, the *wakf's* importance and the mufti's authority strengthen as government resources weaken. Endemic corruption under the Samanid dynasty in eleventh-century Iran encouraged religious leaders to establish their own fiefdoms in cities like Merv and Nishapur, and it was the *wakf* that served as the economic base for their control. It wasn't until the nineteenth century that the *wakf* was brought under the Ottoman sultan's authority and it remains the state's most important tool for domesticating religious groups.

This may be changing, at least in part, due to September 11.

'The *wakf* is a corrupt institution that can make a sheik rich in a year. The government contains and controls the religious centres through the *wakf*.'

Dr Ali‡ is an ex-parliamentarian from the port city of Latakia. He is an orthodontist by profession and a secular Muslim with close ties to Islamist groups. Once, on a reporting trip to Damascus I cold-called him on his cell phone to talk about fundamentalism and the state; Dr Ali said he would be happy to meet me in an hour.

An hour and twenty minutes later he entered the lobby of my hotel, a well-dressed man in his sixties and filled with contrition. 'I'm so sorry for being late, but when you called I was performing a root canal.'

'You took my call in the middle of a root canal?'

'Of course. These mobile phones are very convenient.'

Dr Ali escorted me to a corner table in an almost deserted coffee shop. He requested I sit with my back to the entrance to conceal my

* In the days of the Egyptian Mamluks officials would set up *wakfs* to finance elaborate mosques and *madrassas* and appoint their sons as administrators to preserve their family's control of the income. Such conflicts of interest became so widespread that patrons were sometimes pressured to appoint eunuchs as *wakf* administrators.
† CalPERS, as it is known, is one of America's largest retirement funds with some $150 billion under management.
‡ Many of the names attributed to Syrians and Iraqis in this book are assumed.

note taking. That apart, he spoke freely, even enthusiastically, about Islamic fundamentalism in Syria and the government's relationship to it.

'There is widespread discontent,' he said, 'but it is not organized. The old regime is not yet dead and its successor has not yet been born.'

I asked about the Muslim Brotherhood, the pan-Arab fundamentalist group that had seemingly been dormant since Assad routed it at Hama.

'They are obsolete,' Dr Ali said. 'There is a big ideological crisis within the group between those who have become part of the system, and those who are ready to become suicide bombers. Take the Grand Mufti of Damascus. There are eight thousand families that rely on him, as the mufti, through the *wakf*. He has 100 men and 75 women teaching religion on his behalf, all unofficially. There are 70 mosques in Damascus alone.'

So he has a good thing going, I said. The last thing he'd want is to spoil it by challenging the regime.

'There is a line he cannot cross,' said Dr Ali. 'But he raises the consciousness of Islam so that it could, one day, prevail. At the very least, he doesn't want to be caught out should extremist groups gain momentum. There are some people who cannot be bought, at least not until they achieve some level of power and then they too, will covet the *wakf*. These days, everyone is looking for a vacuum.'

Everyone is playing an angle and marking time. Dr Ali sketched for me a primordial landscape of political bogs, ooze, and tectonic shifts. The circle of power is secure for now; its inner core has pacified most constituencies through the patronage of the *wakf* and other institutions. But it knows the satellite-dish generation is aware it has been defrauded. The people who pass by the magnificent Umayyad Mosque, a monument to Arab achievement lost, know they have been consigned to the slipstream of a global economy driven by others. They also know they have their government to blame for this. The implicit contract between ruler and ruled – submission in return for rising standards of living – is void. Loyalty to the state is coerced or purchased but not earned.

Pressure needs a valve, and that valve is religion. Syrians know the mosque is the one place they can hide where the Ba'ath won't follow so long as they don't cross the line. The United States, in demanding Arab leaders choose a side in the war on terror – just as Eisenhower did battling communism four decades earlier – slashed the old line with a new one.

'The Americans are weakening the regimes by asking them to take a contributing role,' said Dr Ali. 'They don't understand what they're doing. This places the religious elite, which is associated with the regime, on the defensive. It is in disarray and this could be exploited by others. The *wakf* is no longer an iron guarantee of compliance. We are in an economic crisis. The question is whether this is an immediate crisis that will force the regime to restructure and change society.'

I wondered. Very little in Syria happens immediately. The economy's prolonged decline is so gradual that the effects are almost imperceptible. 'It's like the frog in the Chinese proverb,' I said. 'It sits in water that is brought to a boil so gradually it doesn't know it's being cooked.'*

'This is true,' said Dr Ali. 'But the Ba'ath knows it must be seen to do something. Otherwise, it will have no credibility if radical groups express themselves with violence. They can be small, isolated and anonymous, but they can do much damage. This is the next phase for change. The most dangerous time for a regime is when it tries to reform itself. We are in a phase where the future belongs to the fanatics.'

In other words, the Ba'ath and other Arab regimes could become locked into the same kind of asymmetrical conflict with shadowy extremist groups the US is waging today. It will be an attack on their credibility, not their survival.

At least not at first.

Meanwhile the current Palestinian Intifada buys the regime time. Instability abroad is good for the Ba'ath at home.

After Israel invaded the West Bank in the spring of 2002 the government didn't have to recruit people to demonstrate solidarity with the Palestinians. Thousands filled the streets of Damascus, Aleppo, Hama and Latakia during a general call to protest after Friday prayers. The US embassy was menaced; dozens of riot police were posted outside the Egyptian and Jordanian embassies.

Confronted with a dramatic escalation in Middle Eastern violence, President Bush dispatched his secretary of state, Colin Powell, to the region. He ordered Israel to end its siege of West Bank cities and the Palestinians to stop suicide-bomb attacks on Israelis. The next day he

---

* Like everything else Chinese, this saying is also claimed separately by Koreans and Japanese.

shifted his position; the suicide bombings must end, he reiterated, but Israel could do whatever it thought necessary to protect itself. Powell's 'urgent mission' suddenly required detours to Morocco and Madrid. It was not clear whether President Bush's reversal suggested an honest reappraisal of Israel's strategic position or a realization that the Jewish state was long past caring what the White House said.

The Arabs perceived this at the very least as American weakness in the wake of Israeli aggression and at worst complicity with it. Either way it was a gift for Bashar. 'Bush demands an Israeli withdrawal and Ariel Sharon blows a huge raspberry,' a diplomat in Damascus told me. 'This is a vindication for Bashar and Syria's hard line.'

The diplomat's embassy is down the street from an agency with interests in the Middle East that are identical to those held by Washington. I talked to several of the agency's confused and dispirited foreign representatives.

SG: What is Powell doing in Morocco?

FR: Ask him. We sure don't know. It looks real bad. It looks terrible. This region is on the brink of upheaval. There is an explosion of outrage over what is going on in Palestine. There have been a lot of spontaneous demonstrations. People get on their cell phones saying 'let's do something.' We shouldn't be antagonizing the Syrian people. This country is pluralist in nature. We used to have a saying in Saudi Arabia about how America had shared interests with the Saudis. Here, we have shared values but different interests. This society is the one we want work with.

SG: But it is still authoritarian.

FR: The salons were shut down. Riad Saif was given a five-year sentence for 'illegally trying to change the constitution'. He's a member of parliament, for crying out loud. But the trial was open to the public. People do talk about politics even with the crackdown, and that is significant.

SG: Are the Islamists gaining popularity?

FR: Right now, there has been a resurgence of sympathy with the Islamists. In a country with 60 per cent Sunnis, you see more women covered. Could they coalesce? Probably not, but if there is a regime change it would have a greater Muslim flavour. Hassan Nasrallah [Hezbollah's leader] is very popular because he's the only one who did anything about Israel. Al Manar [the Hezbollah satellite channel] is very dangerous. It's one infomercial after another for incitement.

SG: Doesn't the White House know what is going on?

FR: I'm sure it is all in the cable traffic, but is it being read? They are reading it, but not computing it. By simplistically reducing this war on terrorism to the lowest denominator, they're holding the region hostage.

SG: So what is driving US policy?

FR: It's domestic politics and myopia. What is happening is not helping Israel and it hurts us a lot more.

Outside, looking in . . .

The main suk in Damascus, known as Hamadiyyeh, serpentines through what was once the Citadel, the heart of the old walled city. The wall is made of three sets of stones that offer a visual chronology of the three great civilizations that ruled there: the largest were cut by the Romans and the mid-sized ones by the Ayyubids, the people of Saladin, who ruled in the late twelfth and thirteenth centuries. They were succeeded by the Mamluks, who remained in power until 1517. From Turkish stock and suckers for detail, the Mamluks extended the wall with the smallest, most intricately joined stones. A moat once circled the walls but it was filled long ago.

The Mongols besieged Damascus three times but failed to breach its walls. In 1402, the great Turkic leader Tamerlane succeeded where the Mongols failed when he found a weakness in the city's lightly guarded southern gate. There he remained for 100 days before evacuating the city along with its greatest artisans for his home in Samarkand. He also left behind a tower of human heads – one for each Damascene who refused to pay tribute.

Syria today suffers from a new, if less grisly, brain drain. It involves largely middle-class Syrians – educated, secular, moderate – who are exhausted with corruption and stagnation and are emigrating to the modern economies of the West, precisely the kind of people who would be at the heart of a reformed economy; without enough of them, no reform process will fully succeed.

It is worth meeting someone who has vowed to stay. Marwan Abdullah and his extended family of assistants and suppliers buttress their patch of the Syrian economy from their antique shop just around the corner from the eighteenth century Azem Palace, adjacent to the main suk. Marwan is twenty-seven, speaks four languages and is studying for an MBA at a university in Beirut. As an only son, he must one day take over the family trading company, which includes this tiny bazaar on the second floor of a second-hand book-shop.

Marwan is already introducing the latest accounting and manager-
ial theories from the Harvard Business School, which he is learning
in Beirut. 'My father doesn't approve, he is so conservative,' Marwan
told me when he started his first-semester studies. 'He doesn't even
want me to take courses in Beirut. So I am taking the courses anyway,
without his knowledge. When I have my degree, he'll be proud.'

I first met Marwan in 1999. I was ambling about, looking for
antique carpets, and Marwan saw me coming a mile away; I would
leave the shop $3,000 lighter but with a richer understanding of what
winnows Syria's once-mighty middle class.

Marwan was correct and professional as he welcomed me into the
shop. We exchanged business cards and he thoughtfully scrutinized
mine before slipping it into his breast pocket. With the clipped confidence of someone twice his age he instructed his clerk, a Palestinian
refugee named Umar, to rifle through a stack of rugs. We were interrupted by an urgent phone call from Beirut which Marwan took,
alternating effortlessly between Arabic, French, and colloquial English
while summoning his 13-year-old cousin to bring tea.

I approached two gentlemen in a corner of the shop watching a
satellite re-broadcast of an Oprah Winfrey show. 'We like it very
much,' said one of the men, who turned out to be Toufic. 'It's a very
interesting look at society and life in America.'

'Well,' I said, wondering if Oprah was aware her demographic
included oppressed Arabs. 'We Americans love to talk about ourselves.'

Toufic shot me a mischievous grin: 'You should hear what *we* have
to say about you.'

Hanging up, Marwan suggested we go to his other shop a few
hundred yards away. 'There is a much better assortment for someone
with tastes as exquisite as yours,' he said. The Harvard Business
School should include a survey course called 'Secrets of the Suk 101:
The Arab Art of Buttering up the Money'.

We stepped into the torrent of commerce that is the main suk.
Marwan eyed my card a second time. Barely above the market's
tumult, I was suddenly treated to a detailed account of what it takes
to keep a business alive in the Ba'ath Party's worker-paradise.

'We hate it here,' Marwan began, as I dodged impalement by an
incoming litter of *knafeh*, a popular Arab pastry. 'The police come
every two weeks or so, demanding bribes or else they'll take our
licences. We have to bribe customs' officials to get our shipments off
the docks. There are no banks so we can't do business on credit. We
have to go through Lebanese banks, but until recently they were

1. François and Charbell Bassil, Le Chef, Beirut

2. Nazem Ghandour (*left*) and Tarik Arafiri, mushroom magnates, Tripoli, Lebanon

3. Mohammad Hijazi, medical technician and ex-Hezbollah fighter, Beirut

4. The Ummayad mosque, Damascus

5. Palestinian refugees, Hai Qaissieh district, Amman

6. Jordanian journalist Qassem al Katib, Ma'an

7. 'For fifty years we've been waiting for our problems to be solved. Israel still has everything and we still have nothing.' Palestinian refugee Subhi Abu Suleyman, Jenin

8. 'We continued to function. We saved people. We kept morale up. We are the hope of Palestinians and good Israelis.' Dr Mustafa Barghouthi resurfaces after dodging Israeli troops during Operation Defensive Shield, Ramallah, West Bank, 21 April 2002

9. Israeli–controlled checkpoint, Nablus, West Bank

10. 'The Israelis don't take history into account.' Women wander through what is left of a Nablusian soap factory after Operation Defensive Shield

11. Iraqis celebrate Saddam Hussein's sixty-fifth birthday in Tikrit, 28 April 2002

12. Foreign dignitaries join in the merriment

13. Abbasid palace, thought to have been built in the late twelfth century, Baghdad

demanding a bond worth 200 per cent of the value of our deposits before they'd cover our transactions. Everyone thinks Lebanese bankers are so sophisticated but they're greedy and risk averse.'

Marwan ran into a friend and we halted abruptly in front of the Nour Eddin Al-Shaheed bathhouse. A rate card listed massages at SL70 and 'abrasive cleanings' for SL20. A freshly polished bronze plaque identified the bathhouse as particularly distinguished:

The Finnish Sauna Society in Damascus has on 27th January 1992 nominated Haman Nour Eddin in the old city to be the parent sauna of the Society.

Then we were off again, now more quickly, leaving me little time to ponder the implications of the global sauna complex. Around a corner we stopped at an ancient door with battered rusted hinges and climbed a narrow flight of stairs. Suddenly we were alone in a small antique warehouse.

'You have been to Israel?'

I hesitated. Admitting in Syria to have been a guest of the Zionist entity is grounds for immediate expulsion. But the pleading curiosity in Marwan's eyes was irresistible.

'Yes I have.'

'We try to follow the Israeli economy via the Internet. We use a server in Beirut. It seems Israel has become a powerful economy, very modern and high-tech.'

'That's true.'

'Before 1948 we always did business with the Jews. They were a big part of the economy. Back then, there was a strong banking system and my father would write cheques to his Jewish suppliers. One family was particularly close to us but they fled to Israel. We know this because my father checked to make sure they were safe.'

'Would you do business with the Israelis today?'

'Of course. But only if there is a just peace. We have done business with Jews, lived with them, eaten with them, for over a thousand years. It was not us who murdered the Jews but you Europeans. In our hearts we would never accept Zionism, but in our heads, we can accept a Jewish state if it decides to live peacefully with the Arabs.'

Two years later, the Pope was paying homage in Damascus to his sainted namesake. President Bashar was using the occasion to score some public relations points over Israel with pointed remarks about the Jews' persecution of Christ.

The papal visit played out against the blood-spattered backdrop of the current Intifada, now in its seventh month. I was back in Marwan's shop, dropping another couple of grand on antique carpets and furniture. ('You always pick out the most expensive items,' Marwan said, admiringly.) Marwan is a Sunni Muslim; Toufic, the Oprah groupie, is a Christian. In the shop are several icons depicting Jesus and Mary in addition to a prayer rug stored among the antique carpets Marwan often uses for afternoon prayers.

Toufic and members of Marwan's family were watching the latest Al Jazeera reports from Palestine. Israeli troops had shot to death a four-month-old infant, which gave the Palestinians control of a moral high ground measured largely by the age of the freshly slaughtered. When a Palestinian killed a two-year-old Jewish settler some weeks before, it was the Israelis who cried victim. Now the Palestinians had the advantage by some 20 months, and even Israeli prime minister Ariel Sharon felt obliged to issue an apology.

As Marwan's father watched the screen silently, toying occasionally with his hearing aid, Toufic turned away from the graphic images of the infant's wounds. 'They want the Arabs to speak peace but the Israelis only speak of war,' he said. 'Only the US can force Israel to make peace but it doesn't, because if there was peace America would have to pull its troops from the region.'

Marwan shook his head. 'Before all this, three out of ten of my friends were prepared to do business with the Israelis,' he said. 'They were prepared to accept Palestine, and we were prepared to accept Israel. But after this, no. It will take a generation to get over this.'

With tourism flat, Marwan said he was expanding the family business. He was drawing up a master plan, something to do with the hotel trade, which he would submit to banks for funding and as a final thesis for his MBA. 'I'm trying to diversify funding but I doubt I'll get bank loans. That means we'll continue to do business in cash, which means we have to lug around these huge boxes. Yesterday I ran into a farmer who sold his house. He was carrying the money on a donkey in huge potato sacks.'

Syria's best and brightest, Marwan said, were lining up for the exits. But not him.

'Two thirds of my friends have left Damascus and these are people with enough money to live comfortably if they stayed. But I'm not leaving. I'd rather gather expertise abroad and bring it back here. This is my home. My father built this business from nothing. How can I leave?'

I told Marwan I was taking a year off to write a book about the golden age of early Islam, how it was enlightened and tolerant.

'It was those things, yes,' he said. 'But most of all, it was a bigger market.'

I returned to Marwan's shop in spring 2002. The Intifada had witnessed the terrible advent of the suicide bomber and Israel's retaliatory re-occupation of Palestinian land. I arrived near closing time, unannounced. Marwan and Toufic were examining a ledger book. They greeted me warmly and called out to the adjoining sewing stall for tea.

Footage of the Israeli invasion flickered away on Al Jazeera. 'Bush is pushing people to religion,' Toufic said. 'When you have no hope, you go to the mosque. The Arabs finally talk peace [at the Arab League summit held in Beirut a few weeks earlier] and Sharon goes to war. It's true what they say, that the Jews want an empire that stretches from the Nile to the Euphrates. It will take fifteen, twenty years to rebuild what they've destroyed.'

I asked Toufic how all this would affect business.

'Not much,' he said. 'We are insulated from this economically.' He thought for a moment and laughed. 'After all, we have no aid programmes to lose; it's not like Egypt and Jordan, which is burdened with your American aid.'

We adjourned with the tea to a corner of the shop. Marwan told me he had graduated from the masters' programme in Beirut. I asked him if he had completed his business programme, and before I could finish he had retrieved from his desk a thick dissertation written in French.

'This is it,' he said. 'Do you know what a *caravanserai* is?'

I nodded. When Muslim pilgrims made the three-month journey to Mecca – the pilgrimage known as *hajj* – they would stay in hostels in the major cities along the way. Damascus marked the midway point for those travelling from Istanbul, and Hamadiyyeh is loaded with ancient hostels, or *caravanserai*. They were made redundant in the late nineteenth century when the Hijaz railway opened between Istanbul and Mecca, reducing the *hajj* journey from months to days. Most *caravanserai* – also known as *khans* – were subsequently turned into warrens of shops and stores.

Marwan intended to convert the old *khans* into a chain of tourist hotels. His dissertation included charts and graphs mapping out pricing models, break-even points, and depreciation costs. Room rates would start at $60 and peak at $400 for a 'Consular' suite, named after the dignitaries among the pilgrims who always stayed in the *khan's* most elaborate accommodation.

Marwan was not alone with this inspiration. Several entrepreneurs had renovated *khans* in Aleppo and were doing the same in Damascus. His comparative advantage, he told me, would be with the furnishings.

'The rooms will be outfitted with real antiques which patrons can buy,' he said.

'At a huge mark-up to the retail price, no doubt.'

'Certainly there will be a minor premium for the additional hand-ling charges of . . .'

'Never mind. How much will this project cost?'

'With a million dollars in working capital I can open a hostel with two renovated homes,' Marwan said. 'It's not a *khan* of course and it's on a smaller scale. But with the cash flow from the hostel, I can buy and begin work on the *khan.*'

Marwan had already identified the first *khan* on his list and the next evening we inspected it. He chose this particular *khan* both for its location – just off the spice market adjacent to the east wall of the Umayyad Mosque – and also for its large courtyard, which insulates the rooms from the noise of the market place The air is redolent with all manner of exotic smells – anise, allspice, cardamom – so that drunken Europeans can smell their way home through the suk's laby-rinthine corridors after a night's carousing. The *khan* currently housed shops that had cheap home goods for sale – soap, kitchen-cleansers, hair-care products.

I asked Marwan whether he would buy out the shop owners or offer them shares in the enterprise.

'Naturally, I'd rather offer shares,' he said. 'But first, you have to make them understand the concept of equity. Syrians are very conservative. They'd rather have cash in hand now rather than stock that could make them ten times richer five years from now. It's a learning process.'

We had dinner at Jabri House, a converted eighteenth-century villa in the Christian quarter with a huge open courtyard and an enclosed elevated dining room to the left of the entrance. Syria may be on the brink of an economic crisis, but every night Jabri House is packed with Damascenes dining, playing backgammon and smoking hookahs.

'Bottom line,' I asked Marwan over a bowel of chicken lathered in yoghurt, a dish known as *fatteh*. 'Where are you going to get the money for the hostel?'

'I'll find a godfather,' he said. 'I know people who know them. They're like an agent. But I only go to the godfathers task by task. I don't want to become too dependent on them.'

'Godfather' is a euphemism for someone rich and powerful who occasionally patronizes the young and ambitious. It is a common colloquial conceit; Syrians toss around words like 'mafias' and 'consiglieri' without a trace of irony, the way Westerners refer to ministers and civil servants. The Syrian ruling class has become so corrupt and criminalized that no business of any magnitude is done without a cabal of ministers, vice ministers and generals wetting their beaks.

'Basically, a godfather is a vice minister or son of a vice minister,' Marwan explained. 'Why a vice minister and not the minister? Because the minister is usually a political appointee and only lasts a few years before he moves on. The vice minister is a careerist, so he develops the most contacts. Officially, these guys are paid $400 a month but they somehow manage to earn enough to pay for a car for each child, a driver to drive them, mobile phones and large villas.'

Institutional graft is synonymous with any country that lacks the rule of law – including America less than a century ago. But there is a jagged edge to the way Syria's ruling elite horns its way into honest enterprises. Every businessman has a story to tell about the Phone Call, the Tap on the Shoulder or the Rap on the Car Window. Marwan has a friend who owns an apartment building. The sons of a particularly prominent government official decided to buy the ground floor to market products they were distributing for foreign manufacturers – one of several highly lucrative businesses they have acquired since their father's elevation into the circle. They confronted Marwan's friend with an offer, which he refused; it made no sense to sell the ground floor, he explained, which in any case was already let to a tenant of long standing.

The next day, Marwan's friend was summoned to the office of the prominent official.

'Let my boys do business,' he was told. 'It's better for them and better for you.'

End of conversation. The floor was sold and the tenant summarily removed.

Swimming Upstream

'Come Stephen! Tea and coffee!'

Msab Fattahi summoned me from the bus we had taken from Damascus to Hama, the final stop before my destination of Aleppo. This was Msab's home and although it was nearly midnight, he insisted on hosting me during the 15-minute layover.

I had become Msab's responsibility several hours earlier, when we began our journey from Damascus. I duly played the role of inept-foreigner-on-a-Third-World-bus, a regular performance despite having worked in the developing world for much of my adult life. I failed to check my bags in properly. I sat in the wrong seat and had to be escorted by the bus driver to the correct one, next to Msab. When I momentarily lost my ticket, he pointed to it peaking out of my shirt pocket. He showed me how my seat reclined, and directed the on-board steward, whom he knew, to give me extra chocolates and servings of 7-Up.

Msab's English was rudimentary – he had used a trade magazine to explain he owned a furniture-making company – but he insisted on communicating. When I told Msab I was an American he became solemn and, unable to express himself in English, made a gesture with his hands and fingers of something descending to Earth. It was the World Trade Center.

'We are very sorry for what happened,' he said. 'These people are not Muslims.'

The bus station was in the centre of Hama. Msab and I passed ancient stone buildings with the honeycombed archways and basalt-and-limestone façades typical of Mamluk architecture. The buildings had been turned into government office buildings forty years ago; draped in the red, white and black banners of the Ba'ath party, they suggested elegant matrons in cheap polyester gowns. At the centre of the courtyard was a clock tower. It told the correct time.

Before Hafez al Assad's war on the Muslim Brotherhood, Hama was known for its medieval windmills. Though the windmills survived, tens of thousands of people were killed in the government assault on the Muslim Brotherhood base and much of it was destroyed. President Assad ordered the rubble paved over, the atrocity sealed under an epidermal layer of concrete. Fundamentalists in Syria have been lying low ever since, and at least on this night there was little sign of civil war.

But even here, the Intifada was not far away. Msab and I entered a nearby coffee house and watched along with two-dozen or so other patrons an Al Jazeera broadcast of Israel's siege of the West Bank. Palestinian gunmen, holed up in Bethlehem's Church of the Nativity, were locked in confrontation with Israeli troops positioned outside. Earlier that day, a church attendant had been shot dead by an Israeli sniper when he tried to collect food from the entryway. Israeli tanks had rolled into the refugee village of Jenin. Corpses were decaying in the streets, according to the report. Israel would not allow aid workers to collect them for fear they were booby-trapped.

A hip, goateed waiter arrived with two demitasse cups of bitter sludge.

'Welcome to Syria,' he said in perfect English.

Someone turned up the volume. Palestinians were reporting 500 people had been killed in Jenin. The Israelis said the body count was much lower.

'This is an outrage,' Msab said. 'The world does nothing. Your government does nothing. How can your Mr Bush do nothing?'

By now, Msab's question – mercifully rhetorical – was a familiar one.

Aleppo has always been a worthy rival to Damascus as an entrepot for global trade. A milestone in international commerce occurred there in the fourteenth century when the Golden Hamster was introduced to the West via a British trading company. The Golden Hamster, or *Mesocricetus*, is popular in the garment trade for its soft fur, in medicine for laboratory research and – when churning away on its trademark treadmill – as the reigning metaphor for the all-consuming ambition of white-collar professionals. Golden Hamsters also make fine pets.

Not only did Aleppo diversify beyond the Hamster trade, it integrated itself into a global economy that knows relatively few Arab-made products.

In the 1990s it was fashionable among economists and investors to distinguish between 'upstream' and 'downstream' goods in the global economy. Heading the production 'stream' are materials needed to assemble a part or product, such as raw materials and industrial goods. They tend to be commodities produced in great quantity with very low profit margins. The farther downstream an item is produced, the smaller its production volume, the higher the technology needed for assembly and the greater the margin. A petrochemical plant is an upstream producer; it makes the naphtha 'pills' that are used to make the synthetic materials used in kitchens and jet airplanes. Rubber is an upstream resource, a Goodyear tyre a midstream product and a Mercedes Benz a downstream, finished good.

Aleppo is that rare example of an Arab city more or less exactly where it should be on the production stream. Its sophisticated industrial base makes quality items – components and raw materials but also some finished goods – for sale in established consumer markets in Europe. This earns the kind of hard, taxable currency that Syria badly lacks. Aleppo should be an Arab model as an engine for economic growth, employment and political stability. This it manages with precious little support from its own government, let alone the international community.

Mohammed Sabbagh Sharabati is the general secretary of the Aleppo Chamber of Industry and one of the largest investors in the province. His family runs the Nour group of textile manufacturers and he recently opened a weaving mill that employs a thousand people. The factory was built with the company's cash reserves; bank loans are too costly and bureaucratic even for a heavyweight industrialist like Mohammad to secure.

'We are waiting for banks to open,' Mohammad said. 'We hear Société Générale [the French financial giant] has expressed an interest. But it will take time.'

Mohammad praised the government for exempting Syrian exporters from a 36 per cent profits tax last year and for lowering taxes on some imported capital goods – so long as they have no Israeli content. It also instructed Syrian cotton producers to sell to garment manufacturers at international market rates, giving them a crucial advantage when competing overseas, particularly against rival Turkey. Previously, textile makers had to buy cotton at artificially high prices to subsidize Syria's influential but inefficient cotton growers. (The government still subsidizes its agriculture sector, albeit through different channels.)

All of this helps, Mohammad said, but the chamber was still demanding concessions from the Americans. 'If you're an Egyptian manufacturer and you need to import US products to produce for export, you get special low interest rates. Why can't Syria qualify for programmes like this?'

It was no use pointing out to Mohammad that Egypt and Jordan had to sign peace treaties with Israel to win privileged access to the US market and that any bilateral trade agreement with Washington could only be considered once Damascus dropped its support of Hezbollah. Even for moderate Syrians like Mohammad, Hezbollah is fighting a war of resistance against Israeli occupation. For now at least, Syrian industrialists would have to make do on their own.

Mohammad dispatched Nidal Kabbani, his export manager, to give me a tour of the new plant on the outskirts of Aleppo. Nidal had spent time as an agricultural engineer in the Persian Gulf, but returned after a few years, homesick.

'The people of the Gulf never tell you what they're thinking,' Nidal said. 'They never invite you to their homes. They're not like Syrians.'

I asked Nidal about the Syrian economy and the trickle of reforms that Bashar had teased out of the system. Bashar was doing his best, Nidal told me. 'But he cannot jump. He must move step by step, which is better for us. We don't want to happen here what happened to Eastern Europe.'

We turned off the freeway and rumbled across a pastoral landscape of olive trees rooted in Syria's famous 'tierra rosa' – that lush, auburn soil that nourishes the country's northern farm belt. We came to the mill, actually a complex of four factories that process, weave, and dye tons of cotton into natural and synthetic garments for sale worldwide. Each factory was embellished with the 'Nour Establishment' corporate crest.

Nidal led me through the weaving plant, which he said was built in a year by construction teams working non-stop in three shifts. The walls were unpainted, the doorframes unvarnished and the bookshelves bare. But the mills were spinning. Huge machines filtered foreign material from bales of raw cotton that was then washed and dried in blow-chambers. (The extracted waste fertilized the factory grounds, immaculately groomed with indigenous plants and flowers.) Once cleaned, the cotton was spun into yarn, coiled into bins, spun again into thread as fine as spider's silk and mechanically wound around a thicket of spools which were taken to the spinning room

and inserted into dozens of looms that wove thread – 10,000 strands
at a time – into sheets of fabric.

The fabric was transported to the dying factory and doused in a
galaxy of different colours and patterns – ranging from the tacky to
the tasteful – rolled, stamped, hermetically wrapped and stacked.
From there they would be shipped to some Asian garment factory, a
low-margin, upstream commodity for the ready-to-wear world.

All of this utilizes the latest machinery imported from Switzerland,
Japan and Germany and an increasingly canny marketing strategy.
Nour is a vibrant, world-class company in an otherwise geriatric
economy.

'The Europeans know we are becoming an important exporter,'
Nidal said. 'They come here all the time, but the Americans don't
care. We once hosted a group from the US embassy two years ago.
All they wanted to do was promote their machinery. They weren't
interested in buying our products. There was no concept of give and
take.'

As the seat of the Umayyad empire, Syria was once as diverse ethnic-
ally and spiritually as the Umayyad Mosque is aesthetically. In part,
the Umayyads had no choice; as the minority of the three monotheistic faiths, it was in the Muslim's interest to have stable, harmonious
relationships with Jews and Christians. But the dynasty seemed
almost to revel in the milieu of a cosmopolitan, tolerant empire. The
first Umayyad caliph Mu'awiya Ibn Abi Sufyan (reigned 661–680)
kept a boozy Christian poet at his court in Damascus, who would
often arrive, inebriated and unannounced, at Friday prayers. Treaties
like those signed in the mid-seventh century by Khalid Ibn al Walid,
a general who married the daughters of recently conquered peoples
on blood-drenched battlefields, promised Jews and Christians:

> . . . security for their lives, good, and churches. Their walls are not to
> be demolished, neither shall men be quartered in their houses.
> Thereunto we give the oath of God and the covenant of God's
> Prophet, and of the Caliphs and the Believers. So long as they give the
> poll tax, nothing but good shall befall them.

The most prominent theologian at the caliphal court was a Christian,
St. John of Damascus. As a monk St. John was known as *Chrysorrhas*,
or Golden Stream, for his oratorical skills. Centuries later, his writ-

ings would influence such theologians as Peter Lombard and Thomas Aquinas.

Christians and Jews – identified by Muhammad as *al kitab*, or people of the book – were welcomed in the suks of the empire for their skill in management and financial affairs. Forced conversions were rare, except among officials promoted to senior posts such as Khalid al Kasri, an eighth-century governor of Iraq born to Greek-Christian parents. His mother was free to worship as a Christian and her son even built her a church behind the south side of the great mosque at Kufah, near the central Iraqi city of An Najaf.

When the mu'uezzin called the faithful to prayer, he rang a small bell for Mrs. Kasri.

It is important not to overstate the level of ethnic and religious tolerance in Syria today. The Jews are long gone and the various Christian sects are slowly dissolving. But many of the tiles that made up the Syrian social, religious and cultural mosaic are still holding together.

Certainly the audience I was given with Aleppo's most prominent spiritual leader was a compelling, if somewhat scripted, display of inter-faith harmony. I had been recommended to Sheik Dr Ahmed Badr din Hassoun, the Grand Mufti of Syria's Sunni Islamic community, by an Aleppine merchant two days earlier. When I arrived at the main mosque at 10.30 a.m., there, waiting for me at the gate, was George Barbian, my Armenian-Orthodox interpreter and Bassel Kansanrallah, the sheik's Greek-Catholic counsellor.

George and Bassel are respected burghers of Aleppo's main Christian communities. Their families have lived in the city for generations. George is short and prematurely grey, with a well-trimmed moustache and dark circles around his eyes. Bassel is tall and balding and wears aviator glasses indoors as well as out. Both men, conservatively dressed, were visibly excited about the interview. As they escorted me to the reception hall adjacent to the mosque, George resisted when we were asked by an attendant to remove our shoes – following the custom in a faith where places of worship are considered sacred ground.

'Why?' George demurred. He seemed slightly embarrassed, as if taking off his shoes – even in the Muslims' house – was a small but symbolically significant challenge to Christian independence in Aleppo. 'We don't usually do this.'

'It is *necessary*,' Bassel whispered pre-emptively as we walked to the empty overstuffed chairs at the end of the hall. 'We have to do it now.'

I could feel the tension building between the two. 'But why?' George demanded. 'Why *now*?'

The hall was so large – it could have accommodated a regulation basketball court with several rows of tiered seats – and the acoustics so finely pitched that even Bassel's raspy hiss was amplified to a low bellow.

'*Because this is a new carpet.*'

I looked down. Sure enough, the carpet was so new it crunched under our feet.

We sat down to await the mufti. A video camera perched atop a tripod was pointed straight at me. A photographer entered and sat down nearby. We waited in silence for Sheik Hassoun, who finally arrived bearded and beaming in an elegant white turban and grey wool tunic.

The sheik clasped my hand in both of his. 'All people have two homelands,' he said. 'Their native country and Syria. Welcome to your home.'

The photographer began snapping enthusiastically despite the slightly absurd fact that we were alone in the hall. The last time I enjoyed such celebrity treatment was four years earlier, when South Korea's Daewoo Heavy Industries presented me with a photo-album commemorating my tour of their shipyard. Soon afterwards, the entire Daewoo group of companies went bankrupt.

We sat down. The attendant brought us cups of tea on a silver tray.

Sheik Hassoun gestured to George and Bassel, the house Christians. 'There are five million Muslims in Aleppo but I have an Armenian interpreter and Catholic assistant,' he said. 'This is Aleppo and this is Islam. When people say it is permissible to kill people of other faiths in the name of Islam, this is madness. Islam did not conquer by the sword, but by turning dark into light.'

What happened to the Jews? I asked.

'The Jews left in 1948 when a country was established based on religion instead of nationality. Israel is a prophet and we believe in him.* This religiously named country also has a Knesset, which is also a religious word that means place of worship. Now there are people who would have *us* govern from the Mosque. Extremism breeds extremism.'

---

* Also known to non-Muslims as Jacob, whose 12 sons founded the 12 tribes of Israel.

The mufti summarized the Jews' prominent role in the courts of the Abbasids in Baghdad (between the eighth and eleventh centuries) and the later Umayyads (driven from Damascus by the Abbasids in 750) in Andalusia, and how Jewish scientists developed doctrines that were later enshrined in Islamic law. In Syria today, he said, there were Muslims who have mothers of all three monotheistic faiths.

'How is this so?' the mufti asked rhetorically. 'Because many people were breast-fed by a wet nurse of different faiths. Under Islam, if a child is breast-fed by a woman five times or more, even if the woman is not his biological mother, that child becomes her child and in fact it is forbidden by law for that child to marry any of her biological children.'

The attendant presented us with cakes and a box of tissues.

I asked the mufti if he could somehow square Islamic law with suicide bombers.

'Life is holy,' he said, 'but with oppression, death also becomes holy. When the door of life is closed, I will kill myself to blow the door open for others. What is happening in Palestine is being done by Zionists, not Jews. They are changing the holy concepts to serve Zionism at the expense of their own faith and 1,200 years of history.'

Muslims were not behind the events of September 11, the mufti explained.

'Maybe Muslims were flying the planes,' he said, 'but with international organizations behind them. They were toys in their hands. Just as Israel used Jonathan Pollard [the US intelligence officer convicted of passing classified documents to Israel], so were Muslims manipulated into betraying Islam. I wish Americans and the US government could understand we are a civilized nation. We are not struggling against other civilizations. I want you to believe me. Our problems are not with Jews, but oppression.'

The attendant reappeared with coffee and a glazed-ceramic bowl filled with sweets wrapped in plastic.

'There is a new generation of leaders and Bashar al Assad is among them. They want your help to start a new page and end this chapter of bloodletting. I am close to Bashar and he talks about the West with great affection. The problem is that part of the US government is controlled by Zionists and the other part doesn't know what's happening and doesn't care. But remember: if America loses the Arab world, it loses the Muslim world.'

The interview was over. Sheik Hassoun inscribed and presented to me a large, elegantly bound copy of the Koran. George translated the inscription:

In the Name of God the Most Merciful, to my esteemed brother Stephen Glain.

This is a token of friendship so that justice and right would rule among people under the guidance of God.

Your brother, Ahmed Hassoun.

I was running late for my next appointment, but Sheik Hassoun would not let me go until I promised to meet Archbishop Souren Kataroyan, his opposite number in the Armenian Church. I was scheduled to return to Damascus the next day but assured the mufti I would be happy to see the archbishop first thing in the morning.

At precisely 9 a.m. George and Bassel escorted me from my hotel to Archbishop Kataroyan's office at the main Armenian church several blocks away. We stopped on the way for sweets at the pastry shop owned by the nephew of Bassel's cousin. We also ran into George's sister, a civil engineer, on her way to work in a beautifully preserved, vintage Citroën. This was, after all, their turf; the old Christian quarter.

Within a few minutes, the appropriately silver-haired and avuncular Archbishop Kataroyan swept into the room and greeted us in a navy-blue tunic, white collar and blue-striped shirt cuffs that peaked out from his sleeves. A Mont Blanc pen was clipped to his left breast-pocket and he wore the gold and emerald ring that identified him as the prelate of the Armenian church for all of Syria, excluding Damascus.

The archbishop was born the son of a priest in 1939. The Turkish genocide against Armenians in 1915 left his family with nowhere to go but Syria. When his father died, the archbishop's older brother sent him to the clergy. He was ordained in 1962, served as a pastor in Canada eleven years later and briefly led a monastery in Lebanon before returning to Aleppo as a bishop in 1977. When I met him, he was celebrating his fortieth year in the priesthood and his first quarter-century as the prelate of Aleppo.

The archbishop was animated, radiant, his voice booming. He gestured wildly from his desk, framed from behind by a wooden bookcase crested by a carved eagle, Armenia's national bird, with outstretched wings. Like Sheik Hassoun, he revealed himself to be an ebullient ambassador for Syrian ecumenicalism, which he attributed to the late, great Hafez al Assad.

'Our late president is the secret to our stability,' the archbishop said.

'Syria welcomed us in 1915 and Hafez al Assad managed the region when he came to power. In the United States, you have laws for civil society. Let Americans come here and see Christians and Muslims living peacefully without laws.'

'What happened to the Jews?' I asked.

'Emigration is happening everywhere, all the time,' Archbishop Kataroyan said. 'Perhaps it was economics. Perhaps it was the wars. We all want peace. Our late president talked about peace, but peace can't come without justice. The genocide is repeating itself in Palestine and no one is doing anything. We as Christians believe justice is the light that cannot be buried, as Christ said. Our new leader, Dr Bashar, is the branch of the strong tree that was Hafez al Assad. He stands with the Palestinians to have justice.'

I asked Archbishop Kataroyan about suicide bombers.

'There are two essential points in a human being's life,' the archbishop began, demonstrating a peculiarly Oriental faculty for elliptical expression. 'The first is love for homeland and the second comes when you believe in something. When Jesus went into the temple and cast out the moneychangers, he knew that the temple was beloved and he had to use force. When you see there is no justice, you would do anything to get it back. Unfortunately, innocent people die. This love can lead you to take your own life.'

Can innocent lives be justly taken in pursuit of justice?

'I'm against Osama bin Laden and I think he should be killed,' the archbishop said. 'But the US has killed many innocent people. It's the same thing. America is ignoring the Palestinian massacre the way they ignored the Armenian genocide. Arabs are dying by the thousands. When you stand up to injustice, blood will be spilled.'

I broke my journey back to Damascus to call on Hani Azzouz, a leading member of Aleppo's business community and chairman of Syriamica Azzouz, which manufactures laminates and synthetic veneers for building materials and appliances. It is, along with the Nour group, one of Aleppo's largest employers.

At the Syriamica plant, Mr Azzouz was about 15 minutes late for our meeting. He apologized; his secretary, he explained, had only informed him of our appointment an hour earlier.

He sat upright, hands clasped together on the desk, saying nothing. I delivered a rambling brief on precisely why I was so interested in Syria's industrial base. Mr Azzouz listened passively except for his jaw muscles, which he tightened and relaxed like pistons. I droned on. Finally, Mr Azzouz responded:

'I cannot talk to you.'

'Why?'

'You have come at the wrong time,' he said stiffly. 'I would like to talk to you about the business and show you the factory but it is difficult because of what is going on. It is difficult to think clearly with this sense of frustration and despair. Last night, I was having dinner with friends. These people are doctors and engineers, all Western-educated professionals, and we are very upset.'

Mr Azzouz was referring, of course, to events in the West Bank. He apologized for the inconvenience. He assured me I would be welcome at his factory after the situation had stabilized. 'But until then, I've decided I will not say anything without thinking about it for twenty-four hours. Otherwise, I will get emotional and say something I might regret later.'

Very well, I said and prepared to leave. Just one thing, I asked. How many workers does Syriamica employ?

The company employs 900 people, Mr Azzouz said. It was launched in 1980, exports to 42 countries and generates sales of $34 million annually.

I remarked that industrialists like him welcomed government reforms to facilitate exports.

'Now the competition is much more fair,' said Mr Azzouz. 'We're exporting tax-free and are expanding capacity. Our president knows about the economy because he was following it before his father died. He knows what we need, like telepathy. You can tell what he is thinking with the legislation he is signing.'

Bashar al Assad is a man of peace, said Mr Azzouz, but even the president has limits. 'You can only turn the cheek so many times.'

You are talking about Israel?

'And America,' Mr Azzouz said. 'Every day we are watching people die. Syria is a country that is pro-US yet it treats us like terrorists. For the last fifteen years, Syria has worked peacefully with the Americans. We have done our homework, but the teacher is not satisfied.'

Several years ago Mr Azzouz flew to Atlanta to attend a trade show. His Syrian passport triggered suspicion among the immigration authorities and he was interrogated in a tiny room for half-an-hour. What was his business? Who was he going to see?

'I told them I was the chairman of a $34 million-company and had been invited to a major trade exhibition,' he said. 'I had to endure this with my family there in that little room. This was before September 11. What kind of treatment is this?'

It was getting late. I thanked Mr Azzouz and prepared to leave.

'They are in the church!' he suddenly exclaimed, referring to the confrontation between Israeli troops and Palestinian militants holed up in Bethlehem's Church of the Nativity. 'They are in the birthplace of Christ! Where is the Pope?'

I sat back down. Mr Azzouz was rolling.

'Don't think we are happy when Jews are killed,' he said. 'Imagine, people going to work and not coming back. Think of those young soldiers who were killed in the refugee camp. Their parents put their lives into raising them and one day they get a call: Your son is dead. And for what? Politics!'

A few days earlier a US company had bid to supply Syriamica with raw material for laminate. It was offering a good price, about $8 million, for the order, but Mr Azzouz was contemplating giving it to a European company.

'How can I sell to America with all that is going on?' he said.

In the end, Mr Azzouz gave me a tour of the factory. I've never known an industrialist who wasn't proud to show off his operation; Syrians are no different.

Ghosts of Reason

A few blocks from the Umayyad Mosque and close to Damascus' main suk stands a restored medieval hospital, the Bimarstan al-Nuri. It is similar to those constructed by the eighth-century builder of the Umayyad Mosque, Al Walid, who is credited with segregating victims of leprosy, blindness, and other chronic diseases and providing special accommodations for treatment. Al Walid called each one a *Bimarstan* – Persian for 'House of Patients' – thus founding the empire's first hospital chain.

The Bimarstan al-Nuri was erected in the twelfth century by Saladin's uncle, Nur al-Din, a leader of the Abbayid dynasty that succeeded the Fatimids. It was in a hospital like this that Avicenna, the famous Persian physician known as *Abou al-teb* – Pioneer of all Physicians – deployed his manifold skills. An expert in pharmacy, surgery, plastic surgery and therapy, he is credited with writing the leading medical canon of his day.

The Syrian tourist bureau has preserved the Bimarstan al-Nuri as a

museum of early-Islamic science and technology. It attracts few tourists, though it is an important counterpoint to the Umayyad Mosque;
one celebrates early Islam's spiritual achievements, the other its
secular ones.

I stopped by the Bimarstan while covering the Pope's visit in May
2001. At the entrance, a guide offered to give me a tour. We entered
a courtyard that resembled a spa rather than a hospital. The entrance
is embellished with *muquarnas*, the stuccoed honeycombs that hang
like stalactites from Islamic arches and gateways. A fresco of twin pea-
cocks framed the interior of the main arch. Blossoms from Indian
kumquat trees sweetened the air. Four shallow *diwans*, known as
aiwans, faced the courtyard. Recovering patients would sit or recline
here in the spring and summer. Above the main *aiwan* is an ancient
Muslim proverb: 'From the Koran, find what heals you and give the
mercy of God.'

Treatment was free, according to my guide. In addition to the
many innovations and enhancements to medicine credited to the
Arab Empire was nationalized healthcare. 'Early Islam was very merciful,' the guide said. 'It treated people without money. The Umayyad
empire was a prosperous one with few poor people.'

A large fountain gurgled soothingly in the Birmarstan's courtyard.
Physicians in early Islamic times believed the sound and sight of water
aided recovery. In Aleppo, the guide told me, there is a Bimarstan for
treatment of the insane. The most violent patients were kept in a
ward behind heavy doors with metal bars, through which they could
watch and hear a small fountain in a courtyard.

'In general,' explained the guide, 'the less dangerous the patient,
the larger the fountain.'

A wing of the museum, dedicated to the great scientists, physicians, and engineers of the early Muslim empires, serves as a hall of
fame of Islamic Enlightenment. An ancient manuscript shows an
Arab physician lecturing students in Sicily. There is a medical book
edited in the late ninth century by Ibn Abi Usaybi'a, an Arab medical
historian who translated the Hippocratic oath of Greek doctors into
Arabic. There are portraits of Al Battani, one of history's most
famous astronomers and of Al Biruni, who measured the Earth's
diameter four hundred years before the Europeans. There is Al
Farebi, a philosopher the Arabs call the 'Second Teacher' after
Aristotle and the tragically courageous Abbas bin Farnas, who in 861

attempted to fly by leaping from a 180-foot high minaret in Cordoba with homemade wings.

'He flew for some time before losing direction,' my guide said. 'Unfortunately, he forgot to add a tail.'

The hall of surgical instruments is like a showcase of art in miniature. Scalpels of copper and brass are embellished with scrolls and crosses. Less elegant is the 'cupper', a vessel of glass or copper used to bleed patients. Physicians would heat the device, trapping and expanding the air inside to create a vacuum that 'sucked' the blood to the surface of the skin.

'It was said to be particularly valuable in the treatment of melancholy,' my guide told me.

Rational science did not always prevail. In extremis, a desperate physician would don a special camisole embellished with selected verses known as *sura*, from the Koran. Even Avicenna advised mothers to rub their teething baby's gums with hen's fat and a rabbit's head. Some physicians believed patients would recover faster by drinking water from bowls with elaborate inscriptions from the Koran; talismans were filled with mercury and hung around patients' necks.

Both the bowls and talisman are still used, explained the guide, though not the rabbits' heads, hen fat, and camisole.

Quackery abounded. A popular medieval shadow-play features a charlatan named Gharib. 'I have treated people,' he boasts, 'and how many of them I killed with my potions and purges.' An old woman in Cairo promoted an allegedly miraculous well that could cure anything once the afflicted placed food in a container nearby. Medical fraud was so common that the great physician Al Razi was compelled to issue a treatise entitled *Why people prefer quacks and charlatans to skilled physicians*. Al Razi would back-pedal slightly with follow-up papers entitled *On the fact that even skilful physicians cannot heal all diseases* and *Why ignorant physicians, laymen, and women have more success than learned medical men*.

Though men dominated the medical professions, nurses were used extensively, particularly in battle. 'Old wives'' remedies were as popular then as they are today. Women of dodgy credentials would peddle potions, herbs and powders from house to house. A cure for scorpion bites was wingless locusts – to be eaten roasted. A popular aphrodisiac was honey and ground lizard. Citrus peel was used for treating snakebites. The juice from the pulp of a fruit known as *utrujj* was known to moderate the 'sensuousness in women'.

I tipped the guide and made my way back towards the suk, but not before taking in the Bimarstan al-Nuri's sister exhibit, a display of Syrian taxidermy.

I have often wondered where men like Osama bin Laden would have settled in medieval Islam. While in Damascus in 2001 I had asked Albert Aji, who runs a press centre for foreign journalists, if I could meet an expert on early Islamic history. He arranged an appointment with Dr Suheil Sakkar, a professor at Damascus University.

We met in his library, which fronted a narrow street in the south of town. It was a cavernous repository for thousands of books, mostly Arabic, though there were some with English titles. Dr Sakkar worked from a Chinese desk he bought years ago during a study trip to Beijing. Scratchy Arabic hymns drifted from a Sharp radio cassette player on a bookshelf. Suspended from the ceiling was a large fluorescent lamp, incorporating a magnifying glass, used for reading damaged or faded texts.

Dr Sakkar invited me to sit down and made coffee on a ceramic stove perched precariously on a butane burner. Having presented me with a demitasse cup, he excused himself to pray from the northwest corner of the room. On the wall above him hung a framed, embroidered passage from the Koran.

Dr Sakkar got his PhD from London's School of Oriental and African Studies in 1969. He lectured in Damascus, Morocco and Algeria before returning to Damascus. He has written some 200 books, and was currently working on an encyclopaedic history of the Crusades. He had just finished the 42nd of an expected 70-volume work.

I had come to the right place.

We sat in opposing chairs. I explained my interest in Islam's golden age with an emphasis on the economy. It was an under-sourced topic, he told me. Contemporary political commentators wrote about politics and war but little about socio-economics.

Not much has changed, I thought.

'Trade and the economy is just starting to get the attention it deserves,' Dr Sakkar said. 'We have only the Geniza documents, which Jewish scholars have studied but which Arabs have largely ignored.* We focus on political history because it's easier but I think the economy is more important.'

---

* The Cairo Geniza is a trove of medieval documents preserved by Egypt's Jewish communities and edited into a fascinating account of daily medieval life of the era by S.D. Goitein in *A Mediterranean Society*.

The record does show, Dr Sakkar began, that craftsmen and merchants who produced and sold textiles, jewellery and construction materials drove the economy of early Islam. Much of what they made was exported to the Far East in exchange for jewels, silks, and spices. Syria, not Europe, was the epicentre of the global economy of the seventh to ninth centuries. Damascus became the capital of a great Arab nation, Dr Sakkar said, largely because of its location in the middle of the trade route linking Europe and Asia.

The Mediterranean was host to a vast, largely laissez-faire economy. Prefects known as *maktasib* supervised market activity, but the government's hand was generally unseen and duties were limited to export tithes. Monetary and fiscal policy was driven largely by Jews and Christians.

'They were made *wazirs* [high officials] because it was thought they were better at making money,' said Dr Sakkar. 'Religion was more secular then. The old Muslims were more reasonable than we are today. That's why they had such a great civilization. In early Islam, people thought about God before they worshipped him. Now, they don't think at all.'

And the men of Al Qaeda? Where would they rank in the caliphate?

'On the margins,' said Dr Sakkar. 'As agitators, as they are today.'

We were drifting from the past to the present. 'We should re-write the history of Islam for the new millennium,' said Dr Sakkar. 'We need a new generation of scholars, new universities and institutions. But we need money. Where will it come from? Will we pay for the book or for the gun? I've been a professor for forty years and I make less than $300 a month.'

Fundamentalism had plundered popular debate just as the military budget had impoverished public education. The previous year, Dr Sakkar said, he wrote a paper based on new interpretations of the Koran that argued the Prophet could read and write. Islamists opposing the notion that Mohammad could have recited the revealed word by anything short of divine inspiration denounced him. 'Any new word will provoke them,' he said. 'I have been intimidated by these groups. They believe in emotion, not reason. After all, we are not living in Europe.'

I asked him about the new president. 'He is working hard. He is in need of good advisers in many aspects. We have many people who could occupy such offices but the young chap does not have the opportunity to do everything he needs to do. I hope he will in the near future. We need institutions. We need to change many rules and laws. But we can't afford to change like the Soviet Union. I am afraid we may find ourselves with more and new problems. We need to decide on the gun or the book, the hospital or the garrison.'

The secret to an Arab rebirth, Dr Sakkar said, is unity – openness rather than oppression, fusion rather than fission. The early Islamic empires were strongest when ruled as a cohesive block that did not discriminate against its subjects as in the peak years of both the Abbasid and Fatimid empires between the eighth and twelfth centuries. Foreign invasions crushed Arab unity then, he said, and now foreign aggressors in league with corrupt Arab governments conspire to keep the Arabs backward and poor.

'When the Arabs were united, ruled by civilized rulers, they built a great civilization,' Dr Sakkar said. 'Then, Europe was divided and weak. Now, Europe is very, very strong and a great power and ally of the US. The Arabs are divided by unbalanced countries; Egypt has a population of seventy million, but is a very poor country. Meanwhile, Qatar is a petty emirate with great wealth. They think they live well, but this is an illusion. Egypt has everything it needs to live on, because it has the Nile. In the Gulf, everything is artificial. Oil can't live forever. But the Nile is very old.

'In Syria there is a lot of money and only a few hands spending it. The people are very poor. Many people cannot afford tea, bread, or sugar. This is an awkward situation that will change, hopefully without trouble. We tried to solve our problems by coup d'état, and found ourselves deprived of wealth and freedom. Since the tenth century we have been the subjects of soldiers, only now they are our own. The problem of Israel will not be solved by soldiers. We tried that and we lost the land, everything. Israel is not afraid of our weapons but it is afraid of the day Arabs unite and enjoy democracy and freedom.'

Dr Sakkar spoke quietly and methodically. It was a solemn, passionate appeal for democratic Muslim rule.

'Any attempt to unite the Arabs without Islam will fail,' Dr Sakkar told me as we parted. 'People ask me "what kind of Islam?". I tell them there is only one Koran with only one tradition of tolerance and peace.'

3

Jordan

The Royal Expediency

'Monarchy is neither an attractive nor noble institution'

Otanes, a general of the Persian king, Darius I

Tens of thousands of protesters, mostly ethnic Palestinians, filled the streets of Amman on 5 April 2002 shaking their fists in solidarity with their brothers west of the River Jordan. A week earlier, Israel had launched its West Bank offensive and many of the marchers had family members living in cities under siege – Ramallah, Bethlehem, Jenin, Nablus. This was no symbolic gesture of sympathy for fellow, if distant, Arabs, but a visceral expression of anger, hate and frustration over violence done to blood.

It was the largest demonstration in Amman since the second Intifada erupted eighteen months earlier and was directed as much against the Jordanian upper class as against Israel. There was nothing new in this; during the first week of the Intifada, protestors not only threw rocks at the US and Israeli embassies but also trashed luxury cars and apartments in fashionable neighbourhoods like Abdoun and Sweifiyeh. Since then, lower-class resentment had intensified. When protestors chanted 'You who have everything, give us guns,' they referred to a despised, moneyed elite. Driving through the crowd in a friend's Land Rover I was singled out contemptuously by protestors angered by what the vehicle and its occupant represented – a corrupt, wealthy, Westernized nouveaux-rich.*

---

* Because of Jordan's high import duties, licensing fees and sales taxes a luxury sports utility vehicle (SUV) like a Land Rover can cost up to $80,000. A BMW sedan can run into the $150,000 range and a Porsche sports car well over a quarter of a million dollars. The number of such conspicuous vehicles seems to rise inversely to the rate of Jordan's economic decline.

'Know your Koran!' a bearded and pious cab driver roared at me as we lumbered past one another. A Palestinian flag fluttered from his window.

I locked the doors and drove on. The demonstrations had a wild edge. Civil disobedience on this scale is unusual in Jordan and the demonstrators seemed aroused by their own daring. They combined their hatred for Israel with hatred for the United States, which they blamed for abetting Israeli atrocities.

This of course, is bad for the monarchy. The Hashemite dynasty, installed and nurtured by British imperialists, is now cosseted by American diplomatic and financial support. As Washington rises higher in the public odium, so does the throne. America's interests in Jordan are essentially limited to the peace accord King Hussein signed with then-Israeli prime minister Yitzhak Rabin in 1994 which gained Jordan, with its tiny, exhausted economy, a free-trade agreement with the United States. Even under the wily and beloved King Hussein, lukewarm Jordanian support for the treaty turned into disillusionment as hopes for a peace dividend evaporated. Now, with news footage of Israeli tanks rumbling through the streets of Ramallah and Palestinians stuck for days in their living rooms alongside the corpses of dead family members they were unable to bury, Jordanians were agitating for a repeal of the peace altogether. In effect, they were demanding their king relinquish the country's most valuable commodity: a peaceful border with Israel that is convertible into American diplomatic support and hundreds of millions of dollars in financial assistance.

For days after the demonstrations, riot police harassed Palestinian refugees in camps and neighbourhoods. In Hai Qaissieh, a community of Palestinians from the West Bank town of Hebron, police fired tear gas, threw rocks at windows and beat young men. The residents said they did nothing to provoke the violence.

'We were at Fuddruckers having lunch when we heard police were attacking the village,' said an elderly woman who left Hebron in 1948 during the first of the Arab-Israeli wars.* 'They fired no less than a hundred tear-gas canisters at us. They took men and hit them very

---

* Fuddruckers is a US fast-food company that has a successful franchise in Amman. It was renamed 'Oven's Own' after the onset of the second Intifada, in sympathy with an Arab embargo on US products and brands.

hard. We are a peaceful village. Why would they do this? Jordan has never been like this. My grandson is a policeman and he told us Palestinian police were hitting Palestinians because they were under orders to do so.'

I visited Hai Qaissieh a day after the assault. Armed men and *mukhabarat* agents were still milling about. Burned tyres soiled the streets. Occasionally, young boys would throw stones at the police that would fall harmlessly short of their targets.

Rasha, the woman's 20-year-old niece, joined the conversation. She was an English major at Jordan University, spoke fluent English and was covered with a *hijab*.

'The Americans are committing criminal acts and there is nothing but deep silence from the world because the Jews control the media,' Rasha told me. 'They want the world to think we hate the Jews, but we always lived peacefully with them until the Zionists came. I would like to go to the US to educate the American people about who we are. People say the Americans are fair-minded people but they do not understand the Palestinian position. We watched CNN on the Internet, and what it reports is not true.'

I returned to the street and was intercepted by a young man who insisted I talk to his 63-year-old father, Hamad. At their home at the top of a steep rise in the densely populated village, Hamad greeted me warmly.

'Welcome to my son's wedding,' he said. 'Come in and meet the family.'

I peered inside. Sure enough, the women were arranging chairs and an enormous buffet reception. Hamad summoned one of his grandchildren to bring us tea. He wore a wool sports coat over a blue V-neck sweater and an open-necked shirt. Hamad came to Jordan from Hebron in 1955 with his ten family members. He was ten years old at the time and carried his youngest sister across the Jordan River on his shoulders.

The tea arrived. Yesterday's riots and the government's heavy-handed response, Hamad said, was part of a sequence of crimes committed by Israel.

'It begins with massacres like Deir Yassin,' said Hamad.* 'You cannot kick the Palestinians out. These are my grandchildren' – he gestured to a gaggle of curious adolescents – 'they are fighters too.

---

* In 1948, Jewish fighters are said to have slaughtered 250 residents of Deir Yassin, an Arab village near Jerusalem that is now home to one of Israel's largest psychiatric hospitals.

But for what? I would live with Israel, coexist with the Israelis, if they would let me return to my home.'

The wedding party had arrived and Hamad's son pried his father away to greet the guests. They insisted I stay for the reception, but I had to go.

On my way out, a village boy presented me with a spent tear-gas canister. It was a 561 CS 'Lightweight projectile chemical irritating agent,' produced by Federal Laboratories in Saltsburg, Pennsylvania.

The cycle of Middle Eastern violence was burrowing its way under the surface of Jordan's ever-fragile stability; whatever goodwill Washington had with the Jordanians was going down with it.

'If we have to fight the Americans as well as the Israelis, let's go ahead and treat America like an enemy.'

I was in the Amman office of Labib Kamhawi, a Palestinian businessman; we were watching Al Jazeera's news coverage of the violence in the West Bank. The Kamhawis are a prominent family from Nablus. Half fled Palestine during the 1948 war that established Israel; the other half remained.

Because of the difficulty journalists in the West Bank had getting out their reports on the Israeli invasion, the extent of the damage would only become clear after the Israelis pulled out nearly a month later. In the meantime, people like Labib with embattled family members were constantly trying to make contact by a cell-phone network that was frequently jammed.

Labib took a call on his cell phone, crooking it between his ear and shoulder as he took notes. After twenty minutes or so he hung up and sat down wearily on the sofa.

'There's trouble in Nablus,' he said softly. Then, gathering a pen and paper, he gestured for me to join him at the coffee table.

'Come,' he said. 'Let me show you Nablus.' He sketched a street grid. 'This is the entrance to the old city of Nablus. This is where my family has a block of buildings. They were built in 1892.'

He drew a circle where his family had lived for over a century then returned to the sofa.

'The Israelis bulldozed it. They bulldozed the old city and the old soap factory. They occupied the mayor's house and jailed his two sons. The head of Islamic Jihad blew himself up though the Israelis won't say how many Israelis he took with him. Americans ask us how we can tolerate suicide bombers. It's because we don't have tanks.'

The British occupied Nablus in 1936 as part of the mandate, Labib said. In 1948, the British moved out and Jordan's Arab Legion moved in. The Israelis captured the city in 1967 and held it for over three decades before they finally withdrew in 1993 as part of the Oslo peace accords.

'Now,' Labib said, tossing the pen onto the coffee table, 'the Israelis are back.'

Labib is a trader. Among other things, he sells medical and industrial equipment to Iraq under a United Nations programme that allows Baghdad to buy humanitarian items in exchange for oil. For Labib, the monarchy and the Western powers that support it are colonial anachronisms. But with the streets and alleyways of his childhood turned to rubble by America's close ally, he was livid.

'This is the beginning of the end for the Americans in the Middle East,' he said. 'They carried through like the Cold War never ended. They needed a new enemy, and they found it in Islam. Bush is a criminal, public enemy number one. And now Colin Powell is wondering whether he should meet with Arafat. Why should he even bother to come at all?'

The TV switched to a recently convened meeting of Arab foreign ministers.

Labib jabbed an accusing finger at the screen. 'And these idiots are finished. It's over. Egypt is a great country run by twits. Instead of trying to raise Egyptian standards to international levels they are lowering them to their own intellectual depths. Mubarak and the king are scared. They didn't go [to the Arab summit] because they had nothing to say.'

'What do they have to fear?' I asked. 'Is there a credible opposition?'

'Things are still in formation,' Labib said. 'The age of the coup is over. The armies are infiltrated. They're inept and insecure. There will be no civil war in the short term, just civil disobedience. But the younger generation of Arabs and Jordanians, the same ones who were totally disengaged and apathetic a few years ago are now demonstrating. They're using the Internet to organize, thanks to Bush and Sharon. In the long run the Americans will always be seen as the enemy.

'Then there are the Islamists,' Labib continued. 'Just look at the Abdoun mosque. The imam there is young, he's educated. He wears designer jeans.'

I missed the point.

'Usually,' Labib explained, 'the imam is Mr Failure. He's the guy who can't get a decent job elsewhere. Now the imams are yuppies. They are intelligent people going to the mosque because they can't apply themselves anywhere else and they're angry.

'And I'll tell you this: if revolt happens in one country, there will be a domino effect.'

The limits of hilm

In the 3,000-year history of Levantine power-struggles between Babylonians, Hittites, Chaldeans, Assyrians, Romans, Byzantines, Persians, Arabs, Mongols, Sogdians, Turks and finally the French and British, the strip of land known today as Jordan was never much more than a sideshow. It prospered under the Nabataeans at Petra in the second and third centuries BC, when those crafty cave dwellers controlled what amounted to a toll road between Europe and Central Asia. But the Nabataeans were made redundant in 106 BC, when the Romans conquered Petra and developed Palmyra in what is now Syria as their preferred entrepot.*

The land east of the Jordan was always ruled as the frontier of someone else's empire, most effectively under the seventh-century Umayyad Caliph Mu'awiya I Ibn Abi Sufyan. Like the other Umayyads, Mu'awiya was a Muslim-come-lately, having converted to Islam only on the eve of Mohammad's final triumph at the gates of Mecca. Under his 20-year rule the Arab-Islamic empire was transformed from a theocracy confined largely to the Arabian Peninsula to a sweeping and in many ways secular domain. From his ornate throne in Damascus Mu'awiya motivated and manipulated his subjects using charm, diplomacy, and prehensile cunning.[†] He aptly described his management style in an aside to Egyptian governor Amr ibn al As:

> Were there but a hair between me and my followers, it would not snap. If they draw it tighter, I would let it loose; if they loosen, I would tighten.

---

* Outflanked by the Romans, the Nabataeans moved westwards, settled in what is now southern Israel and the West Bank and thrived as olive-oil barons.

† Chapter Four of the *Rules and Regulations of the Court*, a medieval guidebook for palace protocol, ordains the caliph sit on an elevated throne draped in Armenian silk with wooden feet carved into bell shapes. Provincial governors ruled from ebony chairs covered with gold-embroidered fabric and decorated with vegetal motifs, lions, birds, elephants, horses and camels.

Mu'awiya had what Arabs call *hilm*, a soft touch that neutralized potential rivals with charm and wit – what we call charisma. He once asked a delegation of Arabian Jews if they knew how to prepare *haris,* a dish traditionally eaten on the Jewish Sabbath that he remembered as a younger man travelling in the region. Although the first caliph to appoint a bodyguard, he made a point of strolling through the markets and mosques of his realm, chatting with shop owners and patronizing their wares.

Mu'awiya could be ruthless – he once disposed of two ambitious generals with poisoned honey – but preferred to flatter, cajole, or bribe his rivals into submission. In his struggle for control of the empire with Ali, the prophet's nephew, he ladled out generous stipends to rival soldiers and functionaries.

When Ukail, a brother of Ali, paid Mu'awiya a visit, the caliph welcomed him and inquired after Ali's health.

'I have left him as God and His Apostle would wish,' Ukail replied. 'And I find you as God and His Apostle disapprove.'

Mu'awiya smiled but did not reply as he escorted his guest from the audience room. His courtiers were instructed to entertain Ukail lavishly and present him with a large amount of money.

The next morning, Mu'awiya and Ukail reconvened.

'How did you leave Ali?' Mu'awiya asked again.

'I left him better to himself,' Ukail replied, 'whereas you are better for me than he.'

Twelve hundred years later, Mu'awiya would be resurrected in the person of Hussein ibn Talal, the third sovereign of the Hashemite Kingdom of Jordan.*

Until his death from cancer in February 1999, King Hussein was among the most highly respected and best loved of Arab leaders. The timing was auspicious: had he lived much longer, he would have been confronted with the consequences of his own misrule. Instead, he dumped them on his son.

From the day of his coronation at the age of 18, King Hussein balanced the competing pressures of Middle East politics on a fulcrum of charm, finesse, and the occasional use of brute force. Britain created Jordan at the end of the First World War and transplanted the Hashemites from what is now Saudi Arabia for their part in the Arab

---

* King Hussein would have resented the comparison; the Hashemites and Umayyads were bitter rivals.

revolt that drove out the Turks. Jordan also served as a buffer zone to help insulate what would become Israel as ordained by the Balfour Declaration of 1917, which included a commitment in principle to a Jewish state in Palestine. Since then, Jordan has lived off subsidies – first from Britain to protect the young Jewish state from the Arabs and later from the Arab states, to ensure Jordan remained in their first line of defence against Israel.

Aside from its strategic location Jordan has little going for it. Unlike its neighbours, it has no oil and little water. (It is indebted even to sanctions-stricken Iraq, which supplies it with oil at discounted rates.) It has a small population and a primitive industrial base. One of its most important assets, its port at Aqaba, is too shallow to handle anything larger than mid-sized vessels. Jordan's one indigenous mineral worth mining – phosphate – is exhaustible and poorly managed. Pinioned between Iraq and the West Bank, it is a reluctant and perpetual no-man's land, a swamp-pit for political risk.

King Hussein survived by carefully calibrating his actions to suit a realm of rival constituencies. He was a generous patron; as a former palace insider once told me: 'King Hussein's policy was to corrupt his people so they'd be hated and could not form a power base independent of him.' To enhance his pan-Arab lustre in the turbulent 1950s he expelled his British advisors. Then, posing as a brave ally in Eisenhower's war on communism, the king had his security services stage several bogus coup attempts.

When events forced King Hussein's hand he acted decisively. In September 1970, when Yasser Arafat and his fighters challenged his authority after Israel flushed them into Jordan in the 1967 Arab-Israeli war, the king expelled them with armoured units. When Syria deployed a tank column in support of Arafat, the Jordanian air force smashed it.

King Hussein's own *hilm* was an abundant resource in an otherwise parched and parsimonious desert kingdom. When an opposition lawmaker who was jailed for sedition rejected a royal pardon, Hussein drove to the prison and waited outside until the reprieved dissident sheepishly accepted the king's offer of a ride home; when a Jordanian border guard gunned down Israeli schoolchildren at a bus stop, Hussein went to Israel and mourned together with the bereaved parents. The mother of one victim later named a son after him.

Hussein had an instinctive touch for body language. While receiving visitors, he would sit on the edge of his seat, his back upright and his hands placed serenely on his knees in a posture of humility and

respect. No one worked a crowd better: in 1996, after bread shortages in Jordan's southern Ma'an province triggered several days of
rioting, he addressed the restive masses from atop a tank, sleeves
rolled up and smoking a cigarette, and calmly persuaded them to go
home.

While visiting the northern city of Irbid, a man approached the
king to request his son be freed from prison.

'What was his offence?' Hussein asked.

The man looked down. 'He insulted both you and your father.'

The king delivered a perfunctory insult to the man and *his* father.
'We're even,' he said, then turned to his bodyguard and ordered the
boy's release.

The medieval Arab historian Al Ghazali once wrote of monar-
chical authority: 'Nothing is more prejudicial and sinister for the
king than royal inaccessibility and seclusion and nothing impresses
the hearts of the subjects and officials more than ease of access to the
king.'

This wise counsel could have been inspired by Mu'awiya and was
most certainly followed by King Hussein.

Unfortunately, *hilm* doesn't pay the rent. Nor does it reduce the
enormous debt that shackles Jordan's economy and elbows out funds
urgently needed for investment. Hussein was a Sandhurst-educated
soldier-statesman who revelled in power struggles, fast cars, jet
planes, and beautiful women. Trade and commerce was for wimps.

King Hussein's legacy was an economy littered with waste and
corruption along with colourful anecdotes about his winning charm.
A decade after it made peace with Israel Jordan is still run on patronage and *wasta* and even that seems to be in dwindling supply. When I
decided to move my bureau from Tel Aviv to Amman I dropped by
for coffee with the then-vice minister of information. It was a typical
Oriental gesture – a courtesy call that was less about courtesy than
flattering my way into a high-level guarantee against the capricious
gouge of the kingdom's customs mafia.

Things began well. The minister's eyes lit up when I informed him
about the move to Jordan from Israel; he swept up the telephone
receiver to make a hasty call to the *mukhabarat*. 'I'm sitting here with
the *Wall Street Journal*'s Middle East correspondent,' the minister
declared. 'He is moving here from Israel and you are to expedite the
process. This is a great victory for the Arabs!'

Safe inside my Kevlar-coating of ministerial assurance, I proceeded with the move. A few weeks later, my things arrived at a customs depot outside Amman and I was summoned for a 'routine inspection'.

Six hours and a dozen cups of coffee later, I was obliged to pay a $600 'import fee', to clear my belongings – though the documentation omitted to mention such a duty. ('It is a new tax,' one of the customs officials explained helpfully. 'In fact, it just went into effect last night.') Each box was opened and its contents appraised by an assessor, though I had filed an estimated valuation with the ministry weeks before.

Some months later, I warned a senior government official that such treatment would only alienate potential foreign investors. 'Foreigners they treat well,' the official said. 'You should see what they do to Jordanians.'

The Jordanian economy is in an advanced stage of sclerosis and public discontent with the monarchy is at an all-time high. After 1948 and again in 1967, Palestinian refugees generated a demand-led spurt, mostly in the form of new housing, that settled into a structural expansion as Palestinian professionals – doctors, engineers, teachers – found or created niches in the Jordanian economy. In the 1970s to early 1980s the country prospered off wages remitted from Jordanian – mostly ethnic Palestinian – guest workers in the oil-producing Gulf States. Many of those jobs vanished with the decline in oil prices and the lower-skilled expatriates were forced to return home. Then in the early 1990s thousands of white-collar Jordanians were ordered out of Kuwait in the prelude to Operation Desert Storm in an angry response to King Hussein's support of Iraq. Those who returned with their riches intact built palatial homes in greater Amman, triggering another consumption-led boom.

By the time of King Hussein's death the boom was over and the Jordanian economy has stayed flat ever since. Jordan's total debt, at just over $8 billion, equals nearly 100% of its GDP. The average annual wage has grown by 1.1% in the last ten years against a population growth rate of 4%.

As in other Arab countries, Jordan's white-collar expertise is bailing out for the West. I once purchased a digital clock from a young man in an appliance shop in downtown Amman. After the clock gained an average of ten minutes every two weeks, I took it back for a replacement.* The young man, polite and professional, spoke perfect English and had a masters degree in metallurgy from a university in the United Arab Emirates. I asked him what someone with such an advanced degree was doing selling faulty appliances.

'If I could get the funds I would start my own business as a soil inspector,' he told me. 'But no bank will give me a loan. If this keeps up, my brother and I will move to Britain or Canada.'

Illiquidity again. In Jordan, as in Lebanon, Syria and elsewhere in the Arab world, there is a huge demand for capital among hungry and capable entrepreneurs, but only borrowers with a hefty land bank can qualify for loans.

Just as conservative bankers starve Jordanian entrepreneurs of credit, so the United States – which has a fairly useless free-trade agreement with Jordan given the paltry value of goods it buys from the kingdom – is largely responsible for depriving Jordanians of what were once their two biggest export markets. Iraq was Jordan's largest trading partner until US-led sanctions on Baghdad shut it down. The kingdom's second-biggest market, the West Bank and Gaza, has been cordoned off by an array of Israeli-imposed trade barriers that have easily survived lukewarm opposition from Washington. Before the 1967 Arab-Israeli war, trade between Jordan and Palestine was worth billions of dollars in real terms. After Israel occupied the West Bank it erected tariff and non-tariff barriers to keep non-Israeli goods away from Palestinian consumers. Today, Israel exports to the West Bank and Gaza are worth an estimated $1.8 billion compared with Jordan's pitiful $22 million. A year before the second Intifada broke out, the Israelis prohibited imports of Jordanian cement into the West Bank – one of the few commodities it can sell to the Palestinians and an important source of hard currency – on security grounds.

One morning in the autumn of that same year, I drove from Amman to Jerusalem via the Allenby Bridge. Arriving at the bridge at 8 a.m. I was informed by the border guards that I had to wait an hour to cross to the Israeli side. Jordan had just gone off daylight saving time and had recently turned its clocks an hour forward. Israel, as it turns out, adjusts for daylight saving time a week after the rest of

---

* The new clock also gained 10 minutes at the same rate. As it was later explained to me, my building was plugged into a particularly aggressive electrical grid that did strange things to digital clocks. If the Hashemite Kingdom runs on a electrical cycle of 220 watts I was told, my neighbourhood ran on 230 or so.

the Middle East. Several miles and many coils of concertina wire away, it was only 7 a.m. and the border crossing was still closed.

At 9.15 a.m. the Jordanians waved me through and I entered the Israeli side of the crossing. The border guards told me to drop my bags off at the blockhouse by the bridge and I was escorted to an inspection area. It took half an hour before the inspectors arrived. They slid mirrors with long handles under my car, a 1990 Isuzu Trooper, to check for explosives. After 20 minutes I was told to proceed to inspection area No. 2, a tall, corrugated-steel building about 400 yards away, where I joined a dozen other motorists standing alongside their vehicles waiting for the inspector. A half-hour later he showed up only to discover he had forgotten the key to the padlock that bolted the door to the building.*

My fellow travellers inside this sprawling non-tariff trade barrier were Jordanian businessmen with appointments in the West Bank. Delays like this were common, they told me, and unpredictable. A unison of cell phones cancelled morning meetings. One caller was Mitri Al Muna, a regional distributor for Ideal Standard, a sanitary-ware maker and subsidiary of US commode giant American Standard. 'To say this is a disruption of my business is a severe understatement,' he told me.

While we waited, I noticed Jordanian trucks pulling up and unloading their cargo – phosphates, potash, cement – while an Israeli security guard conducted a desultory inspection for bombs and terrorists. The trucks would then re-load. Each procedure took a good twenty minutes.†

The inspector returned with the proper key. One by one we left our vehicles in the building and waited outside until the examination was completed. I could just imagine the inspector snapping on a latex glove, reaching into the crankshaft and saying: 'OK, now turn your head and cough.'

Next came the immigration hall, where we waited an hour for our bags to arrive from the bridge. They were checked twice at two different sites. We were also obliged to buy Israeli auto insurance at around $30 for each day we expected to be in Israel, where Jordanian insurers were not recognized.

---

* Aside from a priest caught with a cache of guns and bomb-making materials, there have been no major incidents of weapons smuggled over the two Israeli-Jordanian border crossings.
† After Oslo, the Jordanians pushed the Israelis to agree to a so-called 'point-to-point' inspection procedure whereby cargo would be searched and sealed at a designated loading area, thus eliminating the time-consuming and costly border procedures. The Israelis resisted and the Jordanians – at least since the current Intifada began – have given up on the matter.

The whole process lasted three hours and cost me two interviews in Jerusalem plus my Trooper's hood ornament. Perhaps it was lost behind the closed doors of the corrugated inspection hall. We'll never know.

The US has repeatedly asked Israel to open the West Bank to competition and give Jordanian businessmen a fair crack at a market they once owned. In March 1999, US Undersecretary of State for Economic Affairs Stuart Eizenstat called on Israel to encourage Jordanian exports to the Palestinian Authority as a way to stimulate economies on both sides of the Jordan River. 'There is a real willingness on the part of the Palestinians to accept more Jordanian goods,' Eizenstat told Israel's *Ha'aretz* newspaper. 'So I think the key is Israel. We are hopeful that they will move promptly. This is critical to Jordan's economic health.'

The Israelis listened, then showed Eizenstat the door. Since then, US comment on Israeli mercantilism and its impact on the Jordanian and Palestinian economies has been muted.

'The Americans seem to understand the importance of economics but their focus is never sustained,' Jordan's then-foreign minister, Abdul Ilah Khatib once told me. 'Only when there is a crisis do they realize they have to do something.'

Anyone who doubts economic despair energizes radical Islam has never considered the current generation of disenfranchised, unemployed young Jordanian men. Islamic groups in Jordan, which are closely watched by government security agents, say their membership has grown by some 30 per cent in the last two years.

The Jordanian government estimates unemployment at 14%, though no one believes this. Private economists reckon Jordan's jobless rate is between 25% and 30% of the working-age population. The government also announced the economy grew by 3.9% in 2000, up from 2.8% the previous year and the highest rate of growth since 1995. No one believes that either. Jordan's traditional growth centres – construction, tourism, mining, financial services – were flat or grew at a marginal level.

'Don't believe this 4 per cent figure,' one of Jordan's ex-prime ministers told me. 'We have no data. We don't see it. There is nothing substantial to prove the quality of life is improving.'

This wouldn't be the first time the palace inflated growth estimates. It released bullish figures in 1998 only to reveal the data was cooked. The information was leaked to Faud Fanek, an economist-for-hire whose weekly column in the English-language *Jordan Times* is largely regarded as a cipher for government policy. So when Fanek's 4 June 2001 column reported that 'everyone in the country is not feeling good' despite near-four per cent economic growth, this was widely received as a between-the-lines admission that the latest figures were bogus.

The government is privatising inefficient, state-owned assets in name only. Take Jordan Telecommunications. The country's state-owned telecommunications monopoly, known as JTC, was sold in early 2001. But this was in reality a partnership with France Telecom, which bought the rights to manage JTC and 40 per cent of its equity. The government still controls 60 per cent of the company that enjoys a five-year monopoly on all services except for domestic cellular calls. As this was being written, it had yet to list on the local stock exchange, nor would it consider connecting its grid to a fibre-optic cable that would enhance the service but erode its control over international traffic.

I once did a story on an Arabic Internet portal called Al Bawaba. It wanted to import into Jordan a device called a V–Sat to allow it to transmit as well as download signals. The government denied its request for national security reasons, though a company with a V–Sat would also be able to sidestep JTC's communications monopoly.*

Fawaz Hatim Zu'bi is Jordan's Minister of Post and Communications. The king tapped him for his youth and vigour to be at the front of Jordan's transformation into an information technology powerhouse. First he commissioned a study on his own ministry. It revealed that half the 4,000 people on his staff were redundant and less than a quarter had high-school diplomas or better.

'You can't just fire 2,000 people,' Fawaz told me. 'You'd have a revolution on your hands.'

Since then, Jordan's high-tech pretensions have languished.

Real privatization is taboo in a country where the government is one of the country's largest employers. The public sector accounts for nearly a quarter of total employment, a by-product of royal patronage

---

* David Kolitz, an Israeli businessman, once told me about how Yitzhak Rabin sent him to help develop information technology in Jordan. The Jordanian *mukhabarat*, he said, throttled the initiative. 'All they could talk about was control; they only wanted to know how they could control the technology.'

and an enormous economic burden. Potential buyers of state assets are increasingly difficult to find. Attempts to sell the Asati Salt Company, a subsidiary of state-owned Arab Potash and a vital source of foreign currency, collapsed when the investor, a company from Qatar, backed out at the last minute. Norsk Hydro, a major Norwegian company, pulled out of a $700 million phosphate project in late 2000.

The depth of Jordan's economic and social problems are largely overlooked by the caravan of Western leaders who make the pilgrimage to Amman, praise the monarchy for cooperating in the peace process, declare Jordan a modern economic success story and then move on to those recalcitrants in Cairo. This political shuffle is not unknown to many pundits, particularly those who parachute in from Washington. For some reason, Westerners are reluctant to spotlight the corruption, malaise and growing frustration within the Hashemite realm. Visitors who confine themselves to Amman with its wide streets, elegant – if largely empty – five-star hotels and luxury automobiles, are easily seduced by Jordan's image as a progressive, peaceful sanctuary in a stormy region.

A visit to the impoverished city of Ma'an makes it a tougher sell.

The Angry Stepchild
Few tourists en route to the rose-colored mountains, plateaus and ravines of Petra notice nearby Ma'an, the largest town in southern Jordan.

They aren't missing much. This unsightly extrusion of cinder-block buildings and rutted roadways occupies a windswept and desolate desert plane, beautiful in its austerity but for that great plague of the petrochemical revolution – the plastic shopping bag. A pestilent horde of black and white bags roll like tumbleweeds across the asphalt stretch of the King's Highway. They cling like non-biodegradable vultures to the branches of trees and huddle, gristle-like, between the spikes of barbed-wire fences. Had T.E. Lawrence come to the Levant in the age of synthetic materials, he'd have gone back to Oxford.

Fortunately for the Arab Revolt, the Welsh eccentric arrived well before then. Many of the tribesmen he led on behalf of Prince Faisel, the son of the Arab leader who inspired the rebellion against the Turks, settled in Ma'an. Not unreasonably they expected to become influential constituents of the Hashemite kingdom and were disappointed when the seat of power shifted to Amman. It was a logical move; in Roman times, Amman was closer to Damascus and the other cities that formed the *Decapolis*, a sort of trade association among regional city-states. Ma'an was a minor rest stop for Muslim pilgrims en route to Mecca, but it was bypassed with the opening of the Hijaz railway and has been a stepchild of the Jordanian economy ever since.

Today, Ma'an is known as a conurbation of angry, impoverished Bedouin clans. The only lucrative businesses is smuggling – narcotics from Saudi Arabia, guns from Iraq. Addiction to metamphetamines, hashish, heroin and cocaine is common and the men are armed to the teeth. Ma'ani grooms receive automatic weapons as wedding gifts. There is little new construction except for mosques, some with minarets made of little more than steel re-enforcement bars. Nearly every woman attending the local university is veiled.

The city has a long history of unrest, including the advent of the poultry-bomb; during the bread riots of 1996, protesters rebuffed the police by chasing ignited gasoline-soaked chickens under squad cars, some of which actually exploded. Residents travelling outside the city complain of police interrogations without cause after being pulled over for minor traffic violations. In March 2002, the city called a general strike after a local teenager died in police custody. A week of violence followed and it took police days to summon the courage to subdue the protests.

I first visited Ma'an in early 1999 for a story on the government-owned Aqaba Railway Corporation, which was earmarked for sale. It was an intimate look at King Hussein's subsidized empty shell of an economy as it laboured to keep an army of idle young men off the streets and out of the mosques.

At the time the ARC was the government's largest employer. Of the 1,200 people on staff, 850 were from Ma'an. The average employee earned between 100 to 600 dinar a year ($138 – $850), and had a below-average education if he was educated at all. At least a third of all employees were hired in the 1980s to upgrade the line, which carries phosphates from distant mines to the port at Aqaba. Those jobs were no longer needed and would be the first to disappear under the privatization plan.

In 1998 the ARC made JD1 million (1 million dinar) in operating profit (approx $1.4 million) but posted a JD5 million loss due to high interest payments on its JD70 million outstanding debt, a burden inflated a decade earlier by the dinar's depreciation against the dollar. The company needed new locomotives, rolling stock and spare parts but the weak currency made such upgrades prohibitively expensive.

The director general of the ARC was Abdullah Alkawaideh Al Kattab, a retired army colonel. He left the army 16 years ago but could not live on his pension. So he returned to his hometown of Ma'an to run the railroad.

'I imposed a military-like regime,' Mr Al Kattab told me in his office. 'We pay people who work hard and we offer bonuses for people who work extra hours. Now, the government wants to sell the company without coming down here and meeting the people. If you have eight children and you're told you may lose your job, what do you do? Where do you go? The ARC employed the fathers and grandfathers of many of my employees. No one wants to leave because there are no new jobs.'

There was a knock on the door and a delegation of Bedouins entered unannounced. Mr Al Kattab received them courteously and called for coffee. The leader of the group was a regally moustached sheik named Saed Jazzi, whose army tunic over his *dishdasha* (an ankle-length shirt) identified him as a *Mukhtar*, a sort of tribal administrator. He said he had ten children but wouldn't divulge his age. 'If my wife knew how old I was,' he said with a wink, 'she'd leave me.'

Sheik Jazzi and Mr Al Kattab exchanged pleasantries and then got down to business: two young men from the sheik's tribe had just lost their jobs and wanted to work for the railway. The families of the two men had appealed to Sheik Jazzi for help and now Sheik Jazzi was dumping the problem on Mr Al Kattab, who nodded thoughtfully and said he would do his best to help. He escorted the sheik to the door and the delegates exited in the same order as they had entered. As the last tribesman filed out Mr Al Kattab lowered his head in frustration and rested it on the door.

'Every day this happens,' he said. 'We want to do the right thing, but my authority is limited. I have to work within my means, but I'm also a Ma'an resident and I must be nice to people when I meet them in the street. Also, we don't want them to resent the government. If there was somewhere else for them to go, it would be easier. But we have no agriculture, no rain, no factories.'

We said goodbye. My next interview was with Ibrahim Bazaya, the head of the ARC's union. As I made my way to his office, I noticed room after room filled with three or four men sipping coffee, reading newspapers and chatting idly.

Ibrahim Bazaya sported a red *keffiyah* (Arab headdress) and a heroic-ally groomed beard. He dismissed privatization: 'Our ancestors built this railroad with their blood. It is mingled with the soil of the rail-road. The people of Ma'an will never leave the railway.'

I returned to Ma'an and the ARC three years later. My driver, Wael, had no problem reaching the city but I had forgotten the location of the railway's headquarters. Though the company is the city's largest employer, no one seemed to understand where we wanted to go. The choicest of our three sets of wrong instructions sent us to an idle, almost deserted train depot 30 kilometres from the Jordan-Saudi Arabian border. Abandoned wood-panelled rolling stock rusted and silvered in the desert sun. Two men sat outside the office, a converted 20-foot cargo container. In response to Wael's inquiry, they pointed in different directions.*

As we returned to the car, a half-crazed and toothless figure then approached us, wearing a faded British army sweater and sporting yellow, oversized sunglasses.

'You are looking for the gold?' he asked, reminding me of Ben Gunn, the mad, marooned seaman in Robert Louis Stevenson's *Treasure Island*. ('Crazy says I! Crazy says you!')

Gold?

'Some foreigners came here ten years ago looking for gold but never found it. Are you here for the gold?'

'Actually I'm a journalist writing about Jordan's privatization pro-gramme. Can you tell us how we can get to the Aqaba Railway Corporation?'

Wael translated. There was a long pause.

'Are you sure you're not here for the gold?'

We gave the man a few dinars and proceeded to the car. The gold would have to wait.

An hour later, we were at the gates of the ARC with Qassem al Katib, a local correspondent for *Al Dustour*, a Jordanian daily news-

---

* The Arabs themselves acknowledge a mild deficiency when it comes to giving directions, a conse-quence perhaps of the elliptical versus linear orientation of the Near Eastern mind.

paper. Most Jordanian journalists are on the state payroll. Not Qassem, who ferrets out official corruption and exposes bureaucratic inefficiency. He is trusted in Ma'an, and many of its residents stop him on the street to say hello.

Qassem is also a former employee of the ARC.

'The railway is the only thing we have,' Qassem said as we headed for the main offices. 'We'd protect it with our blood. In 1998, the government announced plans to privatize it and a US company, Wisconsin General, came and wanted to take it over. But there has been no privatization until now because there is too much debt.'

When the railway was first put on the block, it was thought to be worth $150 to $180 million. The US suitor reached an agreement with the government to cut the ARC payroll from 1,500 to 530 people. This being Jordan, redundant workers were rotated to another money-losing enterprise, in this case a nearby phosphate mine. The company proposed to invest $20 million in new rolling stock and locomotives from a French company.

Negotiations snagged, however, when the phosphate mine refused to pay the transport fees demanded by Wisconsin General. The talks broke down, according to Qassem, and since then the railway had been transporting about half the volume of a year ago.

'The government has pledged to develop Aqaba's cargo-handling facilities so we can pick up as much cargo for import as we do phosphates for export, but nothing has happened,' Qassem said. 'It's like the media city.* There is nothing else in Ma'an. A Chinese company has offered to spend JD6 million to build an industrial park and approval was given two months ago. But they want to use all-Chinese labour and management.'

We parked outside ARC's headquarters. It was eerily vacant. Qassem spoke to a lonely guard who admitted us without checking our IDs or my camera bag. An underling escorted us to the head office. Mr Al Kattab was still there and kind enough to remember me. He greeted us warmly but shot a furtive, 'what-are-you-up-to-now?' glance at Qassem. He was slightly paunchier than I remembered and dressed in a dark suit.

The director's offices had been moved to the southern wing as the company was concentrating its offices since the layoffs, explained Mr

---

* Shortly after he assumed the throne, King Abdullah II announced Jordan would open a commercial park where media organizations could establish their operations tax-free. Interest waned, however, after a palace spokesman declared the park would accept no media outlet that reported critically on Arab leaders.

Al Kattab. His office was larger than the old one, with powder-blue curtains stretched from floor to ceiling.

It was very strange. There couldn't be more than a hundred people in the building, let alone the five hundred or so supposed to be left after the downsizing. Gone were the men in *dishdasha* and *keffiyah*, milling about the hallways or loitering in offices three-at-a-time, smoking cigarettes, sipping coffee and reading newspapers.

We sat down for tea. Mr Al Kattab brushed off my apologies for arriving unannounced.

'It is nothing,' he said leaning back in his chair. 'I have few appointments for the day.'

I believed him.

'So how goes the privatization?' I asked.

Mr Al Kattab sat back in the chair behind his desk. Last year, he said, the company invested millions of dollars in spare parts to replace five locomotives. The railway now had 17 trains and expected to have 22 by the end of the year. A study was currently assessing how the ARC could ship non-phosphate cargo like wheat to Aqaba. A Chinese company was considering investing in Ma'an, which the ARC hoped would generate additional cargo bound for Aqaba. Ma'an offered a 20-year tax holiday for investors and was thinking of lifting taxes altogether. He expected foreign investment to pour in because of Ma'an's cheap labour and electricity.

'The king will see to this,' Mr Al Kattab said, beaming. 'He's focused on Ma'an. He recently opened a university and industrial park in his name.'

I tried again.

'How goes the privatization?'

Mr Al Khattab shrugged wearily. 'Wisconsin General did not sign a contract with Jordan Phosphate Mining Company because of a dispute over pricing. All movement stopped. We are still a government company, but we are on our own. We don't get subsidies from the government and we are expected to make a profit. But people still come for jobs and we try to help them.'

We talked for another twenty minutes or so. I tried unsuccessfully to corner Mr Al Khattab on cargo volume and sales figures. Finally he insisted an aide take Wael and I out to lunch on his behalf. He offered his regrets he couldn't join us and was whisked off in a late-model Mercedes.

Before we broke for lunch, the aide, Omar Chalabi, escorted me to his office. Omar was a pleasant sort with a gentle smile and high, patrician forehead. When I told him he bore a striking resemblance to the late dictator Hafez al Assad, he thanked me. His Directorate of Planning had several offices, nearly all emptied by the downsizing. 'I like it,' he told me, rummaging around for the ARC's most recent financial statement. 'It's lonely sometimes but it makes for better coordination.'

I skimmed through the balance sheet he handed me. Total capacity in 1999 was 2.6 million tons of cargo against a total shipped of a million tons. In 2002, the company expected to handle in excess of its expanded capacity of 3 million tons.

I asked for a profit statement. As Omar went to fetch the information, the company's financial adviser walked in. He was just the person I was looking for.

'Does the railway make money?' I asked immediately, before Omar returned.

The financial adviser shrugged. 'My general manager would not be happy with me for saying this,' he said, 'but basically when the privatization plan collapsed, they spent money upgrading the line to attract a new partner. None came, and we had a loss of JD2 million (approx. $2.8 million) last year. We've lost money since we were established in 1976. We'll have no profit this year and next year it's going to be worse.'

Omar returned. I confronted him with the facts as handed down from the financial advisor.

'No, no,' Omar protested. 'We have cash in the bank. My manager has a different way of calculating profits than the financial adviser. We take a book loss on depreciation charges but we make a profit in the end.'

Whatever, I thought. 'Let's have lunch.'

We chose a dimly lit kebab joint and were joined by Qassem and Wael. Omar explained that Wisconsin General had been taken over by Canadian National Railways, which prohibits its subsidiaries from holding stakes in foreign enterprises. 'That's why it couldn't sign the phosphate contract.'

I nodded numbly. By this time I couldn't have cared less if the Aqaba Railway Company was about to merge with the Chattanooga Choo-Choo, so I decided to change the subject.

'Why are Ma'anis so angry?'

Omar paused. 'We Ma'anis are hot tempered,' he said. 'That is partly because we are in the middle of the desert-sea, but the main thing is we refuse to be humiliated. We like our freedom. It's very simple.'

Until then, Qassem had been sitting quiet and coiled, waiting to strike. 'The government ignores us,' he said sharply. 'We send letters to King Abdullah every year, and every year he never replies. The trade and investment ministry has no electricity. There is corruption and nobody cares.'

Omar offered unconvincing denials. I asked for the check, which Omar insisted on picking up.

Wael and I said goodbye to Omar and Qassem, then waited in the car for Omar to depart so he wouldn't see us following Qassem's car to his house. Qassem lived on the outskirts of town in a modest but well ordered home. We were escorted to the *diwan* and served tea by his four daughters and two sons, who took turns peering curiously at us from the half-wall of the foyer. I could hear someone toiling in the kitchen and guessed it was Qassem's wife, though she never appeared.

Qassem sat in the couch to my right and toyed with his car keys. 'They are afraid of the truth,' he began. 'The truth hurts them.'

As Wael translated, I appraised Qassem closely for the first time. He wore a grey suit and dark tie, his hair and beard were flecked with grey and had the short crop of a pious Muslim. He rarely smiled, his eyes were dark and brooding and he spoke slowly, weighing each word: a man of integrity who could be neither bought nor intimidated.

'I am waiting for some kind of reprisal,' he said. 'I expect it one way or another but I don't care. For fifty years, under his late majesty, no journalist in Jordan was ever arrested. Just this week, one of my colleagues was jailed after he wrote about rising insurance premiums because a minister owns an insurance company. The people can't take this any more.'

Does the new king know of this, I asked.

'The new king gives a lot of authority to ministers,' Qassem replied. 'We can't come out and say the harassment comes from him but we're fed up. It depends on who gives him the information. He goes abroad and talks about standards of living but life here gets worse every day.'

I asked about the Aqaba Railway Corporation.

Qassem had worked at the railway for 18 years. At one time, he said, the company was one of the most successful of all government enterprises. Then it took on enormous debts just as the currency depreciated. There was too much patronage, Qassem said, too much nepotism in management. The staff became demoralized and security lapsed. Railroad spikes were sold as scrap iron. Accidents rose after a team of Egyptian specialists were sent home before properly training engineers to operate the new locomotives.

'Corruption is all over,' he said. 'The railway is corrupted, just like the glass factory.'

The glass factory?

Ma'an's only other major enterprise was a glass factory, Qassem explained. It lost money for years and was finally closed while it still held a huge inventory of unsold glass. One day a truck turned over and plate glass shattered onto the tarmac. The management was selling the surplus glass on the black market.

I asked about the riots.

'There is always a problem with the police,' he said. 'Last month, a kid was arrested and held for five days. He was beaten, sent to the hospital and died. The family said they would not accept the boy's body until the men responsible were identified and killed.'

Bedouin justice. When the police beat someone to death in Ma'an, Qassem said, they pass the baton around so no one man can be fingered for the crime.

'We chased the cops to the roof of their station,' said Qassem, allowing himself a rare grin that quickly vanished. 'One cop was killed. We rioted for three days and there were police checkpoints in and around the city for eight days.' Twenty-two people were arrested but only eleven had been released.

'Until 1989,' said Qassem, 'we never noticed the inequity. We are the poorest people in Jordan and we are treated very badly. The government has pushed us to the breaking point. The amount of drug dealing is scary but we have nothing left to lose. Nobody wants this life. We just wish the government would take us seriously.'

I asked Qassem if Ma'an could ever be the flashpoint for a major confrontation with the government that may spread to other cities.

Again, the fleeting grin. 'After the riots, the cops came to search for our guns. We knew they were coming thirty hours before they arrived and hid everything except the oldest weapons. They got 1 per cent of our stock. We have all we need. All we're waiting for is an excuse.'

*

Later, as we headed north back to Amman, I asked Wael what he thought of Qassem.

'Mr Qassem is a good man,' said Wael. 'He speaks excellent Arabic. He is very brave. And he is afraid.'

I nodded.

We were closing in on Amman. The spare desert flatlands of southern Jordan had given way to verdant green hills.

I stared out the window and wondered if Ma'an could be the next Hama.

The Odd Couple

Wael Farid is an ethnic Palestinian from a West Bank village near Jenin. He is moustachioed, balding and powerfully built, with broad shoulders and thick forearms. Wael is my friend, my ride, my eyes and my ears. As we cruised through Ma'an, he remarked upon the city's poverty.

'Do you know what's wrong with this place,' said Wael in his booming, baritone voice.

'What's that?'

'No *refugees*,' he said. 'Wherever there are Palestinian refugees, there is business.'

No Middle East envoy could have put it better.

If Jordan's rare economic booms are a testament to Palestinian industriousness – they followed the return en masse of Palestinian émigrés and their wealth to the kingdom – the government's failure to capitalize on such growth is a tribute to external political factors, a lack of resources, and official ineptitude.*

'The Jordanian economy is permanently sick,' says Ahmed Chalabi, the head of the dissident Iraqi National Congress. 'The Jordanians have a false sense of prosperity and a $26 billion shortage of foreign exchange. The [government] failed to take advantage of [the Lebanese civil war] and replace Beirut as a financial centre. They could not tolerate new ideas that would get the economy going.'

---

* In 2001 the government unveiled a value-added tax when the economy was already suffering from low spending levels partly because the government declared obscure events as bank holidays, so merchants had to shut their doors. No one could travel because, as business was so bad, they didn't have the money. 'Excessive holidays are economic catastrophe,' declared a headline in the 3 March edition of *The Jordan Times*.

Jordanian society neatly divides into two halves. The civil service and the army are dominated by venerable Bedouin families, otherwise known as 'East Bankers'. They represent the elite of Jordanian society and once included some of King Hussein's wisest and most loyal ministers and chamberlains. The economy is run by the Palestinians. They are the bankers, traders, engineers, and doctors who were educated abroad and pride themselves on being city dwellers.*

Whatever his flaws, King Hussein knew that his economy wasn't going anywhere in the soft hands of his often imperious Bedouin brothers.† (Some of the early Islamic caliphs, particularly Omar I, discouraged their subjects from tilling the soil.) Unlike his more despotic counterparts, who in 1948 and 1967 found themselves host to millions of Palestinian refugees, King Hussein allowed his country's Palestinians to integrate into Jordanian society and encouraged their industry.

This division of labour works well when the economy is stable and the region is at peace. It is not working well now. If East Bankers resent Palestinians as a nuisance imposed on them by Zionism and dismiss them as a petty bourgeoisie – the Jews of the Arabs, as Palestinians are often described – the Palestinians regard East Bankers as temperamental, gun-crazy elitists.‡ Many Palestinians consider the Hashemite throne an illegitimate legacy of Western imperialism and are among the biggest opponents of the peace with Israel. Early in the current Intifada, demonstrations against Israel, America and the Jordanian rich proliferated into anti-Hashemite dissent. At a university soccer match between two teams – one from a college attended predominately by ethnic Palestinians and the other by the children of East Bankers – opposing cheers degenerated into anti-Palestinian and anti-royalist epithets. At one point, the royalists' invective was directed at Queen Rania, the king's ethnic-Palestinian wife.

Discrimination against ethnic Palestinians is undeniable. Though three out of five Jordanians are thought to be of Palestinian origin, election gerrymandering has left them with only eleven seats in the country's rubber-stamp parliament. Few Palestinians are promoted to

---

* Palestinians chafe at proposals occasionally mooted by Israel that they be allowed to settle some of their refugees in the Negev desert, instead of their historic homes in cities like Jaffa and Haifa.
† Jordan cheekily demands international lenders forgive its external debt even as it imports labour in the face of double-digit unemployment.
‡ The rivalry between tribal Arabs and their urban counterparts goes back centuries. Early Arab chroniclers related with amusement the crudeness and ignorance of the Bedouins who conquered the Byzantines; ornate carpets, they wrote, were torn to pieces and divided among the soldiers, dogs were fed from gold plates and camphor was mistaken for salt and used to flavour soups.

senior military positions and Palestinian businessmen who bid for army contracts routinely lose out to companies owned by East Bankers.

The kingdom can ill afford to alienate such a large and important constituency. Look at a map to hear the clock ticking on the monarchy. The Hashemites dwell uneasily between a potentially revitalized Iraq – once the engine of the Arab economy – and an independent Palestine, both of which could ultimately consume Jordan economically. With the Cold War over, Jordan is no longer an indispensable ally in the fight against Soviet communism, and an Israeli-Palestinian peace would eliminate the need for a buffer between the Jewish state and its Arab neighbours. The Hashemites could, in a generation's time, be declared redundant.

'If there is an independent Palestine, Jordan's political system will become Palestine's,' an opposition politician once told me. 'Jordan has thrived so far because Yasser Arafat's corruption has driven the best Palestinians here. A legitimate government in Palestine will reverse that outflow and the centre of gravity will shift to the West Bank. The king will ultimately become the titular head of a Greater Palestine.'

Will the process be so peaceful?

'There could be unrest,' the politician said. 'The danger is that we may not see it coming until it's too late.'

At the time of our discussion, the palace released a copy of a circular issued by King Abdullah, imploring members of the royal family to throttle back on personal spending. The memo was regarded as a bid to pre-empt charges of royal largesse.

'All the royals are overspending,' said the opposition figure. 'This country can't afford a royal family any more.'

Succession in the Middle East has always been tricky. Mu'awiya built up a great empire only to sabotage it by naming his son, Yazid, as his heir. Yazid, a libertine sportsman, preferred the company of falcons, dogs, apes and lynxes to that of his *wazirs* and ministers. An accomplished musician, he introduced the lute to the Muslim world and gave solo performances at raucous drinking sessions. Decline set in, and by the late seventh century, Umayyad rule had spiralled into a profane decadence that isolated the palace from the proletariat.

Abdullah bin Hussein, now Abdullah II, was the last person anyone expected to be a king. Hassan bin Talal, King Hussein's brother, was crown prince for 33 years before Hussein abruptly made Abdullah his heir a month before his death. This bizarre, Shakespearean tale is too lengthy and convoluted to reconstruct here.* Suffice it to say the king's choice of Abdullah II, then 37 years old, surprised some observers who held the scholarly if somewhat arrogant Hassan in high esteem. 'Hussein spent his life holding his country together then crawled out of his death bed to destroy it,' Ahmed Chalabi told me when the king's decision was announced.

There was nothing in the weeks and months following King Hussein's death to suggest Abdullah would be anything less than the charismatic leader his father was. The succession was defiantly smooth. Like Hafez al Assad, King Hussein was a skilled auctioneer who bartered patronage for loyalty among his realm's various tribes – ethnic Palestinians, Islamists, Christians, Circassians – and left behind no debts that might complicate the transition.

Abdullah was known as a Sandhurst-educated major general in the Royal Jordanian Special Operations Command. His military bearing suited the solemnity of his father's funeral. He stood erect and greeted foreign dignitaries with a purposeful handshake. He seemed to have inherited his father's charisma and body language. Most Jordanians looked upon their new sovereign with favour, confidence, and hope.

Within a year, Abdullah had squandered that goodwill. To begin with, he spent more time out of the kingdom than in it, speaking before journalists and congressmen in Washington, promoting Jordan as a high-tech incubator at economic forums, and holding court on American TV talk shows. 'When I want to know what my king is thinking,' a Jordanian woman once told me, 'I watch *Larry King Live.*'

The king travels in an enormous Airbus jet, allegedly a gift from the Sultan of Brunei, and so sophisticated the palace was obliged to hire a German crew to fly it. It is a conspicuous mode of transportation for the head of a tiny economy with a budget deficit worth nearly 8 per cent of its gross domestic product and an average annual wage of $1,200.

Among the king's first controversial acts was closing down the Amman offices of Hamas, the Islamic extremist group committed to the destruction of Israel. Unlike his father, who kept an unspoken truce with Hamas members, Abdullah felt compelled to exile them to Qatar. This was necessary, he said, because Hamas was as much a

---

* Immediately after the announcement a source close to the palace told me that CIA hostility to Hassan was at the heart of it.

threat to the Hashemites as it was to the Jewish state. 'Every good soldier knows it's best to fight his battles at the time and place of his choosing,' the king told a dozen reporters at a press luncheon. 'I was going to have to take these guys on sooner or later.'

The confrontation between Hamas and King Abdullah was forgotten until an ailing Hamas leader flying back to Amman from Qatar was prohibited from entering the country and had to remain aboard the plane in the searing desert heat for two weeks. 'I've always been loyal to the monarchy because it gave me a valid passport and an opportunity to have a life here,' said an ethnic Palestinian friend who runs his own trading company. 'But if this is the way they treat their citizens, it makes me wonder what the passport is worth.'

Then there was the release of the 3.9 per cent economic growth figure. Most businessmen to whom I spoke believed the economy actually contracted in 2000 and were outraged by the government's estimate. 'We don't see any of this growth,' a moneychanger told me. 'All we see are empty buildings. The government keeps talking about this 4 per cent growth so it looks like the economy is keeping up with the population, but only the illiterate believe it.'

Following the second Intifada and September 11, the monarchy has become overtly paranoid and repressive. Turnover among Abdullah's army chiefs-of-staff has been conspicuously high, suggesting concerns they might develop their own power base if left in place for a prolonged period. Parliament was disbanded and an emergency powers act enacted.

Police were empowered to make arrests with impunity and detain people for two weeks without charge. Demonstrations, rallies and political parties were declared illegal, as was any association of more than eight people.

On 12 April 2002, anticipating a huge rally of protesters from all over the kingdom against Israel's West Bank invasion, the government mobilized one of the largest demonstrations of force in its history. There were tanks at every street corner, soldiers in battalion strength and attack helicopters patrolling the sky. The deployment prevented demonstrators from entering the city centre and the government congratulated itself for defusing the rally, though many Jordanians found the heavy-handed display insulting.

Even before the emergency powers were announced there were signs that what was once regarded as a benevolent monarchy was tightening its grip. By early 2001, the Reuters, Agence France-Presse and Associated Press bureau chiefs in Amman – all Jordanian citizens – had been detained or 'asked in for coffee', a euphemism for subtle interrogation. In May, hundreds of Jordanians took to Amman's streets to express their opposition to Israel's use of force against the Intifada. Police in full riot gear put down the demonstration. Protesters were beaten back with truncheons, tear gas, and attack dogs. Security officials arrested journalists and confiscated their videocassettes. A man and his son were arrested for allowing a cameraman to film from the rooftop of their home; they were freed after being held for 48 hours without charge.

A government spokesman, asked by local media to comment on the protests, denied they were even taking place. Only after video footage aired on Al Jazeera was the government forced to acknowledge that, yes, dozens of Jordanians were injured in clashes with police.

The cameraman who filmed the clashes is Tarek Ayoub. He works for Associated Press Television, which shares offices with Al Jazeera and sells its footage to the world's media outlets. On the day of the May protests he was conducting an interview with a prominent Islamic leader when security agents came and took Ayoub away. He spent the night in jail without charge and was threatened with further detentions if he continued to broadcast footage 'that showed Jordan in an unfavourable light'.

Nearly a year later, during the 5 April 2002 protests, I met Tarek at the AP-Al Jazeera studios. He was running a smuggling racket of sorts, figuring ways to spirit the day's videotapes by car to the Al Jazeera bureau in Beirut. From there, Tarek said, the footage could be transmitted worldwide. 'We've got to get these tapes out,' he said. 'Fox News and CNN called and they want footage.'

As Tarek spoke, I suddenly understood why the government restricted – for 'security reasons' – private ownership of a V-Sat to Jordan Telecommunications. 'We can't feed our video to Qatar because we don't have an uplink,' he said. 'Only JTV [Jordanian Television, the state-owned broadcaster] has that facility and they won't let us use it. So we have to smuggle everything to Beirut through Syria.'

Tarek took a call on his mobile phone. A runner had successfully crossed the border into Syria with the videotapes and was on his way to Beirut. They were lucky, he said; Jordanian border police were checking every car.

During the riots in Ma'an, two Al Jazeera reporters with footage of the violence were arrested by intelligence agents as they returned to the studio. The Al Jazeera producer in Amman, Mohammad Ajlouni, went into hiding for three days to evade a *mukhabarat* dragnet. 'They told me if they ever caught me, they'd have screwed me,' Ajlouni told me later. 'And not gently.'

At about the same time, Tarek said, agents held a pencil in the face of a young female journalist and broke it in two. The pencil could be repaired with glue, one agent said, but the chastity of a virgin, once lost, was gone forever.

'The *mukhabarat* gives orders to the ministers,' Tarek said. 'We have rules, but intelligence is breaking those rules. They are the masters of the game.'

A runner returned. Tarek handed him more tapes.

'This would never have happened under King Hussein.'

In such an incendiary environment, even the appearance of corruption is an undesirable ingredient, which is why many in the establishment disparage Abdullah II's association with Khaled Shaheen, the chairman of a Dubai-based company called Ole Holdings. In 2000, this food-processing and auto-distribution company was awarded an exclusive contract to import BMWs and Rovers into Jordan. Not long after the ink on the contract dried, the government dumped Mercedes Benz as its official vehicle and switched to BMW.

'The Shaheens are the talk of the town,' Farouq Kilani, an attorney and proponent of judicial reform told me. 'There is decay in the judicial system and it's going to get worse.'

Farouq said he had just represented an investor who wanted to launch a $150 million media company in Jordan. The investor was introduced to many people, including the king, and the meetings went well. 'Then,' Farouq said, 'he met with a judge who kept getting calls and saying, "Yes sir, that case is coming up, I'll take care of it." So the investor pulled out. He said our judiciary is corrupt and he'd never know if he could get his money out of the country. Investors are running away.'

The Shaheens are currently facing a lawsuit for writing worthless cheques to Standard Chartered Bank plc, which for months tried unsuccessfully to have the Shaheens extradited from Dubai. When the brothers bounced a cheque made out to the Arab Bank – one of the Arab world's most respected institutions – they were arrested and within 24 hours despatched to Jordan on an Emirates Airlines plane.

The Arab Bank is run by an ethnic-Palestinian family named Shoman and it is chaired by the avuncular but formidable Abdulmajeed Shoman. 'The Shaheens know his majesty,' Shoman once told me. 'They promised BMW they'd deliver 2,000 cars in sales and they did by persuading the government to buy BMW instead of Mercedes. This surprised us.'

This candid observation was made by one of the Arab world's most powerful bankers – and in the post-King Hussein era, one of the few people who could get away with saying it publicly.

There is no reason to believe US government officials will sit Abdullah II down and suggest he get a grip on things. US diplomats generally come to the Middle East not to help reform corrupt, mendicant economies but to hammer out the occasional Israeli–Arab peace deal. For Washington, job one in Jordan is to support and protect the monarchy and its peace treaty with Israel. There doesn't seem to be a job two.

There is little evidence that the American government understands the link between Jordan's economic decay and political instability. In Asia, it was easy to meet US commercial attachés, but the lone commercial officer I eventually discover in the Amman embassy – a $80 million fortress behind a security wall that extends several hundred feet from the embassy core, a complex the diplomats call 'Fort Apache' or 'The Reservation' – only agrees to have lunch with me after I have received permission from the press office.

The attaché insists we meet at the embassy grill, designed to resemble a 'home-style' eatery common in American shopping malls, and pronounces himself optimistic about Jordan's future. The economy is doing just fine and the new king is pressing ahead with badly needed reforms. Unemployment is being addressed. The government is developing the Aqaba seaport into a vital entrepot. Privatization is moving ahead nicely.

'Abdullah has got things under control,' the diplomat said. 'Things here are turning around.'

The bill arrives. I thank the attaché, leave the embassy and return to Jordan.

4

Palestine

The Last Colony

We must expel Arabs and take their places . . . and if we have to use force – we have force at our disposal

David Ben-Gurion, in a letter to his son discussing the 1937 Peel Commission, a UK Government enquiry which proposed partitioning Palestine and transferring land and population to create separate Jewish and Arab states.

Sowing the Wind. . .

The living room on the second floor of the Palestinian blockhouse in Jenin had a ratty sofa, tile floors, a cheap, striped throw-rug and graffiti on its unpainted wall alongside a framed photo of Saddam Hussein. I knew this because the entire face of the building had been knocked down a few weeks earlier by armoured bulldozers deployed by the Israeli army. Though the floor had partially collapsed and sagged at a 45-degree angle, three women somehow balanced themselves on the sofa, chatting idly. When one noticed I was photographing them with Saddam's portrait in the background, she smiled self-consciously and rose to take it down.

It was 19 April 2002. The Israelis had just pulled out of the Palestinian refugee village of Jenin, along with other West Bank cities they had occupied for three weeks as part of Operation Defensive Shield. Prime Minister Ariel Sharon had ordered the invasion – based on plans drawn up under his predecessor, Ehud Barak – following a suicide attack that killed 29 people in Netanya over the Passover holiday. Yasser Arafat was holed up in his Ramallah compound,

locked in the crosshairs of every type of conventional Israeli ord-
nance. This of course reprised him as an authentic Arab hero; only
the mighty Israeli army could magnify the vastly diminished Arafat.

The objective of Defensive Shield was to smash what Sharon called
the Palestinian 'infrastructure of terror'. For Palestinians either side
of the Jordan River, it was the first step in Sharon's ambition to
resolve the hundred-year war over Palestine by 'transferring' them
from the West Bank to Jordan.*

Jenin, with its warrens of concrete dwellings and narrow streets,
had been a particularly hard target for the Israelis. After losing 19 soldiers in an ambush it used bullet-proof bulldozers to flatten some 200
square yards in the heart of the village. On the rising ground where
much of the destruction was concentrated, an arcade of shattered
lives competed for media attention. A man named Ibrahim Jebal told
us soldiers rounded up dozens of men – he ticked off their names –
handcuffed them and later dumped their dead bodies at the local hospital.

'Some of them were part of the resistance,' he said. 'We are all part
of the resistance now.'

Saud Abu Anas was using a pickaxe to dig out the rubble of his
home, from which he had shepherded all ten members of his family
before the bulldozers came. Now his passport, life insurance and
some 6,000 New Israeli shekels (ILS6,000) in cash were buried
underneath a thick webbing of concrete and twisted steel.†

'This is Oslo,' he said, referring to the 1993 peace agreement that
ended years of exile for Arafat and was to conclude five years later
with an independent Palestinian state. 'They allowed Arafat back so
they can kill him here. The soldiers told us: "you are destroying
Machane Yahuda [a market in Jerusalem and suicide-bomb target],
we are destroying you here."'

Farther up the rise, a crowd peered down intently from the top of
a crater formed by a backhoe raking noisily through the demolished
home of the Abu Khaleds. Somewhere down there was the body of
Mahmud, Abu Khaled's grandson. At 3 p.m. on the second day of the

---

* 'Listen,' Sharon was quoted in the 29 August 1982 *Washington Post*, 'this Palestinian thing has puzzled
me for 12 years, and the more I think of it the more I decide that Jordan [...] is the only solution. And I
tell you: we shall never permit another Palestinian state [west of the river Jordan].'

A little over a year earlier, Sharon had told *Time* magazine: 'I don't mind who takes over Jordan.'

† Depending on the transaction, the Palestinians are obliged to do business in US dollars, Jordanian
dinars and Israeli shekels. A Palestinian currency was one of the many items left unresolved by the Oslo
process, leaving the Palestinian economy hostage to the capricious swings of three currencies.

invasion, Mr Abu Khaled told us, the Israelis ordered everyone out before they destroyed the building, leaving his paralyzed grandson still inside when the wall collapsed.

'The Israelis wouldn't listen,' the 70-year-old Mr Abu Khaled said through a *keffiyeh* covering his mouth against the dust. 'They bull-dozed the home as we watched.'

Occasionally the backhoe uncovered some relic of daily life – a woman's purse, a pair of shoes – and workers handed it to the boy's father who inspected it thoughtfully before placing it on the pile of quotidian belongings accumulating beside him.

Mr Abu Khaled told us one of his sons was killed in a firefight with the Israelis and another was arrested during the invasion.

'He's still in jail,' said Mr Abu Khaled. 'I have no idea where he is.'

Dr Ali Jabarin, the vice president of nearby Razi Hospital said his staff had to bury 39 bodies in an open space adjacent to the hospital. The bodies were exhumed that morning and given proper burials.

On the invasion's third day, said Dr Jabarin, he was alerted by tele-phone that a wounded man was crawling across the street towards the hospital doors. 'We tried to get him in under a white flag but the Israelis shot at us,' he said. 'We phoned the Red Cross and the United Nations to petition the Israelis for us.'

By the time orderlies reached the man, said Dr Jabarin, he had died of multiple wounds to the chest.

Reporters, aid workers and human rights groups inspected one heap of tangled rubble after another. The Palestinians tugged at us, peddling their misery. Children proudly displayed belts of spent shell casings. The Israelis defaced posters of *shaheeds*, martyrs in the resistance, with spray paint and bullets. Buildings were riddled by shrapnel and automatic-weapons fire, much of it concentrated at windows where Palestinian gunmen might have positioned them-selves.

I found the crumpled page from a child's homework. It was a fill-in-the-blank English exam and the student had scored 75 out of a possible 100.

> The early pioneers tried first to just adapt to the American way of life and not completely ———— to it.

The student had correctly entered 'assimilate'.

An American negative attitude towards the Arabs still fans the winds of racial ———.

'Discrimination' had been entered as the right answer.

On the porch of his blockhouse, Subhi Abu Suleyman, a 56-year-old construction worker, rested his head on his two hands holding the handle of a cane as the backhoe worked the wreckage of the Abu Khaled home.

'I've never seen anything like this,' Subhi said. 'The 1967 war was a ping-pong match compared to this.'

Subhi, born in Haifa, had been living in the Jenin camp since 1948. His family would have fled to Jordan or Syria, he said, but it had no car. A decade ago he visited the villa where he was raised and found it occupied by Iraqi Jews, who told him they bought it from the Israeli government.

'For fifty years we've waited for our problems to be resolved,' said Subhi. 'Israel still has everything and we still have nothing. We have no future. These children need to go to school. The Americans are killing us. It's not the people, but the government, and who dominates the government? The Jews. And the Arab governments are working for them.'

The Palestinians said the massacre at Jenin had claimed some 500 lives. Israel responded that no more than 40 Palestinians, mostly gunmen, were killed. When the United Nations formed an independent committee to investigate the claim, the Israelis, with US support, barred it from entering Israel.

Israel should have welcomed the committee. From the moment journalists swarmed into Jenin – the Israeli-controlled checkpoints outside the city were closed and we had to sneak in – it was obvious there was no massacre. The stench that Norwegian envoy Torgeir Larsen had described for the cameras the day before was rotting garbage. Accounts of Israeli troops dropping corpses at hospital doors bound with plastic handcuffs and shot execution-style never surfaced in a report on the violence later issued by Human Rights Watch.*

Imagined or real, atrocities committed at Jenin would nest in the

---

* The report cited Israeli efforts to minimize casualties during Operation Defensive Shield.

consciousness of young Palestinians and gestate into a symbol for a new generation of killers – in Jenin certainly but also in Ramallah, Tulkarem, Nablus, Bethlehem and every other West Bank town besieged by Israel in the spring of 2002.

Ramallah is no refugee camp; it is the centre of Palestinian commerce. After Oslo, investors from the Palestinian Diaspora launched successful enterprises in Ramallah because of its close proximity to Jerusalem. Before the current Intifada the city was one of the most dynamic Arab economies. New cars choked the streets and storefronts were fully stocked. The atmosphere was secular and ecumenical. Western fashions mingled with traditional Muslim *chadors* (head coverings). Working with Israel was regarded as professional collaboration, not collusion. Ramallans referred to their city proudly as 'our Tel Aviv'.

The assault on Ramallah was therefore in some respects more wanton and traumatic than the Israeli actions in Jenin. True, soldiers arrested suspected militants. But they also sacked automatic-teller machines and tried to open up bank vaults. They broke into the education ministry and carted away student files. They stripped the hard drives from Palestinian Authority computers and raked commercial buildings with automatic weapons fire.

This was a 'terrorist infrastructure' broadly defined.

'This is not the infrastructure of terror, this is civil society. They destroyed what makes us self-reliant.'

Dr Mustafa Barghouthi and his wife Rita were recovering at home hours after the Israelis pulled out of Ramallah, a day after my visit to Jenin. Mustafa was clearly exhausted after three weeks of 'floating around', in his words, to avoid arrest. It was cold and wet, and both Mustafa's cell phone and house phone were constantly announcing calls from friends and journalists to confirm his well-being.

Yes, it was awful, Mustafa and Rita were saying. True, there is so much work to be done. *But we survived.*

There are the two Barghouthis within the Palestinian leadership and they work opposite sides of the Palestinian street. Marwan Barghouthi, an admired and by most accounts uncorrupted Arafat lieutenant, once supported peace with Israel and then opposed it, for what he said was Israel's betrayal of Oslo. As a leader of Arafat's Fatah movement he was implicated in dozens of suicide-bomb attacks. Israeli security forces arrested him in April 2002. More than any Palestinian official besides Arafat, Marwan Barghouthi is associated with the militarization of the Intifada that brought about Operation Defensive Shield.

The other Barghouthi, Mustafa, is the director of the Health, Development, Information and Policy Institute, which provides healthcare and emergency medical services. He advocates peaceful resistance to Israel's occupation and is a leader of Palestine's younger generation of competent, respected administrators.

The Israelis targeted him nonetheless, firing a tank round through his clinic and raking it with 50mm calibre bullets. They stole or burned files, including data from a joint research project with Johns Hopkins University on infant mortality. They removed the hard drives from new computers still packed in boxes and tossed the monitors in a pile. They attacked his ambulances – one was shot five times – and harassed his drivers.*

'We've sent the US consulate a full report,' Mustafa said. 'The Israelis took electronic items and databases. We had the best database in the country. It had information on clinics and schools.'

'Some things can't be replaced,' said Rita, a high-spirited woman with bright eyes and raven-black hair. 'Do you know what they were calling Mustafa as they burned the files? Son of a bastard, which is much worse in Arabic than how it sounds in English.'

She offered me a cigarette, which I declined.

'You smoke?' I asked.

Rita shrugged. 'We die of other causes in this country.'

Mustafa finished a call. 'It will take billions of dollars to rebuild,' he said. 'Rita doesn't like this word but the city has been raped.'

'I don't like it,' Rita said. '"Ravaged" is better.'

'Okay, ravaged. But there is a sense of violation. I was a leader of civil society. If they do this to me, imagine what they would do to a villager. One of our drivers was forced to disrobe naked in front of women in broad daylight. This cannot last. In the case of South Africa it was the Europeans who turned first and America was the last to finally come around. The United States cannot allow its Middle East policy to be held hostage to a war criminal like Ariel Sharon and the Israeli lobby. It's shameful but it cannot last. The price is total instability in the Middle East.'

---

* The Israelis accuse the Palestinians of smuggling bombs and weapons to militants in ambulances; the Palestinians charge the Israelis with exploiting a single incident to restrict emergency medical service in the territories.

Mustafa radiated a degree of pride and optimism, as if the siege and the destruction had discredited the militants and vindicated moderates like himself, whose ambulances symbolized something the Palestinian Authority had failed so miserably to deliver – honest, efficient civic services.

'Ariel Sharon wants us in a collection of chicken cages,' Mustafa said, 'but we continued to function. We saved people. We kept morale up. We created a grass-roots organization. We are the hope of Palestinians and good Israelis.'

Mustafa had spoken with Arafat the day earlier by phone for a half-hour. 'Now is not the time to criticize,' he said, 'but we need democracy. Militarizing the Intifada was a huge mistake, the biggest that was made. Now there must be change. The old system cannot stand. I'm optimistic.'

Later that day I drove to Mustafa's clinic, where I met Dr Mohammad Ishafi, the director of the Union of Palestinian Medical Relief Committees and manager of Mustafa's ambulance service. Dr Mohammad's office was filled with medical supplies and he was wearing the white vest of the clinic's emergency service staff. A yellow badge on his right shoulder bore the letters 'UPMRC'.

Soon after the Israelis occupied Ramallah, Israeli troops used Dr Ishafi as a human shield while searching his offices for militants, room by room. A soft-spoken man with rimless eyeglasses and a grizzled moustache, Dr Ishafi said he wasn't frightened because he knew the building was empty. But his heart sank when the soldiers forced him to do the same in the adjacent building, where gunmen had been exchanging fire with Israeli troops.

'I was scared,' he said. 'If there were fighters in the rooms, they would have killed me.'

The soldiers took two hours to search the building. Fortunately for Dr Ishafi, the gunmen evaded the Israelis.

'Respect for medical teams is very important all over the world,' Dr Ishafi said. 'We have special identification cards. The Israelis are welcome to inspect them of course but they can do this without humiliating us.'

Almost everyone in Ramallah knows Sam Bahour, the businessman from Youngstown, Ohio. He is well spoken, highly respected and until the Israeli invasion relentlessly upbeat. (At six feet four inches and 330 pounds, he is also one of the largest Palestinians in Palestine. A popular West Bank spectator sport is watching Sam Bahour wedge himself into his Hyundai sedan.)

Shortly after meeting with the Barghouthis I had lunch with Sam at one of the few establishments in Ramallah untouched by Israeli tanks and machine guns. Sam is a second-generation Palestinian who came to Ramallah in 1995 with a background in information technology and took an executive MBA course at Tel Aviv University. He now works for the Arab-Palestinian Investment Company, or APIC, a conglomerate run by a Palestinian who made his fortune in Saudi Arabia.

'The Palestinian Authority is over,' said Sam. 'Healthcare, education, security, everything. How do you calculate the destruction of personal property? Just the loss of automobiles [to Israeli tanks, which arbitrarily rolled over vehicles parked in residential areas] is devastating.'

Sam was close to completing a $10.2 million retail centre called The Shopping Plaza that APIC incorporated and listed on the Palestinian Stock Exchange on 28 September 2000 – the same day as Ariel Sharon's visit to the Harem al Sharif which most Palestinians say brought about the current Intifada.

As it happened, Sam was in Tel Aviv at COMDEX, an Israeli trade exhibition of information technology. The Palestinians had opened a pavilion there – a COMDEX first – and Sam was leading it. His scheduled address to the exhibition was upstaged as news of Sharon's visit swept through the hall.

'Israeli officials apologized to me because they couldn't attend,' Sam said. 'Even the head of the Knesset apologized.'

The foundation-laying ceremony for The Shopping Plaza was held on April 1 – April Fool's day. APIC had planned for a total of six outlets and construction on the first was almost finished when Sharon unleashed Defensive Shield.

Sam wasn't sure about his next move.

'Ordinarily,' he said, 'I'd be hiring staff and setting up foreign-supply contracts. But now there are so many questions. After what's happened, will I have to deal only with Israeli suppliers? This was to be our contribution to the modernization of the Palestinian economy, but the situation is so dire now. Prior to twenty-five days ago I didn't think re-occupation was possible. I didn't think the Americans would allow it. But the unthinkable happened and I'm hesitant. If there are economic conditions here imposed by Israel we'll have to re-evaluate. We're back to an NGO economy. NGOs are the only ones hiring.'

I asked Sam where he was on September 11.

'In my office,' he said. 'There was a guy who was real happy when we watched the coverage on CNN and I told him "Look, we'll end up paying for it." A few days ago he called me from Jenin and told me I was right. He's out of work. I had to let him go.'

Sam paid the bill and drove me back to the Israeli checkpoint where I would take a taxi back to Jerusalem. As he navigated man-made barricades and cars smashed like rodents by Israeli tanks, he told me that during the Israeli siege he had read *The Jewish State*, the manifesto written by the father of modern Zionism, Theodore Herzl. 'I had so much time to kill and wanted to know what started all this,' he said. 'So I downloaded it from the Internet and read it. As a Palestinian, it made my blood boil. But then I appreciated it for what it is – a masterpiece. Herzl was a genius. The book reads like a blueprint for how to build a modern country in the Middle East.'

Sam smiled ironically. 'I respect Herzl for being able to design a state and impose it on an indigenous people. The Arabs saw it coming, but they were too incompetent to do anything about it.'

We reached the checkpoint. I shook Sam's hand and lumbered past the guard post. While waiting for a cab, I took out my notebook.

'As Sam Bahour goes,' I wrote, 'So goes the Arab centre.'

Since biblical times, soap has been an important Arab manufactured good, particularly in the Mediterranean Levant.* From Aleppo to Cairo, soap factories boil animal fat, grease and vegetable oil into translucent bars that are usually green and often displayed stacked into towers, like minarets. Some Arab soaps are elaborately coloured and presented as gifts.

In Nablus on the West Bank, soap was a natural downstream product from the city's main export, olive oil. In the Old City, a complex of stone villas, shops and cobblestone streets there were four soap factories that were centuries old, some dating back to the

---

* Though you wash yourself with lye and use much soap, the stain of your guilt is still before me, says the Lord God – Jeremiah, 2:22

Mamluk era of the fourteenth century. They employed hundreds of people and produced what was proudly marketed as the world's only olive-oil soap.

Soap is to Nablus what Panama hats are to Ecuador – an ancient product that has been crafted for so long using the same methods it becomes an iconic reference to the community itself. Like the olive press, soap is a symbol for Nablusian industry and industriousness.

During Operation Defensive Shield, the Israelis alleged that gunmen were sheltering in the factories, and in the subsequent battle that followed they were destroyed. By the time I reached the site, workers were busy carting away rubble-filled wheelbarrows past nearby Saint Dimitrios, the Greek Orthodox church. On the church wall was a sign in Arabic, Hebrew and English. 'Please keep this place holy,' it requested.

Ma'az M. Nablusi, the president of the Nablus Chamber of Commerce, owned one of the factories. 'The Israelis don't take history into account,' he said in his office. 'These were more than factories. They represented the civilization, the history, the economy of Nablus. The Israelis claim there were fighters there, but no bodies were ever found. They claimed there were bomb factories because of the oil and soda, but this is ridiculous. Their plan is to destroy our economy.'

Ma'az's office resembled the offices of all chamber-of-commerce presidents – press kits on the coffee table, framed photographs of factory grand-openings and souvenirs from dozens of trade shows and delegations. There was a plaque with the Palestinian and Greek flags, a token of Greco-Nablusian commercial ties; a cut-glass paper-weight from an EU trade show; a mounted, brass model of a poly-vinyl chloride elbow-joint commemorating a Taiwanese-Nablusian enterprise that produces industrial pipe.

'The siege has affected our economy in a very clear way,' said Ma'az. 'The Israelis let in basic goods like oil and food but they have blocked the kind of raw materials our manufacturers need. So we have to smuggle items in through the fields in bullock carts. It will take us months to dig our way out of this and even when we do the Israelis can move back in anytime they'd like. Who would ever invest in an economy like this?'

Before I left, Ma'az referred me to the matriarch of the city's oldest soap-producing clan who could walk me through the history of the Nablusian soap industry.

An hour later I was in an ice-cream factory getting a further insight into the local economy with the scion to Nablus' premier ice-cream empire. The soap lady was nowhere to be found but along the way I had run into Raed G. Anabtawi, the finance and sales manager of Al Arz Ice Cream Factory Company.

Raed runs Al Arz with his four cousins and holds a degree in finance from Louisiana State University. He was relaxed but polished in a pine-green windbreaker, olive-drab chinos and round, wire-rimmed glasses, with his thinning hair cut close. He didn't appear to be someone in charge of a company bleeding red ink.

'This is a fifty-year old, family-run company,' he said. 'We've never seen such difficulties.'

Al Arz (the cedars) was named after the cedars of Lebanon; it employs 120 people and sells most of its product in the West Bank. Raed's father started the company by selling ice, then ice-cream bars and finally a range of ice-cream products. In 1982, the elder Anabtawi automated the production line with imported Danish equipment. In 1999, Al Arz purchased a new factory line from the same Danish supplier as part of a $1.5 million expansion of its output and product range. When the second Intifada started, sales plummeted and Raed had to inform the banks the company could not repay its loans.

Since then, Al Arz's debt and procurement costs have risen by 15 per cent in tandem with the shekel's 15 per cent depreciation against the US currency. Al Arz's revenue is generated in shekels but its debt is denominated largely in US dollars, the currency with which it pays for its raw materials — milk powder, vegetable oil and wrapping paper.

Sales are well below the estimates Raed gave the bank when he applied for the loans for the new factory line. Before the violence, Al Arz's annual revenue was ILS10 million ($2.5 million). It estimated sales growth of 40 per cent in 2000 but revenue grew by only half that rate, to ILS12 million. In 2001, sales slipped to ILS11 million. For 2002, Raed said, the company needed to achieve sales growth in excess of 60 per cent to cover its loan commitments.

'We'll be lucky to make 10 million shekels,' he told me. 'The banks will have to recognize our creditworthiness.'

Raed showed me the factory. A production run had just ended and workers were hosing down the machinery with hot water. They were running two production lines on a single shift.

'Before the Intifada,' said Raed, 'we were operating three lines on two shifts a day, sixteen hours a day.'

'So you're losing money.'

'A lot,' he said, gesturing to the new line. 'This is a $1.5 million write-off.'

Even before the Israeli siege, Al Arz had to release 20 part-time workers and told many full-timers to stay home. During the invasion, it had to refund vendors for undeliverable stock after a power cut melted its entire inventory.

The company has five containers of raw materials, mostly butter and vegetable oil, sitting at port waiting to be paid for and collected. Worse still, the unseasonably cold weather had discouraged even people who could afford ice cream from buying any.

I asked Raed if he had ever tried to sell into Israel, where the company's products would be about 30 per cent cheaper than locally produced ice cream. However, as he explained, it is easier for a camel to go through the eye of a needle than for a Palestinian ice-cream bar to find its way into an Israeli freezer.

'To get an export license,' Raed told me, 'we needed to send samples of our products to a food-inspection agency for testing. When we passed the test they asked us for letters from the suppliers of our raw materials along with samples for analysis. When this was done, the Israelis wanted confirmation from the supplier of our milk powder that it was registered with the proper agencies in Israel. It was a strange request since we buy our milk powder from an Israeli company.'

After six months of this Al Arz opted to freeze, so to speak, its attempt to crack the Israeli market.

'They never say "no" of course,' said Raed. 'But we've given up for now.'

We ended up in Raed's office, where he produced the much-anticipated ice-cream bars.

'The Israelis are in direct control of us,' he said. 'It used to take ninety minutes to drive to Ramallah, now it's eight hours. If we were smart we would have moved elsewhere. Jordan has cheap labour, a good commercial bank. Here the land is expensive, taxes and electricity are high.'

Raed licked clean the stick from his ice-cream bar and tossed it in the trash bin.

'For thirty-five years, since the occupation,' he said, '$10,000 earned in Palestine is $70,000 anywhere else.'

It was getting late. I said goodbye to Raed and took a taxi to the same unmanned checkpoint through which I had entered Nablus that morning. I was dropped within a hundred yards of it and walked through a small village to reach my driver waiting on the Israeli side. I passed a row of blockhouses and some young Palestinians watering flocks of chickens and turkeys.

Six Israeli soldiers now manned the checkpoint. Several dozen Palestinians were detained on either side of the city limits. The Israelis had arrived about a half-hour ago, I was told, and closed the border after some shooting at a nearby settlement. No one knew how long the wait would be so there was ample time to meet my fellow detainees.

'You are an American?' asked a middle-aged man, whose name was Marwan.

'Yes. A journalist.'

'You are welcome.'

Another Palestinian gently tugged at my arm and gestured towards the Israeli soldiers with a jerk of his head. 'You Americans are always asking why we hate you,' he said. 'This is why.'

Marwan was returning home to his village from the fashion boutique he owns in Nablus. Like many Palestinians, he had family in the US and spoke fondly of the time he spent there.

'It's a wonderful country,' he said. 'Don't you Americans know what your government is doing to us?'

A half-hour passed. It was getting dark – and cold.

'Why don't you just cross over and tell the Israelis who you are,' said Marwan. 'You're an American. America is Israel's ally. Of course they'll let you through.'

By this time several Palestinians were urging me to trudge across no-man's land towards the soldiers, my US passport as flak-vest. I wasn't sure if they actually believed the Israelis would let me pass or were just bored and eager for some kind of incident to break up the monotony.

I suddenly remembered my schoolmates suckering me into a high-speed jump off a dirt track on my sporting bike. I was nine years old and ended up in a bloody heap.

'Everything will be fine,' Marwan assured me.

Actually, I preferred to stay where I was. As the Israeli army is well trained, the troops manning this particular checkpoint should have been no less disciplined than others I had encountered over the years. Certainly they were under orders – let no one pass – and it would have been presumptuous of me to challenge them.

Second, Israeli troops have been known to shoot journalists.

Nonetheless, Palestinian peer pressure being what it is, I eventually found myself walking towards the checkpoint. I was 20 yards away from the Israelis before they gestured at me to stop.

'Journalist!' I shouted, holding my passport aloft.

The Israelis ignored me. I felt like an idiot.

I am generally sympathetic to Israeli soldiers patrolling Palestinian areas. Short of having to put down a rebellion at home, a soldier's worst duty is occupation. The average Israeli army recruit or reservist wants nothing to do with the Palestinians or the Jewish settlers he is ordered to protect.

Most of the troops I have met in the field are good-natured; just that morning I was told at the main checkpoint to Nablus that the city was closed. Some shooting had taken place, the soldiers said, and the borders had been sealed a few hours before my arrival. They acknowledged there was nothing to prevent me from sneaking in but they advised against it – sincere advice, I would like to believe, out of concern for my safety.

We spent the next few minutes discussing the relative merits of the American M–16 assault rifle and the Israeli-made Galil. The Galil is superior, if somewhat heavier, they said. A soldier asked me which Jerusalem hotel I was staying in and how much I was paying for the room. So I told him.

'That's too much,' he said and handed me flyer advertising a hotel in West Jerusalem. His friend Shlomo ran it and his special rate for journalists included discounts on flak vests.

We said goodbye, I sneaked into Nablus, and now here I was – Israelis in front, Palestinians behind, turkeys gobbling in the distance. I decided to find out what $3 billion in US aid to Israel is worth.

'Journalist,' I yelled again. '*American* journalist!'

'*Fuck America*,' one soldier shouted back. 'Get back to where you were!' He assumed the passive-aggressive posture Israeli troops adopt when challenged: rifle raised with butt stock slightly above shoulder, barrel aimed at the checkpoint perimeter – in other words, at my legs.

I sheepishly retreated back to the barricade.

The Palestinians loved it. Marwan said something about the poacher turning on the gamekeeper. It was a translation of a classic Arabic expression, the kind that in its more elegant vernacular would have embellished the absurdity of my situation with references to a ninth-century Arab astronomer and a fifteenth-century poet.

Finally, the soldiers checked our identities before letting us through. I handed a soldier – not the abusive one – my passport.

'Are you the journalist?' he asked gravely.

'Yes.'

'Your driver is waiting for you.'

The Golden Bowl

What was once known as mandated Palestine has little strategic value. True, Israel's economy is the world's 36th largest as measured by per-capita income but it is driven largely by a high-tech sector financed with highly fluid, foreign capital. There is a small domestic market of six million Israelis and three million Palestinians and no natural resources on either side. Neither Israel nor the Palestinians control an important waterway; the principal reason the British wanted author-ity over Palestine in the last century was to protect the Suez Canal and to secure the land approach to India. Gaza was a key port in medieval times but was sidestepped in 1498 along with the rest of the Levant when Portuguese navigator Vasco da Gama discovered a sea route between Europe and Asia. (His Arab pilot, Ahmad ibn Majid, was an unwitting conspirator in what would rank alongside the Sykes-Picot agreement and the collapse of oil prices as one of the biggest setbacks to the Arab economy.)

Nevertheless, the strip of desert on the Mediterranean's eastern lit-toral has seized humanity's viscera for thousands of years because of a small, indefensible city that hardly figured on the old caravan routes. As the home for a constellation of sites considered holy by all three monotheistic faiths – the foundation of Solomon's temple known as the Temple Mount, the Church of the Holy Sepulchre, built on the spot Christ was crucified, and the Dome of the Rock, the third-holiest site in Islam – Jerusalem provides ample inspiration for humans to destroy each other.

The Medieval Arab Jerusalemite Al Muqadassi described Jerusalem as 'a golden bowl filled with scorpions'; Jesus Christ called it 'the city that slays the prophets'; with the possible exemption of Seoul during the Korean war, no city has changed hands more often or more bloodily. Joshua conquered it along with the rest of Canaan with the twelve tribes of Israel in 1250 BC. The Jews were cast out by Babylonian King Nebuchadnezzar in 586 BC, only to be restored by Cyrus II of Persia less than a hundred years later.

Hellenist rule gave way to the Romans, who with Annas and Caiaphas – the Hebrew city fathers of the time – dutifully fulfilled their pre-ordained roles as Christ's killers. Roman authority atrophied into the excesses of Byzantine rule and its confrontation with the Persians, who massacred the inhabitants and burned the churches in 614. In 638 the Muslims came, to rule Jerusalem as *Al Quds* – the Holy – for most of the next 1,280 years until the British occupied Palestine in 1918.

In the dramatic and violent narrative that is the history of Jerusalem, few episodes are more refreshing than the occupation of the city by Omar I, the second Muslim caliph known to this day for his modesty and reverence. Accounts of his entry into the city vary but are united by a common theme: the austerity and piousness of the new ruler that shamed the Byzantines and endeared Islam to the local population, both Jews and Christians. One story has the people of Jerusalem mistaking a lowly attendant for the caliph as the Muslims approached because Omar, dressed in a coarse, patched mantle, had insisted an exhausted supplicant ride his camel. He would subsequently declare Jews and Christians to be *dhimmis*, a minority protected under Muslim rule.*

It was the most peaceful conquest of one of the world's most con-tested cities.†

Jerusalem is the third-holiest site in Islam behind Mecca and Medina. Here one mystical night Mohammad was feted by the great prophets of the past, including Jesus, and then hoisted to heaven from the rock

---

* When it came to Islam's heartland, however, Omar's tolerance had its limits. He expelled Jews and Christians from the Arabian peninsula, doubtless motivated by the words of the Prophet: 'Let there be no two religions in Arabia.' Osama bin Laden cites this admonition to justify one of his primary object-ives, namely the removal of US troops from Saudi Arabia.

† When the Crusaders took Jerusalem in 1099, they indiscriminately slaughtered tens of thousands of Muslims, Jews and Christians. 'In the Temple and the porch of Solomon, men rode in blood up to their knees and bridle reins,' wrote one Frank, justifying the massacre as 'a just and splendid judgment of God' on the unbelievers in a place that had 'suffered so long from their blasphemies'.

Jerusalem returned to Islamic control in 1187 when Saladin marched through the city's western gate. The second Muslim conquest of Jerusalem would be as peaceful as the first.

astride his winged steed, Buraq. To mark this epic journey, Caliph Abd al Malik built between 685 and 691AD what would be Jerusalem's most distinctive landmark and Islam's greatest artistic triumph.* It was less inspired by piety, of which Al Malik had little, than by the caliph's ambition to stick it to his arch rival, Ibn Zubayr, a long-time opponent of the Umayyad dynasty.

By the close of the seventh century, Umayyad naval vessels patrolled the world's most lucrative sea routes and Umayyad armies guarded the empire's frontiers. Damascus controlled the imperial treasury and bankrolled the most gifted artists and brilliant scientists of their time. But Ibn Zubayr, allied to the Qurayshi tribe of Mecca, held the Ka'bah, Islam's holiest shrine. The great, square mosque is the sacred destination of the annual pilgrimage, or *hajj*, that all Muslims are obligated to make at least once in their lifetime. Then, as now, the *hajj* was big business. If Al Malik could divert those pilgrims from Mecca he could throttle Ibn Zubayr's economic lifeline.

Al Malik commissioned his court architects to build the best shrine that seven years' revenue from Egypt could buy. Its dome would out-shine the Christians' Anastasias Church at Golgotha, the Church of the Ascension on the Mount of Olives, and the Church of the Holy Sepulchre.

The caliph hired artisans and engineers steeped in Byzantine trad-ition, many of them Jews and Christians. The dome would rest on an octagon that, if fitted in a circle, would measure 55 metres in diam-eter. Its design combined the early Islamic world's most potent ideals: faith and reason. The shrine's primary colours, blue and gold, suggest the promise of heaven and the fruit of secular knowledge. Geometric shapes – circles, squares, and octagons – emphasize and celebrate through mathematics the eternity and perfection of divinity.

The Dome of the Rock is widely regarded as one of the world's most stunning and flawlessly designed buildings.† It is also one of the few government projects in the Middle East that was finished on time and under budget; upon its completion, the architects reported to Al Malik that 100,000 gold dinars remained unspent. The caliph suggested they keep the money as a bonus. The architects declined, offering instead to hammer the dinars into plating for the dome.

Al Malik ordered the walls of the shrine inscribed with a verse

---

* The site is also venerated by Jews as the place where their first patriarch, Abraham, prepared to sacri-fice his son Isaac.
† The dome is not a mosque as is popularly thought.

from the Koran that rejects the idea that God would ever represent himself in human form:

> The Christ Jesus, son of Mary, was but God's apostle – [the fulfillment of] His promise which he had conveyed unto Mary – and a soul created by Him. Believe then in God and his apostle and do not say '[God] is a trinity'. God is but One God: utterly remote is He in his glory from having a son.

The message was clear: Islam is here to stay. And it did – with the exception of the Frankish interregnum – until June 7, 1967, when a one-eyed warrior restored Jerusalem to Jewish rule.

Occupation from Without. . .

In a famous photograph, General Moshe Dayan, Israel's then defence minister, strides triumphantly through the freshly captured streets of Jerusalem during the waning hours of the 1967 Arab-Israeli war. To his left is his then chief of staff, Yitzhak Rabin, later Israel's prime minister. To his right is Major-General Uzi Narkis, immortalized as the answer to one of the most frequently-asked trivia questions among journalists covering the Middle East: *Who is the guy walking to the right of Dayan and Rabin in the famous photo of them taken after the Arabs lost Jerusalem?*

In fact, Narkis deserves special mention for defying a rabbinical command to blow up the Dome of the Rock. With the Sinai peninsula, the Golan Heights and the West Bank and Gaza Strip in Israeli hands, only one objective remained: to replace the Arab profanity with the construction of the Third Temple. As even secular paratroopers wept with joy before the Wailing Wall, the Israeli army's chief rabbi told Narkis to destroy 'The Mosque of Omar', as he put it, with a hundred kilograms of explosives.

'We'll get rid of it once and for all,' the rabbi said.

'Rabbi, stop it,' Narkis replied.

'Uzi,' the rabbi said, 'you'll enter the history books by virtue of this deed.'

'I have already recorded my name in the pages of the history of Jerusalem,' Narkis replied.

With that, Narkis made himself a human breakwater against a tide of revisionist Zionism that had been growing ever since the arrival of

the first Jewish colonists in the early part of the last century.* Fuelled
by the Balfour Declaration of 1917 and the Nazis' rise to power 16
years later, Palestine's Jewish population rose from 25,000 in the late
nineteenth century – most devoted to prayer and contemplation – to
450,000, largely European emigrants.

Until then, the Arabs and Jews of Palestine lived together as
peacefully as everywhere else in the Islamic world. As I learned
from Sheik Hassoun in Aleppo, Jewish and Arab children in
Palestine born in the same week were treated as foster brothers and
sisters and were nursed by each others' mothers. (The then-Mufti of
Jerusalem, Haj Amin al Husseini, had three such Jewish foster
brothers; enraged by what he regarded British-Zionist collusion
over Palestine, al Husseini allied himself to the Nazis.) Whatever
incidents of intolerance that occurred until then was due to
Ottoman, not Arab incitement. Anti-Semitism was largely a
European problem, not an Arab one.

When foreign Jews flooded in, tension and then conflict was inevitable due to the alien ways of the Europeans and the disruptive effect
of their imported wealth on the local economy.

Though on a macroeconomic level Palestinian output increased
because of Jewish immigration, the rate was conspicuously uneven.
The burgeoning Jewish population established its own institutions,
such as the labour union known as the Histadrut in 1920, whose self-
sufficient economic enclave was based on exclusively Jewish labour
and acquiring what was then designated as inalienable Jewish land.
By 1937, the Jews of Palestine controlled some 10 per cent of the
region's cultivated property, mostly along the coast. The bulk had
been bought in large estates from several hundred landlords, the
majority living outside Palestine. Many of these were Lebanese who
after the Sykes-Picot agreement suddenly found a border running
between them and their Palestinian farms and estates. To enter
Palestine they required exit and entry visas from the French and the
British respectively, neither easily obtained. Consequently they
became net sellers and émigré Jews ready buyers.

By the early 1930s Zionist groups were reduced to buying land in
much smaller lots from different groups of local people; this increased

* Herzl was happy to establish a Jewish state outside Palestine and at one point considered Uganda as an
option. So-called revisionists within the World Zionist Organization overruled him, declaring that only
Palestine would do.

the displacement of those who rented those lands and so deepened the antipathy between Arab and Jew.*

Among the few European Zionists who expected resistance by the Palestinians to Zionism was Ze'ev Jabotinsky. In 1923, he published an article entitled 'The Iron Wall', in which he stated that a settlement between Jews and Arabs over Palestine was impossible, and irreconcilable with Zionism. Therefore:

> We must either suspend our settlement efforts or continue them without paying attention to the mood of the natives. Settlement can thus develop under the protection of a force that is not dependent on the local population, behind an iron wall which they will be powerless to break down.
>
> As long as the Arabs preserve a gleam of hope that they will succeed in getting rid of us, nothing in the world can cause them to relinquish this hope, precisely because they are not a rabble but a living people. And a living people will be ready to yield on such fateful issues only when they have given up all hope of getting rid of the alien settlers.

Only then, said Jabotinsky, will the extremist anti-Jewish settlement forces be sidelined, enabling more moderate groups to 'offer suggestions for compromise'.

He was prophetic. By 1936, support for the Zionists was becoming a liability. With war clouds forming, London needed Arab backing to ensure oil supplies in the event of a conflict.† So to appease the Arab states Britain agreed to limit Jewish emigration to Palestine, thereby provoking Jewish extremist groups like the Irgun and the Stern gang who used tactics that were little different from today's militant Palestinians.

The King David Hotel in Jerusalem was blown up in July 1946, leaving 91 dead – mostly soldiers, but also civilians including 17 Jews; British soldiers were captured and executed; and Lord Moyne, a British Foreign Office minister was assassinated, as was Count Bernadotte, a UN-appointed mediator and a member of the Swedish

---

* For an excellent, comprehensive look at how economic factors have shaped the Middle East over the last century, see Owen and Pamuk's *A History of the Middle East Economies in the Twentieth Century*.

† Similarly, France withdrew its support of Israel to curry Arab favour in its war with Algerian rebels in the 1950s.

royal family, in May 1948. The Jewish extremist leaders included Menachem Begin and Yitzhak Shamir, both future Israeli prime ministers.

The British Mandate ended on 14 May 1948. The Arabs rejected an eleventh-hour UN-sponsored partition plan; the Jews accepted it, although David Ben-Gurion later told members of The Jewish Agency that 'following the establishment of the state – we will cancel the partition of the country and we will expand throughout the Land of Israel'.*

Israel declared statehood and repelled a combined Arab attack plagued by petty feuding and factional disarray. The US and Russia recognized the Jewish state and the rest is well-travelled history.†

The Arab historian Ibn Al Athir once noted of the Crusaders: 'The Franks, may God confound them, gained their conquests by the divisions among the faithful. For in fact the Moslem armies and their leaders were constantly at war with one another, their attitudes were divergent, their aims divided and their imperial resources wasted.'

So it was with Zionism and the Arabs – at least in the eyes of the Palestinians. Eighty years after Jabotinsky's article, the 'natives' are still restless and his iron wall remains an economic as well as a political barrier.

'Watch it!' I said, grabbing the dashboard as Halil casually swerved to avoid an oncoming Mercedes taxi.

I was packed in the front seat of a meat truck hurtling along the West Bank's notorious Fire Valley Road. The second Intifada was a year away. I was reporting a story about the Palestinian economy and decided to spend a day delivering meat products in a Hyundai refrigerator-truck owned by Al Haya Food Industries Company. The firm is based in Ezariya, north of Hebron and according to their logo had been serving quality meats since 1920. Driver Halil Masaud and salesman Iyad Al Amleh were taking me on their morning run from

---

* There is a Muslim precedent for this. In March 628, Mohammad agreed to a ten-year truce in his war with the Quraysh in the village of Hudaibiya outside Mecca. Like Ben-Gurion and the partition plan, Mohammad's consent was a ploy to buy time and prepare for a decisive thrust on the battlefield.

† Harry Truman, the US president who supported Israel, ignored the advice of his closest aides, including Secretary of State George Marshall and his successor Dean Acheson, senior diplomat George Kennan and Defence Secretary James Forrestal.

Bethlehem to Ramallah via Jericho on a two-lane asphalt strip kinked by mountain switchbacks and hairpin curves. The tarmac was pot-holed and the guardrails scarred and twisted. It was 28 miles and 90 minutes of white-knuckled, adrenalin-gushing hell.

Before one blind curve after another, Halil honked his horn to alert any traffic that might be approaching from the other direction. A laminated passage from the Koran dangled ominously from the rear-view mirror. 'God is everywhere,' Halil said. 'He doesn't sleep. He is all knowing.'

The Hyundai was wheezing up a sustained mountain rise with a full load of mortadella, sliced turkey breast, chicken parts and cocktail weenies. We bobbed our heads forward, coaxing the truck and its 2.2-litre engine onward. After yet another blind curve, my blood froze as a Volvo dump truck emerged in the oncoming lane, its grill filling the entire view through the Hyundai's windshield. Halil swerved, this time violently. The Volvo clipped the truck's side-view mirror as it passed.

I instinctively clutched the laminated passage from the Koran, breathless. In Palestine, there are no atheists in meat trucks.

'This road is fit for a thief, not a human,' Iyad remarked. 'It is a danger for all Palestinians.'

We were on this two-lane funhouse because the Israelis denied Al Haya Food Industries permission for its trucks to take the less hazardous Al Quds Road through Jerusalem, a smoother and less eventful one-hour journey. As Jerusalem slowly creeps eastward with expanded settlements, one way to protect the settlers is by strictly limiting the number of Palestinian vehicles passing through the city.

The expansion of Jewish colonies in the West Bank and Gaza has long been regarded on both sides of the conflict as the most provocative obstacle to peace in the Middle East. Israel built the first settlements in the West Bank and Gaza soon after it captured those territories after the 1967 Arab-Israeli war. Settlement expansion has gained momentum over the last decade or so, despite a pledge by Israel to halt such activity as part of the Oslo agreement. The settlements, which the Arabs regard as colonial outposts on Palestinian land, are regarded by many on both sides of the conflict as the most provocative obstacle to peace in the Middle East.

The settlements are inhabited by religious activists who want to repopulate the region with Jews, and secularists lured by the high quality of life – pools, gardens, air-conditioned villas – all subsidized by the state. Some Israelis defend the settlements as 'facts on the ground', that give the country depth in a future conventional war with the Arabs. Others, including senior military men, say the army's requirement to patrol them diverts valuable resources from protecting Israel proper. The settlements, they argue, are as great a threat to security as they are a strategic cushion.

The old warhorse Ariel Sharon once said he would never consider dismantling settlements. His predecessor, the war-hero Ehud Barak, was prepared to exchange some 90 per cent of the West Bank and most of the settlements for peace with the Palestinians during the unsuccessful Camp David peace talks in July 2000.*

The first Bush administration once threatened to withhold American aid if Israel siphoned the money away on settlements. The current Bush administration doesn't seem to care either way.

Jewish colonies account for just over 1 per cent of the total land in the West Bank. This, however, ignores the many bypass roads that join the settlements to Israel proper and the army bases that protect them. The Oslo peace accords honeycombed the West Bank by giving the Palestinians full authority only over major population centres like Ramallah and Jericho. Both sides share control over the rest of the West Bank and in some areas Palestinians have no authority at all. Israeli checkpoints inhibit the free flow of people and goods from one West Bank town to another. Because most of the best roads are reserved almost exclusively for Israelis, the majority of Palestinians are forced to take time-consuming and neglected alternatives like the Fire Valley Road.

Between Jewish colonies, the garrisons that protect them, and the roads that cleave their land it is not surprising that many Palestinians associate their fate with that of native Americans. Unchecked, settlement expansion will eventually subdivide a Palestinian Authority already clustered into tiny, isolated enclaves. If it is possible to Balkanize a Bantustan, it is happening in Palestine.

The Oslo accords, which were fatally flawed by an unrealistically high presumption of goodwill on both sides, called for most settlements to be dismantled. According to Peace Now, an anti-

---

* Camp David was supposed to settle the issues left unresolved in Oslo. However, both sides came out of the negotiations with very different interpretations of what happened.

occupation Israeli organization, West Bank and Gaza settlements since Oslo have grown by 52.5 per cent and the number of Jewish settlers by 72 per cent. B'tselem, an Israeli human rights group, estimates Israel has demolished some 740 Palestinian homes since 1994. According to the Israeli government the homes were built without permits. The Palestinians say these are prohibitively hard to obtain.

One of the largest Jewish settlements is Har Homa, an enormous – and steadily growing – complex of villas and community centres that crowds out adjacent Palestinian villages. Viewed from nearby Bethlehem, wrote correspondent Danny Rubinstein in the 21 February 2000 edition of *Ha'aretz*, 'this new Jewish neighbourhood appears to be the continuation of the Arab town, Beit Sahur. You see Har Homa from virtually every locale in Bethlehem – you see the cranes, the stone walls, the foundations of homes in a neighbourhood under construction. [This] encapsulates Bethlehem's fate as a city which lacks space for development. "We're under siege; they've put us in a ghetto," bemoan members of the city council.'

Some 450 Israeli reserve officers expressed the most recent Israeli outrage over the occupation. In early 2002 they signed a petition declaring they would no longer serve in the territories. In February, the Council for Peace and Security, a group of 1,000 reserve generals, colonels and intelligence officials publicly advocated a unilateral withdrawal from all of Gaza and much of the West Bank. Their gesture, applauded by Israelis opposing the occupation as a threat to the morality and character of the Jewish state, was condemned by hardliners who support the concept of *Eratz Yisrael*, or Greater Israel, as an intrusion of subordination and weakness.

Avraham Avinu – 'Abraham our father', in Hebrew – is one of the largest Jewish settlements in Hebron, with a primary school and a dedicated water supply. It was built in the centre of old Hebron, a city revered by Jews, Christians and Muslims as the burial place of the Old Testament patriarchs. Around 400 settlers, guarded by 2000 Israeli troops, are surrounded by 120,000 Palestinians. Many of the settlers came from large US cities, particularly New York and believe fiercely in a divine writ for Jewish possession of the West Bank, which they call Judea and Samaria.

The City of the Patriarchs, as Hebron is called, is a living symbol of Holy Land implacability. In August 1929, a time of great tension between Arabs and Zionists, 59 Jewish men, women and children were murdered there. The city's centrepiece is the Ibrahimi mosque, built on the Cave of Machpelah, the reputed burial site of Abraham, Isaac, Jacob and their wives. In 1994, a settler gunned down 29 Palestinians in the mosque.* Israeli security forces carefully regulate access to the site in an attempt to separate Jews and Muslims. Peacekeepers known as the Temporary International Presence in Hebron, or TIPH, patrol the area, armed only with cameras.

Few peacekeepers conceal their dislike of the settlers. 'Even if they go on a rampage and attack Palestinians and it's on television it doesn't go too far up the [Israeli] legal system because they are so powerful politically,' said Jens Veng, a TIPH member.

Relations are sour not only between the settlers, the Palestinians and the TIPH, but also between the settlers and the Israeli troops. Soldiers spend their time escorting Jewish children to school and mediating petty disputes. The settlers, when attacked by Palestinians, harangue the soldiers for being too easy on the Arabs; when settlers attack a Palestinian, the soldiers are condemned as biased occupiers.

'This is not the job I was trained to do,' one Israeli soldier told me when I first visited Hebron in 1998. 'I'd rather be fighting in Lebanon.'

Ezeddin Sharabati lives with his extended family in an elegantly refurbished, if cluttered, villa with labyrinthine passageways, open courtyards and vaulted ceilings. The stone floors and stairs are worn and gleaming from centuries of use.

The Sharabati home is literally within a stone's-throw of Avraham Avinu and blocks the settlers' expansion plans. Since the 1967 war, Ezeddin told me, the settlers offered the Sharabati family from $100,000 to 1 million dollars to leave. Bidders came to him through Arab brokers, he said, 'to save me the scorn of selling to a Jew'.

Ezeddin was 50 years old when we met in September 1998; his face bore the scar of a wound inflicted during the 1967 war.

'They don't want Palestinians on the land of Palestine,' said Ezeddin. 'Is this the meaning of their Western democracy? What right do they

---

* The assailant, an American-born doctor named Baruch Goldstein, was killed in the mêlée. Not long after the incident, settlers built a marble shrine to Goldstein in the Judean hills. 'Here is buried the martyr, the doctor', reads the inscription. Though the Israeli government declared the shrine illegal, Jewish pilgrims flock to it.

have to live on my land, these American Jews? I won't let it happen. I will not go the way of the American Red Indian.'

When the settlers aren't offering Ezeddin fat cheques through proxy buyers, said Ezeddin, they engage in low-grade terrorism. California property lawyers would call it 'creative eviction'.

Upstairs in his bedroom Ezeddin produced his journal, a spiral-bound green notebook with yellowing pages. I asked him to read passages at random.

He opened to September 22, 1996: *I had workers here to renovate the house. While the workers were on scaffolding some women* [from the settlement] *started hurling sand bombs, stones, empty bottles and eggs. At 8.05 a.m., the Israeli army came and stopped them.*

He turned to June 15, 1991: *I came home at 7.30 p.m. to see settlers praying in the house. I asked them to leave and they hurled verbal abuse at me. I didn't respond so as not to provoke them. They left, then returned [. . .] and beat me. My neighbours came to help and finally the Israeli army.*

On 6 October 1996, while Palestinians and Israelis negotiated a special agreement on Hebron – it is known as Oslo II and was a response to a spat of sectarian violence – the Sharabati women, while hanging out their washing, were the targets of a similar bombardment as Ezeddin described in the 22 September diary entry. He produced one of the stones for me: on it the settlers had written 'a gift from the Jews' along with the date.

At 6.15 p.m. on 28 February 1994, three days after the 1994 massacre, Ezeddin was reading the Koran in his bedroom when he heard a loud pop. Shards of broken glass spewed onto the floor and covered his head and chest. Ezeddin raced to the window and saw the settler who had just fired the shot.

Ezeddin covered the bullet-hole with cellophane, as it has been ever since.

The side of the Sharabati home that faces Avraham Avinu is matted with chain-link fencing and barbed wire. A corrugated steel cover over an open-air courtyard keeps soldiers from relieving themselves into it. An electric lock was recently installed on the door.

Across the narrow strip that separates the Sharabati villa from the settlers is the vault-like Avraham Avinu. Its stone walls are high and smooth.

Ezeddin says the Israeli army tries to be fair but is burdened by a handful of unruly soldiers and the settlers' political clout. He often consults with the TIPH and only once took matters to the Palestinian Authority.

'I called to complain,' Ezeddin said, 'and the Arafat crony who picked up the phone didn't know where Hebron's old city was.'

Ezeddin has kept his journal since the 1967 war. He opened it to 5 June 1967 – the peak of the fighting – but then spoke from memory. His father, he said, ordered the family to flee what they feared were Jewish vigilante groups seeking revenge for the 1929 Hebron massacre. They packed themselves into an ambulance bound for the village of Sair on Hebron's outskirts but were diverted to a refugee camp near Jericho. There they came under fire from an Israeli tank. Ezeddin received the second-degree burns that scarred his face, his father and mother were injured and his 17-year-old brother and two sisters, aged 14 and 17, were killed.

An Israeli patrol arrived at the camp, he said. 'They set aside everyone between the ages of fifteen and twenty-five, lined them up and shot them. They left me for dead. The last thing I remember was a sign that said "Welcome to Jericho".'

Ezeddin was found by Bedouins and taken to a Jerusalem hospital to be cared for by an Israeli doctor named Hamadipsi. Ten weeks later, he returned to his home.

Ezeddin put away his journal. He told me about how Jordanian troops who administered the West Bank after the British mandate ended quietly abandoned Hebron in 1967 without firing a shot. 'Political theatre,' he said. 'They fled, offered no resistance.'

When Egyptian President Anwar Sadat signed the Camp David peace accord with Israel in 1978, which left the status of the West Bank and Gaza unresolved, said Ezeddin, the Palestinians lost all hope of recovering their land.* 'It was clear then the Arab regimes would protect Israel and accept its policies automatically,' he said. 'They are my enemies as well as Israel. When Oslo was signed, I watched it on TV and cried. That was the final blow.'

Ezeddin introduced me to his children, who have known nothing but occupation. His oldest son, Samir, works at a shoe factory. Samir scored well in school but could not attend college because of the disruption of the first Intifada. Efifeh, Ezeddin's 31-year-old second cousin, teaches English in a nearby secondary school.

---

* Saddled with a failing economy and an ambition to regain the Sinai Peninsula originally lost to Israel in the 1967 Arab-Israeli war, Egyptian President Anwar Sadat risked the ire of the Arab world by travelling to Jerusalem in November 1977 and addressing the Israeli parliament, the Knesset, as a prelude to the Camp David peace accord signed in March 1979.

'The Sharabatis have been here for a thousand years,' Efifeh told me. 'We will survive for another thousand.'

I asked Ezeddin if he or his sons sympathized with militant groups committed to Israel's destruction. He shook his head.

'Hamas?' he said. 'Islamic Jihad? No. Sometimes, I say to myself that terrorism is the answer but I know it is the state's responsibility to protect the individual, not the other way around. Europe is the reason for the crimes against the Palestinians. It is enough to know that Israel was created by Europe. My war is not with the Jews, but the people who planted them here.'

The settlers I met at Avraham Avinu assured me they had close Arab friends in Hebron but warned me about the Sharabatis. Thugs, they told me, violent. Ezeddin's father was a prominent leader of the 1929 massacre, they said; one of the Sharabati boys once attacked the settlers with a knife.

'He wasn't there to cut tomatoes,' said 38-year-old Orit Struk. She showed me photos of the incident after Israeli soldiers came to restore order.*

Israel Zev is a 48-year-old carpenter from Chicago. He had been living in Israel for the last 25 years, in Avraham Avinu for the last five. He was powerfully built and wore a lime polo shirt and denim overall. He had three siblings, of whom two lived in Hebron, nine children and three grandchildren.

'This is the land of the Jews,' he told me, munching an apple. 'It's where we belong. This is where the front line is. I'm a carpenter by trade, but my identity is as a Jew and a soldier. We're all soldiers.'

'What exactly,' I asked, 'do the settlers do in Hebron?'

'We settle,' he said. 'The Bible talks about restoring the land. [Arnold] Toynbee wrote about how all great peoples rise and fall, except for the Jews.†

'I have Arab friends,' he went on, 'but I am not sympathetic to a

---

* Yarden Vatikay, the Israeli army's Central Command spokesman at the time, corroborated Ezeddin's account of his experiences with the settlers and soldiers. The knife-wielding son, according to Yarden, 'is not exactly normal. There was no reason to believe he was dangerous'; the elder Sharabati was 74 when he died, which would have made him five years old at the time of the 1929 massacre.

† In *A Study of History*, Tonybee also wrote: 'The evil deeds committed by the Zionist Jews [. . .] were comparable to crimes committed against the Jews by the Nazis . . . [the Arab massacre] at Deir Yasin was on the head of the Irgun; the expulsion after the 15th of May, 1948, were on the heads of all Israel.'

Palestinian state. They already have a state, in Jordan. They can go to Jordan.'

A little over two years after meeting the Sharabatis, with the current Intifada in its second month, I visited Hebron with Ahmed Mashal, a Palestinian journalist who shepherds countless foreign correspondents in the West Bank and Gaza. It was cold and wet. The Israelis had blocked the main roads into Hebron so we had to try several approaches before entering the city.

We called on Ishaq Al Natsheh, the deputy mayor. Soldiers had sealed off Avraham Avinu for the security of the settlers, he told us, and thereby effectively cut the old city in half. Curfews and closures had all but shut down Hebron's traditional industries: stone-cutting and glass-blowing. It was nearing Ramadan, the Muslim holy month, and residents on one side of the city were finding it difficult to unite with family members on the other.

'People have lost faith in the peace process,' said Ishaq. 'This violence started because Israel doesn't respect its agreements. The Palestinians want their own state as allowed under Oslo but nothing has been implemented. There are peace treaties, UN resolutions, human rights covenants, all these things. But if the Israelis were serious about peace they'd end the occupation.'

I wanted to see the Sharabatis but they, along with the settlers, were locked away behind the barricades. Produce normally sold in the Hebron suk in the centre of town near the Sharabati home was displayed at a temporary market in the city's main square a few hundred yards north. Here the retractable tables were laden with fresh produce and the women of the city were pinching, patting, sniffing, squeezing and buying every manner of spice, meat, fruit and vegetable.

We walked south until the city square and the din of the makeshift market were behind us. Suddenly, an Israeli concussion grenade exploded about thirty yards in front of us. I looked around and saw Palestinian teenagers huddled behind buildings and on rooftops. Another hundred yards or so away I could make out Israeli soldiers behind huge cement blocks, drawing the odd bead on stone-throwing youths. They were armed with M-16 rifles adapted to fire rubber bullets.

Such is the banality of evil in the Middle East; we had managed, within a few metres of the market, to stumble into a street clash.

Prior to the militarization of the second Intifada, conflict like this was the most violent expression of Palestinian outrage. Through the sulphurous haze of today's suicide bomber the image of teenagers throwing rocks at Israeli soldiers seems almost quaint.

It was not the kind of cross-border trade I liked to cover, but since we were there I suggested to Ahmed we interview some of the kids. Khalil Mohammad seemed eager to talk after we found him in the queue of teenagers lined up to hurl stones. These would almost certainly fall well short of their targets, but not before placing the Palestinians who threw them within lethal range of Israeli gunfire.

Khalil was 19 years old, so he was born 14 years after the Israeli occupation began. What did he expect to accomplish throwing rocks at armed men?

'This is my right,' he said. 'By throwing stones I am exercising my right to reclaim the land we lost in 1967. We are here because of Sharon's visit to the Al Aqsa mosque but our main goal is to end the occupation.'

'Do your parents know you come here?'

'Only when I return home injured. I've been hit four times.' He lifted his trouser leg to reveal the bruise from a rubber bullet.

'Two days ago,' Khalil said. 'We won't stop coming . . .'

He was interrupted by a shuddering exchange of live fire. It seemed to be coming from the market but it was impossible to be sure. Everyone froze for a moment, then bolted towards a nearby mall.

We clustered by the main entrance. I needed to compose myself before resuming the interview but Khalil and his comrades were *laughing*. This was resistance, true, but also a great adventure for a generation of young Palestinians who, after seven years of a stingy peace, had almost nothing to look forward to. Throwing rocks at Israeli soldiers may be the most exhilarating thing they ever do with their lives – until perhaps, they detonate themselves at a Tel Aviv nightclub or a Jerusalem coffee house.

'Where did the firing come from?' I asked.

'God knows,' Khalil said. 'We don't use guns because we can't get them. Instead of donations from Saudi Arabia, we should be given guns.'

'What happens if Israel withdraws from the West Bank and Gaza?'

'If Israel gives us back the land it took in 1967 and East Jerusalem,' Khalil said, 'there will be peace.'

I asked Khalil what he was doing before the Intifada. He said he was working for an Israeli company on a Jerusalem construction site.

Occupation from Within . . .

'A Palestinian,' so goes an old saying, 'is someone who can buy from a Jew and sell to an Armenian and still make a profit.'

Throughout the Arab world the Palestinians are respected, even feared, for their business and entrepreneurial acumen. Until the end of the First World War Palestine was a thriving Mediterranean entrepot with a small but sophisticated banking sector. Even today the Arab Bank is considered the best, if somewhat conservatively run, financial institution in the Middle East.* Started in Palestine by the Shoman family, it moved to Amman in 1948 to escape the war. Through five decades of conflict the Arab Bank has protected its depositors and honoured every withdrawal request.

The Shomans still run the Arab Bank and own an orange grove in Jaffa. 'We're the soul of the Palestinian economy,' Abdulmajeed Shoman once told me. 'The crisis made us smart. It made the Palestinians smart.'

Like many other minority populations – the Chinese in Southeast Asia, ethnic Koreans in Japan and Armenians almost everywhere – the Palestinians are more prosperous outside their homeland than inside it. Since the second Intifada, the Palestinians have blamed Israel – its invasions, assassinations and checkpoints – for destroying their economy.

Before the Intifada they blamed Arafat.

Edward R. Murrow, the great broadcast journalist who as a young man helped Jews escape Nazi persecution in Europe, interviewed David Ben-Gurion at the Jewish leader's home soon after the Suez Crisis of 1956. When the interview finally ended – it was well past 1 a.m. – Murrow said goodbye and shuffled out with his film crew to their car. Realizing he hadn't thanked Ben-Gurion and his wife for their patience, Murrow returned to the house to find the prime minister of the newly established State of Israel in Mrs. Ben-Gurion's apron, washing the dishes.

---

* Aboudi Najia, the Lebanese financier profiled in Chapter One, spent months trying to persuade the Arab Bank's board to list part of its equity. 'They said no,' Aboudi said. 'They weren't rude, they just weren't interested.'

It is hard to imagine Yasser Arafat scrubbing coffee cups let alone building the institutions needed for a viable state. The Palestinian leader has cloaked himself in the vanities and accoutrements of statehood – 17 security agencies, private compounds, a personal jet and bagpiping colour guards – without constructing an effective administration to go with it. While Palestinians loathe Ben-Gurion and the other Zionists for building a nation at their expense, they respect them for doing it so skilfully. Arafat and his cronies command no such regard.

By the time this book is published, Yasser Arafat may be retired, exiled, voted out of office or dead, just another ex-Third-World potentate whose years in office were measured by how many US presidents he survived. So much has been written about Arafat – his duplicitous links to terrorists, his contempt for human rights – there is no reason to dwell on him here. What is worth noting is the economic framework this most resourceful of despots will leave his people. Before the current Intifada the Palestinian Authority had a gross domestic product of just over $5 billion and an average annual wage of $1,780. That places the Palestinians slightly on the high side of the Levantine-Arab average, a distinction they earned despite, not because of, Arafat. To paraphrase a maxim on revolution: You can build an economy with the government or without a government but you can't build an economy *against* the government. Since the Oslo accords and Arafat's triumphant return from exile in Gaza, the Palestinians have struggled against their leader and the inept kleptocracy he brought with him.

Corruption is often cited as the greatest strain on the Palestinian economy. Stories abound of Mohammad Dahlan and Jabril Rajub – Arafat lieutenants rumoured to be his potential successors – taking hefty equity stakes in Palestinian monopolies. The Oasis casino at Jericho was once the Palestinian Authority's most lucrative enterprise and widely regarded as a palatial slush fund for the black economy. Arafat himself, though outwardly frugal and known for his spare official lunches, is suspected of keeping billions of dollars in a Swiss bank account.

In fact, corruption in Palestine is no worse than elsewhere in the developing world. 'It's overestimated,' a US diplomat told me in mid-2001. 'Things that cause indignation here would be taken for granted elsewhere in the Arab world. They [Arafat's cronies] were much more heavy-handed four or five years ago but donors complained and we pressed for reform. Until December they were moving in the right direction.'

Yet the main burdens on the Palestinian economy – simple neglect and bad management – are overlooked. As a product of his generation, Arafat never cared much for economics. He inaugurated the Palestinian Securities Exchange but never returned, even in 1999 when it was the Arab world's top-performing stock market.* His most senior economic advisor is Mohammad Rashid, a diligent and intelligent man but whose frame of reference is somewhat dated. 'Rashid does understand economics but in a 1950s kind of way,' was how one Western diplomat put it.

Below Rashid is a gallery of petty functionaries and novices appointed for their loyalty to the regime, not for their ability or qualifications. Take that once-formidable Palestinian banking sector. The chairman of the Palestinian Monetary Authority – Arafat's Alan Greenspan – is Faud Besseso, a former researcher for the Bank of Jordan and advisor to the sultan of Oman. He is a nice man but clearly not the right choice as central banker to an economy with no modern banking law and three currencies. Prior to the second Intifada, the Palestinian banking sector suffered from the same problems that hobble financial services throughout the Arab world – too many banks, a concentration of borrowers holding a disproportionate ratio of deposits and lending officers who can't read a balance sheet.

A ham-fisted, typically risk-averse bureaucracy smothers Palestinian industry. While putting together a story on how the second Intifada was ruining Palestine's olive harvest I met Said Assaf, the director general of his own agriculture think-tank. Said is an expert on the Jojoba nut, a cousin to the olive and used in cosmetics and lubricants. The Jojoba nut fetches higher prices on commodity markets than the olive and is ideal for a rural economy with a small labour force.

Said is something of an endearing nut himself. His resumé – all 16 pages of it – frequently deploys the third person and lists his most noteworthy writings. These include his 1994 monograph 'A Study on the Recent Growing of a Rapidly Propagating Olive Cultivar Misnamed "Improved Nabali" and Its Effect on Impeding the West Bank Olive Industry'.

That said, Said knows his nuts. He stunned a 1990 nut conference in Asuncion, Paraguay by announcing he had discovered how to

* The Nablus-based Palestinian Stock Exchange escaped much of the carnage of Operation Defensive Shield because of its close proximity to a hotel used by journalists as a base during the siege. According to PSE general manager Hasan Adnan Yassin, the reporters phoned US diplomats and asked them to persuade the Israelis to stop shelling the hotel.

enhance the Jojoba's fecundity, thereby increasing its oil yield. He also developed a Jojoba press that could be slowly integrated along with the higher value-added Jojoba into Palestine's olive farms.

In 1993, armed with reams of data about the potential of the Jojoba, Said asked the agriculture ministry for a loan – and was rejected. The ministry 'mafia', as he described it, refused to finance what it did not understand and could not control. He tried to finance the project himself but no bank would give him a loan. Years passed before two investors, a Briton and Norwegian, backed him. The enterprise was just moving into profit when the second Intifada spoiled Palestinian agriculture along with the rest of the economy.

'It's bad enough we have to contend with the occupation,' Said told me, 'without this mafia that came with Oslo.'

Arguably the most important company in the Palestinian Authority is the Palestinian Telecommunications Company. It is known as Paltel and was once chaired by Hatem Halawani, a man with no previous telecommunications experience. Paltel averaged steady sales growth until the market matured and Halawani's inexperience asserted itself.

Among Halawani's legacies as Paltel chairman were the frustrated ambitions of a small but highly motivated group of Palestinian software writers. I once wrote a profile of Bisan, the West Bank company launched by Marwan Totah in 1987. Although Bisan's world-class products included an Arab-language accounting program, it was constantly fighting state-imposed red tape and incompetence.

In 1995, Bisan spent months designing an invoice program to compute in the Palestinian Authority's three currencies only to discover the government had not bothered to announce the introduction of new invoicing standards. In 1997, Marwan spent $80,000 building a switching network in Jerusalem to allow an internet-service provider he co-owned to carry data to and from the West Bank. The network used an Israeli lease-line that charged Palestinian users local rates. In February 1998, Paltel quietly re-classified calls between the West Bank and Jerusalem as international. For thousands of Palestinians, dialling Jerusalem for Internet access was suddenly prohibitively expensive, which customers only discovered when their bills arrived a month later. Paltel subsequently offered a monopoly lease-line service via the Israeli grid, charging users four times the cost of what had been a local call between the West Bank and Jerusalem.

'With rates like these,' Marwan told me, 'who needs enemies?'*

When I phoned Paltel to request an interview with Halawani, the company spokesman told me to come by the next day for a meeting. Having driven for two hours from Jerusalem to the company's head-quarters in Nablus, I then endured 20 minutes of meaningless chit-chat in the spokesman's office before asking when I could see the chairman.

The spokesman crooked his head. 'Mr Halawani is not here,' he said.

'Then what am I doing here?' I asked.

The spokesman explained that he had to interview me before I would be allowed to interview Halawani.

'Now,' he said, producing a notebook, 'what questions will you be asking the chairman?'

I spent the next 40 minutes providing the spokesman with sample questions that he wrote down by hand – slowly. I was to make a follow-up phone call a week later. Halawani never found time for an interview until after my story on Bisan appeared.†

In addition to Israel and Arafat, the Palestinians face another problem: the international foreign-aid community.

Over the years, donor organizations and governments have com-mitted some $3.4 billion to the Palestinian Authority to help the Palestinians build a self-sustaining economy. The result has been a cruel chaos of good intentions.

Well before the current Intifada began I interviewed Anis 'Al Qaq, who was then Arafat's European fund-raiser, in Geneva. From the open-air Swiss chalet where we met one evening for grilled trout, Palestine had never seemed farther away as I took in the fresh moun-tain air, the snow-covered Alps, sailboats wafting across the lake and the fierce but elegant geyser of water that billows from it.

Against this refined backdrop I expected Anis to outline aid pro-jects that were doing wonders for Palestine's Great Unwashed. So I

---

* Marwan is currently testing the latest version of his accounting software in Ramallah and is busy attending IT conferences with Sam Bahour.

† A Palestinian with Jordanian citizenship, Halawani ended up in Amman as the minister of water and irrigation, one of the desert kingdom's most vital portfolios. It was another curious posting; Halawani had as much experience in water as he did telecommunications when he took the Paltel job.

nearly choked on my sorbet when the interview turned into a bitch session.

'It's out of control,' Anis said. 'I see all this money coming in and no results.'

Anis guided me through the get-it-while-you-can world of foreign aid. Since it was established, the Palestinian Authority has become home to hundreds of NGOs funded by governments and run by directors who earn six-figure salaries. They are part of the global 'conference class' as he put it, a self-perpetuating culture of workshops, seminars, and PowerPoint presentations.

On a per capita basis, the average Palestinian is far richer than the average Bangladeshi or Pakistani, a tribute to Palestinian hard work and enterprise. Part of Arafat's price for making peace, however, was a litter of donor programmes that has mushroomed into a huge business; nearly half of foreign funding in Palestine returns to donor countries as contracts or consultancy fees.

All this would be fine, Anis said, if donors took his advice and concentrated on sectors where Palestinians really needed it, for example, transportation, agriculture and energy. But projects in these areas were often too small scale for the deep pockets of the aid community.*

'They have to spend their money or lose their budgets,' Anis said. 'Two years ago, the Europeans took members of my staff on a tour of Europe for a multi-week course on Western diplomacy. They came back knowing all about Metternich and Talleyrand when I really need someone who understands how to raise goats.'

Anis's mobile phone rang. He chatted briefly and hung up.

'That was the Japanese,' he said. 'They want to build another hospital. Why don't they do something with the one they already built?'

Before Oslo, Anis belonged to one of the few NGOs working in the occupied territories. Most secretly monitored Israeli human rights abuses, which made fund-raising difficult. Any money that trickled in came from anonymous sources who didn't want to know how it was used.

'We knew all the tricks for getting around the authorities,' he told me.

Now, Anis said, the tricks were on him. He competed for funds with an army of independent aid workers – including many Palestinians

---

* In some ways the Palestinian Authority can't get a break; one of its largest projects was an electricity grid to be developed by Enron shortly before the Texas energy giant famously collapsed in late 2001.

who quit their jobs because working for an NGO is more profitable – who were evolving into a parallel government beyond the
Palestinian Authority's control. A year earlier, Anis said, the United
Nations launched an investigation into the $10 million in aid ear-
marked to help restructure the Palestinian judiciary.

'It turns out we only received $2 million,' Anis said. 'The rest went
to NGOs. A lot of these groups issued reports and bulletins condemning the Palestinian Authority for being corrupt and abusive of
human rights.'

Anis lowered his voice, embarrassed.

'Arafat was not amused.'

No one really knows how much aid money sloshes about in the
Palestinian Authority. The Italian government once financed a
project to promote West Bank–Italian business ties. Anis found out
about the project only after someone pointed out that the director's
salary consumed half its entire budget.

'I had to go to Rome to ask the programme be cut,' said Anis. 'The
Italians finally did but only after doing their own investigation.'

Back in the West Bank a month later, I checked up on that Japanese
hospital. In 1994, the Palestinian Authority asked donors to refurbish
their medical centres. The Japanese government declared it would
build a brand new $20 million hospital in tiny Jericho. The authority
pleaded with them to build it in Ramallah but the Japanese, believing
Arafat would make Jericho his capital, resisted.

The new hospital opened in 1997 equipped with the latest
Japanese medical equipment – and lots of empty beds. Yet to operate
at full capacity, it remains short of qualified staff.

'There is all this money and no training,' Hassan Barqawi, the hospital director, told me. 'We are trying to establish ourselves as a
regional facility but the running costs are too high.'

From his office window, Hassan had a nice view of the Oasis
casino, which in pre-Intifada days was churning out millions of
dollars a month. I asked if the casino's management ever donated
money to the hospital.

'No,' Hassan said. 'They gave us a photocopier once. It broke.'

What the Japanese did in Jericho the Europeans did in Gaza. In 1994,
the United Nations World Relief Agency announced it would build

a new hospital in Gaza with $45 million in European Commission funding. In 1997, the UN declared the facility completed but the Palestinians wouldn't accept it. The air conditioning wasn't operating, surgical and lab equipment had not yet been ordered, let alone installed, and the place was riddled with termites. The EC agreed to spend another $10 million to finish the hospital and hire an international management team but it took them two years to find one.

When I visited the Gaza hospital in April 2000 the UN, EC and the Palestinians were haggling over who would run it. 'Looking back,' said Gavin Evans, who had just arrived as the European Commission's representative in Jerusalem, 'you could argue it would have been better to upgrade the existing facilities.'

A year later I met Anis 'Al Qaq at The American Colony Hotel in Jerusalem. While still dividing his time between Geneva and Palestine, he was no longer working for Arafat. Anis was vague about this, though I was later informed he had antagonized the Palestinian leader with some annoying questions about how certain funds had been allocated.

Anis was in buoyant spirits. I asked what he was doing now he had quit the government. He told me he had started his own NGO.

The Rorschach Summit
On 25 July 2000, after two weeks of marathon negotiations at the Camp David compound outside Washington DC, the Israeli and Palestinian delegations left without a deal. The most intense bid to end some 80 years of Jewish-Palestinian conflict failed spectacularly. In January 2001, the two sides met again at the Sinai resort town of Taba for a last-ditch attempt to reach a settlement before Bill Clinton, the then-lame duck US president who led the talks, stepped down; again, no success.

It is a measure of the distance separating Israelis and Palestinians that dozens of their most senior leaders could confine themselves in one place for two weeks, hold hundreds of meetings and take reams of notes, spend hours with reporters in post-mortem interviews and still leave the world guessing about what really happened. Ever since the July 2000 Camp David talks collapsed, it has been impossible to determine if Yasser Arafat rejected a deal offered by the then-Israeli prime minister Ehud Barak that almost anyone else would have accepted – thereby setting the stage for the current Intifada – or if no such deal existed.

'Ask Barak, and he might volunteer that there was no offer and, besides, Arafat rejected it,' was how Robert Malley and Hussein Agha put it more than a year later in an article about the summit published by the *New York Review of Books*. 'Ask Arafat, and the response you might hear is that there was no offer; besides, it was unacceptable; that said it had better remain on the table.'

Such ambiguity has turned the Camp David summit into a Rorschach test that validates the fears and suspicions of both sides. For the Israelis it proves that Arafat is not a serious partner for peace; for the Palestinians it is a cautionary tale of how the US and Israel – in lockstep, as ever – conspired to box the Palestinians into an unfair agreement. Such is the confounding, collective dissonance of Middle East diplomacy.*

Maher Masri was a participant at Camp David. He is the Palestinian trade minister and a prominent member of the Masri family, a clan with serious economic and political muscle on both sides of the Jordan River. From their headquarters in Amman and Nablus the Masris control telephone grids, water projects, supermarket chains, real estate holdings, auto dealerships and an investment bank. They are as wealthy and influential as they are respected. In the years I have covered the Middle East I have heard stories of Masri honour and generosity from tycoons to taxi drivers.

The Masris are pro-peace and friendly to the West. If there was one Arab constituency America and Israel need on its side, it is the Masris.

Nearly two years after Camp David I met with Maher at his Amman home. The Israeli invasion of the West Bank was in its third week and he was hoping the siege would end soon so he could return to his office in Ramallah. He hobbled to the door in his stocking feet to greet me; all the excitement, he said, had enflamed a minor case of gout.

We discussed the Israeli invasion and its impact on the already traumatized Palestinian economy. Finally, I asked him about Camp David.

---

* The fault lines even divide officials on the same side; Robert Malley's account of the Camp David summit contrasts markedly with the one constructed by his then-boss, Middle East envoy Dennis Ross.

'It was an ill-planned meeting from the start,' Maher began. 'For some reason the US administration insisted on convening it. Perhaps they thought they could get something by gathering everyone together, some kind of broad agreement.'

'We keep hearing about Barak's big deal,' I asked. 'What specifically did the Israelis put on the table?'

'We talked about refugees, but only in broad terms,' Maher said. 'The Israelis insisted on sovereignty over Jerusalem. As the days progressed the Israelis came up with back-up plans, such as dual sovereignty in certain areas outside the Old City. The Israelis would build a flyover from Abu Dis [a village on the outskirts of Jerusalem] to the Old City so Muslims and Christians could pray at their holy sites.'

The talks shifted to the land issue, according to Maher. At one point the Israelis offered to return 78% of the West Bank and Gaza to the Palestinians in addition to 12% the Palestinians would lease to Israel for twelve years.

This was unacceptable. 'Settlements occupy only 1.2% of the West Bank,' Maher said. 'Why did they need 12% of the land?'

The Palestinians' principle objection, said Maher, was to Israel's insistence on three zones in the West Bank – two in the Jordan Valley and one farther north – where Israel could deploy militarily to meet a conventional threat from a third country, presumably Iraq.

'They would do this with no advance notice,' said Maher. 'At any point they could send tanks across our territory and amass their forces. These three zones would have meant we would never have full sovereignty. They'd be able to criss-cross us with impunity.'

'What about Taba, where they say the real concessions were made?' I asked.

'Even before Taba we were meeting with the Israelis in secret at a West Jerusalem hotel. There were follow-up meetings and revised proposals from what had been discussed at Camp David. On land, the Israelis went from offering 78% to 90% to 94% of the West Bank, swapping 3% of land here for 1% of land there. We met seven times, holding one, two meetings a week.'

Israel's then-foreign minister Shlomo Ben Ami and Arafat aides Saeb Erekat and Mohammad Dahlan led the teams. They discussed things as arcane as ensuring Armenians would have access to their holy sites and which side would have jurisdiction in certain areas over jaywalkers. Solid meetings, Maher said, but nothing conclusive.

'At one point Ben Ami said we could have 100 per cent of the West Bank but then nothing was done. On the contrary, they'd go back on their word. I was in constant touch with those working the security issues. When the Israelis would come back after consulting with Barak they would change their position. On the Old City, Barak suddenly says he wants full sovereignty over the holy sites, from the Al Aqsa Mosque to the Mount of Olives.'

What came at Taba, said Maher, came too late.

'The Israelis said they could not negotiate because of the upcoming election and that was the end of it. But the bottom line is this: even with the best deal the Israelis were insisting on dividing the West Bank into three parts. They even wanted to build three bridges from one to the other. That is independence? They simply do not want us to have a viable state.'

I asked Maher why, as the Palestinian trade minister, he was not involved directly in the follow-up discussions.

'There is nothing to discuss,' he said. 'We have agreed in principle for a free trade zone but there are no details. Nothing on transport of goods, nothing on labour. We disagree on every single issue.'

Maher explained that in the seven years since the peace process began there has never been a meaningful economic pact established between Israel and the Palestinian Authority. The Israelis, he said, have completely ignored the vague commitments on trade and commerce spelled out under Oslo. Both sides are so absorbed with Jerusalem, borders and refugees that economics has been sidelined. This distinguishes Arabs and Israelis from modern history's other famous antagonists like China and Taiwan and even, increasingly, the two Koreas, who have made trade an important basis for the prospect of reconciliation. Not so Israelis and Palestinians.

'The Israelis like the status quo,' Maher said. 'The West Bank is a $1.5 billion-market for them, Gaza is worth $700 million. It's been that way since 1967. They have divided and conquered the market. Why would they want to change?'

Taher, Maher's brother and a former Jordanian prime minister joined us to say hello on his way to a dinner party. There were rumours the Israelis would be pulling out of the West Bank soon, he informed us, but this was no cause for optimism.

'If you create a structure of hate, there will be no peace,' Taher said. 'Believe me, Yasser Arafat cannot control this violence. There will be more suicide bombings. Give it a few days.'

5

Iraq

The Show

In Italy, for 30 years under the Borgias they had terror, murder, and bloodshed, but they produced Michelangelo, Leonardo de Vinci, and the Renaissance. In Switzerland, they had brotherly love. They had 500 years of democracy and peace, and what did that produce? The cuckoo clock.

Orson Welles, 'The Third Man'

By the time Saddam Hussein's understudy emptied an automatic pistol into the air, sending a horde of already ecstatic Iraqis into an ululating rave, the world's press corps had more than paid its way.

The occasion was Saddam's sixty-fifth birthday celebration at Tikrit, the dictator's birthplace. It was 28 April 2002 and the Iraqi image factory had transformed a cast of thousands into raucous political theatre. A swarm of journalists had accepted invitations to the event, if only for a rare sight of one of the world's most opaque, oppressed, and oil-rich countries. This was my fifth visit to Iraq in four years. My earlier visa application and those of other Western journalists submitted since September 11 had been rejected. But with Saddam's birthday only a few weeks away, the Iraqi information ministry went into hyper-drive, flinging entry permits at anyone with a video camera and a shoulder to hoist it on.

We arrived by the plane-full and a week in advance. Film crews dutifully transmitted footage of Iraqis bashing the West and praising Saddam. The Iraqi association of journalists held an anti-American rally outside the old US embassy, under Polish administration since it was abandoned prior to Operation Desert Storm. They harangued the Polish diplomats inside, celebrated Saddam, ate cake and left peacefully.

What the rallies lacked in spontaneity they made up for in numbers. Bands of young men stopped buses at night and paid passengers to attend the next day's events. They carried automatic rifles – with empty magazines, so I was told; no one in their right mind would give street thugs loaded weapons – and a simple message: Show up or else.*

Baghdad was layered in cloth banners extolling Saddam as Iraq's 'Eternal Spring' amid the nuclear winter of America's imperium. 'Lead on Saddam – Quitting is no option', one proclaimed; 'Pride & Triumph', declared another. The Al-Rasheed Hotel lobby featured a display of Saddam portraits designed to appeal to Iraq's key constituencies: Saddam in Palestinian *keffiyeh* (the pan-Arabists), in sheik's gowns (the tribes), kissing the Koran (the Islamists).†

There was a well-attended exhibit of contemporary Iraqi art at the Saddam Art Gallery and a play allegedly from the dictator's pen. Islamic clerics opened a huge mosque with a dome shaped like the helmet of Saladin, the twelfth-century Kurd and Tikrit native who drove the Crusaders from Jerusalem in 1187. Municipal officials unveiled a new statue of Saddam, his right arm cocked in a sweeping gesture of paternal goodwill and framed by a half-circle of stone columns carved in the shape of papyrus reeds.

The *Iraq Daily*, the country's only English-language propaganda sheet, bubbled with poems and paeans to the great leader alongside its usual murky photographs and such evocative human-interest stories as 'Chills Cause Colds, Study Finds' and a six-column treatise on how to cope with bee stings. ('Remove the stinger as quickly as possible [. . .] Get away from the hive.')

In the run-up to the Big Day, each edition of the *Iraq Daily* featured on its front page the following Saddamism:

> The trodden road is not always the best road but it is wise not to neglect it completely.

---

* That is not to say ordinary Iraqis are not armed to the teeth; only days before, tracer bullets from small- arms fire lit up the night sky after the Iraqi national football team won an important match.
† The Saddam personality cult is noteworthy for its populist conceit. He is portrayed with a Leica camera at the Iraqi Photography Association, in Panama hat and pleated, short-sleeved shirt before the tourism ministry and as a chef ladling soup from a saucepan on behalf of the Iraqi Culinary Institute.

Exactly why Saddam said this or what he meant was never spelled
out, leaving journalists with a decryption challenge worthy of China-
watchers during the Cultural Revolution: What, we asked diplomats,
United Nations officials and chambermaids, is the trodden road? If
the road most trodden is not always the best road, why is it well
trodden? And what of the road least trodden? Was Saddam, the
Renaissance Tyrant, revealing himself to be a fan of Robert Frost and
American Transcendentalism?

All of this was a warm-up for the main event in Tikrit, about a two-
hour bus drive from Baghdad for the assembled journalists. Like all
dictators' hometowns, Tikrit is a monument to official largesse, brist-
ling with new public-works projects, sports stadia, government
bureaus and new mosques, each larger and more hideous than the
other. The roster of Iraq's ranking army officers – the country's top
growth industry given its association with a huge smuggling trade – is
top-heavy with Tikritis.

Having reached the parade grounds, we were herded towards a
pavilion facing a strip of tarmac and a reviewing stand. Some of us
mingled with foreign dignitaries and diplomats, others lingered on
the grounds. North Korea, Iraq's partner in the axis of evil, was represented by a reed-thin brigadier-general in red mortar-board epaulettes and slicked hair seated, appropriately enough, next to the
Russian representative – a portly major-general with blue mortar-
board epaulettes and thinning hair. Iran, the other member of the
terror trio, boycotted the celebration, apparently still sore at Baghdad
for starting the Iran-Iraq war in 1980.

In the reviewing stand a band was warming up the crowd with
trumpet blasts and thundering kettledrum rolls. Young girls sang
patriotic songs and waved banners. Helicopter gun-ships buzzed
above. A circle of young men in white gowns and *keffiyehs* performed
traditional tribal jigs. The reviewing stand's lintel featured a mounted
tribal war party on one side and the Dome of the Rock on the other.
At the centre, in high relief, was Saddam's heroic profile. The
message was obvious: Saddam as Saladin, his young charges behind
him, prepared to march on Jerusalem.

By 10 a.m., the Iraqi cabinet had assembled in a stone-and-marble
pulpit to the left of the main pavilion, elevated from hoi polloi and
safe from the kind of terrorist human wave that killed Egypt's Anwar
Sadat in 1981 as he reviewed a military parade. Reporters squinted

for signs of Saddam but were disappointed; though most of the cabinet showed up – Deputy Prime Minister Tarik Aziz was seated alongside an ex-president of Namibia. Saddam assigned as his stand-in Ali Hasan Al Majeed, who in 1988 slaughtered thousands of restive Kurds in the northern city of Halabja with chemical weapons. He has been known ever since as Chemical Ali.

The ceremony began. The cabinet rose in salute as the band played the Iraqi national anthem. Chemical Ali left his perch and descended to the grounds where Tikrit's city fathers presented him with Saddam's birthday present: a diorama depicting a sword-wielding, mounted Iraqi soldier leaping over a Russian T-72 battle tank amid schematic reproductions of Babylon, the Sheik Omar Mausoleum, the Dome of the Rock and two palm trees. It was all done up in gold plate and sealed in a display case.

Chemical Ali, besieged by reporters and film crews, accepted the gift and then turned to Saddam's giant pink-cream and pistachio birthday cake, shaped like a red rose, the symbol of the ruling Ba'ath Party. Cameramen filmed Chemical Ali as he cut the cake, which was then wheeled away from the midday sun and the feral appetite of the working press. We were hungry for the rights to an epic boast – '*I ate Saddam's cake!*' – but were disappointed yet again.

Ali returned to the pulpit and there followed a procession of hundreds of young girls obviously hand-picked for their beauty from the expanse of Saddam's realm. They wore tribal gowns and dresses unique to their provinces – except for one group in the blue gowns and black hoods of Palestinian suicide bombers. Their motion was perfunctory, their expressions blank. I thought of trained seals. In fact, for a country known for Stalinist brio and huge military deployments Saddam's birthday party had all the magnitude and intensity of a local farmers' fair. The brigadier-general from North Korea, the world's leader in mass placard displays, fan dances and human geodesics must surely have been snorting in disapproval.

A human stratum of labour unions, women's groups and trade associations followed the girls. Early in Saddam's reign, these organizations were the most robust and progressive in the Arab world. Now they were fossilized shells in the Ba'ath party's concrete façade. Each group carried banners that identified themselves and congratulated the leader for reaching retirement age.

'Saddam = Our choice!' declared placards, copying 1970s American campaign posters.

'Nixon's the One!' I shouted back, but was drowned out by

ululating virgins and young men chanting: 'Palestine is Arab' and 'By soul, by blood, we praise you O Saddam!'

At one point, a white-robed, sword-wielding fanatic rushed the cameras, preparing what appeared to be some kind of self-mutilation in solidarity with the Palestinians. The crowd, aroused by the prospect of something both violent and spontaneous, egged him on. Chemical Ali seemed to be encouraging the man to sacrifice something, at least a digit or a similar minor extremity, for Saddam, pan-Arabism and the CNN-Al Jazeera complex. But the man was bluffing, and attention returned to the tedious delirium of the parade.

I watched the procession with Hugh Pope, the *Wall Street Journal's* chief Orientalist and roving Middle East correspondent. As Hugh translated the banners (he is fluent in Arabic, Turkish, Farsi, French, and German and can get by in just about everything else), it became clear that secular clans and religious fundamentalist groups dominated the spectacle – a Semitic version, if you will, of Chicago's St Patrick's Day parade.* Saddam's power base, constructed from the ancient, decentralized tribes and religious hierarchy of the *ulema* – the Muslim nation – has supplanted the secular and modernist Ba'ath Party. (Several years earlier Saddam had *Allah Akbar* – God is great – inscribed on the Iraqi flag.) Like most Arab states Iraq is in political and intellectual retrograde, and like most Arab leaders Saddam panders to it.

This was not Hugh's first encounter with a gang of excitable Iraqis. Two decades earlier, as a recent Oxford graduate of Arab studies travelling through Syria, he was nearly deflowered by a herd of Iraqi truck drivers bunking in his hostel in Aleppo.

'Mr Q, Mr Q!' the Iraqis shouted, banging on Hugh's locked door, 'We LOOOOVE you!'

Fortunately for Hugh's chastity, the door held and he made an early escape the next morning.

Now, 20 years later, Hugh was in the ancestral home of Saladin deciphering the cosmic relevance of Saddam's appeal to clerics and tribal sheiks. He suddenly spied a delegation of Sufis. 'I think I'll have to talk to them, maybe plumb the depths of Iraqi fundamentalism at last,' he declared.

Hugh hurled himself into the crowd and was quickly consumed by it. Looking back, I suppose I should have been worried.

---

* Both Syria and Iraq embraced Ba'ath Party socialism but differed over its role as an agent for pan-Arabism. While Damascus believed the Arab world should develop in lockstep, Baghdad insisted each state evolve independently. Syrians of Hafez al Assad's generation consider this a heretical interpretation of party doctrine.

Over two hours later, with the bus nearly filled with journalists anxious to depart, Hugh appeared, sweating, breathless, and agitated as he collapsed into the seat next to me.

'Well,' he began. 'Everything I've ever said about Iraqi men is true.'

Was he threatened? Did they try to kidnap him?

'My *bum*,' Hugh said, 'is black and blue from getting pinched! It was Aleppo all over again. They even said it: "Mr Q, Mr Q, *we love you!*" They were lifting up my jacket from behind to get a better look at my bum!'

The bus shifted into gear and we bumbled back to Baghdad.

That night, a surprisingly underwhelming firework display for a country suspected of developing weapons of mass destruction burst over the Tigris River. Yet the celebrations, for all their oafish choreography, marked a success for the regime. No matter that Saddam himself made no public appearance or that the White House was planning to sweep away Saddam and his family. He had survived another year thumbing his nose at the West, and for the majority of the world's 250 million disillusioned Arabs with a satellite dish, that was enough; the dictator had won a small but not insignificant skirmish in the airwave war.

The next day, with the celebrations over, the cream-and-pistachio cake digested and the gold-plated diorama no doubt melted down, the *Iraq Daily* saluted Saddam's humility. The headline read:

'President Orders to Cancel Birthday Celebrations in Solidarity with People of Palestine'

It pays to have a sense of humour in Iraq.

Of all the Arab states, Iraq is and always will be, The Show.

In American baseball, the Major League is referred to as The Show to distinguish it from the grapefruit, or minor leagues. For the global community of multinationals, merchants and investors, Iraq is The Show, the main event, the big time. Even before the expected US assault on Iraq, foreign investors and businessmen had laid their markers down on what had been and what would one day be again: the Arab world's most vibrant consumer-led economy.

The primacy of the Fertile Crescent was fully appreciated by the Arabs in the ninth century, when Umayyad decadence and corruption in Damascus provoked rebellion in the eastern provinces that ultimately swept them from power. Descendents of Abbas, a member of the Quraysh tribe in Mecca and Mohammad's uncle, prevailed in the ensuing power struggle and moved the caliphal seat to Baghdad. The Abbasids recognized the economic and cultural dividends to be gained from a close association with Persia and its orientation to the markets and technologies of India. After the First World War, the British identified Iraq and its port at Basra as a vital corridor to the Raj and supply base for its new oil-powered fleet when they included it in their mandate.* The Americans wooed Baghdad as its agent in the Iran-Iraq war, one of the last century's bloodiest conflicts and one the few in modern history that pitted a secular nation-state against a theocracy.

Then there is oil. Iraq's reserves are estimated at some 120 billion barrels – 10 per cent of the world's supply – the largest behind Saudi Arabia. Many of Iraq's oil resources, particularly to the south and east of Baghdad, are untapped. Removing sanctions would unleash a torrent of investment that could double the country's proven reserves and production capacity in less than a decade.

'In the north,' Faisel Al Shahin, an Iraqi vice minister of oil once told me, 'we find oil in lakes.'

Iraq is no Cuba or North Korea – countries with small populations and nothing to offer the world in their current dilapidated state beyond sugar cane and ginseng. Iraq is a real market with vital resources; like a beach ball, it cannot be submerged. Iraqi assets are too vast to be isolated, its people too proud and resilient to subdue. The US may succeed in removing Saddam by force and the Iraqi people may even hail American GIs as liberators. But any attempt to impose on them a regime associated too closely with the US and its interests – increasingly, Iraqis identify this as Israel – would be rejected like a deficient donor-organ.

Ordinary Iraqis dismiss Ahmad Chalabi, the Pentagon's leading candidate among a US-backed cabal of exiled Iraqis to lead a post-Saddam Iraq, as a western stooge if they know him at all. Like the Egyptians with the Suez Canal, Iraqis are no strangers to great-power intrigue and would rather be governed poorly by their own government than well by a foreign contrivance.

Iraqi history is a relentless cycle of rehabilitation and vitality

---

* The United Kingdom declared at the 1921 Cairo Conference its 'mandate' to administer Palestine, Trans-Jordan and Iraq. It did this with the approval of the League of Nations Council but not of the people to be administered.

followed by violence and destruction. The grandeur of ancient Babylon was brought down by Alexander the Great in 330 BC. The enlightened domain of Caliph Harun Al Rashid in the late eighth century was consumed by civil war waged between his sons – one born of Harun's Arab wife, the other by his Persian concubine in an eerie precursor to the Iran-Iraq war. The cosmopolitan, modern Iraq built by oil wealth in the second half of the last century was bludgeoned by twenty years of war and sanctions.

The Iraqis are the Texans of the Arabs. In a region known for subtlety, Iraqis swagger. Size has always mattered in Iraq, from the Tower of Babel to Babylon's Hanging Gardens to the grand edifices of modern pre-sanctions Baghdad. The Iraqis are as big in generosity as they are in brutality, and the current generation of Iraqi tyranny is of suitably outsized proportion. Amman's biggest, most grandiose hotel, designed like the great minaret at Samara outside Baghdad, was built largely as a money-laundering scheme and financed by an Iraqi speculator who lives in Europe. Every so often, Saddam's sons ask the speculator for money. On the one occasion he didn't stump up, his brother living in Jordan was murdered.

Extremes of suffering and achievement inform and harden the Iraqi character. Any Iraqi born in the 1950s knows his country once represented something other Arab states aspired to – a prosperous, diversified economy with a large middle class. He also knows he has Saddam Hussein to thank for much of it; just as Saddam was the wrecking ball of modern Iraq, he was also its engineer. In the Iraqis' battered consciousness, Saddam is just another tragically flawed Arab leader who destroyed what he built and the US is just another superpower having its way with the region. Both will pass. The Fertile Crescent, with Baghdad as its heart and the Tigris and Euphrates rivers as its arteries, is eternal.

Until two years ago the only way to enter Iraq was by a 12-hour drive from Jordan, traversing some of the world's most forbidding desert valleys and escarpments. Drivers occasionally fell asleep during the journey, sometimes with lethal consequences. The Iraq-Jordan border compound comprises a sprawl of corrugated steel huts in the middle of nowhere, with visitors hustled into each one for tea and a shakedown. Immigration officials palm $20 or so for stamping passports, customs authorities another $10 to $15 for potentially subversive items foreigners are bringing into the country – a satellite phone perhaps, or a bottle of Scotch. Another $50 or so buys foreigners out of an AIDs test that may or may not utilize a clean needle. (Visitors are advised to bring their own syringe.)

Extortion thrives on war. Whenever a US bombing raid on Baghdad seems imminent, security officials bribe their way to the border anticipating the ritual fleecing of deep-pocketed journalists.* With the introduction of chartered flights to Baghdad I assumed the Baksheesh Welcome Wagon had run its course. Plundering foreigners at a border hundreds of miles from anywhere is one thing; demanding bribes at an international gateway like Saddam International Airport is quite another.

I was wrong. As Saddam's birthday neared, the border sharks converged on the airport's arrival lobby where they corralled journalists into a warren of offices and relieved us of their sundry commissions. It is for the uninitiated a telling introduction to sanction-era Iraq, where blackmail and bribery lubricate an ossified civil society.

A pestilent haze due in part to the over-aged vehicles that choke its roads and highways afflicts Baghdad. Lacking quality construction materials, most sanctions-era buildings are made of bricks formed from the yellow mud of the Tigris, giving the city a sallow, sickly pallor. Yet behind this gloomy façade, Iraq – in a typically perverse Middle Eastern way – has become one of the most dynamic of Arab economies. Despite more than a decade of sanctions, there is more buying and selling in Iraq than in neighbouring Jordan or Syria.

During a lull in Operation Desert Fox, the Anglo-American bombing campaign against Iraq in December 1998, I visited the Baghdad Stock Exchange, a compound of small, concrete and stucco blockhouses.† Expecting a veritable morgue, I found instead a hectic trading floor, with brokers taking orders from a mob of investors huddled behind a metal guard rail that separated them from the wall of white boards that listed the dozens of publicly traded Iraqi companies and the bid/offer prices for their shares, updated by dealers with erasable ink markers. It was a noisy showcase for the surreal warp between the dramatic video images of Desert Fox as they were

---

* Such outlays would appear on my expense reports as 'emoluments'.
† Operation Desert Fox, the largest air bombardment since the 1991 Gulf War, was launched in response to Saddam's obstruction of UN weapons inspectors. It was widely interpreted in the Arab world – and in parts of the West – as a pyrotechnic display staged to distract Americans from the Monica Lewinsky scandal menacing then-President Clinton.

beamed around the world, and the mundane if chaotic reality at ground zero. Even as cruise missiles were raining down on Iraq during the four-day operation, there were shares to be traded.

It was there I met punter Abdullah Mohammad, a 54-year-old lawyer who had just cashed in the bulk of his shares in Albadia Company, an oil refinery, for a cool return of about ID20,000 (20,000 Iraqi dinars), or about $12 at the then-black market exchange rate. That's about the same amount Abdullah made every month in legal fees, which was why he was spending so much of his free time trading stocks.

'I could have made more,' Abdullah told me. 'But prices have been sluggish recently.'

No doubt due to the political risk associated with the bombing, I offered.

'Not really,' Abdullah said. 'It's the end of the year, and a lot of companies are closing for Ramadan [the Muslim holy month].'

The Baghdad Stock Exchange was established in 1992 as part of Saddam's drive to boost the private sector. The 100 or so listed companies were once wholly state owned, but the government has sold down its collective stake to about 25 per cent of their boards' capital base. Any Iraqi company with a capitalization of ID500,000 and a year's profit can register on the market, according to exchange bylaws. In a good session, turnover hovers between ID200,000 and ID300,000.

'This is the beginning of Iraq's private sector,' Baghdad Stock Exchange Director General Sabih H. Al Dulaimi told me. 'We have computers and everything.'

On any given trading day, between 200 to 300 stockbrokers and direct investors would gather behind the guard rail and gesture to dealers, who took down orders and jotted down the names of buyers and sellers. During Desert Storm the hot stock was Baghdad Soft Drink Company, which was trading at ID60 a share, up from ID58 when Desert Fox commenced.

I met Hythan Medhat, a stockbroker who purchased 25,000 shares of Baghdad Soft Drink on behalf of certain high net-worth individuals he would not identify. He wore a flecked burgundy blazer and carried a vinyl clutch bag. 'It's a good price,' Hythan said of Baghdad Soft Drink's shares. 'After the downturn last week, I think it will have a good run.'

Is the stock attractive on a price–earnings basis?*

---

* The price-earnings ratio is calculated by dividing the price of a share by its earnings, providing an indication of its value.

'It's a popular company because it employs a lot of people,' Hythan shouted above the din of fresh orders.

How about return on equity?

'Everyone likes soft drinks.'

Strong balance sheet?

'It's owned by a rich Iraqi businessman.'

Hythan was also touting Modern Paint Company and National Chemicals & Industrial Plastic Company, two 'sanction plays' that would be among the first to lure foreign investment once sanctions were lifted. 'They have good assets,' he said. 'They were developed in the 1970s and they would be the first to benefit.'

Hythan was trading through dealer Mazen Azizi, who like the other 50 dealers in the Baghdad pits got his license after taking a two-week course. They made a 1% commission on the value of each confirmed trade recorded, he told me.

'We learned how to buy low and sell high,' Mazen said. 'We have to move on instinct or else we'll miss the trade.'

Mazen acknowledged a broker waving his arms frantically behind the guardrail as he peered through a pair of mini-binoculars. It was another order for Baghdad Soft Drink.

He filled out a ticket and handed it to Subhi Azawi, the exchange's 40-year-old head dealer, who had a master's degree in securities trading from a local university and helped pioneer Iraq's security industry. 'I helped to build this market,' he told me. 'I'm an important part of Baghdad's private sector.'

A dealer jammed a written order into Mr Azawi's hand: 10,000 shares in brewer Baghdad Alcohol Company at ID21 a share. Mr Azawi initialled it and passed it to a runner, who deposited it at the counter of the exchange's clearing room, where one of the four women manning it entered the details into a bank of computers.

On my way out of the exchange I re-encountered Abdullah, who was wondering how he would reinvest the day's profit. The index of banking shares had just had an impressive spurt – up 2.12% on the day, and was looking expensive. Agriculture stocks continued to underperform the broad index, rising only 0.45%, though Abdullah was not counting on an agri-business rally just yet.

Finally, Abdullah decided to wait for an opportunity to pile back into Albadia, which he sensed was due for a correction. 'It's the cycle of things,' he says. 'Our stock prices rise and fall. We're no different from America.'

*

Iraq's annual trade fairs get larger each year. European and Asian governments have opened de-facto embassies euphemistically called 'commercial offices' or 'special-interests sections' out of mock respect to the sanctions regime. Showrooms display the latest kitchen appliances and electronic shops carry the latest video games and DVD players. New cars – BMWs and Mercedes as well as economy cars from Malaysia – are slowly replacing corroded, pre-Gulf War automobiles.

Iraq, isolated and closed, may be a rogue state: not so its economy. Long before the White House began pounding the war drum for an invasion of Iraq, the world came to Baghdad, hard currency in hand. Saddam, in his Orwellian ubiquity, controls every deal and transaction.

In this regard at least, the dictator is winning. And in the zero-sum calculus of the Middle East, that means the US and Britain are losing.

For much of the last decade, the most popular items on sale in the old market district of downtown Baghdad was the patrimony of Iraq's depleted middle class – candle sticks, watches, army compasses, cigarette lighters. Now these goods have given way to bootleg copies of American movies and music, the kind of wares routinely sniffed at by the European culture snobs but which no developing economy can resist. The entire spectrum of western pop culture is represented here on CD and DVD and stacked in grimy glass cases: Shanya Twain and the Spice Girls, *Black Hawk Down* and *The Time Machine*. Each disk, with crudely labelled, plastic slipcovers, costs the equivalent of $3 a copy.

Against the backdrop of Saddam's birthday hoopla, Hugh Pope and I entered the market in search of some authentic Arab-in-Suk insight. This is not as easy as it sounds. Upon arrival in Iraq, all foreign correspondents should register their names, organizations and satellite phones at the information ministry and be assigned a minder. Officially an interpreter and facilitator, he is really a petty spy under instructions to frustrate his designated journalist. The minder then drafts a report on the day's inactivity for an equally petty spy who may or may not read it before filing it into the vast slagheap of make-work intelligence gathering.

Not surprisingly, the presence of a minder makes vox populi an elusive quarry. During Desert Fox, I attempted some man-on-the-street interviews, minder in tow.* In a coffee house thick with blue smoke from unfiltered cigarettes and water pipes, my minder introduced me to two men who spoke perfect English. I asked them what they thought of the bombing and by the time we got to 'Our great father, Saddam Hussein' the minder's attention had drifted. At this point, one of the men predicted Special Prosecutor Kenneth Starr would indict Bill Clinton, then under pressure for his affair with Monica Lewinsky, and that Senate Majority Leader Trent Lott would lead the Republican Party to a successful impeachment of the president.

'How do you know about Trent Lott?' I asked.

The man gestured to the preoccupied minder, winked to me and whispered: 'We listen to BBC every night.'

So it was with a sense of great liberation that I accompanied the Arabic-enabled Mr Q as we penetrated the market minder-free. Soon, a 32-year-old shop owner greeted us warmly. He sold old Soviet-made cameras alongside used DVD players, but pirated films and music provided his cash flow. He offered us tea, coffee – 'whatever you like' – as we leaned over a glass display case. A curious crowd gathered – including a few Nubians, most probably refugees from Sudan's civil war – though I wasn't sure if they were interested in us or the bootlegged copies of rock videos on the nearby television monitor.

The shop owner had five children. They were not afraid of American air raids, he told us, and – in unwitting tribute to Raytheon Corp.'s guidance systems – even climbed to the roof of their apartment building to watch the government ministries explode.† He said that business was better because of the United Nation's oil-for-food programme, but only like a drip feed for a sick man. Before the Gulf War, he was studying for a degree in petroleum engineering. In 1991 he had to quit school to take care of his family. His second job was teaching Arab literature.

---

* In the aftermath of Desert Fox, I pointed to a freshly demolished building and asked my minder what it was. He demurred, and when I persisted explained it was a commercial office complex. I later found out the building was the Iraqi Ministry of Defence. Left unanswered was how one could jeopardize Iraq's national security by identifying a building that had already been located and destroyed several times by American cruise missiles.
† During Operation Desert Fox, an Iraqi swore to me he witnessed a U.S. Tomahawk missile cruising through downtown Baghdad at street level and stopping for a red light before resuming its attack.

'Do you feel less isolated as sanctions erode?' Hugh asked.

'You can get a satellite dish with a licence,' the shop owner said. 'This is hard, but even if it was easy we would not allow all Western culture into Iraq. We are a conservative people – rich, poor, it makes no difference. There would never be Western pornography here, for example.'

The television featured a video of MTV's latest peroxide Lolita, grinding her way in wet leather to Next-Big-Tartdom.

Hugh pressed. 'What did you think of the terrorist attacks on the US?'

'We were glad,' the shop owner said. 'Do you know how many Iraqis have been killed because of the sanctions?* America is the mother of all terrorists and Israel is her child. Was not Jenin a form of terror?'

Had the shop owner ever heard of Ahmad Chalabi?

'He's a puppet,' the shop owner replied. 'All the opposition leaders are puppets of the Americans and Israel.'

Iraqis occasionally speak fondly of the British Mandate while simultaneously condemning the United States for its alleged imperialist designs in the Middle East. This is not a contradiction. The end of the mandate in 1932 came well before the creation of Israel and the wars that followed. The first years of independence were relatively peaceful and the Second World War affected the Maghrebi Arabs more than the Levantine ones. The economy was stable and Baghdad modern and cosmopolitan for its time. Urbanization was years away from turning Iraqi cities into steamy conurbations.

Iraqis also yearn for the multi-polarity of the mandate days, when small but strategically important countries like Iraq could leverage their influence by playing one global power against another. Having seen Haj Amin al Husseini go over to the Nazis and with growing violence in Palestine feeding popular support of Germany, the British were increasingly attentive to the Iraqis and their strategic assets. London replaced the mandate in Iraq with a treaty of alliance as early as October 1922 and the country enjoyed greater autonomy than other Arab states under British occupation. In 1955, Britain invited

---

* Quantifying the human costs of the U.N. embargo is difficult. Baghdad estimates a million people have died from sanctions-related causes. Several years ago, questioned on the morality behind a policy that has led to the deaths of 500,000 children, then-U.S. Secretary of State Madeleine Albright said sanctions were 'worth the price'.

Iraq to join a defence pact established to contain the Soviet Union and in exchange gave Baghdad control of its Iraqi air bases.

Today, countries like Iraq can no longer indulge in great-power games. This is a dilemma for Arab leaders but especially so for men like Ahmad Chalabi who would challenge them. It is bad enough they require the patronage of the world's only superpower; even worse when that same superpower is so deeply unpopular with the people they aspire to lead.

Ahmad Chalabi, the leader of the Iraqi National Congress (INC), is a designer-suited metaphor for the paradox of America's ambition to remove Saddam Hussein. According to Chalabi and his acolytes, INC forces nearly toppled Saddam in March 1995 when it destroyed two Iraqi infantry brigades and took a thousand prisoners. Just over a year later, Saddam retaliated against the INC's bases near the Kurdish north and the two sides fought savagely for 15 hours. When it became clear the Americans would not provide air support, the INC was forced to flee. Many INC officers were executed but its rump leadership escaped through Kurdish territory to Turkey, Syria and Iran.

An MIT-educated mathematician, Chalabi is undeniably talented. Even his numerous detractors call him brilliant. He has kept a dissonant cluster of Iraqi opposition groups – Sunnis, Shiites, Kurds, royalists, democrats, socialists – in favour with important sponsors in Washington. Using intellect, charm, and marketing skills he has persuaded Congress to fund the INC despite allegations of corruption and ineptitude within its ranks. The bills Congress hasn't paid Chalabi has covered with his personal fortune.

Chalabi is a scorched-earth personality, engendering either loyal support or fierce mistrust. People I respect and who agree on many things diverge sharply over Ahmad Chalabi. Chibli Mallat, a Lebanese human rights lawyer and an astute reader of men calls Chalabi 'the best alternative' to the rogues' gallery of would-be Saddam usurpers. An American woman I know, an analyst with a finely nuanced understanding of Iraq and the Arab world calls Chalabi 'a total opportunist, someone who knows how to make a quick buck and recognized an opening to become leader of the opposition'.

All of this is white noise in the Beltway echo chamber. No matter how dedicated Ahmad Chalabi is to liberating Iraq, what has kept the INC alive – America's imprimatur – virtually nullifies him as a legitimate leader of the Iraqi people. The closer an oppositionist to the

United States the less likely the Iraqis are to embrace him, so deeply has Washington managed to burrow its way into the popular contempt.

Iraqis know Saddam is a thug, a sadist, and a killer.* But outrage at US policies has, like a magnet, so distorted their emotional compass that even the path trodden by a dictator seems worth taking, so long as it faces 'the aggressor'.

The Smuggler's Republic

As with other Arab states, Iraq has a Yin-and-Yang economy. The formal one is built around the 'oil-for-food' programme or 'MOU', for the Memorandum of Understanding between Iraq and the UN that provided for it. This allows Iraq to sell as much oil as it chooses to buy UN-approved civilian goods. The programme is divided into 180-day cycles, during which Baghdad may sell as much as $5 billion worth of crude.

The US hopes this will assist the Iraqi people while preventing Saddam acquiring materials for his conventional and non-conventional war machine. Its record is mixed. The funds generated by the oil-for-food trade, while considerable, are only a fraction of those needed to rehabilitate Iraqi society. As one UN employee told me: 'What good is medicine if you have to take it with dirty water?'

A $5 billion market is a $5 billion market, however, and everybody wants in. In Cairo I once met with George A. Youssef, the chairman of the Luna Group, an Egyptian lotion and soap conglomerate which make products for companies like Procter & Gamble and Unilever. It also sells Iraq raw materials and packaging for pharmaceuticals under the MOU trade.

I asked George how things were going.

'Very bad,' he replied, collapsing into a threadbare easy chair. He then delivered his version of what I call the MOU Lament. It seemed the European custodian bank that settles oil-for-food transactions was withholding funds owed Luna going back several months.

'When we get an order under MOU,' George said, 'we have to furnish the bank with letters of credit, bills of lading and confirmation of delivery. They then take three to four months to settle

---

* Saddam's sons, Uday and Qusay, are no better. Uday once murdered his father's most trusted bodyguard and has a reputation for pulling up at street corners in his red Rolls Royce and inviting women to be his companions for the evening. (Polite rejection, needless to say, is not an option.) With Uday too impetuous to rule, Saddam is widely thought to be grooming Qusay as his successor.

payment, if they do it at all. We complained about this in New York in February – Egypt, China, Japan, Russia, Thailand, Malaysia. There are billions of dollars at stake. It is a European conspiracy against everyone else.'

Every businessman and trader I know who participates in the MOU programme complains about the bureaucracy involved. If the bank isn't dragging its feet on settlement, the UN sanctions committee that vets Iraq's applications for goods is capricious and draconian. The committee, which some businessmen say is heavily American-influenced, checks for possible leakage into Iraq of any items that could have a non-civilian application. Labib Kamhawi, my Jordanian friend, made a decent living from selling medical equipment and service vehicles to Iraq until the sanctions committee tightened restrictions. His most recent application to sell fire trucks to Iraq was rejected without explanation, though he had been selling such vehicles to the Iraqis for years.

Yet still the businessmen come. No matter how bureaucratic or discriminatory or politicized it is to trade with Iraq, they cannot ignore an economy with 22 million people and the world's second-largest oil reserves. It all resembles the fanatical will of businessmen who, seduced by China's 1.2 billion consumers, make for its ports despite shoals of red tape and eddies of corruption.

In Iraq, the MOU trade has turned a once-great white-collar class into a subculture of agents, brokers and godfathers. Using Iraqi government contacts, a merchant will anticipate a major MOU order and strike deals with foreign distributors for the right product at the best price. The agriculture ministry, for example, may budget several million dollars for a new irrigation system. A resourceful agent, getting wind of this, will set up an order of pipes and water pumps with a German company. He then approaches a godfather, usually a senior military officer, to pimp the ministry on his behalf. If the deal goes through, the agent can expect a commission worth tens of thousands of dollars, over half of which may go to the godfather.

This is the *legal* side of the Iraqi economy.

The illegal side – as defined by the US and Britain – is the smuggling trade. Its main artery runs through the Turkish-Iraqi border crossing at Zakho in northern Iraq, where an ethnic Kurdish population enjoys an informal autonomy and profits handsomely from it. This has continued for so long and has become so enormous that few

Iraqis consider it smuggling. It is worth billions of dollars and trickles down from the elite who control it – Saddam, Kurdish kingpins, and Turkish generals – to a new bourgeoisie the Iraqis call the *Intiha'ah al Basebis*, or 'embargo cats'. Saddam alone is thought to make an estimated $2 billion from the trade each year.

When I visited the Zakho crossing for a story on the Kurds, Iraqi trucks rigged to carry crude oil were lined up for miles facing north and matched by Turkish trucks heading south and loaded with every manner of consumer good, appliance and luxury item. The head of customs at the time was a Kurd named Abdullah Raheem. His building was being renovated – the lobby floor covered with shiny granite tile and the walls trimmed with aluminium moulding.

'Isn't this entire trade illegal?' I asked Abdullah over tea.

Abdullah clearly thought my question ridiculous. 'It's no secret,' he replied. 'Everyone sees it. If volume reaches a certain point the United Nations intervenes. But that's rare. This is the main resource of the Kurdish economy. We have no factories. This is it.'

It is perhaps the world's largest contraband racket and the US tolerates it for three reasons: First, it keeps the habitually fractious Kurds happy and any campaign to remove Saddam will require their support. Second, it softens the impact of sanctions on the Turks, whose annual two-way trade with Iraq was once worth some $2.5 billion. For this, the US gets unrestricted access to Turkey's Incirlik airbase, from which American jets raid Iraqi radar installations and other military sites. Third, Washington can't do much to stop the smuggling trade even if it wanted to.

Taken together, the US-led sanctions and air raids amount to a policy double-negative; the former has enriched Saddam with the money he needs to buy support, the latter enhances his credibility on the Arab street for hanging tough against US aggression. So profoundly ineffective is America's Iraq policy that many Arabs are convinced the Pentagon wants to keep Saddam in power to justify its $380 billion defence budget. This is not as strange as it sounds; because the Arabs don't understand Washington, they tend to give it too much credit for foresight.

'Saddam controls everything,' a senior diplomat told me over dinner in Baghdad's increasingly upscale Masbat district. 'He takes a slice of every business deal. He runs the restaurants and boutiques you see on this street. He completely controls the smuggling trade.'

Some of Saddam's take finances a vast patronage network. For the Islamists he builds mosques, most recently the 'Mother of All

Martyrs' mosque a few kilometres from the airport. With minarets
resembling Scud missiles, it has all the pious dignity of a NASA test
site; to burnish his pan-Arab credentials, Saddam sends thousands of
dollars to the families of Palestinian suicide bombers and victims of
Israeli aggression. He donated $2,500 to each household destroyed in
Jenin and 1 million Euros to the Palestinian Authority's education
ministry after it was ransacked by Israeli troops in Ramallah.

Saddam, however, focuses principally on the secular tribes. Like
Jordan, Iraq was settled centuries ago by clans from today's Yemen
and Saudi Arabia seeking water and a cooler climate. Though much
of Iraq is urbanized, tribal sensibility still informs Iraqi culture. The
tradition of Bedouin hospitality is carefully observed as is the eye-for-
an-eye, Old Testament justice that predates Islam. In the 630s, when
the early Muslims were beginning to expand beyond Arabia, the
Byzantine emperor Heraclius cut subsidies to the Christian tribes of
Syria to cover debts incurred in his wars with the Persians. The tribes
responded by allying with the Muslims in their push against the
Byzantines into the central Levant.

Then, as now, rulers neglected the tribes at their peril. 'If anything
happens to one tribe member the whole tribe rises up,' Sami Alzara
Al Hajem, a dissident sheik of the Bani Hajam told me in London.
'That's why the state doesn't like to mix it up with us.'

The tribes hate Saddam because their sons died in his wars,
Alzara said. Ordinary Iraqis rebelled against Saddam immediately
after Desert Storm largely as tribes lusting to settle old scores, though
larger tribes loyal to Saddam crushed them.

Because sanctions have degraded both the government's ability to
provide basic services and the army's capacity to patrol the frontiers,
Saddam uses tribal sheiks to keep the population in line. This alliance
of convenience is expressed in the proliferation of road-signs along
the country's desolate highways: 'Territory of the Al Dulaimi Tribe'
reads one posted en route to Mosul. 'A sword in the Hands of the
Leader.'

'This signals a 180-degree turn from the modern Ba'ath party,' a
French diplomat once told me. 'It is physical evidence of the revival
of the tribe and is becoming very conspicuous. The elites are complaining of a return to the middle ages.'

In exchange for loyalty Saddam ladles favours and concessions in
various forms. Tribal communities get schools and roads and the sons
of prominent tribal elders attend university in Baghdad. He invites
sheiks to his palaces for elaborate dinners. The meetings are broadcast

on state television and give the tribal leaders and their people face.

So pronounced is the resurgence of tribal influence over the last few years, that it has become fashionable for young Iraqis to flaunt their tribal identity, particularly those from powerful ones like the Al Dulaimi and Al Jabur to the northwest, or the Al Izraj and Beni Tamin in the south. This would have been unthinkable two decades ago when Iraq's large and growing white-collar class haughtily dismissed the tribal code as backward. Today, obeisance to an often illiterate sheik is the only way to get things done.

'I have an Iraqi friend who is very cosmopolitan,' a Western businessman told me in Baghdad. 'He decided to return to Iraq fifteen years ago. Something went wrong with his flat and he had a dispute with the landlord. They went to the police and the courts, but nothing worked. Then he remembered he had a friend who was a tribal sheik. So they went to see him and in two days the problem was solved.'

Some sheiks are less powerful than others. Take Bassem Abed Al Shammar, a lesser sheik of the Al Shammar tribe, who lived in a modest home with several generations of family members. Bassem made a living driving journalists and businessmen between Amman and Baghdad in a huge General Motors SUV and administers to some 500 members of the two-million strong Al Shammar tribe. He proudly showed me the Al Shammar family tree, hand drawn on a centuries-old, tattered parchment. The clans and sub-clans that constituted the Al Shammar thrived before Islam, Bassem told me. Once Iraq's strongest tribe, over the years it has lost much of its influence.

Though relatively minor in his authority, Bassem was an 'original' sheik who inherited his position through blood. Occasionally, he said, Saddam appoints a 'shadow sheik', endowing him with money and influence to undermine the real sheik's authority and weaken the tribe. This divide-and-rule tactic goes back to the Ottoman Turks.

'The state does what it can to manage us,' Bassem said as lizards shuffled across his living room walls. 'It will try to divide a tribe and make it less powerful or make one tribe stronger than the other. But since the 1991 war the government needs all the sheiks. Otherwise, it cannot control the people.'

As we parted, Bassem strongly recommended I meet Sheik Rashid Abdula Salem Al Jabur, a prominent elder of the powerful Al Jabur.

'Sheik Rashid is a big original sheik,' Bassem said. 'He has many cars and wives. Saddam knows he is a real power.'

*

A few days later, sadly tethered to the unavoidable minder, I called on Sheik Rashid. We waited for him in the *diwan* of his villa, built in 1953 on a date-palm and orange grove. A 1970s Chevy Impala was parked in the driveway outside. Two enormous Oriental rugs covered the floor and on the walls hung oil portraits and photographs of Sheik Rashid's ancestors, sheiks and farmers all. The centrepiece of a long table in the middle of the room was a porcelain decanter shaped like a horse and adorned with the White Horse-scotch label.*

The doors to Sheik Rashid's villa are never closed, symbolizing such an important leader's power, authority, and hospitality. Adjacent to the main villa was a large guesthouse where any Jaburi could stay for three days before the sheik was permitted to ask why he had come. Under tribal law, the sheik and his family would be obligated to furnish the guest with food and drink during the three-day period even if it meant going hungry themselves.†

Sheik Rashid finally arrived dressed in a check-brown *dishdasha*, a white silk *keffiyeh*, a bamboo walking stick, worn shoes, and tattered, rag-wool gloves. His thick black moustache had white roots. He received me with a studied courtesy and seemed mildly suspicious; what, I could hear him thinking, does a foreign journalist want with the Al Jabur?

Sheik Rashid gave me a tour of the grounds. It was a hot April afternoon and the date palms shaded us generously as we walked. The Al Jabur migrated 'to the land of Shem' from the Arabian Peninsula centuries ago, Sheik Rashid said; his own bloodline dates back 18 generations.‡ He became sheik in 1990 aged 45 when his father abdicated due to old age. He is responsible for some 20,000 Jaburis scattered throughout the country, though mostly in the cities of Mosul, Kirkuk, Baghdad, Ramadi and Waset.

After spending each morning tending to the groves, Sheik Rashid boards his Chevy Impala and travels in a four or five vehicle caravan

---

* This is a central paradox of the Arabs; the same people who brought us the kilim, the Great Mosque at Cordoba, Damascene mosaic and Persian lustreware have a weakness for kitsch.

† According to another Bedouin custom, any foreigner who touches the flap of a family's tent must be feted as a welcome guest for several days, regardless of his tribe.

‡ In the Old Testament, Shem is the eldest son of Noah and uncle of Canaan. Among his descendants are thought to be the Hebrews, the Arabs and the Aramaeans. It is widely believed the word 'Semite' is derived from his name and Arabs thus resent the term 'anti-Semitic' when applied exclusively to Jews. However, others trace the word Semitic to a German scholar of the late eighteenth century, who coined the term to designate a group of languages with common roots, such as Hebrew, Arabic and Ge'ez, the ancient language of Ethiopia. Because of this, they regard any reference to Middle Eastern peoples as 'Semitic' as simplistic and misleading.

to meet the leaders and families of the Al Jabur clans. He mediates disputes ranging from petty theft to murder. On particularly import- ant issues, he may consult a government official appointed to work with the Al Jabur.

I asked Sheik Rashid why the tribes are so important in Iraq.

'The government's problems have been transferred to us,' he said. 'The people are poor and need help and they come to me. Before, when a young man wanted to marry he could buy his own house and leave his family. Now, he and his wife stay with the family and that leads to problems. The tribes are stronger now and more concentrated.'

On Friday, the sheik would be in Dialla to discuss the killing of a Bani Said by the hand of a Jaburi. Leaders from both sides would sit down opposite one another in the middle of a *diwan* with family members of both victim and assailant seated along the wall behind them. The sheiks would decide who was responsible and negotiate a *fasal*, or settlement. Typically, this would include money, possibly millions of dinar, and perhaps the marriage of a prominent Bani Said male to an Al Jabur female. Only then could a blood feud be averted.

I asked Sheik Rashid about his relationship with the government. If an Al Jabur village needs a new school, hospital equipment, or electricity, he told me, it contacts him and he contacts the govern- ment. Last year an Al Jabur community held a foundation-laying cer- emony for a new library and Saddam attended.* When Sheik Rashid's father died not long afterward, Saddam sent a delegation to the funeral.

I asked Sheik Rashid if he had ever known the government to appoint its own sheik to the Al Jabur.

'*Appointed* sheiks?' Sheik Rashid asked.

I repeated the question, which annoyed him.

'That doesn't happen,' said Sheik Rashid. 'The government can't appoint anyone. Only *original* sheiks command the respect of the tribe.'

The Big Tease

Tyranny is nothing new to Iraq. Al Mansur, the first and greatest of the Abbasid caliphs, once threatened to behead the rightful heir to

---

* For security reasons Saddam usually deploys look-alikes at public functions. I once interviewed an Iraqi civil servant in his office in Basra. The official was called away briefly and I inspected photos on his desk of a ceremony where 'Saddam' was the guest of honour. Though the man was clearly a stand-in, the assembled civil servants, journalists and citizenry played along with the charade.

his throne to secure the succession for his son. Harun Al Rashid, who ruled as caliph for 23 years beginning in the late eighth-century, tried to conceal a homosexual affair by marrying his lover to his sister, Abbasa. When the imposed union unexpectedly produced a son, Harun in a jealous fit had Abbasa and the child strangled and his lover beheaded.

Yet historians are kind to men like Al Mansur and Harun al Rashid because they were visionaries who built great societies. Under the Abbasids the Islamic empire evolved from a chauvinistic, parochial realm administered by and for Arabs into a global faith with a strong Persian influence. Al Mansur summoned the region's greatest crafts-men to build a vast city – *Medinat al-Salaam* – 'the City of Peace' later known as Baghdad. It attracted the greatest physicians and engineers of the era, though they were required to pass a stiff examination before advertising their services on the city's thick double walls. Baghdad boasted 27 public baths at a time when Europeans regarded bathing as unhealthy. Agriculture, once considered beneath Arab dignity, boomed under a growing Persian bureaucracy. Iraq became the heart of a regional canal system that nurtured crops unknown to Europe until centuries later, such as oranges, sugar cane and water-melons.

Religious tolerance thrived and Baghdad became the cultural centre for the three monotheistic faiths. The largest of Baghdad's 28 synagogues had columns of various colours overlaid with silver and gold and verses from the Psalms in gold letters. According to the twelfth-century Jewish scholar Benjamin of Tudela, Iraq's 40,000 Jews 'dwell in security, prosperity and honour under the great Caliph.' Every five days, wrote Tudela, the spiritual leader of the Jews would meet with the caliph and the two men would sit together in a special throne.

Commerce flourished. The wharves at Basra hosted ships that carried silks, potions, dyes, spices, furs and textiles from China and India. Basran merchants could make the equivalent of $100,000 a year. Syria exported its glass products and Samarkand its paper from Canton to Cordoba. The emerging Islamic bourgeoisie embraced popular pastimes like chess and polo, imported from India and Persia respectively. Also from India was to come an arithmetical system that Abbasid Islam would adopt and use to pioneer algebra. The counting system – today's Arabic numerals – would be re-exported to Europe in the thirteenth century by an Italian, Leonardo Fibonacci, who studied in North Africa under a Muslim teacher.

All of this was done on a strict budget. A fiscal conservative, Al Mansur balanced the empire's books and earned the nickname 'father of farthings'. By the time Harun al Rashid assumed control 32 years later in 786, the Abbasid Empire was powerful and rich enough to rival Carolingian Europe. Even Charlemagne had sufficient regard for the Arab-Persian combine to exchange envoys with the Abbasids.

By the eleventh century, corruption had so diminished the Abbasids that they became easy prey to greater powers, beginning with the Seljuk Turks. In 1258 Hulegu, the Mongol warlord, took Baghdad and in the sixteenth century Iraq, along with the rest of the contemporary Levant, was bottled up into the Ottoman empire.

It is a measure of the turbulence of modern Iraq's history that 400 years of Turkish authority doesn't look so bad. For the last half-century Iraq has known nothing but war, coups and dictatorship. A generation ago, one Iraqi emerged from the ooze of military rule and accomplished what no modern Arab leader has done before or since: he built his country into a modern, semi-industrialized state.

The fact that it was Saddam Hussein should not diminish the achievement.

In 1958, a cabal of army officers took power in Iraq after massacring the ruling monarchy of transplanted Hashemites and their ministers. Saddam emerged several years later as the protégé of another coup leader and eventually took control of Iraq's security apparatus and quietly replaced his mentor, General Ahmed Al Bakr. By then, he was well advanced with the building of a powerful nation. Iraq's oil revenue was invested in roads, schools and factories. Engineers and doctors received scholarships to study in the US and Europe. Ali Shukri, a confidant of Jordan's late King Hussein, once remarked to me how many Iraqis studied with him at Cardiff. 'Every one of my classes had Iraqis,' he said. 'Most were doing post-graduate work in engineering and radiology.'

By 1980, the number of physicians per 1,000 people had tripled. Nearly all children attended primary school and nearly 60 per cent went to secondary school. Saddam ordered sweeping land reform, healthcare and minimum-wage laws. He opened male-dominated professions to women. The Ba'ath Party and Iraqi society were unashamedly secular.

With Nasser dead, Jerusalem in Jewish hands and Palestinians and Jordanians at war in the Hashemite Kingdom, Saddam and his economically energized Iraq emerged as the only counterweight to Israel. Western states queued up to sell Iraq everything from un-husked rice to modern weaponry – including the bomb-making facilities that now bedevil the US and Britain – provided Saddam kept the oil taps open.

Had Saddam dropped dead in 1980, Iraqis say, he would be remembered as a great Arab leader.* Instead, he would strangle his creation just as it was leaving the crib by making war on Iran.†

Iraq invaded Iran in part to settle a long-standing border dispute, and the instability that gripped Tehran in the aftermath of the 1979 revolution seemed to provide him with an opportunity. To pay for this Baghdad borrowed some $80 billion, principally from the Gulf States as insurance against Iranian expansionism. After the war, with Iraq intact but its economy in shambles, Saddam asked his Gulf lenders to refinance their loans. Not only did Kuwait and its neighbours refuse, they aggressively pumped oil on to the market, keeping prices low and frustrating Saddam's attempts to revive his economy with petroleum revenue. After several warnings, Saddam made good his threat to unleash a second Gulf War.

What the Iraqi economy would look like had Saddam not invaded Kuwait is an arcane parlour sport for economists.‡ For 22 million Iraqis and much of the Arab world, it is a bittersweet look back at what was, for a while at least, a rare Arab triumph.

Said Aburish, the writer, was among the many non-Iraqi Arabs who flocked to Baghdad to participate in what they hoped would be the epicentre of an Arab revival. 'We believed Iraq was where the Arab dream was,' Said says. 'Iraq had wealth, population, and first-class technocrats. There is a reason why they call Iraq the Fertile Crescent and war and sanctions really did it in.'

---

* Similarly, some historians say Hitler would figure as a great German chancellor had he died after the Nazi invasion of Austria.

† According to Saddam biographer Said Aburish, Saddam travelled to Amman before his invasion of Iran to consult with King Hussein and the CIA agents whom he had asked to meet. There, he received an implicit message of US support in an Iraqi war against Khomeini's Iran. 'There is a great deal to show that the United States wanted both sides weakened,' Aburish told the American public-broadcast programme *Frontline*. 'They didn't like Khomeini. They didn't like Saddam. They sold stuff to Saddam, they sold stuff to Khomeini secretly. They didn't want either side to win and they didn't want either side to lose. And that is what happened.' More than 360,000 Iranians and Iraqis were killed and twice as many wounded during the eight-year conflict.

‡ 'The speed and wide-ranging nature of [Iraq's economic reforms] would certainly have produced significant economic consequences had they not been interrupted by the Iraqi invasion of Kuwait,' is how economists Roger Owen and Sevket Pamuk describe it.

If this is how non–Iraqis reflect on Iraq's rise and fall, you can imagine how Iraqis feel.

Is this any way to run an airline. . .?
'I miss the travel. I wish to see Cairo again, to see Athens and Paris.'

Sufa was sitting on the couch in a friend's office in Baghdad. We had first met two years earlier when I was doing a story on Iraqi Airways. Sufa is an Iraqi Airways flight attendant.

I asked her how she had been. She responded with a self-conscious smile and a quick glance at my friend buried in work behind his desk. He had introduced me to Sufa who is a close friend of his sister. But there is no unconditional trust anywhere in Iraq, even between blood.

'We are fine,' she said finally. 'Considering the circumstances. And you?'

Everything has changed since September 11, I told her. What was it like in Iraq?

'Some people were very happy, I'm sorry to say, to see Americans die after what they've done to us. I felt sad because these were inno-cent people and the flight crews, they were like colleagues of mine. It was not their fault. But now Bush wants to start another war on Iraq. Why? We had nothing to do with what happened.'

'How do people feel about Osama bin Laden?'

'They don't think about him,' Sufa said. 'We just think about sur-vival. If we think about anything going on outside, we think about the Palestinians. We feel this in our hearts. Why do Americans let Israel get away with these crimes? What is happening is not because of Israel but because of America. What Israel gets, the weapons it uses to kill Palestinians, comes from America.'

Sufa had been working as an air hostess for Iraqi Airways for over ten years. Until 1990, Iraqi Airways was regarded as one of the finest airlines between Vienna and Tokyo and its crew, from pilots to line managers, were considered the pride of Iraq's thriving middle class. My Hong Kong–based friend Jim Eckes, an aviation specialist, once told me the engineers and pilots of Iraqi Airways were among the best in the business. 'They were highly motivated, wonderful people,' Jim told me. 'They did an extraordinary job.'

Sufa joined Iraqi Airways six months before Saddam invaded Kuwait. She learned of the invasion watching television in her hotel-room following a flight from Baghdad to India. She couldn't have known it at the time, but she and her colleagues would spend the next decade on the ground. In the run-up to Operation Desert Storm, Iraqi Airways sent its aircraft to regional airports, mostly in Jordan, where they remain to this day.

Iraqi Airways refused to shut down. It arranged bus-tours, ground transportation and annual travel packages for pilgrims making the *hajj* to Mecca. The women who staffed the main ticket office were ex-flight attendants. They kept track of the flight crews so they could be re-activated once sanctions were lifted and the airline could fly again.

One of them is Captain Akram Hasan. When I met him in 1999 he was selling used machine tools from a tiny stall in central Baghdad. Although he greeted us courteously, his eyes – dark and vacant – declared a deep melancholy. He was unshaven, but his shirt was neatly pressed. He smiled only once in our half-hour conversation and even that was contrived.

In 1975, Captain Hasan came to Britain and began two years studying aviation at Carlisle. A year later he soloed in a single-engine Cherokee Piper Cub. In 1982 he returned to Baghdad certified on every jet Boeing makes. His last flight was on 16 January 1991, when he evacuated his aircraft and its passengers to Amman.

He heard about the first Desert Storm offensive in mid-flight. In his diary that night he wrote: *Everyone is dark. They don't know where their future lies.*

Captain Hasan returned to a country bombed-out and broken. The Iraqi dinar's collapse diminished his former salary that was equivalent to $1,500 a month – more than a government minister's pay – to the $2.50 he earns today. He opened his machine tool shop in 1994. Many of his colleagues drive taxies and buses.

'I'm forty-three, which is the best age for a pilot,' he said. 'I'm not giving up now.'

I also met Captain Saad Majeed, the proprietor of a small, joyless amusement park near Baghdad. The sky was overcast. Only a handful of families were enjoying the park, which could have been bought from a corrupt road-show manager for 20 cents on the dollar. Several game booths clustered at the base of the park's centrepiece: a three-storey metal slide, the kind you read about after it collapses at a small-town carnival, killing three people and crippling a fourth.

Captain Majeed met us with orange sodas. Several times during the one-hour interview he apologized for being unable to see me in the city, closer to my hotel. He had just completed his refresher course on Iraqi Airways' sole operating simulator. The other three had broken down and were being cannibalized for parts. He visited the company's headquarters at least once every year, he told me, if only to renew his identification card.

He was also teaching his son the fundamentals of flying. 'I'm still waiting for the call,' he said. 'I just hope I'll be alive when it comes.'

A few days later I arrived at Iraqi Airways' main headquarters on the invitation of Rubieh Salieh, the airline's then-chairman. Security guards interrogated us at the gate and wouldn't let us in. An airport, they explained, is a strategic asset. We bribed our way past.

The headquarters' building was dark and dispiriting. The windows were criss-crossed with strips of masking tape to minimize shattered glass in the event of a missile strike. Exposed wires hung from the ceiling. In the lobby, a model Boeing 747 in Iraqi Airways' livery was sealed in Plexiglas – a sadly appropriate display.

Yet on the second floor the building hummed with life. I was introduced to Chief Engineer Fariz Ani, a tall man and every inch the engineering geek in grey cardigan sweater, plastic bifocals, and pocket protector. As we hurtled to the main hanger through narrow corridors and staircases, employees thrust memos at him to sign and alerted him to upcoming meetings. After we passed an open door to a large office, a woman rushed out and called down the hall after us. 'Fariz, the printer is broken again. Can you fix it?'

Mr Ani barely broke stride. 'Yes,' he replied. 'But not today.'

I struggled to keep up. If the Iraqi Airways folks are this busy now, I thought, what happens when they start flying again? We entered the main hangar. It was nearly empty except for the decaying remnants of the personal airplane of King Faisel II, the Iraqi monarch killed in the coup. 'It gives the hangar a purpose,' Fariz told me, 'as a kind of museum.' Birds flitted among the high rafters. A tangle of war-damaged metal scaffolding used to service jumbo jets awaited repair forlornly in the corner.

A training course had just begun, held in a small addition to the main hangar under a fluorescent light tube that flickered over a Pratt & Whitney J93D-7 jet engine suspended from a hoist. The day's lesson: removal and disassembly of the gearbox for cleaning and re-assembly. At the time this was among the few commercial-jet engines left in Iraq and it had been stripped and reassembled countless times since the Gulf War.

Back at the ticketing office, I was introduced to Captain Kamil Al

Messhedani, assistant director general of flight operations. He was helping the airline's catering arm prepare for an upcoming banquet for diplomats.

Captain Al-Messhedani lit a Marlboro Light, courtesy of the smuggling trade, then smiled. 'My daughters won't let me smoke at home,' he said. 'They keep saying "Remember Daddy, you'll fly again."'

They were right. On a cold morning in November 2000, an Iraqi Airways jet departed from Baghdad with 42 passengers to Mosul. Minutes later, another jet took off with 114 people to Basra. The aircraft were Russian-made and the flights were in direct defiance of the no-fly zone. After a decade of taxiing, Iraqi Airways was finally airborne. Soon after that, Jordanian, Syrian, and French airlines launched regular charter services to Baghdad and Saddam International Airport buzzed back to life.

Sufa first learned the airline would resume limited domestic service from a bulletin on television. The next day she reported to the headquarters to enquire about her schedule. About 30 of the original flight attendants were still with the airline. After three months of refresher courses, both pilot and flight crew were declared good-to-go with a skeleton fleet of two Russian Ilyushins and a new Boeing 747 donated by the United Arab Emirates.

I asked Sufa about her first day back in the air.

'I took my uniform out of my closet and laid it on the bed,' she said. 'And I cried. When we lifted off the first time, that trip to Basra, I cried again. Many other hostesses cried as well.'

Was no one concerned about violating the no-fly zone?

'Oh no,' she said. 'Occasionally US fighter jets fly alongside us. We wave, though they don't wave back. Aside from that, they leave us alone. Actually, the real danger comes from a lack of spare parts. A lot of the equipment are no-go items.'

'No-go items?'

'Items that don't work — like the slip-slide that is supposed to inflate for emergency evacuations. That's a no-go item. If IATA [International Air Transport Association] knew about how many no-go items we had, I expect it would shut down the airline.'

The domestic flights were a welcome relief, Sufa said, but she yearned to travel abroad. International flights would only come with a removal of sanctions and the complete overhaul of the Iraqi Airways

fleet – a potential contract worth billions of dollars that may go to
Europe's Airbus Industrie, rather than Boeing.

'It's better now,' Sufa said, 'but it is just a beginning. Only to Basra
and Mosul, and all these Iraqis demanding soda and cake from us.
They demand so much. This is why we want to see other cities. I
hope to see America one day. And New York. I see New York in my
dreams.'

'You have no animosity towards Americans?' I asked.

'Of course not. Why should I hate American people when it's the
American government that is doing this to us. We wish no war with
the Americans. We want to return to the way things used to be.'

I lowered my voice. 'Some people say your president has done this
to you. If the US army came to Baghdad with a new leader, would
the Iraqis resist?'

Sufa did not hesitate. 'Of course. This is Iraq. We've done nothing
to America.'

She looked down for a moment and then back up. 'Ten years ago,'
she whispered, 'we'd have welcomed the Americans. Now, it's too late.'

Soon after I arrived in Baghdad for Saddam's birthday I put in a
request with the information ministry for interviews with Iraqi
Airways. The inevitable minder and I drove to the Ministry of
Transportation where I was told the new director general was
working. I waited in the parking lot as the minder – his name was
Hazem and he was terribly nervous – disappeared in search of the
director general.

He returned 20 minutes later. The director general was busy celebrating President Saddam's birthday, Hazem explained, and could not
see me.

'Saddam's birthday was yesterday,' I said.

'Yes,' Hazem stuttered, 'but the president is so beloved by his
people they can't stop celebrating it.'

I asked if I could informally introduce myself to the director
general, present my business card and ask when might be a convenient time for us to meet.

Inappropriate, Hazem said. I should submit a written request for
an interview at the information ministry, which would fax it on to
the transportation ministry.

A half-hour later we were in the information ministry's protocol
department. Hazem consulted with a man in a chocolate-brown

dishdasha who made a series of calls on a new Panasonic fax machine. A television showed a woman demonstrating how to sew infant's clothing. The sound had been turned off.

Hazem informed me it would take two hours to write the letter and another hour to fax it to the transport ministry. At 7 p.m., he said, the protocol department would call my hotel and inform me if the director general would be available for an interview.

The call never came. The next day I checked in with the ministry. The director general had been in Basra all week and wasn't expected back in Baghdad for several days.

Only what was here before. . .

For years, the two items Iraqis most frequently requested from visiting journalists, UN staff and businessmen were pharmaceuticals and reading material. The oil-for-food program is slowly meeting demands for the former but Iraqis still crave the latter. This too is a legacy of sanctions: the city that a thousand years ago pioneered the first bookshops is starved of books and magazines.

The Arabs have a saying: 'Books are written in Cairo, published in Beirut and read in Iraq.' It still applies; every Friday after mid-day prayers, Baghdad's most well attended event is the book market on Al Rashid Street in the old downtown shopping district. Here, the city's malnourished readers buy, sell or trade books that are at least a decade old. The selection, ranging from textbooks to lurid paperbacks plucked a generation ago from some distant airport kiosk, are scattered on sheets or displayed in boxes. Thamer Kassem was selling some of his shop's volumes to generate enough revenue to keep the business going. I picked up a 1939 Modern Library edition of Dostoyevsky's *The Possessed* (*'including a hitherto suppressed chapter never printed in America!'*) for the equivalent of $1.20.

'Books are like food,' Thamer told me. 'And our students are famished.'

The next day, Thamer invited me to his shop, only a few blocks away from the book market, behind a modest storefront. The Kassem family has owned the shop for the last 40 years. Since 1991, it has become a depository for personal collections unloaded by emigrating Iraqis or those who have remained behind and were forced to sell their books to survive.

'Each time someone brings their books to me they leave a part of themselves behind,' said Thamer. 'And sometimes they cry.'

Here, stowed away in shelves, packed into cartons or stacked in columns was the discarded intelligence and passion of a generation. In all, some 30,000 volumes were stored in a honeycomb of chambers and passageways. The inventory was heavy with technical manuals and textbooks: *Facts and Fantasy in Freudian Theory* . . . *Plankton Behaviour* . . . *Asphalt Paving Technology* (by the Association of Asphalt-Paving Technicians) . . . *Radio Circuits and Signals Feedback Control Systems – Analysis & Synthesis.*

Clearly, someone had picked the collection clean of Harlequin romances.

'Without the embargo I could offer a whole section of new books,' Thamer said. 'We used to have books from India, Egypt and London, from all over the world. Now, there is only what was here before.'

Thamer introduced me to his assistant, Tahsin Ridha, a trained air-traffic controller. But with no air-traffic to control he winged his way from job to job before landing at the bookshop. He had been working for Thamer for three months and liked it.

'This is a very special place,' said Tahsin, whose father was a librarian. 'It's the perfect way to wait out the sanctions.'

Al Rashid Street was once the heart of Baghdad's shopping district and an oasis for the country's prosperous middle class. Well after the coups of the 1950s and 1960s, patrons would park their Fords and Buicks and stroll down the colonnaded row of two-story boutiques and department stores. The world's top brands were represented here – designer clothes, shoes, jewellery and perfumes.

Today, Iraq's newly rich – the embargo cats – shop across town in the Al Mansur district and Al Rashid Street is a tapped-out arcade that sells cheap wares to the city's poor. People are as likely to travel here by bullock cart as by automobile, though many of those old Fords and Buicks are still lumbering about. Fashion boutiques display gaudy polyester gowns made in China alongside *chadors* for pious Muslim women. Many of the top-floor storefronts, once embellished with wooden railing and elaborate moulding, are derelict and near collapse.

Two establishments from Al Rashid Street's golden era have survived. One is a juice-bar that specializes in grape juice made from raisins. It is distinctive for its juice of course, which has a sugar content of 20 per cent, but also for its décor. The walls are covered with framed, grainy photographs of the Hashemite era. There are photos of Faisel I with his ministers in traditional tribal gowns and of his son and successor Ghazi astride a racing car. (The populist Ghazi would die in a car wreck that many Iraqis believe was a British-inspired assassination.) There is a framed news clipping and photo of Faisel's doomed grandson, Faisel II, opening a new bridge over the Tigris. Um Kalthum, the legendary Egyptian singer is pictured in a packed concert hall. There are mounted proofs of Iraq's original dinar – the one worth $1.50. An icon of the Holy Trinity competes with the inevitable, framed photos of the Unholy Triad – Saddam and his two sons.

There are also photos of Nuri Said, a close adviser to Faisel II and prime minister to more than a dozen Iraqi governments. This interested me. Nuri Said is considered one of the most brilliant and agile diplomatic fixers of his time. A native of Baghdad, he rode with T.E. Lawrence during the Arab revolt where he feuded constantly with Lawrence's Bedouin comrades – he thought them undisciplined and corrupt – and wasted precious resources on conventional, rather than hit-and-run attacks on the Turks. But he distinguished himself as a cunning diplomatist who manipulated agents of larger powers with flattery, bombast and chicanery.

Nuri Said spent most of his career lobbying for, and ultimately getting, British support for Iraq's economic development. One British ambassador described him as the greatest beggar he had ever known. But the price was a pandering association with the West that Iraqi nationalists found treasonable. Nuri Said was ripped to shreds in 1958 by the same mob that killed Faisel II. The man who once remarked – perhaps in self-parody – that Arabs cannot be bought but can be rented found himself on the wrong side of a sadistically aroused Arab street.

I stared again at the photos. An amazing man, Nuri Said – charming, intelligent, duplicitous, brave; an ardent nationalist who insinuated his way into the confidence of superpowers at the cost of being seen as a quisling by his own people.

Then it dawned on me: *Ahmad Chalabi is the Nuri Said of the 21st century!*

I pointed to the photos and asked one of the juice-bar regulars who Nuri Said was and what contemporary Iraqis thought of him.

'Under Nuri Said, Iraq was strong,' the patron told me. 'He was very smart and a good negotiator. The British respected us then.'

What a difference forty years of coups, dictatorship, war, and sanctions make.

Directly opposite the juice bar stands cosmopolitan Baghdad's other relic: the barbershop of Hikmat Mahmoud Al Hilli, who was sitting outside the shop window reading the paper when Hugh Pope and I noticed him. We strolled over, juice in hand, to find out who he was and what he could tell us about old Baghdad. Plus, Hugh badly needed a haircut.

Hikmat was born in Baghdad in 1922 and had cut hair since he was ten. He sported a full head of shimmering white hair, his mouth sparkled with gold fillings and he was wearing a navy-blue shirt, a red polka-dot tie held by a silver clip and black trousers suspended by equally black braces. The walls of his shop were covered with clippings of articles written about him over the decades. One from 1975 identified Hikmat as 'the king's hairdresser, the oldest barber in Baghdad'. There were photos of Hikmat in a variety of poses – standing, sitting – though none of him cutting hair.

Hikmat's premises were no larger than a walk-in closet. The rotted vinyl on its two chrome chairs exposed the foam rubber padding underneath. A fan rotated languidly from the brick ceiling that was someone else's brick floor.

Hugh slid into one of the chairs. Hikmat considered the mop before him disapprovingly, adjusted his thick glasses and then snapped a cotton cloth around Hugh's neck. He picked up a pair of scissors with serrated blades and approached Hugh's head as if it was a commemorative ribbon.

It was clear by now that Hikmat was not only an Al Rashid Street institution but quite thoroughly and delightfully mad. I have never admired and respected Hugh Pope more than when he agreed to have his hair cut by a man whose fly was held together by a safety pin.

'The last British man I serviced was a British officer,' Hikmat said. 'That was in the 1940s. We were never better than under the King and the British. They treated us with respect.'

'Why did the people rise against it?' I asked.

Hikmat kept snipping at Hugh's hair. For a moment I thought he hadn't heard my question.

'We don't talk about that,' he said finally. Apparently, Hikmat was not as barmy as he seemed.

I asked what Baghdad was like before the coups and Hikmat's eyes

14. Rashid Abdula Salem Al Jaburi, sheik of the Al Jaburi tribe, Baghdad

15. Hugh Pope meets Baghdad's oldest barber and 'hairdresser to the King', Hikmat Mahmoud Al Hilli

16. The Brazilian Coffee Shop, Alexandria

17. Saber Mohammad Abu Leila, octogenarian, shoe-shiner and street historian, Alexandria

18. Al Azhar mosque, Cairo

19. The Cairo and Alexandria Stock Exchange during peak trading hours.
Note the empty seats

20. Abdel-Raouf Essa (*right*), imitation-furniture baron, and Ahmed, master craftsman

21. Ben Ezra synagogue, Cairo

22. Dr Mohammad Morsi, engineer, professor, parliamentarian and Islamic fundamentalist, Zaqaziq University

23. Patients await care at a clinic sponsored by the Muslim Brotherhood and run by Dr Abu Hashem Abdullah, Muslim Brotherhood member, Zaqaziq

24. Amin el Mahdy and Ashruf Radi, intellectuals and Greek Club regulars, Cairo

25. Egyptian dissident Saad Eddin Ibrahim awaiting trial, 18 March 2002

brightened. 'Baghdad was a city of light,' he began. 'Seventy-five thousand people visited this city every year. We had a higher quality of people then, before all these peasants from the village came.'

By now Hikmat was attacking Hugh's mane like it was an unruly boxwood hedge. Then, holding Hugh's head steady with his left arm, he dragged a comb deep across Hugh's scalp. The comb, thick with hair, soon resembled a mid-sized rodent. Hugh grimaced and his hair filled the air. I had to brush it from my notebook and as I reached down for my glass of raisin juice found it clogged with hair, like a bathtub drain. I felt I had wandered into a back-alley cat fight; there was enough natural fibre to weave a Bedouin tent.

'I only cut the hair of gentlemen,' Hikmat said, continuing to rake his comb mercilessly through Hugh's crop. 'This is the way I cut all the ministers' hair.'

No wonder they all wear army berets, I thought.

'They must have loved you at the British Club,' Hugh gasped.

Hikmat went on. 'I have cut the hair of [coup leader] General Kassem and Nuri Said. And I had that Saddam Hussein in my shop.'

'You cut Saddam's hair?' Hugh asked, catching his breath.

'No,' Hikmat said, 'but he stopped by once. I was cutting the hair of a senior security officer, and a tall man came in with a briefcase. He said he would meet the officer in 20 minutes "in the hotel to the north", whatever that meant. Anyway, when he left the officer asked me if I knew who the man was. I told him no, and the officer said, "That's Saddam Hussein and one day you and everyone else in the country will know who he is."'

Hikmat surveyed his work. He picked up a straight razor and steadied it with both hands as he peered through his glasses at the nape of Hugh's neck.

Hugh was silent. Hikmat closed in. A few last swipes and it was over.

Hikmat graciously received Hugh's tip as he escorted us out to Al Rashid Street.

'I miss the king,' he said. 'The best way for all the world is a kingdom. It was paradise back then and it will be that way again. Not soon, but some day. We Iraqis are a very patient people.'

6

Egypt

The Towering Dwarf

It is better to move the affairs of the king in the wrong direction than to let them stand still.

Ibn al Furat, an Abbasid minister

The street-corner of Rue El Nabi Danial and Boulevard Sa'ad Zaghloul is two blocks north of Alexandria's main thoroughfare, El Horreya Road. Close by is the recently restored Metropole Hotel, one of the town's nicer hotels and home to some of the Levant's most expensive cappuccino. From the nearby Raml tram station you can catch a tram that for miles shadows the city's famous Corniche and the Mediterranean Sea it so gracefully envelops.

But the corner has its own attractions. The first is the old Brazilian Coffee Shop, founded in 1929. I had passed by the coffee shop several times during visits to Alexandria and finally dropped in for a visit in May 2002.* I learned that a Greek named Dimitry Kolopolis first owned and operated the shop and the Greek ambassador to Egypt attended its inauguration. Now Mohammad Yusef Meligy manages it on behalf of the current owner, a man named Tarik who is usually away on business.

That apart, the shop hasn't changed much since it opened. The marble-tile floor has worn down and the shelves are now stocked with instant coffee jars and the red-and-yellow cartons of Lipton Tea.

---

* Unless otherwise indicated, all the interviews in this chapter took place during the author's most recent visit to Egypt in the spring and early summer of 2002.

But the beans are still Brazilian, fed daily into the vast funnel of the original British-made roaster and stirred, 25 kilos at a time, into a broad pan to cool. They are still ground, spiced or flavoured in metal machines of faded olive drab, with the coffee stored in 24 kilo bins. On a good day – and most days are, regardless of the economy, according to Mr Meligy – the Brazilian Coffee Shop sells between 40 to 50 kilos of coffee.

There is also a French roaster, more beautiful but much less capacious than its British counterpart and kept only for display. '*Les Cafés du Brasil sont Les Meilleurs*' is engraved across its three funnels.

'The new machines may look good,' says Mr Meligy, 'but it takes years for them to age properly and produce the right taste.'

Behind the roasters a triptych-like mirror displays a map of Brazil painted on one side and a chart representing Brazilian coffee production, circa the late 1920s, on the other. In the centre, a bird of paradise is painted on one panel of a glass pyramid in high relief filled with coffee beans – '*the original beans!*' Mr Meligy points out.

The corner's other attraction is the shoeshine boy, Saber Mohammad Abu Leila who was born 85 years ago in the upper-Egyptian town of Sohag. He wears a dark skullcap and a faded, torn *dishdasha*; his hands are cloaked in loose folds of tawny skin and his fingers are dyed indigo blue. He keeps his brushes and rags in a small red wooden box, with tins of Griffin Sterling Paste, made by Brooklyn-based Boyle Midway Inc., stacked neatly against the wall.

Mr Meligy introduced me to Saber and we shook hands. 'He's been shining shoes since he was fifteen years old,' said Mr Meligy, 'almost as long as we've been making coffee.'

I propped one of my smudged loafers on Saber's wooden pedestal and rested my notebook on my knee. If there is indeed an Arab street, certainly no one knows it better – at least from the corner of Danial and Zaghloul – than Saber Mohammad Abu Leila.

I asked Saber how Alexandria had changed in the last seven decades.

'There are so many more people now,' he said, gingerly working a brush into a tin of oxblood polish, 'and they are all Arabs. There used to be so many Greeks, pashas, people in Western hats. And these shops' – he gestured to the storefronts along the boulevard – 'they were all owned by Greeks, Jews, Italians and Armenians. People had style, they were refined. Back then you were prohibited from wearing a *galabeya* (ankle-length shirt) in public. Today, people have no manners.'

Saber spoke of the Second World War, of collecting his polish, brushes and rags during the air raids and heading for shelter. He remembers King Fuad – 'the best king' – and how after he died in 1936 his son Faruk arrived at Alexandria by boat from his studies in England. The Egyptian pound traded at parity with the British pound. Now, Saber said, it isn't worth two milliemes.*

Alexandria was peaceful, tolerant. Saber remembered a pasha (a high official) named Farghali who hired twelve Jews to manage his affairs. 'Today there are no Jews,' Saber said. 'You go to their church, down the street, and there are just a few old women.'

So what happened?

'The wars,' Saber replied. 'The wars came, and then Nasser started his revolution and the Jews were ordered out of the country. Life is difficult for so many people now. Long ago, Alexandria was like Athens. It had the climate, it was the best city in the world for living. There was great commerce. Trading, shipping, fishing, everything that has to do with the sea. A loaf of bread used to cost just a few milliemes. Now it is 10 piastres (just over 2 cents). A brother doesn't want his brother in his own home.'

Saber finished shining my shoes and with them his oral tour of old Alexandria. I said goodbye to him and Mr Meligy and the clerks at the Brazilian Coffee Shop and walked towards the sea.

As I turned the corner it struck me: for the first time in four years of interviewing Arabs I wasn't offered any coffee.

The last time Egypt offered the Arab world intelligent leadership the country was run by a minority class of party-loving Shiite Muslims. An Iraqi Jew was the most influential man in the country and a fraternity of warrior-eunuchs commanded the army. The entire Arab economy, with Cairo and Alexandria at its centre, ran a trade surplus with Europe. Egypt was the capital of global commerce and Egyptian currency was strong and held in accounts from Scandinavia to Canton. Egyptian markets were open, lightly regulated and tariffs, where they existed, were low. The country was home to the world's most prominent scholars and scientists; the most respected physicians in Europe received their degrees from Egyptian universities.

---

* Meaning 'virtually worthless'. In the Egyptian currency, 10 milliemes = 1 piastre and 100 piastres = 1 Egyptian pound (L.E1). Milliemes have disappeared from circulation. At the time of writing, approximately L.E4.60 = $1.00.

That was just over a thousand years ago, under the Fatimid Dynasty. Today, Egypt leads by not leading.

In the nebulae of contemporary Arab statesmanship Egypt was always a dim loadstar. The most populous Arab country is not just newly sovereign but newly Arab, its capital city a full-throated, heaving mass of varying ethnicities – Arab, Nubian, Coptic-Christian, Greek, Italian. Well after the collapse of the Ottoman Empire at the end of the First World War, Egyptians rallied more around their Pharonic past than the glories of Fatimid rule. It wasn't until the late 1950s, after he emerged from the Suez crisis as an authentic Arab hero, that Nasser embraced the pan-Arab cause and Egypt began to perceive itself as part of the Arab bloc. Before that, the father of Arab nationalism always spoke of himself as an Egyptian, a transcendent identity that fuses faith and history with political geography. Egypt is regarded as the custodian of Islamic achievement, the fountainhead of ancient North African culture and since Nasser, the sanctum of Arab unity. If Syria is the beating heart of Arab nationalism, as Nasser put it, and Saudi Arabia its spiritual soul, Egypt is its mind and muscle.

Egypt is also a complete mess. Rarely in the course of modern economic history has so much achieved so little. The country is blessed with one of the world's great rivers, petroleum and natural-gas reserves, a market of nearly 70 million people, a canal rivalling the Bosporus in strategic and commercial importance and some of the world's most lavish tourist draws. Given such resources, Egypt should rank among the world's largest economies. Instead, it churns out a miserable $84 billion or so each year, roughly equivalent to about $1,200 for each Egyptian. It is one of the world's largest mendicants, ingesting some $3 billion in foreign aid, more than half provided by the United States as a reward for keeping peace with Israel. The US Agency for International Development (USAID), the organization that allocates American funding, enjoys a near supra-national authority and is widely condemned among Egyptians as an agent of American corporate-imperialism.

The Egyptian economy stays afloat on the combined strength of its natural and man-made blessings: the canal, foreign aid, energy reserves and the Nile. Of those, only the canal is here to stay. Even the mighty Nile is shrinking as Egypt's population grows. The government talks about modernizing its agricultural base and of using its water resources more efficiently but instead has invested billions of dollars in roads and suburban projects. They were well intentioned but poorly planned and many of the housing units are empty. Egyptians call them *El Fil El-Abyad* – 'the White Elephants'.

Nowhere in the Arab world is the gap between rhetoric and reality so great as in Egypt. The country is officially democratic but election results are routinely manipulated and dissent stifled, sometimes brutally. It is simultaneously a secular republic and home to a thriving radical Islamic order, and it was the syllabi of Egyptian *madrassas* that incubated some of the minds behind September 11. The second-largest bloc represented in parliament is the Muslim Brotherhood, a group officially outlawed by the government but too popular to keep out of the legislature. Cairo proclaims itself a leader in the Middle East peace process and a friend of the US even as its state-owned press reeks of anti-Jewish and anti-Western agitprop. The Israeli 'embassy' in Cairo is perched atop a filthy, 14-floor office building, its tattered flag barely visible from the ground and hanging in limp protest to a hollow peace.

During Fatimid times, between the tenth and twelfth centuries, merchants of all religions travelled freely, without standardized travel documents or identification cards.* Today, many Egyptians who frequently travel to Israel are subjected to official intimidation. In the 30 years since the Camp David peace accord, Egypt and Israel have jointly developed only one enterprise of any significance, the $1.2 billion Midor oil refinery off the Alexandrian coast. It was pioneered by Merhav, an Israeli company that finances infrastructure projects worldwide. Midor's success was due largely to the efforts of Alexandria's governor, an uncommonly fearless Egyptian civil servant who drove the project through thick red tape and fierce political opposition.

While Egyptian officials played down Midor at home, they milked its diplomatic capital in Washington.

'Our profile was hydraulic – it was reduced in Egypt and raised in Washington,' says Nimrod Novik, Merhav's vice chairman and a proponent of Israeli-Arab enterprise. 'Midor was Egypt's fig leaf, its proof of regional cooperation. [Egyptian President Hosni] Mubarak always waved it around in Washington.'†

---

* Letters of introduction were common, however. A twelfth-century letter from the Geniza archive in Cairo, written by the Gaon of Jerusalem, the city's highest-ranking Jewish religious authority, endorses the character of a travelling textile salesman: 'The bearer of these lines is a man from the country of Khorasan. He brought me a letter of recommendation from a merchant in Seville. He is now proceeding to Egypt.'

† Merhav sold its 14 per cent stake in Midor to the Egyptian government in 2001. When I asked Nimrod how much money Merhav made from the sale, he merely smiled broadly.

In Egypt, not losing can be just as good as winning and there is no setback a little spin and self-delusion can't overcome. The October 1973 war with Israel which ended in devastating defeat for the Arab armies is celebrated as a national holiday. The 1956 Suez crisis made Nasser an Arab icon even as Israel, France and Britain routed his forces. Troops returning from defeat by Israel in 1948, when Egypt was a monarchy under King Faruk, were hailed as victors. (This was too much for the military to stomach, and was one of the reasons its officers revolted against the throne in 1952.)

Long before the second Intifada and the war on terrorism had its collateral effects on the regional economy, the Arab world's largest economy sputtered from official sloth and corruption. The government stands by its official estimates of steady growth even as bankers, economists and businessmen agree the country has been in recession for the last three years.

In the annals of global enterprise, Egypt is a stunning mediocrity, a profound slacker, a towering dwarf. Following the October 1981 assassination of Anwar Sadat, the new government of President Hosni Mubarak led a conference on how to repair Egypt's struggling economy. A consensus has yet to be found. Faced with either liberalization at the expense of state control or state control at the expense of an open society and more efficient economy, Mubarak chose not to choose.

Yet Egypt – *Misr* in Arabic – remains crucial. The Arabs first appreciated its importance in their quest for empire in the seventh century. Pious Omar I prohibited his subjects expanding beyond the Arabian Peninsula, fearing unbelievers might corrupt them. Finally, in a rare concession the stubborn caliph bowed to pressure from generals and merchants hungry for the bountiful land west of Sinai. In 640 A.D. he gave Amr Ibn al As, one of his top commanders, the green light for a march on Egypt – then Christian and part of the Byzantine Empire – but only if Amr promised to cancel the attack if so ordered before action had begun. Sure enough, with the Muslim army poised at the Nile facing only a token force of Byzantines, a breathless messenger handed Amr a caliphal edict to recall his forces.

Declaring the message garbled in transmission, Amr attacked and Egypt promptly fell.

Since then, Egypt has been the guest no party can be without. The Umayyad and Abbasid caliphs had to keep their Egyptian viceroys happy lest they form their own independent fiefdom. This happened in the late ninth century under Ahmed Ibn Tulun, who established a brief but illustrious dynasty from Cairo, and again during the Ottoman Empire, when in the mid-nineteenth century Mohammad Ali rose from the ranks of the Albanian janissaries – ex-slaves trained to be elite members of the sultan's personal guard – to become the father of modern Egypt.

'There can be no war without Egypt and no peace without Syria,' so goes a contemporary Middle East saying.* So it was perhaps inevitable that Egypt under Gamal Abdel Nasser would assume the Arab vanguard. But Nasser, unlike Ibn Tulun and Mohammad Ali, plundered Egypt with wrong-headed policies. The Arab world's hunger for competent leadership can be measured by Nasser's exalted rank in the pantheon of Arab heroes; he is remembered not harshly for subverting the most important Arab economy, but heroically for standing up to Israel and the West.

Desert country, dead capital

Anwar Sadat is commonly regarded as the man who made possible Egypt's peace with Israel. In fact, the distinction should go to Aziz Sidqi, a little-known Egyptian technocrat.

In 1960, Sidqi pioneered a five-year plan that tucked nearly every enterprise, from steel making to Arabian horse breeding, under state control. Imports were crowded out; under Sidqi's authority, everything 'from the needle to the rocket' was produced in Egypt by heavily subsidized local industry.

This so undermined the Egyptian economy that by the late 1970s the country's huge military commitment was unsustainable and in 1979 Anwar Sadat was forced to make peace with Israel. In return, Cairo demanded generous amounts of Western aid. Because Egypt was not compelled to dismantle Sidqi's policies, the money accomplished little beyond repairing the country's infrastructure. By the late 1980s Egypt required a massive bailout. The International Monetary Fund stood ready, provided Cairo agreed to restructure the economy. The government accepted this, but backed off after a few gestures towards reform. State assets remain unsold; privatization is on indefinite hold.

---

* The line has been attributed to several sources but has most recently been appropriated by Henry Kissinger.

Egypt insists on defending its currency at overvalued rates, which has cost the government some 40 per cent of its foreign exchange reserves over the last few years. A sometimes creeping, sometimes dramatic devaluation of the Egyptian pound has inflated the price of imports that translates into higher prices and popular unrest. In February 2002, more than a hundred people were jailed after riots in Port Said.

Faced with yet another Egyptian economic collapse, early in 2002 international donors agreed to inject some $10 billion of additional aid intravenously into the country. Currency speculators began profitably selling back black-market dollars for local currency – but not before the government mobilized its two-million-man Central Security Force to close foreign exchange outlets and arrest some 400 people protesting against yet more rising prices on imported goods.

Egypt has been suffering a net dollar outflow since 1999. A regular report on the economy issued by EFG-Hermes, Egypt's largest merchant bank, includes a section called 'Sundry Capital Flow', defined as 'unexplained capital movement by locals'. From 1991 to 1998 there was as much hard currency coming into the country as there was going out. From 1998 to fiscal 2003, the report forecast, a net $12 billion worth of foreign exchange would be funnelled out of Egypt into more stable investments abroad.

'We are forecasting an economic crisis in five years,' Omar Abdullah, the chief strategist for EFG-Hermes Brokerage, told me. 'It will be a turning point. The least painful option will be another IMF program. I'm no fan of the IMF, but compared to the government's capability, it would be a blessing.'

Like brokerage houses everywhere, EFG-Hermes wants to showcase the strengths of its local economy while skimping on the weaknesses. But the suits can no longer ignore Egypt's malaise. A year earlier, the government demanded an apology from investment bank Jardine Fleming after it released a report warning investors away from Egyptian stocks. Jardine issued an apology for the report, according to the government, and after months of not-so-subtle official intimidation, Omar told me, sacked the analyst who wrote the report. Since then, anaemic volume on the stock exchange and the government's inept handling of the currency crisis has emboldened those, like Omar, who would speak negatively about Egypt's economic future.* In August 2002, the

---

* Abdullah wrote the report on sundry capital flows. He left EFG Hermes soon after we spoke and the bank later refuted his data.

Standard & Poor's credit rating agency cut Egypt's foreign currency rating to junk grade.

Uncertainty over exchange rates and dwindling foreign reserves has led to a chronic shortage of hard currency. A month after the Port Said riots, the head of the Arab League, Amr Mussa, was told his state jet, due to carry him and a delegation of Libyan diplomats to a conference in Tripoli, could not take off from Cairo airport until he settled a $152 refuelling charge with the state-owned petroleum company. Only dollars – not Euros or Egyptian pounds – would do. The airport banks claimed they had no dollars to lend Mussa, which was odd given the $15 entry visa foreigners pay on arrival. The jet finally lifted off after a Libyan diplomat left behind his personal identification as collateral.

I asked my friend Mahmoud Sayed Abdel Latif, the vice president of Banque du Caire if he could pull some strings to help me cash travellers cheques into dollars. It was March 2002, following a run on the Egyptian pound and a government-imposed freeze on most dollar transfers. Mahmoud summoned an underling who escorted me across the street to the bank's main branch. It was after 3.30 p.m. and the bank was closed. We entered through a side door, past a guard and into a wood-panelled room where three clerks sat behind desks covered with files and account books. The underling tugged me towards a stern-looking woman in a pink blouse, matching headscarf and blue sweater. She had been entering figures into a ledger.

The two spoke briefly in Arabic. Madam Headscarf nodded, asked me in English for my passport and co-signed cheques, and then summoned a thickset man to deliver them to the banking hall.

'Do-LARS?' the man asked, somewhat agitated.

She frowned at him, and he shrugged and slumped out of the door.

Five minutes later, another man, clutching my passport and cheques, led a troika of minor clerks into the room. A loud confrontation followed. After five minutes or so Madam Headscarf mentioned Mahmoud's name, *sotto voce*, and returned to her ledger. Silenced and defeated, the troika beat what turned out to be only a tactical retreat. Within ten minutes they returned, now a cabal with two bean counters in reserve and a stack of receipts under their arms.

A second confrontation erupted. Once again, Madam Headscarf prevailed.

'Is there a problem?' I asked after the opposition left the room.

'We are only allowed to cash cheques with Egyptian pounds,' she said. 'For this, there will be a 1 per cent commission fee.'

I gestured my consent, as if it mattered.

A quarter-hour passed. Back came the cabal, which now included a man in a black-and-white checked blazer and a strand of hair pasted defiantly over an enormous pate. The cabalists glared at me, the foreign-currency leach, a clear and present danger to Egypt's delicately calibrated exchange-rate regime. After ten minutes of loud words the contest was over, though the opposition never really stood a chance. Banque du Caire may have been government-owned, but in this wood-panelled office Madam Headscarf ruled.

A receipt was produced which everyone signed – twice. By the time it reached me – I had to sign in three places – it resembled an autographed championship baseball. The cabal departed. After a few minutes a clerk returned with a stack of bills.

He counted out one hundred and ninety-six dollars.

I turned to Madam Headscarf. 'You said a 1 per cent commission. This is four dollars short.'

'Actually, the law is a minimum four dollars per transaction.'

In that case, I told her, I wanted to exchange another $200 worth of cheques.

She paused. 'Today, for you, the commission is only 2 per cent.'

Thus more receipts and signatures, followed by another ten minutes before everything was finally settled. Before leaving, I thanked Madam Headscarf.

She looked up from her ledger, expressionless.

'Welcome to Cairo,' she said.

'Cairo,' writes the economist Hernando de Soto in *The Mystery of Capital*, 'is a city of the dead – of dead capital, of assets that cannot be used to their fullest. The institutions that give life to capital – that allow you to secure the interest of third parties with your work and assets – do not exist here.'

Not far from Banque du Caire, in the Sherif El Saghir district, is the Cairo and Alexandria Stock Exchange. Several years ago the government restored Sherif El Saghir in a noble attempt to recreate the romance of 1930s Cairo. It repainted the buildings, replaced the

pot-holed tarmac with cobblestones and installed mock-gas lanterns.
The re-opening was a major media event, attended by politicians,
celebrities, and wealthy businessmen.

Though the stock exchange was the cornerstone of the restoration, it was still unfinished by the time of the opening in 2000. A
year earlier, I talked my way in for a quick preview. Through the
detritus of discarded computers and exposed ventilation ducts I could
make out the outline of a once-regal trading hall. The pit was encircled by a rotunda of Roman columns with Corinthian capitols that
were linked on the viewing floor by a wrought-iron railing.
Underneath the protective canvas lay a floor of imported pine. An
elegant art-deco grill protected the glass door.

I returned in spring 2002. The renovation job had been difficult. Not
long after my first glimpse of the exchange the ceiling imploded after
the columns collapsed from wood-rot. But the technicians, labourers
and artisans had triumphantly matched style and utility. The columns
were given a faux-brown marble finish and the capitols were painted
gold. The ceiling was transformed into a blue sky with graceful cirrus
clouds. There were seats for 150 traders, each plugged into a modern
trading system. Above them flickered huge electronic screens that
displayed the real-time price movement of the market's most aggressively traded stocks.

Unfortunately, there was not much trading. When I visited, it
seemed the closing bell had already rung several hours early.

'A stock exchange is a mirror of the economy,' said Ayman Abdel
Rahman Salah, the exchange's media manager, as we toured the
floor. 'If the economy is weak, the stock exchange does not perform.'

The former is, and the latter doesn't. Average daily turnover had
declined from $250 million in 2000 to about $20 million. Some firms
had closed their seats. Any orders that trickled in were from local
punters; long-term institutional money had been yanked out long
ago, in frustration with Egypt's phantom reform plans. The current
Intifada, US sabre-rattling over Iraq and the recent confusion over
local exchange rates snuffed out any hopes of a revival.

Before Nasser's 1952 coup, Egypt had the world's second-largest
commodities market and the fifth largest stock exchange. Under his
regime, the bourse symbolized human exploitation. 'Back then, a
capital market was thought to be a way for the rich to control the
poor,' Ayman said. 'In films of the time, there was always a greedy

pasha who drops dead on the steps of his huge villa after hearing how he lost all his money in the stock market.'

Now, even the Muslim Brotherhood endorses privatization and universities hold competitions to see who can pick the most high-yielding stocks. Shaimaa Hazem, Ayman's 23-year-old assistant, came second in one. She recently graduated from the Sadat Academy for Management Science, enrolled in the stock exchange's three-month summer training program, and now – in *chador* and conservative trouser suit – celebrates the virtues of market economics.

'A stock exchange is very important for society because it gives people a way to make money and expand their business and employ people,' she told me. 'It is not for the rich, but for all people.'

I asked Shaimaa if she wanted to work in the trading pit one day.

'If I have the opportunity,' she said, 'and if God wills it, I hope to be a stock trader.'

Short of divine intervention there is little that might turn Egyptian share prices around anytime soon. In mid-2002, the Cairo stock exchange's average price-earnings ratio – a calculation that indicates the fundamental value of a given stock – was about as cheap as any listed equity anywhere. No one was buying, suggesting that local and international investors foresaw further decline. In a bone-dry market like this it would be foolhardy for any government to sell its assets.

Munir Fakhry Abdel-Nur is the managing director of Vitrac, Egypt's leading producer of jams and fruit juices. The family-run company controls 65 per cent of the domestic jam market and exports to the world's most developed economies; it makes one in three jam products sold in Japan. The Abdel-Nur family controls 35 per cent of Vitrac's public equity and international investors own the rest. No one is selling, so Vitrac shares don't trade.

Vitrac operates from the Abdul-Nur family's magnificently preserved, 80-year-old villa opposite Cairo's Giza Zoo. The floors are inlaid with intricate mosaics and exposed beams support the ceilings. Jars of jam and bottled juice are proudly displayed in showcases. Outside the compound wall a brass plaque, regularly polished, gives the company's original identification: 'Société Egypto-Française pour les Industries-Agro Alimentaires (SEFIAA) – Confitures Vitrac.'

Mr Abdel-Nur comes to work dressed as the merchant banker he is. When I met him, he wore a grey pinstripe suit with royal-blue tie and matching handkerchief. His blue cuff-linked shirt was mono-grammed below the pocket. Unusually for an Egyptian, Mr Abdel-Nur is precise and laconic, his prognosis clipped and pointed.

'I am not satisfied with the country's economic policy,' he said. 'Real privatization could happen, but only if we get a government that can take the bull by the horns.'

'Do you see anyone like that on the horizon?'

'I don't think so.'

'What does the future hold?'

'We will continue to muddle through.'

I asked Mr Abdel-Nur to identify the biggest challenge facing the Egyptian economy. Certainly political instability and the Intifada were keeping investors at bay, he said, but equally discouraging was an absence of coherent government policy. The mishandling of the exchange rate and the pound devaluation had inflated the cost of imported sugar and the capital goods he needs to keep Vitrac running. A forward market in which he could lock import contracts at a fixed exchange rate would help, but talk about reviving the once-robust Alexandrian commodities exchange has yielded nothing.

'It's been on the table for three, four years and we are tired of waiting,' Mr Abdel-Nur said. 'So we will just muddle through.'

The last time I was in Egypt the only government official who agreed to see me was Mahmoud Mohieldin, a senior advisor to the Egyptian finance minister and one of the few reasons not to write Egypt off just yet. He belongs to a younger generation of Egyptians who understand the depths of Egyptian sclerosis and what needs to be done. He knows how capital markets work and why they are import-ant. He writes thoughtful articles for Western journals about Egypt's economic problems. His perspective is sober and sophisticated, and when we met he was cautiously pessimistic.

'People are forecasting a crisis but we are not Argentina. We have little external debt, no municipal debt and little fiscal debt. So talk of a crisis is not relevant. But severe difficulties may be the case.'

Mahmoud sketched out a problem endemic to the Egyptian economy and common throughout the Arab world – a vast unofficial economy that prevents the state collapsing but is impossible to audit and tax.

'You can assume that the informal economy is equal to 30 per cent of the formal economy,' said Mahmoud. 'What this means is that the economy does not respond to monetary and fiscal stimuli. Most Egyptians don't care about a tax cut because few ever pay tax, except for taxes on sales. So you can reduce taxes as we are doing but it will have no impact, and that erodes the credibility of the government's ability to manage the economy. As a result, what people are seeing for the last ten years is a recession and a lack of confidence.'

The problem, Mahmoud was saying, is not a shortage of capital but its inefficient deployment. Most Arab countries have stock markets, but official reluctance to sell state assets means there are precious few companies in which to invest. The state employee pension funds have highly restrictive conditions on how and where they can be invested. Several countries have mortgage laws, but these are meaningless without banking reform to encourage long-term, retail lending.

None of these problems are new, Mahmoud said, but their strain on an increasingly fragile Egyptian society has never been greater.

'Our political system is focused on short-term management of mistakes made in the past,' he said. 'Egypt is different now. There is instability in the labour market and concern about being made redundant at a time when living standards are declining. Many people are surprised there hasn't been a real crisis yet.'

The man widely blamed for the pound's devaluation is Naguib Sawiris, the most flamboyant of the three brothers who manage the Orascom Group, one of the Middle East's largest conglomerates. Naguib once told me the key to his success: 'You wake up at 6 a.m. every morning, you get ulcers, you succeed. It's a simple formula, but it works.'

In early 2000 Naguib took out a loan worth $670 million to pay for a cellular phone license. About a third of it was dollar-denominated, and when it came due Orascom went to the banks to sell pounds for dollars. The foreign currency wasn't available, so Naguib utilized the black market. The result was a run on the pound and a harangue from the prime minister for his single-handed sabotage of Egypt's exchange-rate stability.

'When the local banks don't provide the dollars you have to go into the market,' Naguib told me. 'What choice do I have other than to sell my company and go live in comfort abroad?'

Naguib is flashy and outspoken in a society that prizes, if not practices, humility. He is also something of a corporate sheik. The

Egyptian government's corruption and weakness – as elsewhere in the Middle East – obliges him to take care of his employees as a village elder does his clan or an imam his congregation. Naguib receives thousands of letters a month from his staff asking for favours or money. He usually delivers and he accounts for every piastre.

When an Orascom employee had a brain tumour, Naguib paid for the surgery. 'This guy came in with all the documentation and X-rays and a letter pleading for help,' an Orascom employee told me. 'So Naguib scrawled "OK" on the letter and we sent him up to the accounts department to draw from Naguib's private account.'

I was sitting in Naguib's wood-panelled office in downtown Cairo. Spring had not yet soured into Egypt's notoriously humid summer and he wore a thick worsted jacket. Occasionally he glanced at the closed-circuit camera perched to his left to see who was waiting outside, but he was unhurried and typically generous with his time.

Naguib is in the front line of the pitched battle between business-men, both small and large, and the bureaucrats who regulate them. This war is going on almost everywhere, but is particularly fierce in developing countries like Egypt. A state's commitment to liberalize and deregulate means nothing without the regulators' consent, which is rarely, if ever, given. So investors like Naguib must fight what is essentially a guerrilla war with conventional weapons. In their arsenal are business practices and standards proven in developed markets on relatively level battlefields. Their armour comprises trade agreements and memoranda of understanding that commit their government to expedite project approvals and import licences. Instead, they are reduced to skirmishing with customs officials, auditors and director-generals of various ministries.

Neither side is intrinsically more virtuous than the other. But the businessman is far more likely to employ people and create wealth than the bureaucrat. If the businessman prevails he may help integrate his country's economy into the network of markets that has, for the last 5,000 years, become increasingly sophisticated, efficient and powerful, a process we know as globalization.

Where the bureaucrat wins, or at least secures a draw, economies collapse – as in Asia in 1997, throttled by red tape and over-regulation – or die a slow, asphyxiating death, like today's Arab economies. Despite this, businessmen like Naguib are often attacked at economic summits as agents of environmental rape and human vassalage.

While the Egyptian government crawls through deregulation,

Naguib prescribes the elimination of entire industries and the immediate privatization of the state's remaining fungible assets. Bureaucrats tend to be stupid or corrupt, he says, and they jam the gears of what could be a well-oiled and efficient free-market economy.

'The government should not be allowed to compete with the private sector,' he said. 'There is no faith in the government's ability to manage the economy. It loses L.E500 million subsidizing the textile sector because it can't find buyers for its product. It should lend that money to help viable small enterprises. We don't even have a small-businessman's association.'

I asked Naguib if he thought poverty and terror were linked, and he pointed out the growing popularity of the Muslim Brotherhood. 'They take advantage of the inefficiency of the government. Their agenda is not democracy but the rule of the sword and the book. People are running to the laps of the Muslim Brothers. The biggest danger facing Egypt is it could become another Iran.'

Urchins of the OEM economy
Ordinarily a currency devaluation is good for a country's manufacturers because it makes their exports more competitive. Egypt, however, makes few products the world wants to buy. In the fiscal year 2000–2001 the country's exports were worth $7 billion – representing a paltry 8 per cent of GDP – largely because the state missed a tectonic shift in the global economy that began two decades ago.

For much of the 1980s, with America's failed economy practically subsumed into the Dai Nippon Co-Prosperity Sphere and business-school students worldwide drinking sake, reading misogynistic comic books and working on their golf swings, it became fashionable to herald manufacturing as the key to economic growth. Using Japan's export powerhouse as the model, a school of economists and pundits prescribed the restoration of America's industrial base – shipyards, semiconductor plants, textile and steel mills – as the only way to revive the mordant US economy. If these industries could not compete with foreign rivals, so they argued, they should be subsidized through higher taxes and protected with tariff and non-tariff trade barriers. Only a country that produces tangible goods could earn sufficient foreign exchange for investment and stable currency rates.

It seemed a compelling argument – just look at what such policies did for Japan. Fortunately for the global economy it was resisted. The US wrote off much of its rust-belt industries, farmed out production to low-cost developing countries and evolved almost organically into an economy led by services and technology.

When US Treasury Secretary Nicholas Darmon resisted calls for the protection of America's semiconductor makers – 'If our guys can't hack it, let 'em fall,' he said – it was a rare act of political courage and a turning point in America's economic transformation.*

Semiconductors have become to the global economy what dry-cell batteries were 50 years ago – low-margin, entry-level tokens in any developing country's journey to industrialization. The US economy is the most powerful in history because it allowed its centre of gravity to shift from the producer to the consumer, which required the emigration of low-margin industry to developing countries.

Egypt should be the opposite side of that transition. Along with the Far East it should have snatched its share of the production contracts available from US manufacturers seeking cheap labour. The evolution is a familiar one: from the production of garments for popular brands like Gap and Levi Strauss to cheap electronic goods for Zenith to circuit boards for Dell and Compaq to knock-down assembly kits for General Motors to composite jet-engine parts for Pratt & Whitney.

Economists and industrialists call this 'original-equipment manufacturing,' or OEM. Anti-globalization activists condemn it as exploitation. On the ground it's called gainful employment.

At each level, the process should yield the host nation a new production technology here, an innovative management technique there. Egypt has missed out, capturing neither the production contracts nor the technology behind them. Like other Arab states, Egypt lacks a range of products and services it can sell to the world for hard currency to invest back into the economy. The country's large domestic market is as much a curse as a blessing; most finished goods produced in Egypt – either by local or foreign companies – are for local consumption and are not of the standard that can compete with rival products abroad. Without an emphasis on exports, both Egyptian manufacturing and the Egyptian economy will atrophy.

Economic planners in Cairo say they understand this. They com-

---

* Darmon worked for President George Herbert Walker Bush, which makes the current administration's pandering to domestic steel and farm interests all the more distasteful.

mission studies and hire foreign consultants to find ways to make Egyptian industry competitive in global markets. They pass laws to make foreign corporations export a certain ratio of their production and work with USAID to arrange export credits for small manufacturers.

And according to bona-fide Egyptian exporters, it's all a load of hooey.

The road from Cairo to Damietta hugs a sinew of humanity packed along the Nile in villages of mud huts, brick homes and concrete blockhouses. Some are freshly painted in elaborate primary colours, others in faded pastels. Many have flat roofs with sprigs of steel re-inforcement bars thrusting up from concrete posts in anticipation of an added income that could finance a second floor. The villages, separated by groves of date palms and paddies of barley, are serenaded by the single-stroke, baritone sputter of ancient water pumps. Every kind of enterprise is represented on the Nile – from auto repair shops and coffee houses to beauty salons. They hug the riverbanks like a child clinging to his mother's dress.

Soon after Amr conquered Egypt for the Muslims, Damietta became an important shipyard for the Umayyad navy. Today Damiettans make fishing boats and furniture – tons of it. Crude shops and showrooms, filled with chairs and tables, mostly unfinished, line the main roads into the city; the closer to the city centre, the more elaborate the premises become.

Damietta's furniture is predominantly sold in Egypt, though some is exported. The industry suits Egypt's development needs perfectly. It requires more labour – ranging from low-cost menial work to high-value craftsmanship – than capital and technology. Much of the factory equipment is built in Egypt, which saves foreign exchange. The business is largely recession-proof; people always need something to sit on.

Therefore the Egyptian government should logically assist labour-intensive industries like the furniture trade with tax concessions, loan guarantees and promotion overseas.

Not to hear Damiettans tell it.

*

'This government is worse than useless. Our ministries don't help us and our embassies do nothing.'

Abdel-Raouf Essa, president of the Domiat Egypt Company, a family-owned enterprise that has been making furniture for four generations, was slumped at an imitation French-inlay desk on the second floor of his factory. I had called him to see if he had time for a foreign journalist. He did.

The factory is a two-storey concrete blockhouse adjacent to a stable filled with sheep, ducks and water buffalo. On the ground floor were stacks of unfinished timber – plywood, chipboard, pine blocks, reed-thin sheets of veneer – alongside large machine tools that cut, shave, edge, sand, polish and glue. Abdel-Raouf was especially proud of a home-built wood-bending contraption that looked like a medieval torture device. He considered filing for a patent to protect it against copyright theft, he said, 'but I'm afraid the government would steal the design'.

For use on wood or people, I wondered.

The second floor, cluttered with finished and half-finished bureaus, desks, corner-shelves, bars, tables and chairs, was where Abdel-Raouf sat at his smudged, obsolete Compaq computer, checking the company accounts and selecting fabric patterns from the thick sample binders piled over and around his desk.

Until ten years ago, Domiat produced exclusively for Egyptian buyers. One day, a Dutchman named Hans arrived with photographs of furniture pieces, most inspired by the eighteenth-century French style, that he wanted reproduced for buyers worldwide. It took Domiat two years to achieve the quality Hans demanded. Since then, Domiat has produced entirely for export to the world's most developed and demanding markets – America, Japan, Austria, Italy. The company makes $3 million a year with a profit margin of 15 per cent. It employs 240 full-time workers.

'We were born in the workshop,' Abdel-Raouf said as we toured the factory. 'The knowledge is handed down from father to son.' (Out of concern for my delicate, foreign innards Abdel-Raouf had ordered tea made with mineral water, and I felt guilty about leaving it on his desk, half drunk.) The air was scented with fresh pine; wood cuttings and sawdust covered the floor.

Abdel-Raouf introduced me to Ahmed, a master craftsman who was embellishing a commode with strips of inlaid veneer. A Finn had ordered the commode for $110. Ahmed dipped bits of the veneer into a vat of hot glue and packed it into narrow grooves that embraced a floral pattern, then smoothed it with a spatula.

Ahmed is 42 years old. He started in the furniture trade when he was six.

'As children, we go to school in winter and in the summer take apprenticeships,' Ahmed said. 'My dream is to own my own shop, but for now, this is what God wills.'

I asked Abdel-Raouf if competition from the developing countries of Asia worried him.

'It comes mostly from Malaysia, the Philippines, China and Indonesia,' he said. 'It is very cheap but the quality is very poor. Even though they sell in great volume, they will need a long time to catch up.'

'Shouldn't Damietta at least diversify into other sectors?'

From the stable outside, a donkey brayed. 'We don't need to diversify,' Abdel-Raouf said. 'All our youth know the business. No one will ever find anyone who can inlay like Ahmed.'

The biggest challenge to the Damietta export machine is not from the Far East, Abdel-Raouf told me, but from the Egyptian government. Egypt lacks hard wood, so Domiat and other furniture makers import lumber from around the world – pine from the United States and Finland, beech wood from Romania and Yugoslavia, plywood from Russia. Because importing is complex and costly, most importers go through agents. The government imposes a tax on wood imports equal to 20 per cent of the shipment value. Under Egyptian law, companies that import materials needed to assemble products for export are eligible for an import-tax rebate if they apply at the finance ministry. But according to Abdel-Raouf, the process is punitively bureaucratic.

'It's a labyrinth,' Abdel-Raouf said. 'We would go to the tax auditors or the finance ministry and they either don't reply or tell us to import on our own, which we can't afford to do.'

What about USAID programmes?

'The Americans have something called Expolink, which is funded by USAID, but it helps the wrong people. They do arrange for the import of wood, but you have to buy it through a USAID-approved bank and sometimes they demand we pay interest anyway. Why don't they just buy the wood for us and we'll pay them?'

*

The Egyptian government is doing at least one thing right. Mahmoud Abdel Latif, the Banque du Caire vice president who helped me pry $198 from his own bank's foreign-exchange turnips, was head-hunted by the government from Chase Manhattan Bank. Having deemed privatization too risky politically, Egypt's finance ministry decided to recruit Western-trained bankers like Mahmoud and restructure the financial sector from within. In the eight months or so since Mahmoud had taken the Banque du Caire helm he had replaced aging apparatchiks with younger staff, winnowed payrolls with early retirement schemes, introduced intensive training programmes and laid the groundwork for new products like mortgage lending.

Basically, this is privatization by stealth – banking reform without the unpopular step of actually selling a bank. But it is better than nothing. The Banque du Caire restructuring is a pilot scheme that, if successful, may be applied to Egypt's other banks.

Mahmoud's biggest challenge, he said, was to diversify his loan portfolio. Nearly 40 per cent of Banque du Caire's outstanding debt was held by only 15 clients. Mahmoud wanted to promote loans to small businesses in allotments of between L.E5,000 to L.E25,000. In the developmental aid community this is known as micro-finance, and it is generally praised as an effective way of funnelling capital to entrepreneurs. Its impact is limited, however, by the donor's finite resources.

Mahmoud's vision, which he was implementing with the help of a USAID training programme, was to graft micro-credit on to Banque du Caire's product line and introduce retail banking to an economy that hardly knows it.

'The default ratio on small loans like this is nil,' Mahmoud said. 'There is a whole army of civil servants, fifteen million or so, who would start their own businesses if they had the funding. If I can loan to two or three million, I can spread my risk.'

I asked Mahmoud for a first-hand view of how it all worked. A week later I was the guest of Mohammad Abdel Basset, manager of Banque du Caire's main branch in the Cairene suburb of Shubra.

Mohammad was very much the natty neighbourhood banker in pressed shirt, blue blazer, and red tie with matching braces and pocket handkerchief. He wore a gold Rolex watch but the hems of his trousers were poorly sewn. He got about with the help of an aluminium cane.

Banque du Caire's new micro-credit programme, Mohammad said, had attracted 612 new clients from between 50 and 60 branches. Each client's initial tranche of between L.E1,000 and L.E3,000 had to be repaid within twelve months at 16 per cent interest, which is roughly what Egyptian banks charge prime customers. If the client meets his obligations his allocation limit rises to L.E4,500 and so on until the fifth cycle, which makes him eligible for loans of up to L.E10,000.

Clients include grocers, shop-owners and small-scale manufacturers producing everything from shoes to iron nails and telephone-cord adaptors. Applicants are required to furnish some documentation – a lease agreement or electricity bill – which is held on their file. This alone is an important advance in a society where so much commercial activity goes unrecorded.

Each client receives a passbook and is requested to make weekly repayments of around L.E75. 'We hold meetings with customers and try to make them feel at home, like they have support,' Mohammad said. 'We ask them to always hold back ten to fifteen pounds in case of emergencies. This is not just about lending money.'

Banque du Caire's credit officers are trained by USAID and then unleashed to inspect inventories, ledger sheets and factory equipment and learn about things like cash flow and depreciation costs. Drinking tea with a client is prohibited as a conflict of interest.

'We try to make them understand the importance of documents,' said Mohammad. 'Though Egyptians are very clever; all they need is a book for very basic things such as expense accounts.'

I asked to meet a client, and within minutes Mohammad and two of his loan officers were escorting me to a printing shop about a mile from the bank. There Said Fat'hy al Wakil, the shop's owner and operator, waded through a thicket of paper cuttings that covered the floor, greeted us warmly and dispatched his assistant to bring us tea.

Said opened his print shop 12 years ago with a paper cutter and a 54-year-old German printing press. He put 50 per cent down on the printer and paid the rest in instalments. In 1996, he upgraded to a 15-year old press that prints four times faster than the old one, kept as a backup. When either breaks down, a blacksmith reproduces the faulty part.

The shop was a study in organized clutter. Rubber stamps were displayed in a wall cabinet that hung out of kilter. Cans of ink were piled in one corner, reams of blank paper in another. An idle fan hung from the ceiling. Said showed us his product line: envelopes for processing laboratories, slips for graduation and wedding photos, blank receipts, day calendars. Last October Said borrowed L.E2,000 from Banque du Caire. He paid this off in five months and then took out another loan for L.E4,000 to pay for raw materials, mainly ink and paper, but also in response to market conditions. Following the pound's devaluation, the price of his imported ink increased from L.E20 to L.E27 a bottle. When the pound recovered and the price of ink receded, he bought ink in quantity to hedge against another run on the dollar.

I savoured the irony; while Egyptian regulators agonize over a revival of their commodities-futures exchange, here is Said, the plucky printer, creating his own.

The tea arrived while we sat in wooden chairs outside Said's shop. The bankers dutifully declined it, and Mohammad's credit officers showed me photos of their families.

'They don't stay in the office and sometimes they work late, so I encourage them to carry the photos,' Mohammad told me. 'This is not only a job for them, it's a source of pride. They work late when no one asks them to.'

Last Saturday was a national holiday, Mohammad said, but he spent it with a businessman seeking to import cyclotrons – three-wheeled scooter taxis – from India for L.E13,000 each. After consulting with importers, they figured they could reduce the shipping costs by half if they broke down each unit before transport into separate components that could be assembled locally.

'Of course we are frustrated with the economy,' Mohammad said, 'but we are fighting it with action.'

Said sported a *zebiba*, or raisin, the dark spot on a pious Muslim's forehead left from years of bowing to the floor in prayer. I asked him if Egypt's failing economy would play into the hands of religious fanatics.

'Poverty leads people to extremes,' he said. 'If people are too rich it is not good and if they are too poor it is not good. This is a problem. I have three children. My eldest daughter is in college. I am not making enough to get by. But these loans help. When I have more capacity, I can hire more people. We have to create an economy that turns on its own without the help of others.'

I was running late, though Said insisted I finish my tea. 'If you leave with your cup half full,' he explained, 'it means my daughter will never marry.'

Faced with being late for my next appointment or jeopardizing my host's bloodlines, I agreed to stay. A few minutes later, my teacup dry, I got up and collected my things. Said took my hand in both of his and shook it vigorously.

'Tell the Americans to treat us the same as they do the Israelis,' he said. 'That is all we ask. My eldest daughter is studying Hebrew. One day, God willing, we will all understand each other.'

Thuggery and its Discontents

People are in the long run what the government makes out of them.

Rousseau

Government ought to be what the people make of it.

John Adams, eighteenth century American
revolutionary and statesman

Most countries are lucky to have one golden age; Egypt has had many. From the Pharaohs to Alexander the Great, from Ptolemy to the Turks, the country's strategic location has proved more compelling than any one conqueror's ability to hold it. Egypt was the centrepiece for many empires and the signature works they left behind – the Pyramids, the Pharos Lighthouse and library at Alexandria, the Nilometer (the device used since Pharonic times to measure the rise and fall of the Nile), the Roman aqueducts, the Al Azhar mosque and the Citadel of Mohammad Ali. Many of these are gone and only one, the Al Azhar mosque, is still in use. It was built by the Fatimids, a Shiite tribe that migrated east from Tunisia to attack the western half of the Islamic world in 969; under their administration from 972 to 1171, Muslim influence over Mediterranean trade, industry and culture reached its peak.

The Fatimids were Shiites, claiming direct descent from Fatima, the prophet's daughter, and her husband Ali, Mohammad's nephew. Apparently bored of the Maghrib and sure of victory over the Abbasids, they journeyed across North Africa with their ancestors' remains packed among their worldly goods. Under Fatimid rule Cairo was transformed from an outpost of the nearby town of Fustat into Egypt's capital and a thriving commercial centre. The Fatimid's early *wazirs* included Yacub ibn Killis, an Iraqi Jew who converted to Islam and is regarded as one of the greatest administrators in Muslim history. Ibn Killis embodied the era's tolerance and enlightenment; non-Muslims were well represented at court, with prominent Jews and Christians invited to the palace for weekly theological debates.

The great mosque and university of Al Azhar was founded in 970 by Jauhar, a former slave who had emerged as general of the caliph's army. The most gifted scientists of the day abandoned the corrupt Abbasids and emigrated to Cairo. They included Al Haythem, known as the Second Ptolemy, who wrote some 200 books, refined the Nilometer and was a master of astronomy, maths, physics and philosophy.

The only blight on Fatimid rule was a 20-year famine and the excesses of the seemingly schizoid Caliph Al Hakim who persecuted Jews and Christians, destroyed Jerusalem's Church of the Holy Sepulchre (he quickly ordered it rebuilt), entombed the minarets of an important mosque in brick and in 1020 proclaimed himself divine. Even Al Haythem feared the crazy caliph and spent much of his workday locked in his laboratory.

As Muslims, the Fatimids were not just a minority in much of the Arab world compared to the more numerous Christians and Jews, but as Shiite Muslims a minority within a minority. Sunnis generally distrusted Shiites for their devotion to Ali and the success of Fatimid rule was a triumph of medieval marketing and propaganda. Basically, they partied their subjects into submission.

Every holiday and event – Ramadan or Eid (marking the end of Ramadan) for example, or the measuring of the Nilometer – a grand procession filled the narrow streets of Cairo followed by a lavish reception. The parade would be led by the educated elite of Islam, both Sunni and Shiite, followed by the palace guard, the regular army – some 5,000 or so in full body armour – and a marching band. Finally came the caliph, dressed in white robes, seated modestly on a donkey and protected by a gold parasol held by a favoured courtier. In general, the weaker the economy the more elaborate the celebration.

Fatimid longevity was due less to pomp, however, than good business sense. Theirs was an ecumenical domain open to foreign goods and ideas. Even during the Crusades, as European Christians clashed with Arab Muslims, commerce flourished.

'In Muslim territory,' wrote Ibn Jubayr, the Arab geographer:

> . . . none of the Christian merchants [are] forbidden entrance or molested. The Christians impose a tax on the Muslims in their land, which gives them utmost security, while the Christian merchants also pay [customs] for their goods in the land of the Muslims. Reciprocity

prevails and equal treatments in all respects. The warriors are engaged in their war, while the people are at peace.

A growing middle – mostly merchant – class began replacing the grey robes of the desert with gowns and turbans of bright colours and diaphanous materials imported from China and India, where Arab seafarers were regular visitors. So easy and frequent were sailings across the Mediterranean – it was known as a *pontos euxeinos*, a friendly, inviting sea – that merchants suffering from chronic disease would regularly sail from North Africa to, say, Toledo or Constantinople for treatment. Deadbeat debtors had to flee as far as the then-Red Sea port of Aydhab (in modern Sudan) to escape creditors because the Mediterranean was too well travelled to provide refuge. Commuting between Tunisia or Sicily or even Spain and the eastern shores of the Mediterranean was commonplace. Like the Pharos Lighthouse, Egypt shined like a beacon for tolerance and globalism. For centuries after Saladin replaced the Fatimids in the twelfth century, Cairo and Alexandria remained cosmopolitan entrepots for foreign ideas and cultures.

It wasn't until midway through the last century that the light was finally snuffed out.

'It was such a happy place. It had telephone operators, cleaners, a nurse, the gardener. They all spoke French but the family spoke Russian when alone together.'

Vera Akerid and her sister Simone were telling me about growing up as middle-class Jewish children in Egypt prior to the birth of Israel in 1948. It was February 2000 and I was writing a story about a trove of Torahs, the Jewish holy book, languishing in Egyptian synagogues since the triumph of Zionism provoked an anti-Jewish backlash that forced most Egyptian Jews to flee. The Torahs – some, centuries old – were being contested by members of the Egyptian-Jewish Diaspora who want to collect them, and the remaining Jews in Cairo and Alexandria who regard them as a vital part of the remains of Egyptian Jewry.

The Jews of Egypt, mostly in their 70s and 80s, are a community in name only. Because all but a few are women, they cannot form a *minion*, or prayer group, which requires at least ten Jewish men. When an Egyptian Jew passes away, the US embassy sends a proxy minion to the funeral. There is no Rabbi, no Kosher butchers and the Ben Ezra synagogue is kept under 24-hour guard by military police. The Torahs, held under lock and key, are only taken out on special occasions.

I met Vera and Simone in a faux-Swiss chalet restaurant with red-and-white checked tablecloths, cheese-boards and cuckoo clocks. The two women radiated a youthful charm and sisterly mischievousness as they recalled banquets and lawn parties held at the Hôtel des Cure in the affluent suburb of Helwan. The hotel was owned by a Dr Glanz, a White-Russian émigré whose eldest daughter Eugenia had married Vera and Simone's uncle. Well into the 1940s, the hotel was a favourite enclave of Cairo's bourgeoisie. Then Nasser nationalized it along with the rest of the economy and leased it to a corrupt army officer who never left the place.

Vera went on describing the hotel, relishing her journey through the past: 'The bedrooms were in the old style – huge, palatial. It was a place where royalty stayed, sometimes for months. The King of Belgium stayed there. They came for the waters, to take the cure. And the garden, it was huge. Mrs Glanz entered her flowers in shows every year and won. There was a solarium separate from the main hotel where people relaxed, took saunas and massages. Except for the New Year's parties, it was always quiet and relaxing. It was open year round.'

'Mrs Glanz was older than Dr Glanz and was very jealous of him,' Simone added conspiratorially. 'Even when we visited them in London in 1982 I remember her getting very cross when I hugged him.'

As late as the mid-twentieth century, Egypt's Jewish community was one of the Arab world's oldest and most robust. Members congregated at the Ben Ezra synagogue in downtown Cairo, which dates back to 606 BC and is thought to stand where Moses was plucked from the Nile. Mohammad Ali, the Ottoman viceroy, encouraged Jews to settle in Egypt as part of his plan to develop a first-world economy. In the art-deco salons of pre-Second World War Egypt, gossip, policy and intrigue found expression in Arabic, French, English and Hebrew.

*

'In the 1930s, the Egyptian Jews prospered,' said Daniel Goshen. 'When I returned to Cairo for a visit in 1981, things had changed. No one spoke a foreign language. It was an Arab nation.'

I met Daniel, who heads the Egyptian Jews Association in the coffee shop of a Haifa hotel with Avnar Assel, also Egyptian born. Daniel's father had fled Russia for Egypt in the 1920s and settled in Port Said, where he worked on the Suez Canal. Avner, a third-generation Egyptian, was employed as a clerk at a major Jewish-owned trading company.

Like Simone and Vera, Daniel and Avner fondly recreated for me the Egypt of their youth. They lived, prosperous and secure, with their families in comfortable homes and owned the latest European and American automobiles. Unlike the Akerid sisters, Daniel and Avnar abandoned Egypt for Palestine to help forge a Jewish state.

'In 1935, my brother joined the Hagana without telling my mother,' Daniel said.* 'When she found out she forced my father to take out his pension and follow him, so we settled there as a family. Two years later, my brother was killed in the Arab-Jewish riots. In 1948, I fought under Moshe Dayan in the war of Independence.'

Avnar's departure was more abrupt. In 1946 his request for a visa to visit Palestine was rejected and his name was placed on a list. On 15 May 1948, the day Israel's statehood was declared, Egyptian police began herding Jews into camps. When Avner arrived at his grand-mother's house, he was met by two cars filled with seven Egyptian soldiers armed with rifles with fixed bayonets, taken to a police station and then driven to a camp in Alexandria. In all, according to Avner, the government incarcerated nearly 400 Jews.

'There were Jews but there were also members of the Muslim Brotherhood and leftists,' Avner said. 'Some of the Jews were Zionists but others had nothing to do with it. The camp wasn't so bad. We had good relations with the commanding officer. He was a brigadier general and allowed us books. I learned Hebrew, because one of the men was a teacher. It was good to have something to do.'†

---

* The Hagana, the Jewish militia, later to become the Israeli army, known as the Israeli Defence Force.
† Not all experiences were apparently so benign. After my story on the Torah dispute appeared I received an email from a reader who claimed he was similarly incarcerated and was forced along with other inmates to run along a makeshift track shouting, 'I am a Jewish dog.'

After 15 months, Avner was driven straight to the harbour in Alexandria to be deported by ship along with hundreds of other Jews. He could take nothing with him – no books nor photos nor college diploma – and had just about $30 in his pocket. The second Jewish exodus from Egypt, the evacuation of some 80,000 to 90,000 people and the cream of Egypt's middle-class, had begun.

Of the myriad Jewish communities who have settled in Israel, the Egyptians are among the most successful. Avner joined a Kibbutz and later worked in the export department of a petrochemical company. Daniel settled in finance.

'We did very well,' Daniel said. 'Many of us went into banking because we knew several languages and we knew how to work with the world.'

More than 30 years after Israel and Egypt normalized relations, Israel's Egyptian-born Jews cannot claim compensation for the homes they were forced to flee. 'We left our cars, our houses with the keys inside,' Daniel said. 'But the Egyptian government is not willing to release these items or compensate us.'

Avner has visited Egypt three times since his deportation. 'The first time I went with my wife, to see the places we left behind,' he said. 'We saw the house where we lived, the school we attended. We saw the maids, who recognized us and were happy to see us. They regretted what had happened. We saw friends, one of whom was a Muslim bank manager who said he was sorry *he* didn't leave.'

Once, while walking through downtown Cairo for an interview, I passed the Ben Ezra synagogue, an imposing, stone-block structure, heavily crenellated and decorated with schematic palm fronds. Carved into the mammoth porticos over the twin entryways is a Star of David.

The synagogue is a monument to Middle-East paradox. Like the flag that hangs over the Israeli embassy it stands boldly against the anti-Jewish propaganda in the state-run Egyptian media. It is also a tragic anachronism, a vaulted archive for a Jewish community orphaned and nearly extinguished by the triumph of Zionism.

I tried to take a photo and was shooed away by military police.

*

The Domesticated Opposition

The halls of Zaqaziq University were plastered with posters and flyers celebrating the Palestinian Intifada and condemning the Israeli response: 'Jews are Jews! They killed the prophet Jesus!' Israeli, US and British tanks were graphically depicted slaughtering stone-throwing youths and converging on the Dome of the Rock. The Israeli invasion of the West Bank was a week away but on 4 March 2002 Zaqaziq's students were already in a lean and hungry mood. 'Boycott American goods!' one poster declared, embellished with a photo of a dead infant with a bullet hole through its chest. Another photo showed the child from behind, its entire left shoulder blown out.

Until the late 1960s, Zaqaziq University, like other Egyptian colleges, was a raucous trading pit of ideologies and ideas, shuddering with debate between royalists, socialists, democrats, fundamentalists and pan-Arabists. These competing voices have given way to a rotelike, monolithic refrain – Free Palestine, death to the Jews, Israel and America, Sharon and Bush. Even on college campuses, dissent in Egypt is permissible only when projected outward, toward Palestine, as a diversion from the oppression at home that imposes itself like a lead weight on the public volition.

Zaqaziq, about 70 kilometres from the Suez Canal, is the main city in Sharkiya, Egypt's second-largest province with a population of six million people. Of the 444 elected seats in Egypt's parliament, 28 are from Sharkiya. Of those, three are held by members of the Muslim Brotherhood, one of the country's most prominent and moderate Islamic groups.*

The Muslim Brotherhood, founded in the 1920s, first won 16 parliamentary seats in 1986. Although outlawed, its grass-roots appeal is so powerful that the government cannot prevent it from contesting elections. In a fair race, most analysts estimate the Brotherhood would win around 70 seats. As it is, they control 17, and form the second-largest parliamentary grouping. The government, in a classic performance of Oriental kabuki, pretends Muslim Brotherhood legislators simply represent themselves.

---

* Throughout the 1990s the government fought a low-intensity but bloody war against Muslim fundamentalists that ended, more or less, with a truce. Islamic Jihad, another Islamic organization with considerable appeal in Egypt, remains in the shadows and its penetration of officialdom continues to confound the government. Every so often, reports surface of a senior military or security officer arrested for having close links to Islamic Jihad.

I had come to Zaqaziq as a guest of Dr Mohammad Morsi, a Muslim Brotherhood parliamentarian and professor of engineering at the university. A week earlier he and fellow party leader Dr Ali Laben had told me about the party platform at their Cairo headquarters. As Dr Ali put it, the Muslim Brotherhood's vision goes back three or four centuries: an Islamic republic modelled on the Turkish sultanate. They also believe in market economics and free trade.

'Our goal is to realize the faith as it was practiced by true Muslims,' said Dr Ali. 'We want to return our system to the early caliphates.'

The Muslim Brotherhood says it rejects violence and strongly condemned the September 11 attacks. Largely as a result, Islamic Jihad and other extremist groups have labelled its members as heretical sellouts. In prisons, Dr Mohammad told me, officials separate militant Islamists from Muslim Brotherhood members to prevent their exposure to the more corrosive doctrine of peaceful opposition.

'We are teachers, not judges,' he said. 'We use legal means for legal objectives. The Egyptian government, the Americans, the Israelis have much more to fear from us than from [Islamic] Jihad. Had America ignored Osama bin Laden he would have faded away.

'In January,' Dr Mohammad went on, 'the prime minister addressed parliament. He said the strength of the ruling party rested on five pillars: the military, the security forces, the media, the judiciary, and the personality of the president. Not once did he mention the people.'

The Muslim Brotherhood supports Hezbollah in what it calls the war of resistance against Israeli occupation. Like Hezbollah, the Muslim Brotherhood has a social network that can administer civic services in areas neglected by the government. In remote villages and towns the party operates hospitals and clinics, schools and potable water systems, even though the government provides significantly greater resources to legislators from parties more friendly to it than the Muslim Brotherhood.

'The government wants to weaken our position,' said Dr Mohammad. 'Just last week it ordered the transfer of two assistants from my office. Sometimes when I speak at a mosque, the government comes and interrogates the imam. It's a game. They need a threat and if you don't have a threat in this world, you get eaten up.'

*

Dr Mohammad asked me to meet him at the university after his 11 a.m. class. He was winding up as I entered a lecture hall filled with a few hundred students sitting on crude benches divided by a single aisle. Nearly all the students were males.

I closed the door gently, afraid to interrupt the proceedings – which I promptly did.

'Ah,' Dr Mohammad announced. 'Here is the American journalist I was telling you about.'

Smiles and giggles from the anti-American, student-horde. I sat down at the back. On the blackboard Dr Mohammad had drawn a diagram of the structural integrity of crystal formations. It was annotated in English and for some reason I found myself taking notes: *Defects & imperfections in solids . . . Triclinics, Orthohombic and the Siberian idocrase . . .*

A quarter of an hour later we were in Dr Mohammad's spare office. He called for coffee but had none himself, for he was fasting in cele-bration of the Muslim holy day that commemorates the exodus of Moses and the Israelites from Egypt.

As Dr Mohammad briefed me on his schedule, students trooped in with vouchers they could redeem for discounts on textbooks. Dr Mohammad spoke to each briefly, signed their slips and then turned back to me.

'Today I will go to the irrigation ministry office to discuss the current water shortage,' he said. 'And after sunset, I'll go to the farmers. This is how I spend most of my time. It takes three-quarters of my day when it should only take 10 per cent. It is an obstacle to our main mission of making laws.'

I volunteered that local politics was important in the formation of any democracy.

Dr Mohammad shook his head. 'This is not America. When I ran for office, the *mukhabarat* broke into my house and took my books from my home. *My books.* They charged my son with trying to over-throw the government and held him for two months. He was distrib-uting leaflets. Even after I was elected, they kept him in jail, though I didn't get involved. I even suggested they take my wife instead but they weren't interested.'

More students knocked on the door. They presented vouchers, discussed term papers, begged for extensions on deadlines.

'When these students graduate where will they go?' he asked. 'The market is saturated. There are no jobs. We have 200,000 graduates in the market and the unemployment rate for students inside their discipline is 60, 70 per cent. It's hard for them to find any work. The government promises, promises, but nothing happens. More than half of Egyptians can't read. Only death is reducing the rate of illiteracy. Last year we earmarked L.E300 million for coping with illiteracy. Where does that money go?'

Like all administrative offices in the Arab world, the Zaqazik Central District for Eastern Delta Sub-Surface Drainage, a branch of the irrigation ministry, is overstaffed. On the wall was a colourful chart depicting the rate of Egypt's water consumption. It pre-dated the assassination of Anwar Sadat and forecast a crippling shortage by 2005.*

Dr Mohammad's appointment with the general manager had been cancelled, as the latter had just been called away by the governor. So Dr Mohammad had to make do with an underling. We filed into his office which had a wall-map installed on a hand crank. The map was painted in exquisite detail and had been in use since the British Protectorate.

We were offered tea, though Dr Mohammad abstained. The underling then briefed us on Egypt's intricate municipal water politics. The rice farmers, he said, had planted their fields a month early which placed an unseasonably heavy strain on existing water resources; a project to enlarge a canal running through the city's main thoroughfares was snagged. The electricity ministry had been forced to remove some underground cables; this cost L.E2 million and the project was now way over budget. Dr Mohammad suggested dipping into the L.E13 million provincial fund.

'What's another two million pounds?' he asked.

These Islamists were more politically evolved than I thought.

While Dr Mohammad was given a tour of the offices I waited in a reception area where I was collared by a staff worker named Maher. He insisted I have coffee with him and I resigned myself to another day of bladder-busting Arab hospitality.

---

* A Mideast water crisis is like an Iranian nuclear bomb; every year someone estimates it will be upon us in ten years.

Maher, it turned out, was the director of the laboratory for soil investigation, with a civil engineering degree from Zaqaziq University. I was hoping to hear about Egypt's looming water shortage or the insidious creep of calcium deposits on the city's galvanized-copper pumping system, but no such luck.

'You Americans hate the Arabs,' he said, clinging to my forearm. 'You are constantly trying to divide us.'

I tried explaining to him that the Arabs were pretty good at dividing themselves, but he cut me off.

'Do you know who is responsible for 9-11?' he whispered. His head shot up straight and swept the room for potential snoops, then angled in towards mine. It seems the September 11 attacks were orchestrated by an alliance of various extremist groups working jointly with Israel's Mossad, the CIA, India, and the Italian mafia.

'Even if we assume Al Qaeda was involved,' Maher said, 'it was intelligence agencies who masterminded it. We simply must ask ourselves who benefited the most from the attacks?'

Madness, I thought. Twaddle. The extremes of Arab conspiracy theories boggled the mind. So what if relations between Israel and the US since the attacks have never been closer. So what if the Pentagon is $40 billion richer. So what if . . .

I paused.

'The Italian mafia, you say?'

'The US has to change its policies,' Maher went on, 'not for itself but for the world. It should carry on not as the strongest country but one that embraces compassion. America has a population from all the world, it should represent all those groups, not just one.'

But what about the billions of dollars of American aid that have been given to Egypt?

Again, Maher's head swept for prying ears.

'It's like I give you money and then beat you with a stick,' he hissed. 'It's like . . .'

The phone rang and Maher was called away to take it. Dr Mohammad collected me for our next appointment. I waved goodbye to Maher who gestured desperately for me to stay and finish my coffee.

Dr Mohammad and I arrived at a computer-training seminar near the university. I was photographing him consulting with the project

director and was suddenly encircled by a half-dozen scowling young
students, all men.

'You are a journalist?' they asked.

I nodded.

'American?'

Another nod.

'We are boycotting American goods,' said the tallest, whose name
was Emad. 'We have something to say to you.'

Grabbing my arm, they hustled me into the nearest office. This is
it, I thought: one order of Early Christian, coming up.

The office was empty except for two young women in *chadors*
copying data into computers. As I barged in with my burly escort
they exchanged a look that said: *This should be interesting; to think I
nearly stayed home today.*

I was seated and surrounded by Emad and his gang who by now
were slapping my back and laughing in surprisingly high-pitched
squeals. They offered me coffee, tobacco, hashish. The Clash of
Civilizations had degenerated into the Fraternal Order of Dirty Jokes
and Loose Joints. Coffee arrived. I asked for their names. They were
very particular that I spell them correctly as I wrote them down.

The interrogation began.

'I wish I could know why the Americans hate us and Islam,' Emad
remarked.

'It's like a blind man being led by someone else,' Yasser said, referring to the relationship between the US and Israel. 'The Jews control
everything – TV, radio, politics. Jews are the spinal cord of America.'

'But Jews were always safe among the Arabs,' I said. 'It wasn't until
less than a century ago. . .'

'Yes, with the Zionists,' said Marwan. 'But now I hate Jews as well
as Zionists. They are a minority and their policy has been to control
everything. We hate those who hate us and we love those who love
us.'

I asked how Egyptians felt about their own government.

'We feel very secure,' said Marwan. 'But we can't trust the government for basic things like our children's education. So much of our
income goes towards tutors. I come from a family of engineers and
doctors and my children can't be any less than my brothers and sisters.'

Dr Mohammad entered the office, having looked everywhere for
me.

I finished my coffee. The students insisted I pose for photos with
them, arm-in-arm.

'Tell the truth,' Yasser admonished as I said goodbye. 'Tell the Americans how you are treated here in Egypt.'

The concrete stairway to Dr Mohammad's office was unfinished and unlit. At the entrance lay a pile of shoes belonging to the dozen or so of his constituents waiting in a reception area. The floor was covered with carpets and the walls with maps of Palestine in all its shifting contours – the borders in 1947, 1967, 1973 and 1982.

'Palestine is ours,' Dr Mohammad said. 'It is not for the Jews. One day we will take it back.'

'What about Egypt's peace treaty with Israel,' I asked. 'That is enshrined in Egyptian law and yet you don't recognize Israel.'

'We have no problem with Jews in Palestine. But only as Jews living there in a Jewish state.'

What about the borders of Palestine prior to the 1967 war? They were established by United Nations resolution.

'This was a canard by Europeans in league with Zionists.'

'But would you tolerate Israel if it withdrew?'

'Do you think this will happen?'

I shrugged.

Dr Mohammad smiled. 'Ask me when it does.'

I waited in Dr Mohammad's office while he performed his ablutions and prayed in a corner facing Mecca. The walls were bare, the furniture modest. There were no posters of Palestinian martyrs or portraits of the Dome of the Rock or the Ka'bah. Except for a set of Islamic law books on the top shelf of a bookcase, nothing suggested this was the lair of an Islamic fundamentalist.

Dr Mohammad leaned around the door and summoned his first petitioner. A man in a *dishdasha* greeted him and sat down. His neighbourhood was denied access to a sewage-extension project and the interior ministry was ignoring him; Dr Mohammad promised to investigate. A woman in a red headscarf and grey sweater collected a textbook for her son. A young man in a white Fila sport shirt asked for a job at the irrigation ministry. Dr Mohammad explained he could only recommend three men a year to the ministry.

'And they must have at least a high school degree,' he said.

The man looked down at his hands.

'I'll look into something,' Dr Mohammad said and escorted the man out.

A woman in full *chador* with paisley trim was being forcibly evicted with her family from her small apartment. Could Dr Mohammad either persuade the landlord to extend the lease or help her find another similarly priced apartment? Dr Mohammad made some notes and promised to help.

As Dr Mohammad received another petitioner, I followed the woman as she left the office and introduced myself. Her name was Soha and she was 32-years old.* She dropped out of high school to get married but would return if she could afford the tuition. Her husband made L.E150 a month and the rent on their apartment was L.E200. She last worked in a law office that paid a good wage, but only temporarily.

'I'd like to be independent from my husband because there are some things about him I don't like,' Soha told me. 'When he gets his salary, he pays here and there and then there's no money and we have to borrow. I don't mind working hard today for a better tomorrow but my husband doesn't feel that way.'

Soha had heard about Dr Mohammad through a friend of her brother-in-law. She doesn't usually cover herself, she told me, but did today to impress Dr Mohammad.

'I was told he is a religious man and could be trusted,' Soha said. 'I know he will help me if he can.'

Later that day I paid a visit to Dr Abu Hashem Abdullah, a professor at Zaqaziq University's school of cardiology and a Muslim Brotherhood member. Dr Abu Hashem settled in Zaqaziq twenty years ago after getting his degree in Cairo. In addition to his university activities he runs a medical clinic where he sometimes spends up to eight hours a day. He also works with a group that helps orphans and occasionally visits a small village clinic outside the city limits.

The reception in Dr Abu Hashem's clinic was mainly filled with covered women who couldn't afford the cost of regular healthcare. He greeted me in a blue shirt with yellow stripes, a muted tie and stethoscope around his neck. In his office there was an examination table covered in worn, imitation leather and on his desk a plaster model of a human heart, its valves painted red and blue.

---

* Even in Egypt many people are reluctant to speak openly with journalists; Soha is a pseudonym.

'So this is the face of radical Islam,' I said.

He smiled. 'The government is struggling against the Muslim Brotherhood. They arrest our most prominent members – doctors and engineers – and we struggle back. It comes from your country. Our president takes his speeches from the US government; Bush today, Clinton before him. This is the price we pay for your imperialism. And they want to convince us that this is a democracy.'

One of Dr Abu Hashem's patients was a 90-year-old woman accompanied by her three granddaughters. The woman had complained of a heart murmur and her family insisted she see a doctor. I asked the women if they knew the clinic was associated with the Muslim Brotherhood. Of course, they said, but that was not why they had come.

'This is the only place I can afford,' said the old woman. 'The care is good and the doctor is honest. What difference does politics make?'

Intellectuals without Names
'Would the Islamists ever accept a Jewish state?'

I was telling Amin el Mahdy and Ashruf Radi, two of Egypt's more astute and outspoken writers, about my day with the Muslim Brotherhood.

Amin looked at me as if beholding a pinhead.

'Are you kidding?' he said. 'The Muslim Brotherhood has secret relations with Al Qaeda, Hezbollah and Hamas. They are Dr Jekyll to the West and Mr Hyde to their own people. When you are driven by ideology everything is black and white.'

'They believe they have a mortgage on the truth,' said Ashruf.

'Even now,' said Amin, 'Al Azhar University finances fundamentalism. They need it to survive. Can you imagine, even after September 11, you can hear [Hamas political leader] Ahmed Yassin broadcast three times each Friday to the Al Azhar mosque? It has a college exclusively for North Africa students that graduates some 400 people each year. Where do they get the money?'

We were dining at the old Greek Club, a restored café in the part of downtown Cairo that flourished in the 1920s and 1930s. Formerly a favourite salon for Cairo's intellectual and artistic elites, it now caters to their rag-tag progeny.

With freedom of expression in the Arab world entering its second half-century of hibernation, the Greek Club is the closest thing to an open political forum in the Middle East outside Israel. Intellectuals mingle here to discuss the peace process, a new article by Palestinian writer Edward Said or the latest Human Rights Watch report on Egypt. Their proxy voice is American columnist Thomas Friedman of the *New York Times* who frequently criticizes Mubarak, something they are forbidden to do; they print his articles off the Internet and trade them like kids with bubble-gum cards.

Their patron saint is the jailed writer Saad Eddin Ibrahim. Officially, Ibrahim was charged with illegally receiving European Union money for his think-tank.* In fact he was punished for asking inconvenient questions about election fraud and religious persecution, and for suggesting Mubarak was preparing to make his son heir to the presidency. A sick man, Saad prior to his trial requested permission to travel abroad for medical attention but the government refused to lift the travel ban it had imposed on him.

Even elliptical references to the regime and its authoritarian ways can have its consequences. A week earlier, while addressing a writers' conference, Mubarak noted an article by writer Mohammad Said Mohammad that compared extremism – the kind the government battled throughout the 1990s – to armed resistance. When Mohammad stood up to elaborate, according to a conference attendee, Mubarak cut him off.

'I read it,' the Egyptian president glowered. 'Now sit down.'

It is in this environment that Egyptian intellectuals hunker down, smoke American cigarettes in defiance of the Arab embargo on US goods, and talk treason. I had been invited to the club by Hisham Kassem, publisher of the *Cairo Times*, a bi-weekly journal that is Egypt's only intelligent source of news and information. It survives on a drip-feed of financial assistance and intermittent advertising revenue and is often worked over by government censors. Unexpected 'paper shortages' disrupt print runs and Hisham gets the occasional menacing call from the *mukhabarat*, but he soldiers on.

The Greek Club has worn parquet floors and cream-coloured

---

* Chief State Security Prosecutor Sameh Seif claimed the Ibn Khaldun Centre for Developmental Studies, established by Ibrahim in 1988 to promote democracy and human rights, 'was on the surface a research centre, but in reality was an intelligence agency'.

walls with green trim. To get there patrons walk up a flight of marble steps with art-deco railings, past reproductions of Hellenistic statues and around a Victorian-era elevator. It is all very retro-Euro chic.

The club was almost empty when we arrived at 9 p.m. but Hisham assured me things would liven up. Within an hour, as if coming out of a theatre, a cast of writers, journalists, retro-socialists, neo-capitalists, artists, and musicians filed in. By midnight the place was lousy with intellectuals who smoked constantly and talked endlessly.

It was here Hisham introduced me to Amin and Ashruf. On the table was a paperback copy of *The Iron Wall*, Avi Shlaim's revisionist account of modern Zionism which an Israeli human rights and peace activist had given him.

Amin is writing a book on terrorism that he says will reveal a shadowy complex involving President Mubarak, the Israeli right wing and radical fundamentalists. Ashruf, who writes for an economic journal, believes Egypt must develop its consumer market before concentrating on exports.

'Privatization and liberalization is very important,' Ashruf told me. 'But domestic consumption is the key.'

Both men are self-confessed leftists. In the ever-changing coordinates of Egypt's political map a leftist favours strong ties with the West, economic reform and free trade, though he may or may not support a genuine peace with Israel. A rightist condemns the West and Israel, favours command economies and may or may not be an Islamist.

'To be a leftist, you have to be Western and secular,' Amin told me, as if revealing the charter for some secret society. 'After the Cold War you have to believe in capitalism but also to allow labour a moderating effect. Compassionate capitalism. That's what you must believe in.'

Thus Amin, a leftist, told me how he was attacked by members of a group who oppose peace with Israel – rightists – for attending a commemoration of the Camp David peace accord at the Israeli embassy. One might assume this would put Amin on good terms with a regime that owes much of its stability to peace with the Jewish state. Not so. A month earlier Amin was arrested by state security, detained for ten days without charge and interrogated about his relations with Israelis.

'This is the paradox of Egypt's peace with Israel,' Amin said. 'Egypt has good relations with Israel, both military and economic. It also has an embassy in Israel but no Israeli cultural centre here. Why? Because the state is afraid its citizens will become contaminated by Israeli democracy. There are 2,600 Egyptians working in Israel and 1,600 inter-marriages between citizens of the two countries but we are never told this. Why? Because the state needs tension to survive. With a real peace the security apparatus would no longer be needed.'

'We have a saying here in Egypt,' Ashruf said. 'If you can find one Egyptian intellectual who is not an informant, you are smart. If you can get five together and there are no informants, you are an expert. If you can get ten together without informers, you are an informer yourself.'

I returned to the Islamists. Could the Muslim Brotherhood or any other fundamentalist group win enough parliamentary seats to exert real influence over the government?

Hisham jumped in. 'In a popular, fair election they may get sixty, maybe seventy seats. But they would be limited to that ceiling because elections outside Cairo are run on clan lines, not politics. Their authority is limited by their numbers. They say they have 10 million members, Saad Eddin says it's a million. I say it's closer to 200,000. Besides, Islam has no political or economic theory behind it so the Islamists are restricted in what they can offer. They are hierarchical and factional. Ask them how many clinics they run. This is a city of 20 million people during the day and 16 million by night. It's like demonstrations at Cairo University. They might attract a few thousand people in a population of 69 million.'

Amin agreed. 'Mubarak is secure. He has the security services, the army, the extremists to play against the Americans.'

The regime sits, Amin said, on a compact with fundamentalists that dates back to the wars Egypt led against Israel. Hamas, Hezbollah and Al Qaeda were all fertilized by the legacy of Gamal Abdel Nasser. 'Nasser exported the security man and the sheik,' Amin said. 'He needed them to attack the Zionists. They [the government] may have arrested the Muslim Brotherhood but they left alone the most radical extremists and sent them to Gaza and Afghanistan. The CIA of course, supported this to get at the Soviets. When the Cold War ended, the regimes made a tacit agreement with the extremists that they would not attack one another at home. There are many deals made in the dark between the regime and the empire the radicals tried to erect.'

Something brushed my leg, and a cat emerged from under my table, one of around a dozen strays in the club. They prowled along the window ledge, nestled in chairs, infiltrated the kitchen. The patrons ignored them.

'What's with the cats?' I asked.

'Nothing,' Ashruf said. 'They're just cats who come and go. Cats without names.'

. Just like the intellectuals, I thought. Strays, with no place to gather but the Greek Club.

We were joined by Sabri Said, a journalist who quit his job as a columnist in a local economic magazine to co-host an Al Jazeera show with a member of Hezbollah. Sabri was in Egypt biding his time; he had been in Saudi Arabia working on a story but was expelled by officials who found it unacceptable that anyone would take issue with Hezbollah. Such is the intellectual anarchy unleashed by the Arab world's leading satellite broadcaster and its unnerving impact on the ruling elites.

A red-haired gentleman in a pinstriped jacket greeted Amin and Ashruf. Another man stopped briefly to say hello.

'That first man, the one with the red hair,' Amin said after the men departed. 'He is the last of Cairo's once-prosperous Italian-Greek community. The other gentleman, he is a prominent Coptic businessman. This is all that is left of a great, secular society. Before 1952 we had free elections. Yes, the King was a fascist who had the fundamentalists on his side, the farmers from the village. They were very, very low class. But on the other side you had a huge middle class, the Copts and the Jews. There were 1.5 million Jews, Armenians, Greeks, Italians, all Egyptian citizens. They formed liberal parties. They were free to speak. It was a golden age.'

Amin threw open his arms as if to embrace this, the wreckage of cosmopolitan Egypt.

'Then suddenly it's 1952 and here comes Nasser with this bastard idea of Arab nationality. Ever since then we've been in the sand with the Arabs.'

Saad Eddin Ibrahim, Egypt's leading dissident, has the worldly and weary grace of a persecuted intellectual. He is balding, with a nimbus of greying hair and a goatee that gives him a touch of John Steinbeck. Until his imprisonment, he lived in the Cairo suburb of Ma'adi with his American-born wife in a spacious but modest apartment with marble floors and Persian rugs. A judge had declared Saad's first case a mistrial, and when I called on him a new one had not yet been scheduled. A security guard loitered outside his home and checked visitors' identification cards.

Saad answered the door in a short-sleeved shirt and wire-rimmed reading glasses suspended on a cord around his neck. He led me to the living room sofa, on which were the proofs of an article he was writing for an English-language journal about how the world perceived the US after September 11. A portable phone lay on the coffee table. In the corner was an upright piano, with a songbook entitled *It's Easy to Play Gilbert & Sullivan* propped up on the music stand.

Tossed casually aside was that day's edition of one of Egypt's several state-run newspapers. It led with a 'scoop': The US was preparing bombing raids on Mecca and Cairo.

'This stuff is in the papers every day,' Saad said. 'The level of anti-Americanism in the press is amazing. The overtone and undertone of its coverage, especially after 9-11, is anti-America and anti-West. The regime uses this to channel local discontent away from itself. Meanwhile, it plays the aid card with Europe and the Americans who are afraid it will collapse into an Iran or Algeria. Then it promotes itself as the proponent of peace.'

'Not a bad strategy,' I said.

'When Mubarak began his regime [in 1981],' Saad went on, 'he was tolerant of Islamists and the middle class felt comfortable with him after the turbulent years of Nasser and Sadat. But he stopped short of economic reform because there was no consensus on how to change without losing control of the state. There is an endemic cultural deficit in the leadership, an inability to admit a mistake and the price for this is more mistakes. It also wiped out the regime's ability to hold down the Islamists.'

'Is there a link between economic disarray and fundamentalism?'

'There is no mechanical correlation,' Saad said. 'But when the regime is not doing well on one front, the opposition asserts itself on another. It took ten years for the regime to make up its mind on the economy. Things deteriorated in terms of equity and distribution. Rising unemployment creates fertile soil for elements of the opposition, Islamic and otherwise. It creates mass resentment and discontent. It is what made the 1990s the bloodiest decade in modern Egyptian history.'

'What of the middle class, the crucial centre?'

'The middle class is a huge sociological category,' said Saad. 'And it is increasingly impoverished. Its fate was delayed by the oil boom that provided opportunities the Egyptian government failed to create. It is easy to have one Egyptian to work in Saudi Arabia or Kuwait or Iraq and remit enough money for his entire family to make do. This allowed the government, in turn, to paper over the failure of the Egyptian economy.

'All this comes to an end with the Gulf War. We now have the huge, lower-middle class, the sons and daughters of people living just over the poverty line and whose parents are struggling to make it. They are committed to modernity and know that education is the key. The fathers and mothers push their children to study, to do well, to get a good state job. This was the legacy of Nasser. But the state is no longer the employer of last resort and the Nasserite social contract is no longer honoured by the state.'

In Egypt, Saad explained, a first-year medical student is called 'doctor' by his family and the people of his village. 'They invest all their hopes and dreams in this young student. All this is squandered when he graduates and can't get a job. He keeps waiting and waiting and this provides raw material for Islamic groups. The system has betrayed you, he is told. It is corrupt. He is embraced by the Islamic groups who emerged victorious from the Cold War. As part of the middle class, he is far more vulnerable to recruitment than those from the lower class because he has something to lose.'

The regime exploits this degeneration, said Saad. For all its public hand-wringing in the aftermath of September 11, it tolerates a measure of radical Islam both as a release valve for discontent and a ghoul that focuses the West's attention.

'It is a proportional, cynical use of popular frustration,' he said. 'It is holding the Egyptian people as a hapless hostage and the West as a willing one.'

'Does the Muslim Brotherhood pose a real threat to the regime? Does it possess the legitimacy that could mould Egypt into an Islamic republic?'

'If the Muslim Brotherhood is allowed to participate in the system, it will moderate. Their seventeen representatives are responsible, their best and brightest members. They do their homework. They are fair, honest and predictable men. The worst thing to do is to keep them underground. You have to allow them to become a party and make them accountable to the people. I know a moderate ex-member of the Muslim Brotherhood. The other day he said he was trying to start a centre party and the government wouldn't issue him a license. So he has no alternative but to support the Islamists. People are afraid.'

'Have you told this to American diplomats here?'

'Yes and many agree with me but they get overruled in Washington. It is all very ironic. The Americans supported the Islamists during the Cold War against Nasser and then washed their hands of them, just as they did in Afghanistan.'

I told Saad I had been covering the Levantine Arab states for several years and found them suffering from the same debilities – inept, illegitimate government, stagnant economies, demoralized populations growing at geometric velocity, well-financed religious groups and bankrupt public schools.

'How,' I asked, 'is all this going to end?'

Saad shrugged. He confined his answer to Egypt but it could have applied to the entire Arab world.

'There is an historical fatalism in this country that it is eternal and will go on,' he said. 'But how long can you continue this hardship and stress? The only alternative is a viable, prosperous democracy. Egyptians are ready and want it.'

He glanced again at the newspaper with the lead story about the imminent US attack on Cairo and Mecca.

'That's what I went to prison for.'

On 29 July 2002, four months after my visit, a state security court sentenced Saad Eddin Ibrahim to seven years hard labour for violating Military Decree No. 4, which prohibits the receipt of funds from abroad without government permission. He was also found guilty of embezzling said funds and of 'tarnishing Egypt's image abroad' by disseminating false information.

The White House said it was 'disappointed' with the verdict.

Conclusion

Whither *Asabiyya*?

*'There is more respect to be won in the opinion of this world by
a resolute and courageous liquidation of unsound positions than by
the most stubborn pursuit of extravagant and unpromising
objectives.'*

George Kennan, testifying before the Senate Foreign Relations
Committee, February 1966

Why do they hate us?
I have heard the question over and again since September 11, 2001 –
on television talk shows, inside Washington, DC and in real life. It is
no longer strange, but it is disturbing. To mistakenly conflate Arab
opposition to US foreign policy with a deviant theology rejected by
the vast majority of the Arab-Muslim world diverts attention from
the challenge ahead: How to restore civil society to the Arab world –
its *asabiyya*, as defined by the great Medieval historian Ibn Khaldun –
and reverse its chronic social and economic decay. Only this can
neutralize the appeal of violent extremism, which is relatively new to
contemporary Islam. When I decided to write a book about the
depths and consequences of Arab malaise, questions of why the Arabs
'hate us' never entered my mind. Nor had I any doubt that the mix
of political oppression, stagnant economies and near-four per cent
population growth is enough to create a hopelessness and despair off
which extremism thrives.

The myth of Arab enmity towards Westerners and their values was
shattered by the Arabs themselves. Though the world will never

257

forget the events of September 11, the fact that nothing else happened in the immediate aftermath was overlooked. There were no mass demonstrations in Cairo, Baghdad, Damascus or Amman in support of Osama bin Laden and his demented interpretation of Islam; the storefronts of KFC franchises and computer stores weren't smashed as they frequently are during global economic summits in the US and Europe; few among the Arab world's army of jobless urban youths trooped to Kabul and Kandahar in solidarity with Al Qaeda and the Taliban against the approaching coalition assault; US and European consulates continued to be overwhelmed by Arabs in search of an entry visa to the prosperous and democratic West.

Just as Egyptian Islamic extremists wrongly believed they would spark a 'people's revolution' when they assassinated Anwar Sadat in 1981 for having made peace with Israel, so too did the engineers of September 11 misread the desire of the Middle Eastern peoples for representative government and not another brand of tyranny garbed in a turban or *burkha*. Islamic militants are as ignorant of the true, largely secular yearnings of the Arab majority as are Western governments. As my Syrian merchant friend Marwan once told me about the limited appeal of Muslim fundamentalism: 'It's been tried in Iran and no one wants any part of it. If someone came to you and said "Here's this great way of life called communism," would you be interested?'

The US assault on the Taliban, Osama bin Laden's hosts, was a judicious use of force against provocative militants in their lairs. But widening the war has created new enemies for Washington while hardening old ones. As Saad Eddin Ibrahim, the Egyptian dissident told me, a government unable or unwilling to admit old mistakes is doomed to make new ones. So it is with US policy in the Middle East. Arab leaders considered allies in 'the war on terror' are saluted and subsidized by Washington no matter how thoroughly they plunder their own economies and mistreat their people. The rest are identified as co-conspirators and placed on a list of prospective targets. All of this is done in the name of destroying Al Qaeda and radical Islam, the heart of what has been characterized as a monolithic threat to Western values.

In fact, the US has vastly misjudged what fundamentalist Islam represents in the Arab-Muslim consciousness, just as it overestimated the credibility, cohesion and motives of the East bloc during the Cold War. (There was no missile gap, the Korean War was the *last* thing Mao wanted and Russia was as estranged from China as

China was from Vietnam.) In a sense, Washington and Al Qaeda are fighting past one another; the latter will most certainly attempt another massacre of Americans and their allies, either in the United States or abroad. But the rising Osama bin Laden doubtlessly expected to erupt after the September 11 attacks did not material-ize – a repudiation that revealed his weaknesses rather than his strength and one Washington failed to see. By focusing exclusively on the horror Al Qaeda had wrought and not the whimper that fol-lowed, the US squandered an opportunity to refine its policies so as to further diminish the appeal of Al Qaeda and its clones.

Instead, the US interpreted the September 11 attacks as the first shot in an epic, Manichean struggle. 'You're either with us or against us,' George W. Bush declared immediately after the attacks. It was a memorable line from a US president but not a new one; Eisenhower used it in 1958 by demanding Arab regimes choose sides in the global war on communism. In so doing, he chased Egypt, Syria, Iraq and half of Yemen into the Soviet orbit.

'The policy of containment was initially correct and necessary,' Arthur Schlesinger, Jr wrote of Eisenhower's strategy in *The Imperial Presidency*, 'but it came under the hypnosis of crisis to confuse polit-ical and military threats, to lose a sense of limit and discrimination and to engender a mystique that poorly served its original aims.'

Nearly a half-century later, little has changed in America's rela-tions with the Arabs.

No war can be won without an honest appraisal of what motivates the enemy. Imperial Japan attacked Pearl Harbor and Clark Field in December 1941 in response to an Anglo-American oil embargo that impaired its ability to wage war on the Asian mainland. Just as Tokyo had to neutralize American might in the Pacific to achieve its ultim-ate objective – control of greater East Asia – so too was September 11 a means towards bin Laden's goal of a modern Muslim caliphate in the Holy Land.

Several important books about bin Laden and the motives driving radical Islamic groups were published or reprinted in the year follow-ing the September 11 attacks. In *Holy War, Inc.: Inside the Secret World of Osama bin Laden,* Peter Bergen enumerates the objects of bin Laden's ire – the US military presence in Saudi Arabia, US support for Israel, its continued bombing of Iraq, and its support for such 'apostate' regimes as Egypt and the House of Saud.

'Bin Laden cares little about cultural issues,' Bergen writes. 'What he condemns the United States for is simple: its policies in the Middle East.'

In *Taliban*, an authoritative account of Al Qaeda's Pashtun-Afghan allies, Ahmed Rashid admonishes Washington for projecting bin Laden as 'an all purpose, simple explanation for unexplained terrorist acts' when in fact 'the CIA had spawned dozens of fundamentalist movements across the Muslim world which were led by militants who had grievances, not so much against Americans, but their own corrupt, incompetent regimes'. Gilles Kepel, in *Jihad: The Trail of Political Islam*, notes that conservative Islam, particularly on the Saudi model, is a relatively new phenomenon. Radical Muslim groups were promoted by the CIA as a counterweight to Nasser; the 1973 Arab-Israeli war, which saddled the Middle East with rising oil prices (for Arab oil importers), double-digit inflation and a dramatic rise in unemployment, provided a fertile recruiting ground for fundamentalists. The failure of secular government, Kepel writes, attracted young Arabs to Saudi-style, conservative Islam, though that affair ended in 1991 when Saudi Arabia called in American troops for protection after Iraq's invasion of Kuwait – the very deployment that aroused bin Laden to wage holy war.

'Nothing fuelled bin Laden's rage more,' wrote William Arkin, the doyen of America's military affairs specialists, in a 6 May 2002 *Washington Post* column. 'His greatest public complaint [is] one the US government has chosen to not take seriously over the years [. . .] Are we capable of admitting to ourselves that bin Laden partly exists because [. . .] those troops never left?'

These conclusions are largely ignored in Washington because they do not fit the narrative around which the Bush administration's post-September 11 policies have evolved. The narrative – peddled by a syndicate of policymakers, pundits, academics, Christian fundamentalists and pro-Israel lobbyists in addition to administration hardliners – goes like this: Al Qaeda and their secular co-religionist Saddam Hussein are card-carrying members of a confederation of evil that, like the Comintern before it, is committed to destroying the Judeo-Christian West and its values. The war is eternal, the terrorists' appetite voracious and insatiable.

This narrative serves a double purpose: it justifies current US policy against terrorists – perceived or real – while obscuring the fact that Al Qaeda's war on the United States is essentially a *political* war waged against US policies opposed vehemently by most Middle

Eastern peoples and violently by a handful of extremists. Osama bin Laden, in dozens of videotaped manifestos issued prior to September 11, never proclaimed he was at war with Western culture or society. On 23 August 1996, two months after an attack on a US military base in Saudi Arabia attributed to Al Qaeda, bin Laden released his *Declaration of Jihad against the Americans Occupying the Land of the Two Holy Places* [Saudi Arabia]. In it, he condemns the 'Zionist-Crusader' alliance and its Al-Saud family – collaborators who, he alleges, soiled Islam and brought suffering to Muslims worldwide. There were no references to Descartes, Burke or Jefferson, to say nothing of Las Vegas, McDonald's, MTV, or any other vehicle of Western excess.

To acknowledge the political seeds of the Islamic terrorists' war would oblige Washington's political elite to take responsibility for the policies that provoked their attacks. An unbiased evaluation of US Middle Eastern policy snatches the focus away from the fiction – dispelled by disinterested experts like Bergen, Rashid, Kepel and Arkin – of a cultural reckoning of Biblical proportion and begs the simple question: Is Washington's military presence in Saudi Arabia, its hostility towards Iraq and nearly unconditional support of Israel, Egypt and Jordan worth the lives of 3,000 American civilians? It is a question no Beltway insider is prepared to ask, let alone answer. The narrative unfolds unexamined, let alone unchecked.

A sub-theme to the narrative is that radical Islam evolved spontaneously and in isolation from the prevailing socio-economic milieu, as if decades of war – both civil and trans-national – flat economies, spiralling population rates, chronic unemployment and illiquidity, and incompetent, oppressive and corrupt administration are not enough to foster the kind of desperation and outrage that feeds extremism. Though it is generally assumed declining living standards have a destabilizing effect on most societies, this is apparently not true in the Muslim East, where people are, well . . . different. Perhaps, the narrative implies, Mediterranean passion, the extremes of the Hindu Kush and Southeast Asian humidity fuels violent expression over reason and restraint. Or perhaps Islam's record of tolerance and moderation going back some 1,300 years is an elaborate hoax. Whatever the cause, the enemy is here to stay and is coming soon to a church or synagogue near you.

The narrative has inflated the danger posed by radical Islam while obscuring the greater threat – the failure of the Arab economy. More than two decades since Anwar Sadat addressed the Knesset on his vision for peace, the combustibility of the Middle East and the influence of radical Islam has risen inversely to Arab living standards. Many in the West sadly consider this ratio a coincidence, if they notice it at all. The Arab-Muslim world has never been more stable and open than when it possessed a robust middle class. It is the fortunes of the Arab bourgeoisie that will determine whether the fundamentalists achieve the critical mass needed to rule, as they did in Iran, or remain on the fringe of society, as jackals stalking a herd.

To subdue Islamic terrorism, the US should ally itself to the Arab middle class and not the despots who lord over it.

The early Muslims established the largest empire the world had yet seen through commerce far more than conflict. In the evolution of global enterprise, this was a golden age, with no borders to inhibit trade, no industrial policies to burden taxpayers, no unions clamouring for protection from cheap imports. The Muslim Middle Ages, though deeply religious in character, were characterized by moderation and tolerance. True, each of the three monotheistic religions preached that it alone was the correct interpretation of God's will and therefore any other faith was deviant, but such biases did not prevent Muslims, Jews and Christians from cohabitating in relative peace. The Geniza archive of letters from Medieval Egypt's thriving Jewish community reveal a very different, almost whimsical place compared to the blighted Middle East of today. Among its thousands of documents is a letter from a Jewish judge from eastern Libya written as he was returning home from a pilgrimage to Jerusalem. After scouting about for a suitable escort to transport himself and his goods home, he joined a caravan of Muslim traders. 'They have promised me to be considerate with regard to . . . the keeping of the Sabbath and similar matters,' the judge wrote a friend in Alexandria. 'For in the whole caravan there is not a single Jew besides myself.' Jews, Muslims and Christians lived side by side in Arab cities, as is made amusingly clear by a letter from a scholar complaining to a prominent notable how he was snubbed by the latter's son-in-law. 'When I came to his house he shut the door to my face,' the scholar wrote. 'I stood at the gate . . . and, while his gentile neighbours were looking on, I stood there and stood, knocking the ring, with him hearing me, but paying no attention.'

There can be no greater contrast between the culture of the early Islamic world and the impoverished and sinister backwater that was central Afghanistan under the Taliban, a derivative of radical Islamic movements that first emerged in the 1930s. It is significant that these groups gained momentum within a generation after the allied powers doomed the Arab economy by atomizing and politicizing what had been a solid and healthy economic bloc. The process continues as Israel, abetted by Washington, shreds the Palestinian territories with relentless settlement expansion. It is a classic divide-and-rule tactic employed by empires in both hemispheres. In 1924 Joseph Stalin fractured Central Asia into five separate republics in order to control that region's restive population. He created states where borders never existed and imposed illegitimate proxy regimes to run them. Today, Central Asia is impoverished despite its vast natural resources, unstable and home to a variety of militant Islamic groups.

There is no difference, neither in kind nor motive, between what Stalin did to Central Asians in his empire and what the British and French did to the Arabs in theirs.* The Western powers – the most vocal proponents of a borderless economy – have an obligation to resolve the consequences of the Balkanized mess they made of the Levantine Middle East at the end of the First World War. As a first step, Washington must shed the petrified logic by which it ladles billions of dollars in funding each year to the three countries that figure most prominently in what remains of its Middle Eastern policy – Israel, Egypt and Jordan. It could start by recognizing that the last thing the Middle East needs is aid because the region is awash with cash.

Israel is by far the most successful of those Middle East states that owe their creation largely to colonial fiat. It has a $100 billion-a-year economy and a world-class military that reduces to negligible the prospect of a conventional challenge from its militarily geriatric neighbours. Still, this country with an annual per-capita income of $18,000 receives $3 billion in aid each year from the United States.† Half is for military assistance, while the other half – incredibly – is for humanitarian purposes.‡ In 1998 it was announced such funding for Israel would be gradually phased out in favour of military aid.

American aid to Israel does more harm than good and should be abolished; it is unnecessary, compromises Washington's role as a broker in the peace process and penalizes the people it is ostensibly

---

* The Russians have a talent, Rudyard Kipling wrote of the divide-and-rule method, 'only second to ours of turning all sorts of clans and races into loyal supporters'.

† Egypt, the Palestinian Authority, Jordan, Syria, and Lebanon have an average per capita income of $1,680 and a combined per capita income of less than $8,400.

‡ The pro-Israel lobby is a master at manipulating Congress into sweetening US aid with supplemental programmes, including soft loans for new housing projects that save the Jewish state tens of millions of dollars.

supposed to help – such as those charged with safeguarding Israeli security in an engine of the Israeli economy.

The Iron Rice Bowls

Israel Aircraft Industries is located near Ben Gurion Airport on the outskirts of Tel Aviv. Its compound of modest buildings has the informal ambience of a college campus, though security is understandably tight for Israel's largest source of export revenue.

IAI, as it is known, symbolizes the heart, soul and brains of Israel's daunting military might and technological vitality. It is a global leader in such products as unmanned aerial vehicles, anti-missile defence systems and upgrade packages for fighter jets. Until the proliferation of Israel's small but robust high-tech sector, the company was home to the country's most skilled engineers and technicians. Many of the Pentagon's precision-guided munitions contain at least some IAI technology. If the US ever produces a viable strategic missile-defence system, for example, it will do so with innovations developed for Israel's tactical version, the Arrow II. So vital is IAI to the global aerospace industry that Arab air forces are deploying aircraft with IAI components; the Boeing F-15s bought by the Saudi Arabian government in 1999 have IAI-built external fuel tanks. In March 2000, the United Arab Emirates announced it would buy F-16s made by Lockheed Martin, which relies on IAI as the sole supplier of the aircraft's fuel tanks and vertical stabilizer.

'The true value of IAI is in people's heads,' Eugene Kim, a South Korean arms broker who knows the Israeli defence sector well, once told me. 'It may lack the production capacity of US companies, but every one of their people are thinkers, individuals. This is how they compete with the Americans.'

Up to a point. And that is where US military 'assistance' to Israel becomes a pair of golden manacles.

All but a quarter of the annual US \$1.5 billion of military aid to Israel is denominated in dollars, which obliges Israel to buy US weaponry even if it can produce comparable or even superior products. So companies like IAI have to compete with foreign manufacturers for a slice of Israel's \$9 billion military budget, only a portion of which is for arms procurement. The casual observer could be forgiven for thinking Israel does not produce its own assault rifle – the Galil, made by Israeli Military Industries Ltd – because it is compelled by US aid programmes to buy the American-made M16. Though Israel is the world's fifth-largest arms exporter, Washington has implicitly defined what it can sell abroad. In 1986 IAI unveiled its greatest achievement, the *Lavi* fighter jet. The United States encouraged the *Lavi* when it was conceived in the early 1980s and covered about 40 per cent of its development costs. But when test flights revealed the *Lavi* to be the near equal of the F-16, US aerospace companies and their lobbyists fiercely opposed it. Congress cut funding for the project and Israel cancelled it, rather than jeopardize its relationship with the Americans. The decision cost some 5,000 IAI employees their jobs.

'The cancellation of the *Lavi* created havoc with the company,' Ovadia Harari, IAI's executive vice president told me in a February 2000 interview. 'It was our backbone.'

In July 2000, Israel backed down from a $250 million deal to sell an airborne radar system to China, partly because of pressure from a US congress that feared the system might be used against Taiwan. Washington compensated Israel by proposing a supplemental aid package – in US dollars.

Crowded out by US funding at home and limited largely to niche-oriented markets overseas, Israeli defence companies like IAI have had a hard time finding a foreign partner that would give them the economies of scale needed to compete in the increasingly concentrated global defence industry. When Israeli Deputy Defence Secretary Ephraim Sneh was quoted in August 2000 as saying Israel had developed its qualitative edge through its own initiative and innovation, it was interpreted by some as an appeal to reason over politics: the country could protect itself without billions of dollars that is starving its own arms makers of business.

Sneh and his comments were rejected, most vocally by talking heads in Washington.* Few Israeli, let alone American, officials will say publicly what many admit privately – that US military aid to Israel is a billion-dollar annual subsidy for American weapons-makers at the expense of US taxpayers and Israel's own defence companies. It is a kind of slow hemlock served in an iron rice bowl that is also being administered to Arab recipients of US largesse, beginning with Egypt.

The United States Agency for International Development in Egypt is headquartered in an enormous glass-panelled office building near the

---

* Many of the Middle East 'experts' quoted in the mainstream American press work for think tanks that owe their budgets in part to patronage from US corporations, prominently among them defence contractors.

Cairene suburb of Ma'adi. It is, like the US embassy in Jordan, one of the few State Department outposts built to the terrorist-proof 'Bobby Inman' specifications drawn up in the 1990s and named after their architect. Every year, USAID gives Egypt hundreds of millions of dollars in economic assistance. Washington is reducing that allotment at 5 per cent a year, so that by 2009 the total amount should have shrunk to $450 million. The US also gives Egypt $1.3 billion annually in military aid, expected to remain at current levels for the time being and, needless to say, denominated in dollars.

Few doubt USAID's pivotal role in modernizing Egypt's infrastructure – sewage systems, water treatment plants, power grids. The agency estimates 90 per cent of Egyptians have electricity and telephones; two decades ago many Egyptians worked by kerosene lamp after sundown and businessmen flew to Cyprus to make phone calls. Yet it is impossible to quantify the agency's overall impact; according to a 2001 survey of USAID by Cairo's *Al-Ahram Weekly*, neither the agency nor the Egyptian government have provided detailed assessments of the aid programme's performance on a sector-by-sector basis.*

Egyptians love bashing USAID as much as they like sipping coffee and smoking hookahs, and often indulge in all three pastimes simultaneously. The agency and its citadel symbolize everything Egyptians see as asymmetrical about their relations with America. They resent the large proportion of the total finance allocated that is conditional on the purchase of US equipment and services. Many of the programmes designed to help small businessmen, at least according to people like Abdel-Raouf Essa, the furniture-maker in Damietta, are cumbersome and ineffective. The peace treaty that made USAID patronage possible is unpopular with the majority of Egyptians. Most would prefer an economy that, as printer Fat'hy al Wakil told me, 'turns on its own without the help of others.'

USAID officials say they understand that existing aid programmes must be adapted to support economic change in Egypt, though they complain privately at the government's lack of initiative. 'We are constantly pointing to Eastern Europe, which reformed quickly,' a senior USAID official told me in April 2002. 'But for whatever reason, they can't get their heads around it. There seems to be more concern on our part than on theirs. You can't separate politics from economics.'

---

* 'Such is the lack of documentation,' the survey reported, 'that save for the most recent seven directors, no one at USAID can remember or provide a full list of the agency's directors in Egypt, thereby leaving a yawning gap in the history of the organization between 1975 and 1981.'

You can, however, separate aid from indolence. Increasingly, Egyptian experts and economists are suggesting that US aid is stifling the government's incentive to reform rather than stimulating the economy. Abdel Beshai, a professor of economics at the American University in Cairo believes US funds should be indexed to Egypt's economic performance and tailored to restructure specific sectors of the economy. A five-percent increase in annual foreign direct investment, for example, might be matched by an aid programme aimed at developing not infrastructure, which the Egyptians can now handle themselves, but institutions – banks, capital markets, management-training centres. It is a sound proposal that should also be imposed on Jordan and the Palestinian Authority, which annually receive hundreds of millions of dollars in US aid.

The term 'institution building' has become popular within the donor-aid community and is therefore in danger of losing any meaning whatsoever. To understand what institutions are and why they are important, it is useful to think of the world as divided not between East and West but between countries that evolved under British dominion and those that did not. Wherever the British planted the Union Jack, they also established an administrative authority based on an efficient and standardized civil service, healthcare, banking and postal systems, and a legal code, stock market and regulatory agencies.

The priority Britain placed on institutions reflected its imperial mission: To develop a global economy patrolled and administered by the Crown. ('One great iron band girdling the Earth,' Kipling wrote. 'Within that limit free trade; without, rancorous protection.') That international marketplace required institutions to run properly and it is those institutions that make the difference between civil society and rule by patronage and intimidation. Institutions are what John Adams, once Britain's most wanted insurrectionist, meant when he referred in the Massachusetts state constitution to 'a government of law, not of men'; they are what Palestinian physician Dr Mustafa Barghouthi is trying to establish in the West Bank with his ambulance service.

The United States and Canada in the Western Hemisphere and Hong Kong, Singapore, Malaysia, India, and Australia in the East all developed societies strong enough to weather political and economic crises in part because they grafted the forms of British colonial jurisdiction on to their own social systems. Even Egypt, Jordan and Iraq established modern institutions during the relatively short period of

British rule, though they have been corrupted by war, oppression and incompetence and must be rebuilt. There is ample precedent for such forms of governance in the Middle East, which a thousand years ago developed the world's most efficient bureaucracies along with durable systems for trade and finance.

Take banking. More important than privatizing Egyptian banks is the diversification of their loan portfolios. The pilot micro-credit programme administered by Banque du Caire with USAID training is a good first step, but the objective must be the availability of cheap, long-term capital to finance larger projects and investments. Only then will the Arab economy develop critical mass and snap out of its current malaise. In Egypt I once shared a ride with stockbroker Shareef Rifaat to a birthday party in Al Fayyum, a district known for its beautiful lakes. Shareef spent most of the two-hour drive on one of his two mobile phones, talking to clients and colleagues in Cairo and London in Arabic, English and French. At one point, he stopped long enough to give me a concise summary of what is wrong with the Egyptian economy – the huge, untaxable, grey economy, tight credit, feeble banks – and how to fix it.

'We need a corporate debt market,' Shareef said. 'That will create liquidity in the private sector which means investment and employ- ment, which will pull people out of the informal economy and into the formal one, which creates taxable income for the government. But for a corporate debt market you need wholesale buyers, meaning the international investment community. They won't come unless you have local investment bankers who can speak their language. You have to create the industry, but you can't create an investment banker overnight.'

While at the USAID headquarters I was told of an International Monetary Fund initiative called the Financial Sector Revision Project that was launched to develop credible Egyptian debt and capital markets. The officials there hailed it as a major accomplish- ment.

Not Shareef. 'The World Bank and IMF have been talking about this for years, but no one is willing to bite the bullet and demand change,' he said. 'Typically they hire a retiree to run one of their pro- jects and he's happy to remain in Cairo because he's well paid and has an interest in perpetuating the study. Their motivation is to keep a four-year study going indefinitely.'

It is a common lament, one echoed throughout the international aid community. As my Palestinian friend Anis 'Al Qaq explained, 'sustainable development' for distressed economies is increasingly interpreted as sustainable employment for those foreigners who run donor-financed programmes. The centrifugal force of NGOs in the developing world has become so great it threatens to eclipse the governments they were established to assist. These organizations tend to be just effective enough to show results but not so conclusively that they are no longer needed.

The growing size and resiliency of the NGO rice bowl has triggered a backlash. In 2001, World Bank veterans Dennis Whittle and Mari Kuraishi launched DevelopmentSpace, which matches small-scale entrepreneurs in developing countries with foreign donors online. The model for the venture is eBay, the online auction service, and it has the potential to annihilate one of the biggest obstacles to economic development in impoverished states – the huge bureaucracy that has coagulated around the global aid industry, which is looking more and more like a racket.

Nowhere is this truer than in the Middle East. 'The aid packages [from the 1979 Camp David accords] made Israel secure and Egypt stable,' William Quandt, who helped broker the Israeli-Egyptian peace accord and is now a professor of political science at the University of Virginia, once told me. 'They are now running off inertia more than anything; bureaucrats hate to let go of something they've got.'

Such lassitude costs Americans more than taxes. The fortune Washington doles out each year to Israel undermines US credibility in the Middle East and makes it a target of Arab and Muslim rage. The financial and military assistance Washington funnels into Egypt and Jordan entangles it with regimes that are antithetical to the spirit of the Aristotelian ideals that were translated into Arabic by Islamic scholars a thousand years ago. The Bush administration's mild rebuke of the imprisonment of Saad Ibrahim – a warning it would 'review' future aid transfers to Cairo – is not the stuff that would reform a despot. Characterizing Jordan as 'moderate' mocks Jordanians who have been jailed, harassed and imprisoned for resisting limitations on free speech and association that grow narrower by the day. (In August 2002, Jordanian journalists protested an embryonic government plan to assign 'minders' to foreign correspondents reporting in the Hashemite Kingdom. That would rank Jordan on press freedom somewhere between Iraq, which requires such minders, and Syria, which does not.)

*

The Bush administration insists it is in favour of political reform in the Arab-Muslim world and wants to rebuild Iraq into a democracy that will stand as a model for its neighbours. This is an encouraging and admirable goal, though Washington must be prepared to abide by the consequences of Arab democratization, even if it means Islamic parties would do well in the polls. The cost of denying fundamentalists electoral gains would be far higher than if they were allowed to stand. Algeria learned this in 1992 after the government suspended balloting when it appeared Islamist parties would end up with control of parliament. The result was six years of bloodshed that killed some 75,000 people.

The notion that freely elected Arab legislatures would be exclusively secular and less hostile to Israel is appealing but naive. Islamist groups would do well in fair elections, at least initially. This is not because their orthodox platform appeals to the majority – witness the contempt young Iranians have for their own discredited imams – but because they are far better organized than the alternatives. Over time, as liberal parties mobilized and expressed themselves, Islamist candidates would have to either soften their agendas or alienate the moderate Arab sensibility that dates back to the early Muslim empires. As Hisham Kassem, the publisher of the *Cairo Times* told me, the Islamists' support is limited by the character of Arab identity, which is informed more by clan than by religion or political party. Over the centuries, Arabs have endured imperialism, pan-Arab nationalism, Ba'ath Party socialism and Islamic fundamentalism, but none have replaced the ancient tribal code – the Arabs' own *asabiyya,* an egalitarian system that is far more consistent with the ideals of Locke and Rousseau than Marx or Khomeini. It is a kind of feudal pluralism, what Laura Veccia Vaglieri of the University of Naples called 'the democratic tendencies of Arab society'. This is not unique to the Arab world; in Confucianist East Asia, the patriarch was respected and obeyed but his authority had to be earned and ineffective leadership could be challenged and replaced by public will. So it is with the Arab sheik. In the Middle East as elsewhere, the consent of the governed was respected long before Magna Carta was signed in 1215.

The elimination of Saddam Hussein and the emancipation of the Iraqi people may be followed by a revival of the Levantine economy, though it will be short-lived without reform of the Arab economy. This is necessary to rehabilitate the Arab bourgeoisie, the most potent agent for political reform. Autocracy knows no greater threat than a thriving middle class. The 1989 pro-democracy rallies in China that climaxed in Beijing's Tiananmen Square were struck down only after

blue-collar workers – the constituency that buffers China's haves from
have-nots and the seeds of a Chinese middle class – joined student
demonstrations. In Korea and Taiwan, an alliance of white- and blue-
collar classes earned representative government relatively peacefully, by
galvanizing its moral authority with a fast-evolving economic clout.

It would be pleasant to believe Washington understands that economic
reform is more important to the Middle East than oil and arms sales.
After all, studies released after the September 11 attacks by the United
Nations and the World Economic Forum clearly associated extremism
in the region with its stagnant and increasingly isolated economies. It
would be logical to assume such reports would be circulating at the
highest levels of the US government. One would also hope that the
US in the aftermath of Saddam's removal, should it come, would allow
the Iraqi people to develop their own form of representational government and rebuild their economy without outside interference.

There are those in the US government who appreciate the need
for change. From inside their bunker-like embassies throughout the
Arab world, some American diplomats privately express their frustration at what they describe as a US Mideast policy warped by the
parochial imperatives of domestic politics. They complain their
cables are filed away and lost in the vapours of Foggy Bottom, as the
State Department offices in Washington are known. Where they see
a region in decay, desperate for leadership and legitimate institutions,
the White House sees only threats – from rogue states and 'homicide'
bombers to 'multiple potential opponents' and 'hostile peer competi-
tors' – all working separately or in tandem and in lethal opposition to
the Bill of Rights. Washington hardliners have openly suggested Iraq
is only the first stop on the administration's warpath. Far from
seeking multilateral solutions to salvage the Arab economy, there
appears within elements of the Bush administration a *jihadist* zeal for
empire, a return to Cold War-style occupations, proxy governments
and alliances-of-convenience to safeguard US 'interests'. (With a
fitting Knights Templar-type flourish, one senior Pentagon official
has even referred to Palestine as 'The Realm'.)*

---

* Douglas Feith is currently the Bush administration's deputy undersecretary of defence for policy, one of
the Pentagon's most influential positions. In a 1996 briefing paper he co-wrote entitled 'A Clean Break: A
New Strategy for Securing the Realm', Feith urged then-Israeli Prime Minister Benjamin Netanyahu to
reassert Israel's claim to the West Bank and Gaza. A year later, in 'A Strategy for Israel', Feith called on
Israel to re-occupy areas under Palestinian control 'even though the price in blood would be high'.

This would be unfortunate, as wise Americans have always known. If America were to become involved in all the wars 'which assume the colours and usurp the standard of freedom', John Quincy Adams declared in his 1821 Fourth of July address, 'the fundamental maxims of her policy would insensibly change from *liberty* to *force*. She might become the dictatress of the world . . . no longer the ruler of her own spirit.' Senator William J. Fulbright issued a similar, if less elegant warning 150 years later: 'If America is to become an empire there is little chance it can avoid becoming a virtual dictatorship as well.'

The men and women of the Beltway Biosphere who counsel empire are apparently unaware that it was imperial ambition – first Turkey's with its malign neglect, followed by France's and Britain's and their malign intervention – that created the modern Middle East and at least indirectly the dictatorship and systemic rot that afflicts it today.

American policymakers and pundits have long neglected the relationship between economics and political stability. This is ironic, as the world's most powerful country was ordained and established by merchants, traders and farmers – not a professional politician or arms manufacturer among them. The most pressing issues facing the infant United States were arcane economic matters involving trade, the merits and demerits of a national bank, the protection of sea lanes, and Britain's forced recruitment of US seamen. Indeed, George Washington's farewell address is well remembered for his admonition against the young republic entering into 'entangling alliances' overseas.* Over the centuries the United States has become so powerful and self-reliant economically – the value of its trade is equal to 15 per cent of its gross domestic product, or half the global average – that Americans seem to have forgotten that among the inalienable rights celebrated by the founding fathers was the right to prosperity through human industry. An entire generation of Arabs has been deprived of that right, either because of the inadequacy and oppression of their leaders, foreign occupation, or both. The assumption taken for granted by most Americans – that their children will have a better education and greater opportunity than they have – remains, for most Arabs, a dream. 'Where flocks and corn are the only wealth',

---

* Dwight Eisenhower – another retired general – is credited with the second most-famous farewell address, in which he warned of the pernicious effects of the 'military-industrial complex'.

as Dr Johnson wrote of the Scottish Highlanders, 'he who is poor never can be rich. The son merely occupies the place of the father, and life knows nothing of progress or advancement.'

Anthony Nutting, summing up his 1964 *The Arabs: A Narrative History from Mohammed to the Present*, dismissed talk then circulating of an Arab political federation and suggested economic union as a more viable alternative. 'It was economic need,' Nutting wrote, 'even more than the proselytizing fervour of the new Muslim faith, that sent the Arabs [. . .] to forge the first and greatest union in Arab history. They did it thirteen centuries ago and despite all their present handicaps and shortcomings, they are unpredictable enough to do it again.'

The Arabs have failed to overcome those handicaps and shortcomings and economic union is as unlikely today as political federation was in Nutting's day. The Arab condition erodes, relentlessly and unnoticed, like a silent scream. So long as their once-legendary entrepreneurial instinct is stifled by despotism and occupation, so long many in their ranks will abet, and some embrace, violent extremism. Unless the Western powers help repair the damage done to the Arab economy a century ago, Ibn Khaldun's prediction that civilizations will collapse if they cannot adapt their societies – their *asabiyya* –to modernity will come true for the Arabs, with consequences both terrible and sustained.

Chronology

AD 570–632: The Age of Mohammad

570	Birth of the Prophet in Mecca.
610	The first vision.
622	Early Muslims escape to Medina.
630	The Muslim army returns and conquers Mecca; Mohammad signs treaties with Jews and Christians, making them protected minorities, a precursor of the *dhimmi* system of the Islamic empire.
632	Death of the Prophet.

632–661: The Hijaz Caliphs

632–661	The first four caliphs who ruled from Medina in the Hijaz region of the Arabian peninsula: Abu Bakr, Umar ibn al Khattab (Omar 1), Uthman ibn Affan and Ali ibn abi Talib.
632	Abu Bakr succeeds the Prophet, decides on title of *Khalifa*; orders expedition into Syria, which is subdued four years later under his successor, Omar.
638	Omar and the Muslim army enter Jerusalem and are welcomed by Christians and Jews oppressed under Byzantine rule; Muslims expand empire West to Egypt and as far East as Azerbaijan, where the remnants of the Sassanian empire are swept away. Victorious Muslim commanders promise 'not to kill or enslave the population' nor desecrate their temples.
644	Omar assassinated by a Persian slave; his successor, Uthman ibn Affan, strengthens the central government and codifies the Koran.
656	Uthman murdered by a cabal of rebellious Egyptians while at home reading the Koran, triggering a power struggle between Ali, Mohammad's nephew, and the ambitious governor of Syria, Mu'awiya I Ibn Abi Sufyan. Compromise agreement leaves Ali severely weakened.
661	*Khawarij* brigands – among the first Islamic militants – assassinate Ali

274

for making concessions to the secular Mu'awiya, who proclaims himself caliph and establishes Umayyad dynasty from Damascus.

661–750: The Umayyads

661–680 Under Mu'awiya, Christians control the financial system and the Byzantine civil service model prevails. The Byzantine currency, the gold dinar, circulates in the Western half of the empire and the Sassanian silver dirhem in the Persian East.

680 Mu'awiya dies peacefully and is succeeded by his son, Yazid. Ali's two sons, al Hasan and al Husayn, attempt to unite with rebellious followers in Iraq and are massacred at Karbala by Umayyad governor, sewing the seeds of the split between Sunni and Shiite Islam.

685–705 Reign of Caliph Abd Al Malik; Dome of the Rock completed. Al Malik succeeded by son Abd al Walid, who presides over a decade of prosperity and public works, including the great Mosque in Damascus; Hajjaj bin Yusuf, governor of Iraq, translates Persian records into Arabic, strikes silver coins with Koranic texts, stimulates trade and commerce, digs canals and irrigation systems; Muslim empire expanded to include North Africa. Muslim armies cross (and name) the Straits of Gibraltar, and conquer southern Spain.

732 Islamic advance into Western Europe halted when Charles Martel defeats the Muslim army at the Battle of Tours.

750 Revolt of the Abbasids led by Muslims in the East, prominent among them Iranians. The Umayyad family is massacred, though Abd al Rahman survives and flees to *Al Andalus* (Andalusia) in southern Spain, where he founds an independent Muslim enclave in 756 that thrives for 500 years.

749–1031: The Abbasids

754–775 Age of Al Mansur, who builds Baghdad – the City of Peace – into the political, economic, and cultural capital of the Arab-Muslim empire. Heavy Persian influence over bureaucracy, art and science. Jews thrive. The port at Basra becomes 'a water front for the world'. Canton opens to Muslim seafarers and Sino-Arab trade flourishes.

786–809 Golden age of early Islam under Caliph Harun al Rashid. Islam goes global with an exchange of embassies between Baghdad and Charlemagne's court. A succession struggle after Al Rashid's death leads to civil war between his sons Al Ma'mun and Al Amin.

868 Rise of Ibn Tulun as sub-autonomous viceroy of Egypt.

908–1031 Abbasid decline begins with Caliph Al Muqtadir. Local revolts proliferate and in 930 rebels sack Mecca and make off with the Ka'ba, or sacred rock. Seljuk Turks slowly consume Iraq, Persia and Central Asia, reducing Abbasids to a protectorate occupied by professional soldiers – including former slaves – known as *ghulam*, the precursors of the Mamluks.

969–1171: The Fatimids

969–972   The Fatimids, a Shiite tribe emigrating from Tunisia, conquer Egypt and establish the last of the great Arab empires. Caliph al Muizz lays the foundation stone for Al Azhar mosque in 970; Yaqub Killis, legendary minister and statesman, emerges as chief counsellor to the caliph; Fatimids retreat in the north as the Byzantines begin the reconquest of Syria.

996   Al Hakim made caliph at the age of eleven, marking a decline of caliphal authority and the rise of military factions in the corridors of power; he responds to disturbances in Palestine by burning the Church of the Holy Sepulchre, though he quickly orders it rebuilt; the Arab empire expands into southern Europe. Trade flourishes and Tripoli, Sidon, Ascalon, and Gaza become important port cities.

1021   Al Hakim disappears under mysterious circumstances. Half a century of famine and violence ends in 1073 with arrival of Badr al Jamali, Armenian governor of Acre in Palestine.

1095   Pope Urban II declares first crusade.

1099   Crusaders massacre Muslims, Jews and Christians en route to victory in Jerusalem.

1124   Fulcher of Chartres celebrates Western colonization of the Muslim east; Islam turns inwards; violence between rival Fatimid ministers opens the way for Kurdish leader Nur al Din and his nephew, Salah al-din (Saladin); Adid, last of the Fatimids, dies in 1171; Arab caliphate replaced by Ayyubid sultanate with Salah al-din as sultan.

1187–1917: Ayyubids, Mamluks, Ottomans and Zionism

1187   Salah al-din recaptures Jerusalem for Islam; emergence of Mamluks; Muslim maritime fleet struggles to keep up with increasingly advanced European merchant and naval vessels.

1242   Mongol army enters Anatolia.

1258   Baghdad falls to the Mongol ruler, Hulegu.

1260   Hulegu dispatches an envoy to Cairo, who demands Egypt submit to his authority and is murdered by then-sultan Qutuz. Hulegu attacks and is repulsed by the Mamluks, who become the legitimate rulers of Egypt.

1291   End of Latin (Crusader) Kingdom of Jerusalem. The Mamluks continue to wage war against the Christians, while simultaneously developing trade relations with Byzantium and Europe.

1299   Osman, a Turkish-Muslim warrior, leads raids on Christian Byzantine settlements in western Anatolia. Dawn of the Ottoman Empire.

1375   Ibn Khaldun writes his famous *Muqaddima*, which notes how Muslim power declined as it took the Koran as 'an object for study rather than an inspiration for life'.

1387   Timur threatens Mamluk sultanate and conquers Damascus three years later, where he is interviewed by Ibn Khaldun.

1448	Mamluk Sultan Jaqmaq issues anti-*dhimmi* decree, prompting some Jews and Christians to emigrate. Muslim economies shift from laissez-faire capitalism to European-style feudalism.
1498	Vasco da Gama discovers a sea route to India. This makes the Arab land bridge to the Orient redundant and begins the slow decline of Arab seafaring. Advances in western firearms allow the Portuguese fleet and European armies to establish their superiority on sea and on land.
1512–1520	Reign of Selim I and the Ottoman conquest of the Fertile Crescent and Levant. Beginning of Ottoman rule over the Arabs.
1881–1882	Persecution of Jews in Russia after Tsar Alexander II is assassinated. First wave of Zionist emigration to Palestine. Earliest Zionist movements founded.
1888	Britain occupies Egypt.
1897	First Zionist Congress in Basle establishes a programme to resettle Jews in Palestine.
1898	Father of modern Zionism Theodore Herzl visits Palestine for first and only time.
1904–1914	Second large wave of Jewish emigrants to Palestine; Nagib Azoury publishes *Le Réveil de la Nation Arabe*, predicting a future conflict between Zionism and Arab nationalism; Palestinian delegates to the Ottoman parliament warn of Jewish domination.
1914	Egypt becomes a British Protectorate and a British army enters Iraq.
1916	British forces moving on Baghdad defeated at Kut al-'Amarah.

1917–2002: The Modern Arab World and Israel

1917–1922	Arabs drive Turks out of the Levant in First World War alliance with Britain, whose troops take Jerusalem and Baghdad. Balfour Declaration endorses the creation of a Jewish state. Sykes and Picot treaty divides Arab world into Western protectorates; divisions enshrined in Cairo Conference; French subsequently given the League of Nations mandate for Syria and Lebanon, the British the mandate for Iraq and Trans-Jordan (including Palestine). French march into Damascus. British install Hashemites princes Faisel and Abdullah in Iraq and Jordan respectively.
1922	Egypt gains independence under King Fuad I.
1928	Hassan al Banna, aiming to revitalize Islam, establishes the Society of Muslim Brothers in Egypt, which King Faruk later uses to counter secular nationalists.
1929	Arab-Jewish clashes leave 250 dead, including 60 Jews in Hebron.
1932	Iraq becomes a fully independent kingdom under Faisel I.
1936–1939	Jewish militias ally with British forces to put down an Arab Revolt.
1939	Faisel II becomes king of Iraq.
1944	Jewish terrorist groups target British administration for limiting emigration of Jews to Palestine; King David Hotel bombed by group associated with future Israeli Prime Minister Menachem Begin.

1947	Michel Aflaq and Salah al-Din Bitar establish the Ba'ath Party, rooted in Western socialist and nationalist traditions.
1948	Israel declared as Jewish state, battles Arab armies to a stalemate. British mandate ends.
1951	King Abdullah of Jordan is assassinated for his suspected ties to Israel. His son, Talal, rules for one year before abdicating in favour of his own son, Hussein.
1952	Egyptian Colonel Gamal Abdel Nasser deposes King Faruk, nationalizes the Suez Canal and crushes the Muslim Brotherhood.
1956–1958	British and French with Israel's help occupy the Suez Canal Zone. Eisenhower orders them out, demands Arab leaders side with America or against it in the war on communism; a bloody coup destroys King Faisel and the Hashemite court; Egypt and Syria enter the Soviet orbit after forming the United Arab Republic.
1967	Second Arab-Israeli war leaves Jewish state with control of the Sinai Peninsula, the Golan Heights, and the West Bank and Gaza.
1970	Hafez al Assad assumes control of Syria in a military coup; Palestinian Liberation Organization ejected from Jordan by King Hussein in a civil war known as Black September; Saddam Hussein emerges as Iraqi strongman. Nasser dies and Anwar Sadat becomes president of Egypt.
1973	Egypt opens third major Arab-Israeli war by re-taking the Suez Canal but then loses it again; Israel finally triumphs, although rattled.
1977	Anwar Sadat visits Israel and addresses the Knesset, the Israeli parliament.
1978	Israel and Egypt sign Camp David peace accords; Iran's Muhammad Reza Shah Pahlavi deposed by Imam Ruhollah Khomeini.
1980	Iraq invades Iran. Washington supports Iraq overtly, Iran covertly.
1981	Anwar Sadat assassinated by Muslim radicals opposed to Camp David accords.
1982	Israel invades Lebanon in response to attacks by Palestinian militias from Lebanese enclaves.
1987–1993	First Intifada, or uprising, of Palestinians against Israeli occupation.
1990–1991	Saddam Hussein invades Kuwait; Coalition forces eject Iraq in Operation Desert Storm.
1991	US hosts Arab-Israeli peace conference in Madrid.
1991–1993	Palestinian and Israeli peace negotiators meet secretly in Oslo, Norway. Oslo Peace Accord signed on September 13, 1993.* Israel and Jordan normalize relations one year later.
1994	Baruch Goldstein, a US citizen and Jewish settler, murders 29 Muslim worshippers in the Tomb of the Patriarchs in Hebron.

---

* This accord outlined a proposal for limited Palestinian self-rule in the Gaza Strip and in the West Bank town of Jericho. It committed Israel to withdraw from these areas within five years, following which the two sides would reach agreement on the final status of all Palestinian areas occupied by Israel since 1967 – including water rights, the fate of Palestinian refugees, and the future of Jerusalem. The settlement also provided for the establishment of a ruling body, the Palestinian National Authority (PNA), as the administrative authority of the Palestinians.

1999   Labour candidate Ehud Barak defeats hardliner Benjamin Netanyahu
            and promises full withdrawal from southern Lebanon and peace with
            the Palestinians; King Hussein dies, succeeded by son Abdullah II.

2000   Israeli troops withdraw from south Lebanon 'Security Zone' in May;
            Hafez al Assad dies, succeeded by son Bashar. US-led efforts to
            mediate an Israeli-Palestinian peace agreement at Camp David in
            July fail. Two months later, Israeli hardliner Ariel Sharon visits the
            Al-Aqsa mosque in Jerusalem, sparking the second Intifada.

Sources

INTRODUCTION

Al Khouri, Riad, 'Arab industry stagnant at end of century', *Jordan Times*, 8 June 2000

Azzam, Henry T., 'The need to attain high economic growth in the Arab region', *Jordan Times*, 3–4 November 2000

——'Foreign direct investment inflows to the Arab world', *Jordan Times*, 17 November 2000

De Soto, Hernando, *The Mystery of Capital: Why Capitalism Triumphs in the West and Fails Everywhere Else*, Basic Books, New York, 2000

Fromkin, David, *A Peace to End All Peace: Creating the Modern Middle East, 1914–1922*, Henry Holt, New York, 1989

Glubb, Sir John Bagot, *The Life and Times of Muhammad*, Stein & Day, New York, 1970

Hitti, Philip K., *History of Syria*, Macmillan, New York, 1951

Hovannisian, Richard G., and Sabagh, Georges (eds.), *Religion and Culture in Medieval Islam*, Cambridge University Press, Cambridge, 1993

Kardoosh, Marwan, 'Foreign investment and the Middle East – growing together or growing apart?', *Jordan Times*, 22 March 2001

Lindsey, Brink, 'Poor Choice: Why Globalization Didn't Create 9/11', *New Republic*, 12 November 2001

Malley, Robert, and Agha, Hussein, 'A Reply to Ehud Barak', *New York Review of Books*, 13 June 2002

Manning, Robert A., and Jaffe, Amy Myers, 'The Shock of a World of Cheap Oil', *Foreign Affairs*, January/February 2000

Nutting, Anthony, *The Arabs: A Narrative History from Mohammed to the Present*, Hollis & Carter, London, 1964

Owen, Roger, and Pamuk, Sevket, *A History of Middle East Economies in the Twentieth Century*, Harvard University Press, Cambridge, Mass., 1999

Petry, Carl F., *The Cambridge History of Egypt: Volume 1, Islamic Egypt, 640–1517*, Cambridge University Press, Cambridge, 1998

Rice, David Talbot, *Islamic Art* (revised edition), Thames and Hudson, London, 1975

Savir, Uri, *The Process*, Random House, New York, 1998

Seale, Patrick, *Assad: The Struggle for the Middle East,* University of California Press, Berkeley, 1989

Tuchman, Barbara, *A Distant Mirror: The Calamitous Fourteenth Century*, Knopf, New York, 1978

Wilson, Jeremy, *Lawrence of Arabia: The Authorized Biography of T.E. Lawrence*, Atheneum, New York, 1990

World Bank, *World Development Indicators*, Washington DC, 2001

CHAPTER I: LEBANON

Ambrose, Stephen, *Nixon: Ruin and Recovery*, Simon & Schuster, New York, 1991

Bergin, Peter L., *Holy War Inc.: Inside the Secret World of Osama bin Laden*, Free Press, New York, 2001

Choueiri, Youssef M., *Arab Nationalism: A History*, Blackwell, Oxford, 2000

La Guardia, Anton, *Holy Land, Unholy War: Israelis and Palestinians*, John Murray, London, 2001

Seale, Patrick, *Assad: The Struggle for the Middle East,* University of California Press, Berkeley, 1989

CHAPTER 2: SYRIA

Ahmed, Akbar, 'Ibn Khaldun's Understanding of Civilization and the Dilemmas of Islam and the West Today', *Middle East Journal*, Washington DC, 2002

Associated Press, 'Syrian activist reappears, alleges he was kidnapped and threatened', *Jordan Times*, 24 June 2001

Ayalon, David, *Eunuchs, Caliphs and Sultans: A Study in Power Relationships*, Magnes Press, Jerusalem, 1999

Carmichael, Joel, *The Shaping of the Arabs: A Study in Ethnic Identity*, Macmillan, New York, 1967

Frye, Richard, *The Golden Age of Persia,* Phoenix Press, London, 1975

Gilmour, David, *The Long Recessional: The Imperial Life of Rudyard Kipling*, John Murray, London, 2002

Guthrie, Shirley, *Arab Social Life in the Middle Ages: An Illustrated Study*, Saqi Books, London, 1995

——*Arab Women in the Middle Ages: Private Lives and Public Roles*, Saqi Books, London, 2001

Hitti, Philip K., *History of Syria*, Macmillan, New York, 1951

Nutting, Anthony, *The Arabs: A Narrative History from Mohammed to the Present*, Hollis & Carter, London, 1964

Reuters, 'Syria faces shrinking economy – US report', *Jordan Times*, 17 March 1999

Rice, David Talbot, *Islamic Art* (revised edition), Thames & Hudson, London, 1975

Zaydan, Jurgji, *Umayyads and Abbasids*, trans. D.S. Margoliouth, Darf Publishers, London, 1907, new impression 1987

CHAPTER 3: JORDAN

Aburish, Said K., *A Brutal Friendship: The West and the Arab Elite*, St. Martin's Press, New York, 1997

Atlas Investment Group, *Jordan Country Report*, Amman, April 2001

Fromkin, David, *A Peace to End All Peace: Creating the Modern Middle East, 1914–1922*, Henry Holt, New York, 1989

http://www.times-archive.co.uk/news/pages/tim/1999/11/25 (for the relationship between King Abdullah of Jordan and the Shaheens)

Kennedy, Hugh, *The Prophet and the Age of the Caliphates*, Longman, London and New York, 1986

La Guardia, Anton, *Holy Land, Unholy War: Israelis and Palestinians*, John Murray, London, 2001

Nutting, Anthony, *The Arabs: A Narrative History from Mohammed to the Present*, Hollis & Carter, London, 1964

'US urges: Boost Jordan's exports to PA – Stuart Eizenstat says move would help to smooth King Abdullah's transition', *Ha'aretz*, Tel Aviv, 3 March 1999

Zaydan, Jurgji, *Umayyads and Abbasids*, trans. D.S. Margoliouth, Darf Publishers, London, 1907, new impression 1987

CHAPTER 4: PALESTINE

Aburish, Said K., *Arafat: From Defender to Dictator*, Bloomsbury, London, 1998

Andrews, Richard, *Blood on the Mountain*, Weidenfeld & Nicolson, London, 1999

Armstrong, Karen, *Jerusalem: One City, Three Faiths*, Knopf, New York, 1996

—— *The Battle for God*, Knopf, New York, 2000

Glain, Stephen J., 'What a way to greet the neighbors: with eggs and bulldozers – for family of Palestinians in Hebron, real estate becomes a surreal issue', *Wall Street Journal*, 12 October 1998

Hourani, George, *Arab Seafaring*, Princeton University Press, Princeton, 1951

La Guardia, Anton, *Holy Land, Unholy War: Israelis and Palestinians*, John Murray, London, 2001

Malley, Robert, and Agha, Hussein, 'Camp David: The Tragedy of Errors', *New York Review of Books*, 9 August 2002

Nutting, Anthony, *The Arabs: A Narrative History from Mohammed to the Present*, Hollis & Carter, London, 1964

Owen, Roger, and Pamuk, Sevket, *A History of Middle East Economies in the Twentieth Century*, Harvard University Press, Cambridge, Mass., 1999

Shlaim, Avi, *The Iron Wall: Israel and the Arab World*, W.W. Norton, New York, 2000

CHAPTER 5: IRAQ

Aburish, Said K., *Saddam Hussein: The Politics of Revenge*, Bloomsbury, London, 2000

Adler, Marcus Nathan, 'The Itinerary of Benjamin of Tudela', critical text, translation and commentary, Feldheim, Phillip, New York, (http://www.uscolo.edu/history/seminar/benjamin/benjamin1.htm)

Carmichael, Joel, *The Shaping of the Arabs: A Study in Ethnic Identity*, Macmillan, New York, 1967

Glubb, Sir John Bagot, *The Life and Times of Muhammad*, Stein & Day, New York, 1970

http://www.pbs.org/wgbh/pages/frontline/shows/saddam/interviews/aburish.html (text of interviews about Saddam Hussein)

Kaplan, Robert D., *The Arabists: The Romance of an American Elite,* Free Press, New York, 1993

Kennedy, Hugh, *The Prophet and the Age of the Caliphates,* Longman, London and New York, 1986

Nutting, Anthony, *The Arabs: A Narrative History from Mohammed to the Present,* Hollis & Carter, London, 1964

Owen, Roger, and Pamuk, Sevket, *A History of Middle East Economies in the Twentieth Century,* Harvard University Press, Cambridge, Mass., 1999

Sevan, Benon V., Executive Director of the Iraq Programme, comments made at the informal consultations of the UN Security Council, 26 February 2002

CHAPTER SIX: EGYPT

Carmichael, Joel, *The Shaping of the Arabs: A Study in Ethnic Identity,* Macmillan, New York, 1967

Dawoud, Khaled, 'Prosecuting Ibrahim – again', *Al Ahram Weekly,* 25–31 July 2002

De Soto, Hernando, *The Mystery of Capital: Why Capitalism Triumphs in the West and Fails Everywhere Else,* Basic Books, New York, 2000

EFG-Hermes Research, 'S&P Cuts Egypt's Foreign Currency Rating to BB+', Newsflash, Giza, 22 May 2002

EFG-Hermes Research, 'Fitch Cuts Egypt's Foreign Currency Rating to BB+', Newsflash, Giza, 21 August 2002

EFG-Hermes, Egypt 'Macroeconomic Update', Giza, 9 January 2002

Friedman, Thomas L., 'Bush's Shame', *New York Times,* 4 August 2002

Goitein, S.D., *A Mediterranean Society: The Jewish Communities of the World as Portrayed in the Documents of the Cairo Geniza,* University of California Press, Berkeley, 1967

'Grounded for Greenbacks', *Cairo Times,* 7–13 March 2002

Hourani, George, *Arab Seafaring,* Princeton University Press, Princeton, 1951

Huband, Mark, 'Egypt demands Fleming reversal', *Financial Times,* 3 March 2000

Kennedy, Hugh, *The Prophet and the Age of the Caliphates,* Longman, London and New York, 1986

McCullough, David, *John Adams,* Simon & Schuster, New York, 2001

Nutting, Anthony: *The Arabs: A Narrative History from Mohammed to the Present,* Hollis & Carter, London, 1964

Owen, Roger and Pamuk, Sevket, *A History of Middle East Economies in the Twentieth Century,* Harvard University Press, Cambridge, 1999

Petry, Carl F., *The Cambridge History of Egypt:* Volume 1, Islamic Egypt 640–1517, Cambridge University Press, Cambridge, 1998

Slackman, Michael, 'Egypt's Dinosaur Economy Lumbers on with Aid', *Los Angeles Times,* 17 February 2002

Zaydan, Jurgji, *Umayyads and Abbasids,* trans. D.S. Margoliouth, Darf Publishers Ltd., London, 1907, new impression 1987

CONCLUSION

Ahmed, Akbar, 'Ibn Khaldun's Understanding of Civilization and the Dilemmas of Islam and the West Today', *Middle East Journal,* Washington DC, 2002.

Bergin, Peter L., *Holy War Inc.: Inside the Secret World of Osama bin Laden*, The Free Press, New York, 2001

Chace, James, *Acheson: The Secretary of State Who Created the American World*, Simon & Schuster, New York, 1998

Diehl, Jackson, 'AID's Egyptian Disgrace', washingtonpost.com, 2 September 2002

Drinkard, Jim, *Israel Benefits From Special Long Lasting US Aid Provisions*, Associated Press, 8 May 1990

FitzGerald, Frances, 'George Bush & the World', *New York Review of Books*, 26 September 2002

Glain, Stephen J., 'With Peace on Hold, Is Either Side a Winner? Camp David Failure Could Fuel Israeli Call for More Military Aid', *Wall Street Journal*, 26 July 2000

Herman, Arthur, *How the Scots Invented the Modern World: The True Story of How Western Europe's Poorest Nation Created Our World & Everything in It*, Crown, New York, 2001

Holt, P.M., Lambton, Ann K.S., Lewis Bernard, *The Cambridge History of Islam: Volume 1, The Central Islamic Lands*, Cambridge University Press, Cambridge, 1970

Israel Aircraft Industries – 'Lavi, Multi-Role Fighter Prototype', http://www.aero-spaceweb.org/aircraft/fighter/lavi/index.shtml

Kepel, Gilles, 'The Jihad in search of a cause', *Financial Times*, 2 September 2002

Khalaf, Roula, 'Arab region "needs 5% annual growth"', *Financial Times*, 9 September 2002

Lind, Michael, 'The Israel Lobby and American Power', *Prospect*, 1 April 2002

Nutting, Anthony: *The Arabs: A Narrative History from Mohammed to the Present*, Hollis & Carter, London, 1964

Owen, Roger and Pamuk, Sevket, *A History of Middle East Economies in the Twentieth Century*, Harvard University Press, Cambridge, Mass., 1999

Rashid, Ahmed, *Taliban: Militant Islam, Oil and Fundamentalism in Central Asia*, Yale University Press, New Haven and London, 2000 (revised edition, Pan Macmillan, London, 2001)

Rashid, Ahmed, *Jihad: The Rise of Militant Islam in Central Asia*, Yale University Press, New Haven and London, 2002

Schlesinger, Arthur M. Jr, *The Imperial Presidency*, Houghton Mifflin Co., Boston, 1973

'USAID in Egypt: 25 years', *Al-Ahram Weekly*, 21–27 June 2001

Vest, Jason, 'The Men From JINSA and CSP', *Nation*, 2 September 2002

Bibliography

BOOKS

Aburish, Said K., *A Brutal Friendship: The West and the Arab Elite*, St Martin's Press, New York, 1997

—— *Arafat: From Defender to Dictator*, Bloomsbury, London, 1998

—— *Saddam Hussein: The Politics of Revenge*, Bloomsbury, London, 2000

Agius, Dionisius, and Hitchcock, Richard (eds.), *The Arab Influence in Medieval Europe*, Ithaca Press, Reading, 1994

Ambrose, Stephen, *Nixon: Ruin and Recovery*, Simon & Schuster, New York, 1991

Andrews, Richard, *Blood on the Mountain*, Weidenfeld & Nicolson, London, 1999

Armstrong, Karen, *Jerusalem: One City, Three Faiths*, Knopf, New York, 1996

—— *The Battle for God*, Knopf, New York, 2000

Ayalon, David, *Eunuchs, Caliphs and Sultans: A Study in Power Relationships*, Magnes Press, Jerusalem, 1999

Bergin, Peter L., *Holy War Inc.: Inside the Secret World of Osama bin Laden*, Free Press, New York, 2001

Carmichael, Joel, *The Shaping of the Arabs: A Study in Ethnic Identity*, Macmillan, New York, 1967

Chace, James, *Acheson: The Secretary of State Who Created the American World*, Simon & Schuster, New York, 1998

Choueiri, Youssef M., *Arab Nationalism: A History*, Blackwell, Oxford, 2000

De Soto, Hernando, *The Mystery of Capital: Why Capitalism Triumphs in the West and Fails Everywhere Else*, Basic Books, New York, 2000

Dunn, Ross E., *The Adventures of Ibn Battuta: A Muslim Traveler of the Fourteenth Century*, University of California Press, Berkeley, 1989

Field, Michael, *Inside the Arab World*, Harvard University Press, Cambridge, Mass., 1995

Fisher, Eugene and Bassiouni, Cherif, *Storm Over the Arab World: A People in Revolution*, Follett, Chicago, 1972

Fromkin, David, *A Peace to End All Peace: Creating the Modern Middle East, 1914–1922*, Henry Holt, New York, 1989

Frye, Richard, *The Golden Age of Persia*, Phoenix Press, London, 1975

Gilmour, David, *The Long Recessional: The Imperial Life of Rudyard Kipling*, John Murray, London, 2002

Glubb, Sir John Bagot, *The Life and Times of Muhammad*, Stein & Day, New York, 1970

Goitein, S.D., *A Mediterranean Society: The Jewish Communities of the World as Portrayed in the Documents of the Cairo Geniza*, University of California Press, Berkeley, 1967

Guthrie, Shirley, *Arab Social Life in the Middle Ages: An Illustrated Study*, Saqi Books, London, 1995

——*Arab Women in the Middle Ages: Private Lives and Public Roles*, Saqi Books, London, 2001

Herman, Arthur, *How the Scots Invented the Modern World: The True Story of How Western Europe's Poorest Nation Created Our World & Everything in It*, Crown, New York, 2001

Herodotus, *The Histories*, trans. Robin Waterfield, Oxford University Press, Oxford, 1998

Hitti, Philip K., *The Arabs: A Short History*, Princeton University Press, Princeton, 1943

——*History of Syria*, Macmillan, New York, 1951

Holt, P.M., Lambton, Ann K.S., and Lewis, Bernard, *The Cambridge History of Islam: Volume 1, The Central Islamic Lands*, Cambridge University Press, Cambridge, 1970

Hourani, Albert, *A History of the Arab Peoples*, Belknap Press, Cambridge, Mass., 1991

Hourani, George, *Arab Seafaring*, Princeton University Press, Princeton, 1951

Hovannisian, Richard G., and Sabagh, Georges (eds.), *Religion and Culture in Medieval Islam*, Cambridge University Press, Cambridge, 1993

Kaplan, Robert D., *The Arabists: The Romance of an American Elite*, Free Press, New York 1993

Keller, Werner, *The Bible as History* (revised edition), William Morrow, New York, 1981

Kennedy, Hugh, *The Prophet and the Age of the Caliphates*, Longman, London and New York, 1986

Kepel, Gilles, *Jihad, the Trail of Political Islam*, Belknap Press, Cambridge, Mass., 2002

Kubiak, Wladyslaw B., *Al-Fustat: Its Foundation and Early Urban Development*, American University in Cairo Press, Cairo, 1987

La Guardia, Anton, *Holy Land, Unholy War: Israelis and Palestinians*, John Murray, London, 2001

Lewis, Bernard, *What Went Wrong? Western Impact and Middle Eastern Response*, Oxford University Press, Oxford, 2002

McCullough, David, *John Adams*, Simon & Schuster, New York, 2001

Nutting, Anthony, *The Arabs: A Narrative History from Mohammed to the Present*, Hollis & Carter, London, 1964

Owen, Roger, and Pamuk, Sevket, *A History of Middle East Economies in the Twentieth Century*, Harvard University Press, Cambridge, Mass., 1999

Petry, Carl F., *The Cambridge History of Egypt: Volume I, Islamic Egypt, 640–1517*, Cambridge University Press, Cambridge, 1998

Rashid, Ahmed, *Taliban: Militant Islam, Oil and Fundamentalism in Central Asia*, Yale University Press, New Haven and London, 2000 (revised edition, Pan Macmillan, London, 2001)

——*Jihad: The Rise of Militant Islam in Central Asia*, Yale University Press, New Haven and London, 2002

Reston, James Jr, *Warriors of God: Richard the Lionheart and Saladin in the Third Crusade*, Faber and Faber, London, 2001

Rice, David Talbot, *Islamic Art* (revised edition), Thames and Hudson, London, 1975

Rodenbeck, Max, *Cairo: The City Victorious*, The American University in Cairo Press, Cairo, 1998

Savir, Uri, *The Process*, Random House, New York, 1998

Schlesinger, Arthur M. Jr, *The Imperial Presidency*, Houghton Mifflin, Boston, 1973

Seale, Patrick, *The Struggle for Syria*, I.B. Tauris, London, 1965

——*Assad: The Struggle for the Middle East,* University of California Press, Berkeley, 1989

Shlaim, Avi, *The Iron Wall: Israel and the Arab World*, W.W. Norton, New York, 2000

Sperber, A.M., *Morrow: His Life and Times*, Freundlich Books, New York, 1986

Toynbee, Arnold J., *A Study of History*, Vol. VIII, Oxford University Press, London, 1954

Tuchman, Barbara, *A Distant Mirror: The Calamitous Fourteenth Century*, Knopf, New York, 1978

Wallach, Janet, *Desert Queen*, Doubleday, New York, 1996

Wilson, Jeremy, *Lawrence of Arabia: The Authorized Biography of T.E. Lawrence*, Atheneum, New York, 1990

Zaydan, Jurgji, *Umayyads and Abbasids*, trans. D.S. Margoliouth, Darf Publishers, London, 1907, new impression 1987

ARTICLES, REPORTS, WEBSITES AND JOURNALS

Adler, Marcus Nathan, 'The Itinerary of Benjamin of Tudela', critical text, translation and commentary, Feldheim, Phillip Inc., New York (http://www.uscolo.edu/history/seminar/benjamin/benjamin1.htm)

Ahmed, Akbar, 'Ibn Khaldun's Understanding of Civilization and the Dilemmas of Islam and the West Today', *Middle East Journal*, Washington DC, 2002

Al Khouri, Riad, 'Arab industry stagnant at end of century', *Jordan Times*, 8 June 2000

Arkin, William, 'Our Saudi "Friends"', washingtonpost.com, 6 May 2002

Associated Press, 'Syrian activist reappears, alleges he was kidnapped and threatened', *Jordan Times*, 24 June 2001

Atlas Investment Group, *Jordan Country Report*, Amman, April 2001

Ayyoub, Tareq, 'King instructs Royal family members to avoid overspending, accumulating debts', *Jordan Times*, 15 March 2001

Azzam, Henry T., 'The need to attain high economic growth in the Arab region', *Jordan Times*, 3–4 November 2000

——'Foreign direct investment inflows to the Arab world', *Jordan Times*, 17 November 2000

Dawoud, Khaled, 'Prosecuting Ibrahim – again', *Al Ahram Weekly*, 25–31 July 2002

Diehl, Jackson, 'AID's Egyptian disgrace', washingtonpost.com, 2 September 2002

Drinkard, Jim, 'Israel benefits from special long lasting US aid provisions', Associated Press, 8 May 1990

EFG-Hermes Research, 'S&P cuts Egypt's foreign currency rating to BB+', Newsflash, Giza, 22 May 2002

——'Fitch cuts Egypt's foreign currency rating to BB+', Newsflash, Giza, 21 August 2002

EFG-Hermes, 'Egypt Macroeconomic Update', Giza, 9 January 2002

FitzGerald, Frances, 'George Bush & the World', *New York Review of Books*, 26 September 2002

Friedman, Thomas L., 'Bush's Shame', *New York Times*, 4 August 2002

Glain, Stephen J., 'With peace on hold, is either side a winner? Camp David failure could fuel Israeli call for more military aid', *Wall Street Journal*, 26 July 2000

——'What a way to greet the neighbors: with eggs and bulldozers – for family of Palestinians in Hebron, real estate becomes a surreal issue', *Wall Street Journal*, 12 October 1998

'Grounded for greenbacks', *Cairo Times*, 7–13 March 2002

http://www.pbs.org/wgbh/pages/frontline/shows/saddam/interviews/aburish.html (text of interviews about Saddam Hussein)

http://www.times-archive.co.uk/news/pages/tim/1999/11/25 (for the relationship between King Abdullah of Jordan and the Shaheens)

Huband, Mark, 'Egypt demands Fleming reversal', *Financial Times*, 3 March 2000

International Museum with no Frontiers Exhibition Cycles, Islamic Art in the Mediterranean, *The Umayyads: The Rise of Islamic Art*, 2000

Israel Aircraft Industries, 'Lavi, Multi-Role Fighter Prototype', http://www.aerospaceweb.org/aircraft/fighter/lavi/index.shtml

Kardoosh, Marwan, 'Foreign investment and the Middle East – growing together or growing apart?', *Jordan Times*, 22 March 2001

Kepel, Gilles, 'The Jihad in search of a cause', *Financial Times*, 2 September 2002

Khalaf, Roula, 'Arab region "needs 5% annual growth"', *Financial Times*, 9 September 2002

Lind, Michael, 'The Israel Lobby and American Power', *Prospect*, 1 April 2002

Lindsey, Brink, 'Poor Choice: Why Globalization Didn't Create 9/11', *New Republic*, 12 November 2001

Malley, Robert, and Agha, Hussein, 'A Reply to Ehud Barak', *New York Review of Books*, 13 June 2002

——'Camp David: The Tragedy of Errors', *New York Review of Books*, 9 August 2002

Manning, Robert A., and Jaffe, Amy Myers, 'The Shock of a World of Cheap Oil', *Foreign Affairs,* January/February 2000

Menocal, Maria Rosa, 'Where Muslim and Jew once lived in tolerance', *International Herald Tribune*, 2 April 2002

Reuters, 'Syria faces shrinking economy – US report', *Jordan Times*, 17 March 1999

Sevan, Benon V., Executive Director of the Iraq Programme, comments made at the informal consultations of the UN Security Council, 26 February 2002

Slackman, Michael, 'Egypt's dinosaur economy lumbers on with aid', *Los Angeles Times*, 17 February 2002

UN Arab Human Development Report, http://www.undp.org/rbas/ahdr/

'US urges: Boost Jordan's exports to PA – Stuart Eizenstat says move would help to smooth King Abdullah's transition', *Ha'aretz*, Tel Aviv, 3 March 1999

'USAID in Egypt: 25 years', *Al-Ahram Weekly*, 21–27 June 2001

Vest, Jason, 'The Men From JINSA and CSP', *Nation*, September 2, 2002

World Bank, *World Development Indicators*, Washington DC, 2001

Glossary

Asabiyya: Theory of social cohesion developed by Ibn Khaldun, the fourteenth-century Arab historian. Translated roughly as 'solidarity' it refers to the component parts of traditional society – family, clan, tribe, kingdom and nation – and the forces of modernity that can disrupt and ultimately liquidate them.

Ba'ath (Renaissance) Party: Established in 1940 to spearhead an Arab-nationalist movement pioneered by Lebanese socialists Michel Aflaq and Salah al-Din Bitar. It has since degenerated into a vehicle of patronage and intimidation that sustains dictatorships in Iraq and Syria.

Burkha: An all-enveloping garment of various colours used in Central Asia to cover women in conservative Muslim societies.

Caravanserai: Hostels patronized by Muslims on holy pilgrimage to Mecca and made redundant in the late nineteenth century with the introduction of a railway grid linking the major cities of the Levantine Arab world. Also known as *khans*.

Chador: A black cloak worn principally by Arab-Muslim women to cover the head and upper body while leaving the face exposed.

Dishdasha: Ankle-length shirt worn by men and occasionally women of the Levant. Also known as *galabeya*.

Dhimmi: Medieval Jews and Christians living as 'protected minorities' under the Islamic caliphates. In exchange for a small tax, law-abiding members of these communities were allowed to live and worship more or less as they pleased.

Diwan: A long meeting room where men of authority – from tribal elders to municipal officials meet in the Arab-Muslim world to discuss and negotiate administrative affairs.

Fasal: A meeting of trial sheiks to resolve disputes between separate tribes.

Hajj: The Muslim pilgrimage to Mecca.

Hilm: An Arab term for charisma, particularly as a leadership trait. Commonly used in medieval times.

Hijab: Head covering common among pious Muslim women, similar to a scarf or handkerchief.

Intifada: Palestinian resistance to Israeli occupation. The first Intifada began in 1987 and ended with the Oslo peace accord of 1993; the second began in September 2000 in response, say Palestinians, to a provocative visit by Israeli hardliner Ariel Sharon to the Harem al Sharif in Jerusalem, a site sacred to Muslims.

IPO: Initial Public Offering. The sale to investors of a company's equity, either existing or new, usually to raise funds for expansion or debt reduction.

Jihad: A spiritual struggle all Muslims are obligated to wage against threats to Islam, whether internal or external. A Muslim may wage *jihad* simply by choosing to do good over evil, or by making war against a perceived aggressor hostile to Islam.

Jihadist: Someone who wages *jihad*. Also used colloquially in reference to anyone in fanatical pursuit of an objective, whether spiritual or temporal.

Ka'bah: The central shrine of Islam in Mecca. Legions of pious Muslims trek to the *Ka'bah* each year on the *hajj*. According to Muslim doctrine, every Muslim is supposed to visit Mecca once in his life.

Keffiyeh: White Palestinian scarf, checked in either black or red. Believed to be inspired by British occupational forces following the First World War, the *keffiyeh* has become a symbol of Palestinian resistance to Israeli occupation.

Kharijite: Order of militant, fundamentalist Muslims who assassinated Ali, the Prophet's nephew, for negotiating a political deal with a secular rival.

Madrassas: Orthodox Muslim schools established at the dawn of Islam and today regarded warily by moderates as incubators of extremism.

Minion (Hebr.): A group of ten Jewish men, the minimum required under Judaism for a religious service.

Mukhabarat: A generic reference for the extensive internal security agencies that currently oppress many Arab countries.

NGOs: Non-Governmental Organizations. Not-for-profit groups and agencies involved in a range of issues and causes, from charitable work to environmental protection and economic development.

Pasha: A high-ranking official in the Ottoman empire.

Shaheed: Someone who has sacrificed himself in *jihad* or political struggle.

Sura: A chapter of the Koran.

USAID: United States Agency for International Development. USAID is particularly active in Egypt and Jordan, which receive the vast majority of US foreign aid not allocated to Israel.

Ulema: A body of Muslim scholars who interpret *sharia*, or Islamic law.

Umma: Community of the faithful within Islam.

Vizier: Ministerial officers who often exerted considerable influence over the Turkish sultans and the Arab caliphs before them.

Wasta: Arabic shorthand for the network of connections, usually filial, often needed to achieve even the most basic tasks in lieu of an unresponsive or unreliable central government. Arabs will use *wasta* to attain a government job, secure a loan or find their children a place in a decent school.

Wakf: A charitable trust within Islamic communities.

Zebiba: Arabic for the dark, oval-shaped mark pious Muslims often develop on their foreheads from bowing regularly in prayer.

Acknowledgements

Journalists call them 'fixers', a short-hand reference to people who set up interviews, act as interpreters, arrange transportation, translate print and broadcast reports, recommend story ideas and somehow manage to keep the world spinning on its correct axis even as everything else goes unhinged. They are in equal parts journalists, assistants, sounding boards and seers. In strange and sometimes hostile worlds, they serve as a foreign correspondent's eyes and ears, and the ones I have been lucky enough to work with are all heart.

In Israel and the Palestinian territories, Ahmed Mashal bailed me out of one predicament after another even as bigger and more extravagant media groups bid for his attention; Amin Andraus, who worked for me during those first six months in Tel Aviv, is the nicest kid ever to become a lawyer; Nancy Shektar-Porat, with help from husband Doron (another nice lawyer), knows no peer for efficiency and acumen when it comes to navigating the complexities of Israeli society, politics and business; Mirna Ishac of the Beirut Information & Studies Center is as smart as they come, and Curlie Reem persuaded Hezbollah to meet me – no small feat given my chaotic schedule at the time; Mandy Fahmy in Egypt did everything on my behalf short of parting the Red Sea, and I was never sure if Rania al Kadri in Jordan was working for me or I was working for her, but somehow we got the job done. These people are professionals in every way and – *inshallah* – friends for life. What I know about the Middle East is due to their patience and hard work.

What I know about the global economy I owe to my years working for the *Wall Street Journal*. Managing Editor Paul Steiger was good enough to allow me a sabbatical to write this book; Foreign Editor John Bussey took a chance assigning me the Middle East after I had clearly burned out covering Asia; Mike Williams put up with me during a rocky transition from one side of the Orient to the other; Steve Yoder, my boss in Tokyo, was a valued *sensei* and showed by example the smart way to run a news bureau; National News Editor Marcus Brauchli was, as ever, a faithful, fraternal confessor; and if Hugh Pope ever needs someone to carry his bags on his next adventure, all he has to do is call.

Danny Pearl was my mentor, colleague and friend.

At John Murray, editor Gail Pirkis persuaded her bosses to 'take a punt' on a book about the Arab economy and I hope I haven't let her down. Writing it was more therapy than work, thanks to Gail and line-editor Andrew Maxwell-Hyslop; I will miss Andrew's transatlantic wake-up calls as well as his superb editing. His is a light and expert touch and any mistakes are mine.

Writing a book can be an expensive enterprise, and the generosity of the Pew International Journalism Program at Johns Hopkins University's Paul H. Nitze School of Advanced International Studies significantly lightened my load. As the program's journalist in residence in the final quarter of 2001 I was supported by the able John Schidlovsky, Louise Lief, Jeff Barrus and Denise Melvin, as well as force-of-nature Katherine Reese and her unruly charge, the sage Steve Muller. They are the greatest. Quill Lawrence of *The World* alerted me to the fellowship in the first place and Peter Bergen, a Pew alumnus, gave me an idea of what to expect during my formative book-writing months and suggested ways to improve the early drafts.

I was also lucky enough – thanks to Nancy Birdsall and Sonal Shah – to serve as journalist-in-residence at the Washington DC-based Center for Global Development, a new think-tank that is distinguishing itself by formulating refreshingly subversive ways to create wealth and nurture economies in the developing world.

Tony Emerson, the business editor of *Newsweek International*, was receptive to ideas for columns related to the theme of Arab economic decay and actually managed to get some in the magazine; Tony was introduced to me by Carroll Bogert, my guiding light.

In covering the Middle East I was privileged to stumble into the lives of extraordinary people who showed me that courage and decency are honoured in equal measure on both sides of the conflict. In Israel, journalists Danny Ben Simon and Oded Granot were patient with my endless questions; Labour party leader Ephraim Sneh and Meretz leader Naomi Chazan, and businessmen Nimrod Novik, Yosi Maiman, Yosi Vardi and David Kolitz taught me that an Israeli-Palestinian peace accord will mean nothing without a viable Palestinian economy to go with it; peacemaker Alon Liel always had time for coffee, no matter how busy he was: Einat Mitrany, Meron

Meilich and Menachem Feder welcomed me into their homes as family.

In Jordan, Beit Oweis adopted me, and Reuters correspondent Khaled was a valuable escort in Lebanon and Syria. He also read drafts of the book and offered corrections and helpful comments; Rania and Adi al Kadri kept me well-fed, well-informed and laughing all the way; philosopher-entrepreneur Omar Salah leavened many an idle evening with Scotch and polemics; Suleiman al Kalidi, also of Reuters, embraced me when I arrived in the Hashemite kingdom and was the last of its subjects to see me off when I left; Jamal Lattouf is an honest businessman and friend; the Masri clan – Omar, Taher, Maher, Monib, Sabih and the others – are the best Greater Palestine has to offer; dear Hayem, Suad and Mr Bisharat of Bisharat Tours managed most of my transport needs and buoyed my spirits; Alberto Fernandez is a model civil servant and I miss our lunches.

The American Colony Hotel in Jerusalem was my second home and the folks who run it made me feel like I owned the place; bookseller Munther M. Fahmi provided me with the books I needed to write my own; in Iraq, Samir Al Jaburi was a gracious host; Lebanese investment adviser Samir Beydoun dropped everything for me when I cold-called him in Beirut; Albert Aji at the Orient Press Center in Damascus was a huge help; in Egypt, Drew and Roxanne Dowell made Cairo fun and introduced me to the elegant and thoughtful Samir Raffat. They escaped to New York but left me in the good hands of Mandy Fahmy; retired Colonel Norvell 'Tex' De Atkine at the Regional Studies Detachment at Fort Bragg, North Carolina, is that rarest of commodities – an objective source on matters of Middle East security; Said Aburish, the Palestinian writer, always made time for me in London or over the phone and graciously offered advice and news tips; Leon Bijou approached me as a source, but quickly became a vital friend, confidant and personal stand-up comic.

Fellow journalists often set aside professional rivalries and offered me a much-appreciated helping hand. Trudy Rubin, a columnist for Knight-Ridder newspapers was a felicitous travel mate as we crashed about the West Bank during that cold, chaotic April 2002. Trudy introduced me to the Barghouthis and shared with me her valuable perspective shaped from years of covering the region; it was the persistence of the *Washington Post*'s Howard Schneider that netted the interview with Bashar al Assad and he was kind enough to let me sit in; Beirut-based Gareth Smyth of the *Financial Times* was generous with his insights and hooked me up with the mushroom lords; Randa Habib, the Amman bureau chief for Agence France-Presse was my oracle and a courageous fount of truth in an increasingly intimidated Hashemite kingdom.

My parents, John and Josephine Glain, sister Sandy and her husband David have been my greatest source of strength and inspiration, and I am blessed that Christina Balis will join this circle.

Finally, I am indebted to the countless peoples of the Middle East – Jews, Christians and Muslims – who raised the blinds from the window of their world and gave me a real-life glimpse at the malaise and oppression that enslaves it. They sometimes did this at their peril and they asked for nothing in return; it was enough that I listened.

Index

Abbas, uncle of Mohammad, 183
Abbas bin Farnas, 100–1
Abbasa, 199
Abbasids, 19, 95, 104, 198, 200, 218, 235–6
'Abd al Malik, 45, 64, 152
Abd Rabbo, Waddah, 70
Abdel Basset, Mohammad, 232–4
Abdel Latif, Mahmoud Sayed, 220, 232
Abdel-Nur, Munir Fakhry, 223–4
Abdullah, Dr Abu Hashem, 248–9
Abdullah, Crown Prince of Saudi Arabia, 8
Abdullah II, King of Jordan: anger in Ma'an, 126; at Arab League summit, 8; crackdown on dissent, 134; and succession, 130–3; and Shaheens, 135
Abdullah, Marwan, 81–7, 258
Abdullah, Omar, 219
Abraham, 152, 159–60
Abu Dis, 175
Abu Leila, Saber Mohammad, 213–14
Aburish, Said, 201
Adams, John, 235, 267
Adams, John Quincy, 272
Aflaq, Michel, 54, 62
Agence France-Presse, 133
Agha, Hussein, 174, 176
Airbus, 131
Airbus Industrie, 206
Ajlouni, Mohammad, 134
Akerid, Simone, 237–9
Akerid, Vera, 237–9

Al-Ahram Weekly, 266
Al Amleh, Iyad, 156–7
Al Aqsa Mosque, 13, 165, 176
Al Arz Ice Cream Factory, 146–7
Al Assad, Bashar, 95, 98; at Arab League summit, Beirut, 8; and Hezbollah, 70–1; interview, 67–9; and Lebanon, 38–9, 43; and liberalization, 69–70; and succession, 65
Al Assad, Basil, 27
Al Assad, Hafez, 69; in Aleppo, 96–7; and Ba'ath party, 72, 75–6; and corruption, 75–6; death of, 65–7; in Hama, 88; and Lebanon 27–40
Al Assad, Rifat, 65
Al Azhar Mosque, 235–6, 249
Al Battani, 100
Al Bawaba, 118
Al Biruni, 100
Al Dulaimi, Iraqi tribe, 196
Al Dulaimi, Sabih H., 186
Al Dustour, 122
Al Farebi, 100
Al Fayyum, 268
Al Ghazali, 113
Al Hajem, Sami Alzara, 195
Al Hakim, Fatimid caliph, 236
Al Haya Food Industries, 156–7
Al Haythem, 236
Al Hilli, Hikmat Mahmoud, 210–11
Al Husseini, Haj Amin, 154, 190
Al Izraj, 196
Al Jabur, Iraqi tribe, 196

Al Jabur, Sheik Rashid Abdula Salem, 196–8
Al Jazeera, 71, 84–5, 89, 108, 133–4, 181, 253
Al Katib, Qassem, 122–8
Al Kattab, Abdullah Alkawaideh, 121, 123–4
Al Manar, 53
Al Mansur, 198, 200, 208
Al Mawla, Mahmoud, 48, 51
Al Messhedani, Kamil, 204–5
Al Muna, Mitri, 116
Al Muqadassi, 150
Al Natsheh, Ishaq, 164
Al Qaeda, 16–17, 103, 245, 249, 258–61
'Al Qaq, Anis, 170–3
Al Quds Road, 157
Al Rashid, Harun, 184, 199–200
Al Rashid Street, 207–8, 210–11
Al Rassoul Al Azzam, 55
Al Razi, 101
Al Sadr, Musa, 53
Al Shahin, Faisel, 183
Al-Shahr, 70
Al Shammar, Iraqi tribe, 196
Al Shammar, Bassem Abed, 196
Al Wazani, 49
Al Wakil, Said Fat'hy, 233–5
Al Walid, Umayyad caliph, 61, 99
Alawites, 65, 69, 74
Albadia Co., 186–7
Aleppo, 62, 79, 86, 100; history of, 88; Hugh Pope in, 181–2; industry in, 90–1; religious communities, 93–4, 96–7; shadow economy, 75–6; soap industry, 144
Alexander the Great, 235
Alexandria, 212, 214–16; commodities exchange, 224; and Geniza letter, 262; Jewish community, 238–40; stock exchange, 221
Alexandria, library of, 235
Algeria, 12, 270
Ali, nephew of Mohammad, 19, 111
Ali Hasan Al Majeed (a.k.a. Chemical Ali), 180–1
Ali, Mohammad, 218
Ali, Mohammad, Citadel of, 235
Allenby Bridge, 1, 115
American Colony Hotel, 173

Amr ibn al As, 110, 217
Anabtawi, Raed G., 146–8
Anastasias Church, 152
Ani, Fariz, 204
Anjar, 43, 45
Annas, 151
Aqaba, 112
Aqaba Railway Corp. (ARC), 120–8
Arab Bank, 134–5, 166
Arab League, 8
Arab Legion, 109
Arab Re-insurance Group, 30–1
Arab Revolt, 111–12, 119
Arafat, Yasser, 50, 109, 162; at Arab summit, Beirut 7–8; and Barghouthis, 140–2; at Camp David summit, 173–6; and corruption, 130, 167; and donor aid, 170–3; and economic mismanagement 166–8; in Oslo, 137; and September 1970, 112
Arafiri, Tarik, 34–7
Aramco, 56
Arkin, William, 260–1
Arrow II, 264
Asabiyya, 60, 257, 270, 273
Asati Salt Co., 119
Assaf, Said, 168
Assel, Avnar, 239–40
Associate Press, 15, 133
Associated Press Television, 133
Asuncion, Paraguay, 168
Australia, 1, 267
Avicenna, 99, 101
Ayman Abdel Rahman Salah, 222–3
Ayn Ibil, 46, 47
Ayoub, Tarek, 133–4
Ayyubids, 81
Azawi, Subhi, 187
Azem Palace, 81
Aziz, Tarik, 180
Azizi, Mazen, 187
Azzouz, Hani, 97–9

Ba'ath (Resurrection) Party, 72, 82, 88; Al Assad and Alawites, 74–5; and Hafez al Assad's death, 67; and Islamists, 78; origins of, 62–3; role in secular Iraqi society, 200; and Saddam Hussein, 180–1; and 'tribalization' of Iraq, 195

Babylon, 180, 184

Baghdad, 4, 24, 185, 188, 190, 195–7, 202–3, 205–11, 258, 270; Abbasid, 19, 95, 199; and oil for food, 109, 192; and Saddam's birthday, 178–9, 182; sanctions, 6, 115; and smuggling, 194; United States and Saddam Hussein, 183

Baghdad Alcohol Co., 187

Baghdad Soft Drink Co., 187

Baghdad Stock Exchange, 186

Bahour, Sam, 142–4

Baksheesh Welcome Wagon, 185

Balfour Declaration, 112, 154

Bani Said, 198

Bank of Jordan, 168

Banque du Caire, 220–1, 232–4, 268

Banque Libanaise Pour Le Commerce, 32

Banu Qaynuqa, 17

Banu'l-Nadir, 17

Barbian, George, 93

Barghouthi, Marwan, 140

Barghouthi, Mustafa, 140–2

Barqawi, Hassan, 172

Bassil, Charbell, 22–5, 28

Bassil, François, 22–5, 28

Bazaya, Ibrahim, 121–2

Begin, Menachem, 156

Beirut, 7–8, 22–7, 29, 31–2, 38–40, 42, 46–50, 53–5

Beirut, American University in, 27, 55

Ben-Ami, Shlomo, 175

Ben Ezra synagogue, Cairo, 238, 240

Ben Gurion Airport, 264

Beni Tameem, 17, 196

Benjamin of Tudela, 199

Bergen, Peter, 259–61

Bernadotte, Count Folke, 155

Beshai, Abdel, 267

Besseso, Faud, 168

Bethlehem, 89, 99, 105, 140, 157, 159

Bimarstan al-Nuri, 99, 102

Bin Laden, Osama, 5–6, 16, 97, 102, 202, 242, 258–61

Bint Jubayl, 46, 49

Bisan, 169

Bitar, Salah al-Din, 54, 62

Boeing, 203–6

Boulevard Sa'ad Zaghloul, Alexandria, 212–13

Brazilian Coffee Shop, Alexandria, 212–14

British Broadcasting Corporation (BBC), 189

Brunei, Sultan of, 131

Buraq, Mohammad's steed for the Night Journey, 152

Burke, Edmund, 261

Bush, George W., 16, 25; and Intifada, 79–80, 85, 89, 109, 241; and Iraq, 202; and Jewish settlements, 158; and trade subsidies, 228; war on terror, 259

Bush, George H. W., 158, 228

Byzantines: 2, 110, 151, 217–18; Anjar palace, 45; defeat by Arabs, 18–19, 129; Dome of the Rock, 152; and Maronites, 22; Umayyad Mosque, 61

Cable News Network (CNN), 107, 133, 144, 181

Caiaphas, 151

Cairo, 3–4, 9–10, 29–30, 50, 102, 119, 223–24, 226, 192, 202, 207, 242, 256, 258, 266, 268–70; Cairo conference, 183; Camp David accords, 218; and economic reform, 219–21; and export promotion, 229; under Fatimids, 214, 236–40; intellectual community of, 249, 252–4; and Israeli embassy, 216, 242; soap industry in, 144

Cairo, American University in, 267

Cairo and Alexandria Stock Exchange, 221

Cairo Times, 250

Camp David Peace Accord, 162, 216, 251, 269

Camp David Peace summit, 158, 173–5

Canada, 267

Canadian National Railways, 125

Canton, 199

Cave of Machpelah, 160

Central Intelligence Agency, United States, 25, 201, 131

Central Security Force, Egypt, 219

Chalabi, Ahmed: and Iraqi opposition, 183, 190, 191–2; and Jordanian economy, 128; on King Abdullah II, 131; and Nuri Said, 209
Chalabi, Omar, 124–5
Charlemagne, 200
Chase Manhattan Bank, 232
China, 59, 66, 72, 176, 179, 193, 199, 208, 231, 237, 258, 265, 270
Church of the Ascension, 152
Church of the Holy Sepulchre, 150, 152
Clayton, Gilbert, 10
Clinton, William Jefferson, 249
Comintern, 260
Compaq, 228, 230
Confucianism, 270
Constantine, 61
Constantinople, 3, 237
Cordoba, 3, 101, 199
Council for Peace and Security, 159
Crusaders, 19, 102; capture of Jerusalem, 151; and Ibn Jubayr, Arab geographer, 237; Saddam, Saladin and, 178; and Zionism, 156
Cyrus II, Persian king, 105

Daewoo Group, 94
Dahlan, Mohammad, 167, 175
Damascus, 44, 67–8, 81, 91–2, 95–7, 99, 102, 152; and Aleppo, 88–9; banking in, 73; *Decapolis*, 120; and Finnish Sauna Society, 83; French occupation of, 11; and Hezbollah, 52; history, 60–2; Islamic enlightenment in, 2–3; and Lebanese civil war, 26; Pope John Paul II's visit to, 39; military capability, 64, 71; and Mu'awiya, 110; relations with Beirut, 39–42
Darmon, Nicholas, 228
Dayan, Moshe, 153
Defensive Shield, Operation, 136–7, 139, 141, 143, 145, 168
Deir Yassin, 107, 163
Dell Computers, 228
Descartes, René, 261
Desert Fox, Operation, 185–6
Desert Storm, Operation, 114, 178, 185–6, 188–9, 195, 203

Dhimmis, 19, 151
Dome of the Rock, 150, 152–3
Domiat Egypt Co., 230–1
Dostoyevsky, 207
Druze, 20, 24, 26, 39–40, 76

eBay, 269
EFG-Hermes, Egypt, 219
Egypt, 11, 13, 21, 24, 79, 85, 91, 104, 109, 152, 179, 207, 212–56, 261–2; as Arab world leader, 215; Cairo Geniza, 102; cheap oil, 15; economic 'crisis', 219; and Eisenhower Doctrine, 12, 259; foreign direct investment, 14; Jewish community in, 237–41; likely succession, 16; liquidity crunch and currency devaluation, 220–7; low exports, 228–32; Mamluks and *wakf*, 77; micro-credit, 232; Muslim Brotherhood, 249; Muslim conquest of, 18–19, 217; Nasser and Ba'ath Party, 62; peace process, 216; privatization, 30–2; Saad Eddin Ibrahim on, 253–6; and US aid, 265, 269
Egyptian Jews Association, 239
Eid, 236
Eisenhower, Dwight D., 11, 259, 272
El Faves, Nawaf, 65
El Horreya Road, Alexandria, 212
Erekat, Saeb, 175
Essa, Abdel-Raouf, 230–1
European Commission, 173
Evans, Gavin, 173
Expolink, 231

Fadallah, Abdul Halim, 54–5
Faisel I, King of Iraq, 209
Faisel II, King of Iraq, 2, 24, 209
Fatima, 235
Fatimids, 19, 99, 104, 215, 235–7
Ferdinand, King of Spain, 19
Financial Sector Revision Project (IMF), 268
Finland, 231
Fire Valley Road, West Bank, 156
Friedman, Thomas, 250
Frontline, 201
Frost, Robert, 179

Fuad, King of Egypt, 214
Fulbright, William J., 272
Fustat, Egypt, 236

Gadhafi, Moammar, 8, 53
Galil, Israeli assault rifle, 149, 264
Gama, Vasco da, 50
Gap, 228
Gaza, 3, 13, 50, 153, 162, 167; and
    Camp David summit, 175; EU
    hospital in, 172–3; and Israeli trade
    barriers, 115, 176; settlements, 157,
    159, 165
General Motors, 228
Geneva, 170
Geniza archive, 102, 216, 262
Ghandour, Nazem, 34–7
Giza Zoo, Cairo, 223
Glubb, Sir John Bagot, 2
Golan Heights, 42, 71, 153
Goldstein, Baruch, 160
Goshen, Daniel, 239–40
Greek Club, 249–50, 253
Greenspan, Alan, 168

Hagana, Zionist militia, 239
Hai Qaissieh, Jordan, 106
Haifa, Israel, 239
Halabja, 180
Halawani, Hatem, 169–70
Hamadiyyeh, 81, 85
Hamas, 163
Harari, Ovadia, 265
Hariri, Rafik, 23, 27, 43
Hasan, Captain Akram, 203
Hashemite dynasty, 66, 111; and
    Hamas, 132; and Intifada, 106, 119;
    and Ma'an, 120; Palestinian
    resentment of, 129–30
Hassan bin Talal, 130–1
Hassoun, Sheik (Dr) Ahmed Badr din,
    93–6
Hazem, Shaimaa, 223
Hebron, 159, 163–4
Helwan, Cairene suburb, 238
Hezbollah, 25–6, 38, 40–3, 46–8, 50–6
Hijaz Railway, 55–7
Hijazi, Mohammad, 55–7
Histadrut, Israeli labour union, 154
Homs, 62

Hong Kong, 202
Hôtel des Cure, 238
Hudaibiya, 156
Hulegu, 200
Hull, England, 9
Human Rights Watch, 139
Husain, 19
Hussain, Qusay, 192
Hussain, Uday, 192
Hussein ibn Talal, 8, 24, 75, 106, 111,
    120, 134–5, 200; charm of, 111–13;
    and Glubb Pasha, 2; and Palestinians,
    129; and September 1970 civil war,
    112; succession, 130–1
Hussein, Saddam, 4, 37, 136–7, 188,
    209, 211, 260; birthday celebration,
    177–82, 206; and Iraqi
    modernization, 200–1; and Iraqi
    National Congress, 191–2; possible
    elimination of, 270–1; and smuggling
    trade, 194–6; and tribes, 195–8

Ibn Abi Usaybi, 100
Ibn al As, Amr, 110, 217
Ibn Al Athir, Arab historian, 156
Ibn al Furat, Abbasid minister, 212
Ibn al Walid, Khalid, 92
Ibn Khaldun, 60, 257, 273
Ibn Khaldun Centre for Development
    Studies, 250
Ibn Killis, Yacub, 235
Ibn Tulun, Ahmed, 218
Ibn Zubayr, 152
Ibrahim, Saad Eddin, 250, 252–6, 258
Ideal Standard, 116
Ilyushin, 205
Incirlik, 194
India, 208, 234
Indonesia, 231
Inman, Robert, 206
International Air Transport Association
    (IATA), 205
International Monetary Fund (IMF),
    47, 218–19, 268
Intifada, 8, 13, 15–16, 26–7, 42, 50,
    52–3, 68, 70, 79, 84–5, 89, 105–6,
    115–16, 129, 132, 140–3, 146–7,
    156, 162, 164–70, 172, 174, 217,
    222, 224, 241
Iran, 20, 25, 38, 51–3, 179

Iraq, 2, 4, 6, 12, 14, 16, 21, 63, 74–5, 77, 139, 255, 259–61, 267, 269–71; and Sykes-Picot agreement, 9; and King-Crane Commission, 11; Muslim conquest of, 18; economy, 193; and Jordan, 112, 114–15, 120, 130; and Israel, 175; and possible US war with, 222

Iraq Daily, 178, 182

Iraqi Airways, 201–5

Iraqi Culinary Institute, 178

Iraqi National Congress, 128, 191

Iraqi Photography Association, 178

Islamic Jihad, 163, 241–2

Israel, 1, 8, 9, 15, 20, 29, 31, 83, 91, 104, 169, 202, 270–1; and Balfour Declaration, 10; and Camp David summit, 173–6; and Egypt, 215, 235, 238–240, 241, 245; and Hashemites, 130, 132; and Iraq, 183, 190, 202; and Intifada, 13; Jerusalem, 153; and Jewish settlements, 155–66; and Jordan, 105–9, 113, 129; and Lebanon, 26–7, 39–40, 46–53, 55–7; and Operation Defensive Shield, 7, 79–81, 84–5, 89, 99, 105–9, 129, 132, 136, 136–50, 241; and Osama bin Laden, 259–61; and Palestine, 136–50; and Nasser, 217; and Muslim Brotherhood, 241–2; and Saddam Hussein, 195; and Syria, 42, 64, 68, 71–2, 76, 94–6; trade barriers on West Bank, Gaza, 115–17; and US aid, 263–5, 269

Israel Aircraft Industries (IAI), 264–5

Israel Military Industries Ltd, 264

Isaac, 160

Jaber, Imad, 47

Jabotinsky, Ze'ev, 155

Jacob, 94, 160

Jadid, Salah, 65

Janissaries, 218

Japan, 41, 171–2, 230

Jauhar, Fatimid general, 236

Jazzi, Saed, 121

Jefferson, Thomas, 261

Jenin, 89, 105, 128, 136–7, 139–40, 144, 190, 195

Jericho, 157, 162; at Oslo, 158; Oasis Casino, 167–72

Jerusalem, 1, 13, 61, 71, 107, 115, 117; Muslim conquest of, 18

John the Baptist, 61, 92

John Paul II, 39

Johnson, Dr Samuel, 273

Jojoba nut, 168

Jordan, 1–2, 8, 20, 24, 40, 47, 59, 85, 91, 105–35, 147, 164, 168, 184–5, 203, 261, 263, 265, 267, 269; Aqaba Railway Corp., 120–7; British Mandate, 182; crackdown on dissent, 132–5; and Operation Defensive Shield, 105–9; economy, 114–15; and ethnic Palestinians, 128–30; and Hashemites, 16, 38; Israeli trade barriers, 117; and King Hussein, 66–7, 75, 200; and King Abdullah II, 111–14, 130–5; Ma'an, 119–28; Masri family, 174; and privatization, 13, 118–19; and Six-Day War, 162; and Sykes-Picot agreement, 9; and Syria, 79; US aid to, 267; and tribes, 195

Jordan Phosphate Mining Company, 124

Jordan Telecommunications, 118, 133

Jordan University, 107

Joshua, 151

Jumblatt, Kamal, 40

Jumblatt, Walid, 39–43

Ka'bah, 152, 247

Kabul, Afghanistan, 258

Kamhawi, Labib, 108–10, 193

Kandahar, Afghanistan, 258

Kansanrallah, Bassel, 93–4, 96

Kassem, Abdel Karim, Iraqi coup leader, 24, 211

Kassem, Hisham, 250, 252

Kassem, Thamer, 207–8

Kepel, Gilles, 260–1

Kennan, George, 257

Kerbala, 19

Khadija, wife of Mohammad, 73

Khalaf, Samer, 33

Khalif, Lama, 33–4

Khamenei, Ayatollah, 53

Kharijite, 16

Khomeini, Ayatollah, 53, 57
Kilani, Farouq, 134
Kim, Eugene, 264
King David Hotel, 155
Kipling, Rudyard, 263, 267
Knesset, Israeli parliament, 94, 143
Koran, 16, 18
Korea, North, 12, 66, 72, 119, 176, 183
Korea, South, 12, 14, 32, 59–60, 66, 72, 94, 166, 176, 271
Korean Peninsula, 41
Korean War, 150, 258
Kuraishi, Mari, 269
Kuwait, 15, 30–2, 114, 201–2

La Clauss, Imad, 46–7
Laben, Dr Ali, 242
Lahoud, Emile, 27
Larson, Torgeir, 139
Latakia, 65
Lavi, Israeli fighter jet, 265
Lawrence, T. E., 1, 11, 119, 209
Le Chef, 22–25
Lebanon, 3, 60, 64, 96; Anjar palace, 43–5; Arab League summit, Beirut, 7–8, 12, 15; and Bashar al Assad, 68; and Hezbollah, 46, 48, 51–7; sectarianism, civil war, economy, 25–8; and Sykes-Picot agreement, 9,11; and Syria, 38–40, 42–3; and Syrian banking sector, 71, 73–4
Levi Strauss, 228
Lewinsky, Monica, 185, 189
Libya, 8, 14, 30, 220
Locke, John, 270
Lockheed Martin, 264
Lott, Trent, 189
Luna Group, 192

Ma'adi, Cairene suburb, 253, 266
Ma'an, Jordan, 119–128
Maghrib, 191
Magna Carta, 270
Majeed, Said, 203
Malaysia, 193, 231
Mallat, Chibli, 8, 191
Malley, Robert, 174
Mamluks, 77, 81
Maronites, 22, 26, 39, 40, 42

Marx, Karl, 270
Masarjawayh, 3
Masaud, Halil, 152, 157
Mashal, Ahmed, 164
Masri, Maher, 174–6
Masri, Taher, 176
Mecca, 6, 17, 19, 73, 83, 110, 120, 151–2, 156, 183, 203, 247, 254, 256
Medhat, Hythan, 186–87
Medina, 6, 17–18, 50, 151
Medinat al Salaam, 199
Merhav, 216
Metternich, Prince, 171
Midor, 216
Modern Paint Co., Iraq, 187
Mohammad, the Prophet, 2–3, 17–18, 110, 151, 183, 235
Mohammad, Abdullah, 186–7
Mohammad, Said Mohammad, 250
Mohieldin, Mahmoud, 224–5
Mongols, 19, 81, 110
Morsi, Dr Mohammad, 242–8
Mount of Olives, 152, 176
Moyne, Lord Walter, 155
Mu'awiya I Ibn Abi Sufyan, 19, 92, 110–11, 130
Mubarak, Hosni, 8, 16, 109, 216–17, 250–4
Mukhtar, 121
Mukhtara, 40–2, 43
Muslim Brotherhood: in Egypt, 216, 223, 239, 241–2, 248–9, 252, 255; in Syria, 65, 76, 78, 88
Mussa, Amr, 220

Nabataeans, 110
Nabatiyah, 47–8, 50
Nablus, 108–9, 140, 144–6, 148–9, 174
Nablusi, Ma'az M., 145–7
Najia, Aboudi, 29–31
Narkis, Uzi, 153
Nasrallah, Sayyed Hassan, 39, 52–3, 71, 80
Nasser, Gamal Abdel, 8, 56, 67, 214, 238, 254; and Arab nationalism, 200, 215, 253; and Ba'ath Party, 62, 74; coup, 222; and radical Islam, 252; and Suez crisis, 217; and Socialism, 218, 255

National Chemicals & Industrial Plastics Co., Iraq, 187
Nayyouf, Nizar, 70
Nebuchadnezzar, King of Babylon, 151
New York Times, The, 250
Nilometer, 235–6
Nomura International plc, 29–31
Norsk Hydro, 119
Nour Group, 91–2
Novik, Nimrod, 216
Nur al Din, 99

Oasis Casino, West Bank, 167, 172
Ole Holdings, Jordan, 134
Omar I, second caliph, 73, 129, 151, 153
Operation Desert Fox, 185–6, 188–9
Operation Defensive Shield, 136, 139, 141, 145, 168
Operation Desert Storm, 114, 178, 186, 195, 203
Orascom Group, Egypt, 224–6
Oslo Accord, 13, 27, 29, 109, 116
Ottomans, 1, 10–11, 19, 62, 77, 196, 200
Oweis, Khaled Yacoub, 40–5

Palestine, 2, 14–15, 43, 45, 50, 53, 56, 80, 84, 95, 97, 115, 130, 173, 181–3, 190, 239, 241, 247, 271; and Balfour Declaration, 112; Operation Defensive Shield, 136–41, 143, 148; and foreign aid, 170; history, 150–1; and King-Crane Commission, 11; and Jewish settlements, 157–8, 160, 166; and Jordan, 115, 130; Muslim conquest of, 18; and Zionism, 154–55
Palestinian Authority, 9, 13, 117, 140, 142–3, 158, 162, 167–8, 169–72, 176, 195, 263, 267
Palestinian Monetary Authority, 168
Palestine Securities Exchange, 14, 168
Palestinian Telecommunications Co., 169
Palmyra, 110
Park, Chung Hee, 59–60
Peres, Shimon, 30
Persia, 2–3, 18, 45, 99–100, 105, 110, 151, 183, 184, 197, 199–8

Persian Gulf, 32, 50, 91
Petra, 110, 119
Phalange, 26
Pharos Lighthouse, 253
Philippines, 231
Picot, François, 9
Port Said, 219–20, 239
Powell, Colin, 79–80
Pratt & Whitney, 201, 228
Procter & Gamble, 192
Ptolemy, 235
Pyramids, 235

Qatar, 30, 104, 119, 131–2, 133
Quandt, William, 269
Quraysh, 17, 152, 156, 183

Rabin, Yitzhak, 106, 118, 153
Raheem, Abdullah, 194
Rajub, Jabril, 167
Ramadan, 76, 164, 186, 236
Ramallah, 14, 106, 136, 140, 142–3, 174
Rania, Queen of Jordan, 129
Rashid, Ahmed, 260–1
Rashid, Mohammad, 168
Raytheon Corp., 189
Reuters, 133
Ridha, Tahsin, 208
Rifaat, Shareef, 268
Romania, 231
Ross, Dennis, 59, 174
Rousseau, Jean Jacques, 235
Rowihab, Michael, 32–4
Rubinstein, Danny, 159
Rue El Nabi Danial, 212–14
Russia, 41, 58, 156, 179, 193, 231, 237–9, 258, 263

Sabeel, 76
Sabra and Shatila, 56
Sadat, Anwar, 179, 217–18, 244, 254, 258, 261
Sadat Academy for Management Science, 223
Saddam Art Gallery, 178
Saddam International Airport, 185
Sahur, Beit, 159
Said, Edward, 250
Said, Nuri, 209

Said, Sabri, 253
Sakkar, Dr Suheil, 102–4
Saladin, 81, 99, 151, 178, 179, 181, 237
Salieh, Rubieh, 204
Saudi Arabia, 16, 24, 26, 31, 80, 122, 143, 151, 215, 253, 255, 264; and Arab League summit, Beirut, 7–8; and Aramco, 56; and Osama bin Laden, 259–61; and birth of Islam, 17; economy 14–15; and Hashemites, 111; Ma'an, 120; and oil, 183; and Tribes, 195
Sawiris, Naguib, 225–7
Scandinavia, 73
Schlesinger, Arthur Jr., 259
Seif, Sameh, 256
Seljuk Turks, 200
Sfeir, Nasrallah, 39–40
Shaheen, Khaled, 134–5
Shamir, Yitzhak, 156
Sharabati, Ezeddin, 160–4
Sharabati, Mohammad Sabbagh, 90–1
Sharkiya, Egypt, 241
Sharon, Ariel, 7–8, 13, 50–1, 56, 80, 109, 136–7, 141–3, 158, 165, 241
Sheik Omar Mausoleum, 180
Sherif El Saghir, Cairo, 221
Shia, 39
Shiite, 8, 19, 25–7, 53, 191, 219, 235–6
Shlaim, Avi, 251
Shoman, Abdulmajeed, 135, 166
Shubra, Cairene suburb, 230
Shukri, Ali, 200
Sicily, 3, 100
Sidqi, Aziz, 218
Sinai peninsula, Egypt, 217
Sneh, Ephraim, 265
Solidere, 27
Soviet Union, 11, 64, 72, 130, 259
Spain, 3, 19
Stalin, Joseph, 263
Stamets, Paul, 35
Standard Chartered Bank plc, 134
Star, Kenneth, 189
Struk, Orit, 163
Suez Canal, 9, 183, 215, 239, 241
Sunni, 19, 24, 26, 66, 80, 84, 93, 191, 236
Sufis, 24
Sykes, Christopher, 12

Sykes, Sir Mark, 9–11
Sykes-Picot agreement, 9–11, 63
Syria, 21, 24–5, 139, 258; and Iraq, 181, 185, 191, 199, 205, 215, 218; and Jordan, 112, 115, 133; and Lebanon, 26–7, 38–44, 46–7, 52–3, 63
Syriamica Azzouz, 97–9
Syrian Computer Society, 67

T-72, Russian battle tank, 143, 180
Taba, 173, 176
Taif Accord, 26–7, 29, 31, 34, 38
Taiwan, 60, 145, 176, 265, 271
Taliban, 258
Talleyrand-Perigord, Charles Maurice de, 171
Tamerlane, 81
Tel Aviv, 15, 113, 264
Temporary International Presence in Hebron (TIPH), 160
Tiananmen Square, 270
Tikrit, 179–80
Tlas, Mustafa, 70
Toledo, 237
Torah, 237–8, 240
Totah, Marwan, 169–70
Toynbee, Arnold, 163
Tunisia, 295
Turkey, 20, 45, 62–3, 76, 90, 191, 193–94, 272

Ulema, 180
Um Kalthum, 209
Umayyad Mosque, 3, 61, 86, 92, 99–100
Umayyads, 19, 43–44, 61, 64, 78, 92, 95, 110–11, 152, 182, 218, 229
Umma, 17
Unilever, 192
United Arab Emirates (UAR), 8, 15, 30, 205, 264, 271
United Arab Republic, 63
United Nations, 179; embargo on Iraq, 190; and Jenin, 138–9; oil-for-food programme, 109, 189; and peace-keeping, Lebanon, 46–7; Security Council resolutions on Palestine, 57, 247; and smuggling in Iraq, 194; World Relief Agency, Gaza hospital, 172

United States, 9, 97, 267, 271–2; and Osama bin Laden (and radical Islam), 20, 259–62; and Egypt, 215, 231–3, 265, 268; and Syria, 78–9; and Iran-Iraq war, 201; and Iraq, 192, 201; and Jordan, 106–9, 115; and *Lavi*, 265; and oil, 15; and Palestine, 141; US Agency for International Development (USAID), 215

Veccia Vaglieri, Laura, 270
Veng, Jens, 160
Vietnam, 259
Vitrac, 223
V-Sat, 118, 133

Washington, George, 272
Wakf, 76–9
West Bank, 15, 267, 110, 112, 115–17, 169–70, 172; and Camp David summit, 174–6; and Operation Defensive Shield, 50, 52, 105–6, 108, 128, 136–8, 143, 144–6, 241; and Hashemites, 130, 132; and Jewish settlements, 13, 156–9,

162–5; and Six-Day War, 153; and Zionism, 153, 156–8
Whittle, Dennis, 269
Wisconsin General, 124–5
World Bank, 47, 73, 268
World Zionist Organization, 9, 154

Yassin, Ahmed, 249
Yassin, Hasan Adnan, 168
Yazid, 19, 130
Young, Michael, 53
Youssef, George A., 192
Yugoslavia, 23
Yusef Meligy, Mohammad, 212

Zakho, 193–4
Zaqaziq, 241–2, 244
Zenith, 228
Zev, Israel, 163
Zionism, 16, 56, 70, 83, 129; and Egyptian Jews, 240; and Theodore Herzl, 237; and Sykes-Picot agreement, 10, 144, 153–6, 159, 163, 167; and *The Iron Wall*, 251
Zoroastrianism, 18